Reading Education: Foundations for a Literate America

Jean Osborn
Paul T. Wilson
Richard C. Anderson
University of Illinois at
Urbana-Champaign

Lexington Books
D.C. Heath and Company/Lexington, Massachusetts/Toronto

Library of Congress Cataloging in Publication Data
Main entry under title:

Reading education.

Papers from a conference convened at the Wingspread Conference Center, organized by the Center for the Study of Reading.
1. Reading—United States—Congresses. I. Osborn, Jean. II. Wilson, Paul T. III. Anderson, Richard C. (Richard Chase), 1934–0000. IV. University of Illinois at Urbana-Champaign. Center for the Study of Reading.
LB1049.95.R43   1985   428.4´0973   84-47505
ISBN 0-669-08280-5 (alk. paper)

Published simultaneously in Canada
Printed in the United States of America on acid-free paper
International Standard Book Number: 0-669-08280-5
Library of Congress Catalog Card Number: 84-47505

Contents

Part III   Foundations for Better Reading Instruction   195

Preface and Acknowledgments

The conference "Foundations for a Literate America" was convened at the Wingspread Conference Center with the express purpose of communicating the best available knowledge about reading to decision makers who influence how reading is taught in American schools. The main themes of the conference were advances and answered questions. Research experts in reading and schooling presented papers on what is presently known about reading, reading instruction, classrooms, and schools. Also participating in the conference were chief state school officers, administrators from large city school systems, state textbook adoption committee officials, textbook publishers, federal aides involved in educational policymaking, and educational writers. As the researchers spoke, conference participants considered the realities of implementing the research findings in classrooms across the country. The papers from the conference, as presented in *Reading Education: Foundations for a Literate America*, are grouped into three parts, "Taking a Look at Published Programs," "The Organization of Classrooms, Schools, and Instruction," and "Foundations for Better Reading Instruction."

Part I, "Taking a Look at Published Programs," reports recent research about the characteristics of published school materials—the readers, textbooks, workbooks, and teachers' manuals that school systems purchase for use in classrooms. The chapters in this part will be especially useful to members of textbook adoption groups. In chapter 1, Dolores Durkin analyzes the manuals that accompany basal reading programs, finding many more examples of "mentioning" and "assessing" than of genuine instruction. In chapter 2, Jean Osborn suggests how evaluators of the workbooks that accompany basal reading programs can assess effectiveness of the tasks in these books by "counting, matching and judging." In chapter 3, Bertram Bruce provides six versions of a children's story to demonstrate the ingredients of a good story. He discusses the teaching of story understanding and the differences between stories in basal readers and stories in trade books.

Some research-based guidelines for evaluating content area textbooks are presented in chapter 4 by Bonnie Armbruster, who asserts that good textbooks should promote understanding and, in particular, should encourage the learning of important information. In chapter 5, Andee Rubin describes common applications of readability formulas and the unfortunate results that arise when these formulas are used inappropriately. She proposes a new view of the reading process as the basis for choosing appropriate texts. In chapter 6, Walter MacGinitie discusses what teachers and materials must offer if students are to develop their potential as readers.

Part II, "The Organization of Classrooms, Schools, and Instruction," deals with social, administrative, and classroom factors that influence the nature and quality of reading instruction. Teachers and administrators who are interested in the organization of classrooms and schools will be particularly interested in the chapters in this section. In chapter 7, David Berliner presents a new view of classrooms as complex and dynamic workplaces that require management by a teacher who is an executive of considerable skill and talent. He outlines nine executive functions of teachers and reports on some classroom-based research into each function. One function of a teacher is organizing students for instruction; in the early grades, children are typically grouped by ability for instruction in reading. In chapter 8, Courtney Cazden reviews the research on ability grouping and points out how children in low ability groups do not receive the kind of instruction they need to become proficient readers.

Most people would agree that reading instruction must occur in school and that effective instruction is most likely to occur in schools that are well organized. In chapter 9, Ronald Edmonds reviews recent research on the characteristics of successful schools and describes procedures that have been used successfully to improve schools. Some very specific components of a successful reading program—instruction, teacher training, and classroom monitoring—which were used in a large U.S. Office of Education study, are detailed in chapter 10 by Douglas Carnine and Russell Gersten. They discuss the design of instruction and procedures for monitoring student and teacher performance. They find that these practices are the basis for improving reading instruction and raising teacher expectations for their students.

Students in the United States are tested frequently, and they will probably be tested even more frequently over the next decade. The history of minimum competency testing and the goals and hazards of this testing movement are discussed by Roger Farr in chapter 11. He warns of the dangers of relating reading instruction and reading programs to "teaching for the test" and points out the need for more varied and encompassing evaluation of student progress.

A description of the content of reading curricula is the concern of Richard Venezky in chapter 12. He proposes a systematic organization and representation of the major steps in planning reading instruction. The representation scheme he presents will be useful to curriculum designers and to those who must analyze and evaluate instructional programs. In chapter 13, Robert Calfee offers a conceptual framework that integrates some of the ideas in this section. He intends this framework to be an aid to educational practitioners who are establishing and maintaining quality programs for instruction in literacy.

The chapters in part III, "Foundations for Better Reading Instruction," describe research about reading instruction that has immediate (and tested) application to how reading should be taught in classrooms. Each of the chapters presents aspects of some of the most current research on reading.

In chapter 14, Dorothy Strickland notes that through reading aloud, discussions of picture books, and creative dramatics, teachers help children learn to appreciate stories and to want to read. She presents research evidence documenting findings that engaging children in literature-related activities supports their literacy development. Writing about another aspect of learning to read in chapter 15, Joanna Williams makes the case for explicit decoding instruction and urges that teachers and publishers expend the time, money, and effort to incorporate good decoding instruction into their comprehensive reading programs.

Jay Samuels defines the concept of automaticity in chapter 16 and applies it not only to decoding but also to comprehension. He argues that accuracy and decoding speed are necessary (but not sufficient) conditions for good comprehension, and he delineates several procedures for developing automaticity through repeated reading. In chapter 17, Patricia Cunningham compares the teaching of good readers with the teaching of poor readers and offers specific procedures for teachers working with all groups of students.

To understand better why students have difficulty comprehending what they read, Isabel Beck, in chapter 18, analyzed the responses of students who read and answered questions about a short story in a basal reader. She found more than eighty "difficulty candidates" within the story that could lead to student problems in comprehension. From this analysis, she identifies five categories of comprehension problems and proposes solutions (based on theory and research) for teachers to use. Chapter 19, by James Cunningham, summarizes much of the current research on comprehension instruction. Cunningham combines ideas from reading education, teacher effectiveness training, and cognitive psychology and concludes with three research-based recommendations for teachers who are concerned about the comprehension of their poor readers.

In chapter 20 Kathryn Au and her colleagues at the Kamehameha Early Education Program describe a system for reading instruction that was developed by a team of teachers and researchers. This chapter not only characterizes a successful reading program but also describes how researchers and teachers can work together for the continuing improvement of reading instruction.

Recent advances in comprehension teaching are presented in the final four chapters. A prereading discussion plan modeled on the inferential connections people make between familiar and unfamiliar information is described in chapter 21 by Jane Hansen, who also reviews other procedures emphasizing thinking strategies that teachers can use in working with their students.

In chapter 22, Annemarie Palinscar and Ann Brown report their research on four reciprocal teaching activities designed to improve students' comprehension and comprehension monitoring. Because of the clear and positive results of their studies, Palincsar and Brown encourage practitioners to include reciprocal teaching procedures in their repertoires of instructional activities.

Carl Bereiter's concerns in chapter 23 are the incomplete reading strategies fostered by much school reading instruction and the impact these strategies may have on the ability of students to develop knowledge through reading. He proposes a plan to improve reading comprehension that includes teaching students to summarize, improving text materials, and direct teaching of more complete reading strategies.

Finally, in chapter 24, Paul Wilson and Richard Anderson point out that student interests and prior knowledge have been sadly neglected in classroom instruction, yet they are highly significant determiners of comprehension. Wilson and Anderson discuss these factors and synthesize ideas from other chapters in the volume in making recommendations about how to improve school reading programs.

The truly unique aspect of the Wingspread conference was the audience it addressed. Traditionally, educational researchers have spoken to other researchers and occasionally to teachers and administrators. In 1980, the Center for the Study of Reading broke with this tradition and held a conference for educational publishers because of what new research was revealing about the shortcomings of the texts used in schools. Teachers, teacher trainers, and publishers do not make educational decisions in a vacuum, however, nor just in interaction with each other. Administrators and legislators at local, state, and federal levels make significant decisions about educational policy that affect and often constrain what teachers and publishers can do. The administrators and legislators, in turn, are influenced not only by their own concerns but also by broader social factors. For the Wingspread meeting, representatives of these new constituencies were asked to participate because it was considered vital that researchers begin to discuss with them how to improve instruction.

The reactions of the conference participants were wide-ranging. One concern was for better integration of reading and writing tasks in the classroom. Another was to improve teacher education to provide both a strong general education background and much more intensive preservice involvement in classrooms. The administrators agreed that they had to rely on in-service training to help prepare teachers to cope with classroom demands. Discussion of this point led to the suggestion that sound guidelines be produced for teachers that would provide information on how to teach in ways that would help children comprehend better.

The loudest voices were raised about the findings regarding published school materials. One school administrator exhorted the Center for the Study of Reading to disseminate a list of educational publishers that included descriptions of what was wrong with their materials. Cooler heads prevailed, however, and subsequent discussions led to a different recommendation—that the Center for the Study of Reading should undertake to produce a set of guidelines for evaluating basal readers and content area textbooks. Adoption committees nationwide could then follow these guidelines as they made decisions about how to spend public funds on school materials. The Center has accepted this responsibility and is working on the project. Also, as suggested at the meeting, the Center has continued to inform the educational publishing industry about new research on reading.

These efforts, by themselves, are not enough, however. Every reader of this book can help as well. Teachers, teacher trainers, administrators, publishers, legislators, education writers, and researchers all have roles to play. The more everyone involved in education knows about how to improve instruction, the better our prospects become for improving our children's education. If we can act on what we know now, it will be possible to build a more literate America.

Acknowledgments

The conference and the book—"Reading Education: Foundations for a Literate America"—originated in conversations among the staff of the Hegeler Institute and the Center for the Study of Reading. The Hegeler Institute made an initial donation to the project. M. Blouke Carus and Robert J. Willmot of the Hegeler Institute staff took the responsibility of raising additional funds. The Exxon Education Foundation contributed generously, as did the Monsanto Fund, and the University of Illinois Foundation supported the conference at a time of great need. The National Institute of Education, the funding agency of the Center for the Study of Reading, has provided continuing support both for the conference and for the book.

To the great good fortune of the project, the Johnson Foundation made their Wingspread Conference Center available as the site for the conference. Located just north of Racine, Wisconsin, Wingspread is the last and largest of Frank Lloyd Wright's "prairie houses"—an ideal setting for a small conference focused on discussions of defined topics.

Henry Halsted, vice-president of the Johnson Foundation, was very helpful in working out details of the conference and was an attentive, affable host. Kay Mauer, the conference coordinator for the Johnson Foundation, made sure that the on-site arrangements went smoothly.

Special thanks must go to two special people without whose efforts the task of producing this book would have been impossible. Joan Levy was responsible for editorial help in many indescribable, yet invaluable, ways; and Delores Plowman, our indefatigable typist, treated every word, and every revision, as if it were the most important thing we were ever going to say. On such a foundation, a more literate America might actually be built.

Part I
Taking a Look at
Published Programs

1
Teachers' Manuals
in Basal Reading Programs

Dolores Durkin

The Center for the Study of Reading has been charged with a tremendously important responsibility: to improve reading comprehension instruction in elementary schools. Since improvement is impossible unless we know what is already being done, a classroom-observation study was conducted to identify the kind and amount of comprehension instruction that exists in grades three through six (Durkin, 1978–79). Those grade levels were selected on the assumption that more comprehension instruction is offered in the middle and upper grades than at the primary level.

For the study, teachers in thirty-nine classrooms in fourteen school systems were observed for three successive days each while they were teaching reading and social studies. Everything that was done during the 17,997 minutes of observation was timed and described. Because data from the study prompted the research described in this chapter, it is necessary to summarize some of the observations.

Findings from Classroom Observations

In the classroom-observation study, comprehension instruction was never seen during social studies lessons. Of the 11,587 minutes of observation during reading periods, only 45 minutes were spent on comprehension instruction. The 45 minutes were divided among twelve separate episodes, which means that the average length of an instance of comprehension instruction was only 3.75 minutes.

Whereas the amount of time spent on teaching comprehension was unexpectedly small, the time spent assessing comprehension was ten times greater. Large amounts of the teachers' time also went to giving and checking written assignments suggested in basal reader manuals. The constant assignments in workbooks and ditto sheets reinforced a conclusion reached by Charlotte Taylor in *Transforming Schools* (1976): "Teachers keep their classes so perpetually occupied with busy work that neither chaos nor learning takes place" (p. 169). The large number of assignments in all the classrooms was associated with mentioning—saying just enough about a skill, requirement, or topic to allow for an assignment related to it.

Basal Reader Manual Research

After the classroom-observation study had been concluded, a study of basal reader manuals was begun. The purpose of this study was to learn what manuals offer for comprehension instruction and, in the process, to see whether what had been seen in the classrooms might be linked to the contents of the manuals. The five basal series that were examined were chosen because each had a current copyright date and also met at least one of the following criteria: (1) it was a leading seller, and (2) it was widely promoted. Definitions of the activities in the manuals and the frequency with which the activities were found are shown in table 1–1.

Comprehension Instruction

What was counted as an instance of comprehension instruction varied considerably across the five basal series and within each series. A recommendation that was one sentence long counted as an example, as did a recommendation that was well developed. Since all the series contained both kinds of recommendations, it is unlikely that any series was penalized by this procedure.

It should also be noted that certain recommendations were considered comprehension instruction even though they were nonspecific suggestions. For example, "Lead the children to generalize that . . . "; "Guide the pupils to conclude that . . . "; "Help the students to understand that . . . "; or, in preparing for initial work with main ideas, "Introduce the word *idea*." This points up a problem

Table 1-1
Procedures Related to Comprehension in Five Basal Reader Series for Kindergarten through Grade Six

Series	Instruction	Review	Application	Practice
A	128	346	436	693
B	122	158	253	746
C	98	418	538	832
D	92	121	303	662
E	60	85	111	495

Definitions: *Instruction*—A manual suggests that a teacher do, say, or ask something that should help students understand or work out the meaning of connected text. *Review*—A manual suggests that a teacher do, say, or ask something for the purpose of going over instruction offered previously. *Application*—A manual suggests a procedure that allows for the use of what was featured in instruction; this is carried out under a teacher's supervision. *Practice*—A manual suggests a procedure that allows for the use of what was featured in instruction; this is carried out by students working independently.

common to all of the series: they offer precise help (such as obvious answers to assessment questions) when it is least needed, but they are obscure or silent when specific help is likely to be required. Even some of the specific help is of questionable value. First-grade teachers who say to their students exactly what the manuals tell them to say, for example, would be using such advanced language as *literal meaning, logical, infer, main idea, pause momentarily, evident, situation, refer to,* and *prepositional phrase.*

Lest anyone think that the judgments made for the basal reader study were based on excessively demanding criteria, it must be remembered that some manual recommendations categorized as comprehension instruction were only one sentence long. More specifically, if a manual suggested that a period be described to students as something that shows where a sentence ends, that was considered comprehension instruction. Although it was lean, the directive was judged to be both relevant and instructive, since readers do need to know where sentences end if they are to understand them. Before being told about this function of periods, however, they need to know what a sentence is, but manual authors overlooked this need.

In essence, what was counted as comprehension instruction was not always dealt with in a way, or a sequence, that made sense. Is it sensible, for example, to offer information about an ellipsis (three dots) as early as grade one (as did two of the five series) or grade two (as did two others) and then restate that information on twenty-four subsequent occasions? Does it make sense to explain the function of italics *after* students read a selection in which italicized words appear? Providing instruction after it would have been useful was characteristic of all the series. If the instruction could be applied to the next selection, the sequence would not be questioned, but that was not the practice. Instead, it was typical for something entirely different to be highlighted in the subsequent selection.

When considering the frequency with which comprehension instruction is offered, it is also important to remember that a manual procedure may meet the study's criteria for comprehension instruction yet not be instructive for the target audience. One of the five series, for example, deals with the linking function of *and* in a first-grade manual by recommending that children be told that *and* is used to connect two words. A list is put on the chalkboard to allow the children to name the words connected with *and* (for example, *Mary and John, up and down*).[1] Although this recommendation was judged to fulfill the criteria of comprehension instruction, it is highly unlikely that first-graders would be able to grasp the intended meaning of "connect." It is possible, therefore, that all they would derive from the recommended procedure would be word identification practice. Nonetheless, the recommendation was classified for the research as comprehension instruction, since it dealt with a signal word that is important for understanding connected text.

An unexpected characteristic of many manual recommendations for comprehension instruction is that they are more pertinent for writers than for readers.

One manual, for example, directs teachers to show students how simple, brief sentences can be made more interesting by adding adjectives and adverbs, but it makes no suggestion for relating this to how the meaning of long, seemingly complicated sentences can be worked out by readers. Instead of emphasizing that a rhetorical question might be followed by the answer, which is pertinent for readers to know, another manual desribes rhetorical questions as something authors use to hold readers' attention.

Teachers who adhere to one manual's recommendations would tell students that whatever is at the beginning or end of a sentence attracts attention. Elsewhere, the same series teaches that variety in sentence structure keeps a reader's attention. With another series, instructors would teach that short sentences can convey excitement. Meriting attention in all these cases is the fact that the possible significance for reading of what was being discussed was never treated. (Whether what was discussed is correct is a different but also important matter.)

Another questionable pattern found in all the series pertains to what could be interpreted as an eagerness to get to written exercises. Such a pattern can be illustrated by the handling of pronouns. The manuals suggest that teachers use one or two sentences to point out that pronouns refer to other, previously mentioned words and that they should then switch to application. The teachers are thus directed to use additional sentences with pronouns to see whether the students can name their referents—and that is all that is to be done. Predictably, workbook or ditto sheet assignments come next.

What should be emphasized about this illustration is that no suggestions are made for what to do if students are unable to name referents, nor are teachers ever encouraged to link what is being done with reading. More specifically, they are not directed to explain that understanding a sentence may require knowing who or what a referent is and that, if a mental substitution cannot be made for pronouns or for certain adverbs, rereading may be necessary. Instead, what is suggested is a brief, isolated event that is never linked to reading; that is, a means is treated as an end in itself. It is as if doing little exercises and getting right answers are all that count.

In the earlier discussion of the classroom-observation study, mentioning was said to characterize teachers' behavior. What manuals do with pronouns exemplifies mentioning: saying just enough about a topic to allow for an assignment. Mentioning is further illustrated by what the manuals suggest for a reader's use of contexts to learn the meanings of unfamiliar words. Essentially, the manuals' instruction for that topic is vague and circular, stating that the meaning of a word is sometimes suggested by the context and that the context sometimes suggests what a word means. Next comes application and practice; that is, teachers are told to list sentences and have the students explain the meanings of specified words. All the while, the concern is for right and wrong answers; consequently, teachers are not encouraged to probe with such questions as "How do you know it means that?" "What words in the sentence tell you what it means?" "Why couldn't it mean

_____ in this sentence?" That such brief, nonspecific instruction, with little or no probing, inhibits transfer to those times when students are reading on their own is a possibility that both authors and users of manuals should consider.

What may also inhibit transfer is the failure of the manual authors to keep in mind that reading is the concern. In one of the series, grammar seemed to be the issue. At the start, grammar instruction and its relevance for reading was clear. As the instruction became more advanced, however, explicit attention to the link between sentence grammar and sentence meaning disappeared. Instead of continuing to relate what was being taught about grammar to comprehension of sentences, the recommended instruction turned into a technical treatment of grammar as an end in itself. In this case, the unfortunately common practice of turning a means into an end not only deprived students of information that is useful for working out the meaning of complicated sentences but also required that they learn new terms concerned with grammar. Such an approach might be unwise, especially for students who have to struggle to become readers even when a reading program stays on target.

One more noteworthy pattern in all the examined series is a tendency to equate definitions with comprehension instruction and, by so doing, to stop just short of being helpful for reading. This can be illustrated by the way first-person and third-person narration is handled. Characteristically, much attention goes to defining each type of narration. Receiving far less coverage (or no coverage) are (1) the limitations of first-person narration in contrast to the omniscience allowed by a third-person perspective and (2) the implication of this contrast for reading.

The way in which the manuals handle fact and opinion reinforces the same conclusion. All the examined manuals encourage teachers to spend considerable time on defining *fact* and *opinion* and on having students do exercises in which they make distinctions between sentences that state facts and sentences that express opinions. Neglected, however, is how knowing the difference between a fact and an opinion should enter into the reading process—for instance, the reading of an editorial or an ad in a children's magazine. It is as if definitions are all that count, when, in fact, defining terms is just a beginning in the process of improving comprehension.

Review

When considering the data in table 1-1 on the frequency of review, it is important to keep in mind that suggestions for review in all the series are often one sentence long; consequently, they are also nonspecific (for example, "Remind pupils that authors sometimes give clues to when things happen"). When how to review *is* specified, the suggested procedure merely repeats what was recommended earlier for comprehenison instruction.

It is also important to note that the frequency with which information or a skill is reviewed appears to have no connection with its difficulty or importance for reading. The amount of review in all the series seemed to be the product of random behavior more than of a preestablished plan.

How review is spaced throughout a manual also seems to be the result of random decisions. Sometimes a topic is reviewed frequently after its initial coverage. At other times, a topic is introduced and then forgotten for a long while or forever. Thus, like the amount of review, the timing of review did not indicate a carefully constructed, predetermined plan for developing the manuals.

Had there been such a plan, it is likely that efforts to review as a whole what had been said intermittently about a given topic would have been common, not unusual. An obvious need to synthesize is illustrated by the series that taught that shifting the placement of phrases changes the meaning of sentences but then, in a subsequent manual, showed that rearrangements do not alter meaning. Nowhere were the two opposite conclusions ever brought together and compared so that students could understand when a change affects meaning and when it does not.

Application

Before the manuals were analyzed, it was assumed that a suggestion for comprehension instruction would be followed by a suggestion for application. Although this did not rule out the possibility of more than one instance of application for each instance of instruction, the large discrepancy actually found between frequency of instruction and the frequency of application was unexpected (see table 1–1).

This discrepancy stems from the tendency of all the examined manuals to teach by implication rather than by direct, explicit instruction. Thus, if an objective has to do with the ability to draw conclusions that are not stated, it is highly unlikely that manuals will describe an instructional procedure for teaching students how to reach unstated conclusions. Instead, the manuals are apt to provide teacher-supervised exercises (application) in which the concern is to see whether the students can arrive at the conclusions.[2] If the students are unable to do the exercises, all that is offered is more exercises.

One reason the labels assigned to manual segments by their authors were ignored during the analyses is that the manuals provide for application even when what is to be applied has not been taught. In one case, for example, a manual page directs teachers to read a paragraph aloud, after which students are to be questioned about the sequence of events that it describes. Even though the paragraph contained signal words, such as *first* and *after that*, they were never referred to in the suggestions. Only assessment questions were offered. Nonetheless, the activity is explicitly described in the manual as "instruction for following a sequence." For the study, it was classified as application.

Practice

Even a cursory look through basal manuals makes it abundantly clear that the one thing that is never forgotten at any grade level is practice in the form of workbook and ditto-sheet exercises. The effect of large numbers of exercises on students' conceptions of and attitudes toward reading merits consideration, as does the possibility that the content of the practice does little to develop reading skills. One common problem is that practice exercises tend to focus on brief pieces of text, even when what is to be practiced seems to call for larger units of discourse. This means that if the concern is to teach students how to make predictions while reading fiction, the practice is likely to be with sentences, not stories. The task for the students might be to connect sentences listed in one column (*Suzie was cold*) with sentences in a second column (*Suzie went inside*). Although such practice ought to help clarify the meaning of "making a prediction," its value for helping a person make predictions while reading a story must be questioned, especially since the manuals never urge teachers to point up the relationship—if one exists—between the practice exercises and reading a story.

Besides relying on brief pieces of text for practice, the manuals' descriptions of practice are themselves brief. In addition, one brief reference to practice is typically followed by another for still more practice dealing with something entirely different. The result is that many manual pages flit from one topic to another as they make suggestions for practice. A page in one manual, for example, deals in quick succession with identifying words by using contexts and sounds, distinguishing between main idea and supporting details, recognizing time order, interpreting figurative language, recognizing descriptive words, using dictionary skills, and getting information from diagrams.

Is it any wonder, then, that the thirty-nine teachers in the classroom-observation study were classified not as instructors but as mentioners, assignment givers, and assignment checkers? Why they were also called interrogators is explained by a quick look through the manuals: if teachers used all the questions found in the manuals, they would be questioning their students constantly—sometimes about trivia.

Concluding Comments

Presumably, those who are responsible for preparing basal reader series have a rationale for how they deal with comprehension. Although it is recognized that marketing data must be considered when decisions are made about the content of manuals, everyone who purchases, uses, or analyzes a series has the right to expect publishers and authors to assign equal importance to pedagogy. It thus seems appropriate to pose four questions for which the research that has been partially reported here did *not* uncover answers:

1. How do those who are responsible for manuals make decisions about what will be taught for comprehension and when it will be presented? A related question has to do with the content, timing, and frequency of review.
2. What is the reason for relying on practice to teach instead of on direct, explicit instruction followed by practice?

3. Why is there so much practice, typically carried out with brief exercises that may not apply when students read longer pieces?
4. When manuals discuss what writers do, why do they not also discuss its significance for readers? More generally, why are means so often treated as ends in themselves? Finally, why do so many procedures in the manuals stop short of being instructive for reading comprehension?

Although nobody can claim to know all that needs to be known about helping students become proficient comprehenders, those who prepare and publish basal reader series should be fully prepared to respond to the foregoing questions.

Notes

1. Throughout this chapter, the wording of examples is altered to avoid identifying a series. The essence of the recommended procedure, however, remains intact.

2. Because application procedures sometimes replaced (rather than followed) instruction, strict adherence to the definition of *application* in table 1–1 was not always possible.

References

Durkin, D. What classroom observations reveal about reading comprehension instruction. *Reading Research Quarterly,* 1978–79, *14,* 481–533.
Taylor, C. *Transforming schools.* New York: St. Martin's, 1976.

2
Workbooks: Counting, Matching, and Judging

Jean Osborn

Basal reading programs have three major components: (1) a teacher's guide, which provides procedures for the teacher to use in teaching reading; (2) a text, which contains narratives, expository passages, and poetry for the students to read; and (3) workbooks and ditto masters, which contain tasks for the students to work on independently. This chapter focuses on the workbook materials associated with basal reading programs.

My interest in workbooks derived from a classroom study that documented how student time was spent during reading periods (Mason & Osborn, Note 1). For this study, each of forty-five first- through sixth-grade classrooms was observed for two complete reading periods. The observations were made in classrooms that used basal reading programs. Workbooks were used regularly in these classrooms, as was evident from an examination of the data obtained by the classroom observers and from an analysis of interviews with the teachers. Furthermore, the observations revealed that, in most of the classrooms, the students spent as much or more time working independently in their workbooks as they did working with their teachers. (This is not to say that students spent all of the reading period with either their teachers or their workbooks; they were also observed reading silently, listening to tapes, and occasionally writing. Sometimes they were not doing much of anything.)

Two types of classroom organizations (self-contained and cross-class groupings) were observed. Workbooks were used for about the same amount of time in each type of classroom organization. In a self-contained classroom, workbooks have an obvious management function; that is, the teacher can give undivided attention to one group of students only when the other students are doing something that engages them and that the teacher thinks is worthwhile. In cross-class grouped classrooms, teachers have to deal with only one group of students; even in these classrooms, however, workbook activity was a regular feature of the reading lesson. It was evident that these teachers organized their reading periods to include workbook time for the students, even when there was no management need to do so.

Although some reading educators warn against the use of workbooks, the evidence from this study is that teachers use workbooks a great deal. Several reasons can be given for this widespread use. First, teachers want to provide their students with practice on the most difficult parts of the instruction in a lesson, with a review of what has already been taught, and with an integration of what has been taught into what is being taught. Also, in classes made up of small groups, workbooks are used to keep some students busy while the teacher works with others.

In addition, workbook tasks have some properties that are not often discussed. Workbooks provide the teacher with what is often the only clear and uncompromised feedback about what each student can do. Typically, a teacher working with a group of students will ask one student to read a passage aloud or to answer some questions. If that student's response is acceptable, the teacher will move to another student. The teacher must assume that the students who are not reading aloud or responding are able to read the passage and answer the questions. In contrast, workbook activities require students to work independently. Their performance on the workbook tasks provides teachers with information about each student, and such knowledge allows the teachers to make decisions about whether the students need additional instruction or can skip ahead to new material.

Finally, workbook activities train students to work independently. In most classrooms, students work on their workbook tasks independently. What is important, of course, is that the work provided in the workbooks is possible to do independently, is worth spending time on, and leads up to the task demands of other, more complex independent work that the students will face in junior high and high school.

An Examination of Workbooks

The amount of time I saw students engaged in workbook activities inspired me to examine some of the workbooks that accompany basal reading programs. I was interested in getting a sense of how what is taught in a basal reading program appears in its workbook components. Since workbooks are supposed to be part of a delivery system, I wanted to evaluate how well they support the rest of the system.

As I examined workbooks, I posed questions about *sufficiency, efficiency,* and *effectiveness:* Were there a sufficient number of activities to give students practice with new learning? Were the activities efficient—that is, were they well conceived, well written, and well correlated with the teacher instruction prescribed in the teacher's guide and the text provided in the reader? Most important, were the activities effective—that is, were they capable of making a positive difference in the students' reading performance? I realized that a definitive answer to this last question could be given only after serious and long-term classroom studies. I decided, however, that until such studies were done, the effectiveness of workbooks would have to be judged on the basis of such criteria as sufficiency and efficiency. It also became apparent that, since there is almost nothing in the educational literature about the sufficiency, efficiency, or effectiveness of workbook activities, workbook examiners would have to evaluate workbooks on the basis of their own experiences, some educated guesses, and a belief in the notion that meaningful practice of what is being learned makes a difference.

When I began, I was determined to apply my classroom experience to the analysis of the workbooks that were piled on my desk. My professional life has included work as a reading supervisor with teachers and students. I have spent a great deal of time looking over students' shoulders as they worked in workbooks and even more time analyzing the workbook pages of students who had completed their assignments. When I worked in classrooms, my special concern was for students who found it difficult to learn to read. Such students were also my concern as I looked through the workbooks on my desk. Relevant and challenging workbooks are probably important to most students, but they may be critically important to students for whom learning to read is difficult. These students probably do more workbook tasks than other students, because workbooks (and supplementary workbooks and additional exercises on ditto masters) are what teachers turn to when they seek additional practice materials for students who are having trouble.

The procedures I used were simple. I analyzed tasks, keeping in mind the sufficiency and efficiency criteria. As I examined a workbook, I followed along in the teacher's guide and the text to see what was going on in the rest of the lesson. What I saw (and did not see) prompted me to compile a set of twenty guidelines for publishers to consider as they develop workbook materials. Most of the guidelines were illustrated by counterexamples, which were pulled from various workbooks to demonstrate what can go wrong with the design of workbook tasks (Osborn, 1984). In this chapter, the twenty guidelines are put forth for consideration by workbook evaluators—teachers who are using workbooks with their students and adoption committees who are examining the workbook components of basal reading programs.

Some Guidelines for Evaluating Workbook Tasks

1. A sufficient portion of workbook tasks should be relevant to the instruction that is going on in the rest of the unit or lesson. A procedure is needed for analyzing the contents of workbooks and determining their relationship to the rest of the lesson and to previous lessons. Figure 2–1 shows a tabular format that can be used to record and compare the teaching events described in the teacher's guide and the types of tasks that appear in the accompanying workbooks. The vocabulary comprehension, decoding, study skills, and optional activities included in the teacher's guide are matched with the tasks in each workbook. A more complete table would include listings of the words included in the word recognition and vocabulary activities in the teacher's guide and the words the students use in the workbook tasks. Such list-

Program _____	Level _____	Unit _____	Lesson _____

Teacher's Guide	Workbook 1	Workbook 2
Word recognition: forty-six words	Word meaning tasks, with nine words from Lesson 10	Word meaning tasks, with eight words from Lesson 10
Word meaning: twenty-two words		
Sequencing of story events (six events)	Sequence task, with two sets of five events (independent of story in reader)	Sequence task, with six events (based on story)
Phonetic skills: introduce/spl, *sp;* review/ftl, *ft*	Sentence completion task, with thirteen sp words (one word from Lesson 10, no review words)	Sentence completion task, with six *sp* words (three story words) and six *ft* words (no story words)
Locating information on a contents page	Table of contents task	Table of contents task
Optional: 1. Noting action and conversation as a means of characterization 2. Dramatizing good safety habits	No task	No task

Figure 2–1. Sample Comparison Table of Teaching Events and Workbook Tasks

ings are useful in determining the amount of vocabulary practice and review included in workbook tasks (see guidelines 2 and 5).

2. Another portion of workbook tasks should provide for a systematic and cumulative review of what has already been taught. The goal of this guideline is not only to ascertain how the workbook pages relate to what is being taught in a given lesson but to document how much review activity is provided for students. Comparison tables (such as figure 2–1) for at least three consecutive lessons (or units) will give evaluators a sense of how much review is available in the workbook.

3. Workbooks should reflect the most important (and most workbook-appropriate) aspects of what is being taught in the program. Comparison tables for three consecutive lessons, combined with the experience of the teachers evaluating the workbooks, are probably the best means of determining importance and appropriateness in a program. If the teacher's guide for a program directs the teacher to teach about the sequencing of ideas, for example, yet the workbook tasks associated with that lesson (or the next lesson) do not provide practice on sequencing tasks, evaluators may judge that importance might be a problem with the workbooks of this basal program. Additional checks should follow on the relationships between topics covered in the teachers' guides and workbooks in other lessons. It is important to remember, however, that not all instruction is workbook-appropriate. If listening to the sound patterns in poems is part of the teacher-directed lesson, the decision not to include a written practice task for such auditory activity is probably appropriate.

4. *Workbooks should contain, in a form that is readily accessible to students and teachers, extra tasks for students who need extra practice.* Most basal programs provide supplementary workbook materials for students who need extra practice. These extra tasks should be especially valuable tasks, not just more of the same (unless the same is evaluated as valuable) or, worse yet, busywork activities with minimal instructional value. Compare, for example, a syllabication task that requires students to color, cut out, and paste words into shapes with one that has the children marking the syllables in words—perhaps following models that illustrate different syllabication generalizations. The cutting, pasting, and coloring task might keep the children busy for a long time, but it is unlikely to give them much useful practice in dividing words into syllables.

Figure 2–2 shows a table that can be used to tally the number and appropriateness of tasks for different topics. The table is filled out for four topics found in a second-grade workbook. (The extra help tasks appear in a supplementary workbook.) This part of the table shows that, in this workbook of this series, extra help tasks are available and that the workbook evaluator has judged about half of the tasks to be appropriate.

5. *The vocabulary level of workbook tasks should relate to that of the rest of the program and that of the students using the program.* A completed table similar to that

Program _____   Level _____   Unit _____   Lesson _____

Topic	Workbook Tasks		Extra Help Tasks	
	Number	Appropriate/ Not Appropriate	Number	Appropriate/ Not Appropriate
Main idea	6	2/4	6	2/4
Syllabication	6	3/3	6	3/3
Vowels: *er, ir, ur*	4	0/4	6	4/2
Structural analysis	8	7/1	10	6/4

Figure 2–2. Sample Table for Tallying Number and Appropriateness of Tasks.

described in guideline 1 (figure 2–1) can display both the vocabulary presented in the teacher-directed part of the lesson and the vocabulary requirements of the workbook tasks. By comparing the two lists, evaluators can identify programs that include in the workbooks a great deal of vocabulary that is not taught in the rest of the program. If, for example, a workbook task directs students to underline words in passages that show feelings of *hostility, mystery, hilarity,* and *bewilderment,* but these concepts do not appear in any vocabulary taught before the appearance of that task (nor in any of the stories the students read), the evaluators should be alert to further instances of a lack of relationship between components of the program.

6. The instructional language used in workbook tasks must be consistent with that used in the rest of the lesson and in the rest of the workbook. It seems obvious that the language (or explanations) used to teach a new skill or concept should be consistent with the language used in practice materials. To evaluate workbook tasks for consistency with the rest of the program, the instructions given for the teacher to explain new skills and concepts should be compared with those given to the students in the workbook tasks. If, for example, the teacher's manual directs the teacher to describe the differences between *fact* and *fiction,* but the students must decide if paragraphs they read in their workbooks are *real* or *not real,* there is an inconsistency between components of the program. Inconsistency might also be found from task to task within a workbook or even within a single workbook task.

7. Instructions should be clear, unambiguous, and easy to follow; brevity is a virtue. If workbook evaluators are experienced teachers, they know very well that many students do not read instructions but simply go ahead and do the tasks. When easy-to-teach students decide that they must read instructions, they are usually able to follow them, even if the instructions are confusing, ambiguous, or unclear. In contrast, when hard-to-teach students are confronted by unclear instructions, their inability to follow the instructions only confounds their tenuous ability to perform the tasks. It is for these students that clear instructions are especially important.

Probably the best way for workbook evaluators to evaluate instructions is to read several instructions on consecutive pages of workbooks. While reading, they should watch for the following:

Excessive wordiness—for example, "Use the words letters stand for and the sense of the other words to find out what the new word in heavy black print is."

Ambiguity—for example, "boxes" mentioned in instructions might not be evident on the page. Also, unclear uses of such words as *first, second, last, over, under, before,* and *after* are common.

Embedded steps—for example, "Read the first sentence and fill in the missing word. Read the second sentence. Find the word from the first sentence that makes sense in the second sentence and print it where it belongs. Then do what the last sentence says. Repeat for all the other sentences."

Lost steps—for example, "Fill in the blanks at the bottom of the page." If this instruction appears near the top of a page and is one of several instructions, the students are likely to forget it by the time they get to the bottom of the page.

Confusion—directions that even adults would have trouble figuring out; for example, "Four things are named in each row. Three of the things named are part of the other thing. Put a ring around the thing that the others are part of in each row."

Extended complexity—complex instructions that are continually repeated in the same complex form. As students become acquainted with task forms, surely the complexity of the instructions can be reduced; for example, an initial instruction for a workbook task might be, "Read the sentence and the words below it. Decide which word will best complete the sentence. Write that word on the line." Subsequent appearances of the same task could have a much shorter instruction, such as, "Complete each sentence."

Negation—instructions that require students to process words indicating negation, which are more difficult than instructions written without such words; for example, "Circle the word in each row that has a short vowel sound" is easier to process than "Circle the word in each row that does not have a long vowel sound."

Insufficient information—for example, an instruction that asks students to underline the words with the same sound as the word that names the picture. This does not contain sufficient information, because the word represented by the picture contains several sounds.

8. *The layout of workbook pages should combine attractiveness with utility.* Evaluators should watch out for workbook pages that appear cluttered, busy, or disorganized and for long lines of type that are difficult to read. Page layouts should help students understand the requirements of the tasks; for example, the performance requirements of the task in example A may be obscure to some students, whereas in example B each part of the task is labeled and the requirements of the task are more evident.

Example A

Draw a line between the syllables of each word. Then write the number of the rule you used.

1. between double consonant letters
2. between unlike consonant letters
3. between a vowel letter and a consonant
4. between two vowel letters

scaling _____   duty _____   letter _____

battle _____   potato _____   person _____

butter _____   explain _____   jelly _____

Example B

Draw a line between the syllables of each word. Then write the number of the rule you used.

> *Rules*
> 1. between double consonant letters
> 2. between unlike consonant letters
> 3. between a vowel letter and a consonant
> 4. between two vowel letters

Words	Rule Number	Words	Rule Number	Words	Rule Number
scaling	_____	duty	_____	letter	_____
battle	_____	potato	_____	person	_____
butter	_____	explain	_____	jelly	_____

9. *Workbook tasks should contain enough content so that there is a chance that a student doing the task will learn something, not simply be exposed to something.* Enrichment tasks that contain difficult (and sometimes important) concepts frequently appear only once. Tasks that require students to make analogies may be worthwhile, for example, but unless the tasks appear within a well-planned sequence of activities, those students who would most profit from practice with such an important language concept are not likely to benefit. A workbook with a large number of exposure tasks is probably a poor risk for hard-to-teach students.

10. *A task that requires students to make a discrimination must be preceded by a sufficient number of tasks that provide practice on the components of the discrimination.* When students have practiced and mastered component tasks, they have a better chance of coping successfully with tasks that require them to apply what they have learned to more complex tasks. If a task requires students to identify metaphors and similes, for example, evaluators should check that the task has been preceded by exercises in which students work separately with each of these figurative language forms. The opportunity to practice component tasks is especially important for hard-to-teach students.

11. *The content of workbook tasks must be accurate and precise; workbook tasks must not present wrong information nor perpetuate errors.* Phonics, word analysis, and comprehension tasks should be looked at with a critical eye to make sure that students do not practice, for example, that "the sound of *o* in *hope* is short" or that "the

main idea is the first sentence of a paragraph." A workbook with more than one or two such tasks should be viewed with caution—perhaps with alarm.

12. At least some workbook tasks should be fun and should have an obvious payoff. Workbook evaluators should not expect all tasks to be fun and games, but occasional puzzles, word games, cartoons, and other gamelike tasks are probably appreciated by students. It is important, however, that these tasks be worthwhile, not pointless.

13. Most student response modes should be consistent from task to task. The use of an X mark, for example, may cause errors. Students are likely to be confused if they are directed to use X to mark incorrect words in a group of sentences in one task and to use X to mark the sentences that indicate the correct details from a story in the next task.

14. Student response modes should be as close as possible to reading or writing. Except for workbooks designed for children who have not yet developed writing skills, student response modes that call for more rather than less writing seem desirable. Tasks that require students to fill in letters that stand for words, as in example C, probably teach less about word meaning than tasks that require students to write in words.

Example C

Write the letter for the word that belongs in each blank.

a. jumprope
b. stars
c. pouring

1. Where did you leave your ___*a*___ ?

2. The rain was ___*c*___ from the sky.

3. Marcy got seven ___*b*___ on her papers.

Surely, a student checking over the sentence "Where did you leave your *a*?" will not be encouraged to check the next sentence. The same task cast in a format closer to the tasks of reading and writing is shown in example D:

Example D

Write the word that belongs in each blank.

jumprope
stars
pouring

1. Where did you leave your *jumprope* ?

2. The rain was *pouring* from the sky.

3. Marcy got seven *stars* on her papers.

Another example of evaluating response modes can be drawn from main idea and sequencing tasks. The purpose of main idea and sequencing practice tasks is to help children identify what is important in what they read. Underlining the main idea sentence in a paragraph (if one exists) is closer to real reading than finding the appropriate main idea sentence among three sentences in a multiple choice task. Requiring students to write out main ideas (whether they be stated or implied in a paragraph), however, is even closer to the challenges of reading and studying. By the same token, asking students to write out the sequence of ideas in a paragraph, as in example E, seems to be much better preparation for reading and studying than having them write numbers next to an array of phrases or sentences, as in example F.

Example E

Rochelle did five jobs before she and her mother went skating. List those jobs in the order she did them.

1. _____ made the bed
2. _____ cleaned her room
3. _____ sorted the laundry
4. _____ carried the baskets
5. _____ washed the dishes

Example F

Number the sentences to show the order of events in the story.

__5__ Rochelle practiced the flute.

__1__ Rochelle made her bed.

__3__ Rochelle sorted the laundry.

__2__ Rochelle did the dishes.

__4__ Rochelle carried the laundry baskets to the car.

Example E requires more writing by the student (and more time correcting for the teacher) than example F does, but it seems more like a real study task.

15. *The instructional design of individual tasks and of task sequences should be carefully planned.* A well-designed task makes the performance requirements of the task clear, helps the student attend to the important elements of the task, and permits the student to move without hazard through the task from beginning to end. So little has been written on task design that it is difficult to provide precise guidelines for workbook evaluators, but a few illustrations will indicate some aspects of instructional design that should be considered.

The exercise in example G purports to give students practice in reading sentences that use two different meanings for the same word. The students are told to put a circle around the sentence that goes with the picture:

Example G

Flowers grow in the earth.

The earth moves around the sun.

The students have to read only as far as *flowers* in the first sentence to get the correct answer. The task is written so that no further reading is necessary, which makes it unlikely that the students will practice reading the target words.

Example H shows a similar item written so that the students are much more likely to read the target words:

Example H

Her dog sleeps in that shed.

I wish her dog didn't shed.

Another problem is two-part tasks in which the student's success in working the second part depends on getting all of the items correct in the first part. Such tasks are neither instructionally sound nor fair to students.

Some tasks are written so that student responses do not indicate to the teacher what the students know. Responses to the syllabication task in example I, indicate only whether the students know how many syllables are in words, not where the divisions occur:

Example I

Read each word. Color the circles to tell how many syllables there are in each word.

outside	oooo	everyone	oooo	vegetables	oooo
Tuesday	oooo	point	oooo	Saturday	oooo
potato	oooo	stopped	oooo	morse	oooo

It should also be noted that coloring the circles carefully is probably a big waste of time.

Some tasks are written so that student responses do not indicate whether or not they are correct. In example J, the teacher has no way of telling whether the student has identified the before events or the after events; the lines the students draw indicate only that two obviously connected events have been matched.

Example J

Draw lines from the sentences that show *before* to those that show *after.*

The girl fell on the sidewalk.	Mail fell in the mailbox.
The mailbox was full.	The girl hurt her arm.
The water spilled from the bucket.	The man filled the bucket.

Some tasks make unreasonable demands on students. The task in example K would be difficult (and tedious and boring) for even the most compulsive adult to complete, and it surely would be frustrating and self-defeating for most second-grade students. (Such tasks usually present many sentences for the students to analyze.)

Example K

Read each sentence. Decide which consonant letter is used the most. Underline it each time.

1. My most important toy is a toy train.
2. Nancy, who lives in the next house, has nine cats.
3. Will you bring your box of marbles to the party?

The following is another example of unreasonableness:

Example L

In these sentences, some words end with these blends: *lf, lp, lt, nd, nt, cut, ft, mp.* Underline the letters for these blends in the words in these sentences.

1. The cat and dog are sitting on a shelf.
2. We will plant a tree in the camp.
3. The snow and ice will slowly melt.

One question that often arises after a task is labeled unreasonable is "What good is this task anyway?" Such questions should be honored and answered truthfully by workbook evaluators.

16. Workbooks should contain a finite number of task types and forms. The repetition of task forms is not a common practice in workbooks. On the contrary, there are usually almost as many task forms as there are pages in a workbook. Frequent use of the same task forms, but with differing content, has two advantages: it reduces the need for teacher help, and, once students have learned to work with a task form, they can concentrate on task content.

One procedure for charting the task forms in a workbook is as follows:

1. Select thirty consecutive pages from a workbook.
2. Write down a topic for each page—for example, "practice with words with *sw*," or "alphabetical order."
3. Mark any tasks that have the same form.

Figure 2–3 is an example of such charting, representing thirty consecutive pages in a third-grade workbook. The topic labels enclosed in boxes, circles, and wave circles show the number of times task forms are repeated. Only three forms being repeated, one time each, may not seem to be frequent repetition, but it is more

Page	Task Topic	Page	Task Topic
21	Practice with words with *ine*	36	Syllables
22	Practice with *oo*	37	Puzzles
23	Choosing titles	38	Word identification
24	Word identification	39	Practice with words with *ash*
25	Using common syllables *a, be, un, ful, ly, ness*	40	Base words and endings
26	Vocabularly identification and use of *cl, bl, pl*	41	Practice with words with *spr* and *str*
27	Word referents	42	Practice with *and,* comprehension
28	Plural *ves* on words ending with *f*	43	Classifying words
29	Following directions	44	Contractions
30	Alphabetical order	45	Sequencing
31	Classifying words	46	Practice with words with *sw*
32	Practice with words with *ie*	47	Long and short *e* sounds, comprehension
33	Compound words, comprehension	48	Multimeaning words
34	Commas as a comprehension aid	49	Practice with words with *ward,* comprehension
35	Noting details	50	Noting details

Figure 2–3. Sample Charting of Task Topics and Forms

than occurs in many workbooks. Note that not all similar task labels imply a similar task form.

Since counting task forms also involves counting task topics, the other benefit of such evaluation is that it reveals the number of topics covered in a workbook. The variety of topics and the lack of repetition of either topics or task forms may lead workbook evaluators to wonder about the sufficiency of practice available to students. They should consider whether the workbooks contain a sufficient number of tasks to provide the massed practice that might help hard-to-teach students master the skills and concepts of the program.

17. The art that appears on workbook pages must be consistent with the text of the task. Pictures that are confusing and inappropriate to the task are bad, no matter how nice they may look. Inappropriate and confusing art can turn a task into a guessing game. Sometimes, pictures are extraneous to the content of a workbook page and seem to exist solely as decorations—and as occupiers of space that could perhaps be used more profitably.

Workbook evaluators can sample the appropriateness of art by the following procedure:

1. Randomly select twenty illustrated pages from a workbook.
2. Examine each page according to the following criteria:
    a. Clarity of drawings. (Does the picture illustrate what it is supposed to illustrate?)
    b. Relationship of pictures to items. (Do the pictures relate to the text?)
    c. Appropriateness. (Are the pictures necessary? Is their presence a help or a hindrance in completing the task?)

Particular attention should be given to an examination of the sound analysis tasks that frequently appear in beginning levels of a program. Example M represents a hazardous task.

Example M

Circle the pictures whose names begin with the beginning sound of the word *cat*.

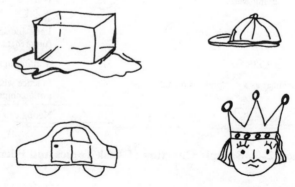

The ice cube could be identified as beginning with the same sound as the word *ice*, the car could be identified as an automobile, the cap as a hat, and the crown as a king. None of these perfectly reasonable identifications would do much for the score of the student who thought of them. Teachers should be aware that such tasks need a great deal of teacher direction if they are to achieve their intent.

18. Cute, nonfunctional, and space- and time-consuming tasks should be avoided. One person's fun task may be another's nonfunctional task, and workbooks with large numbers of nonfunctional and space-consuming tasks should make teachers uneasy. The proportion of nonfunctional tasks in a workbook can be calculated by counting them. Even though the success of this effort will depend on the agreement (or near agreement) of the people who are evaluating the workbooks, such an effort is worth pursuing. If more than 5 percent of a workbook's tasks are judged nonfunctional, the practice function of that workbook would have to be questioned, especially for hard-to-teach students.

19. When appropriate, workbook tasks should be accompanied by brief explanations of purpose for both teachers and students. Explanations of the purpose of the tasks should be available to the teacher. When headings to explain purpose are written for students, they should be written in language the students are likely to understand.

The following task titles selected from several workbooks do not seem to reveal to students the purposes of the tasks (a description of what each task is about follows in parentheses):

The Boy Roy (practice with the *oi* sound)

Putting Down Roots (practice with root words)

Now Hear This (a vocabulary/picture task)

That's Not a Ship (a task with *sh* and *th* sounds)

The following more straighforward set of titles, also selected from several workbooks, are probably more communicative of their tasks' intents:

Cause and Effect

Alphabetical Order

Compound Words

Fiction and Nonfiction

20. "English major" humor should be avoided. This final guideline is the perhaps desperate cry of someone who has looked at too many workbooks. Adult humor and adult use of language, which will pass right by most students, should be discouraged. Perhaps tasks featuring such language are attempts at cleverness by the underemployed English majors whom I suspect are responsible for the development of many workbook tasks. An overriding guideline for all instruction (whether it be delivered in the written mode or in the oral mode) is clarity of communication. Asking second-grade students to "match the consonant clusters with the grape clusters" or (in a dictionary task) to "have your fingers do the walking" is of questionable communicative value.

Recommendations

The evaluation procedures described in this chapter should help workbook evaluators get a sense of the sufficiency and efficiency of the workbooks that they are using or that they contemplate using. The procedures employ counting (to ascertain the number of tasks devoted to various topics), matching (to compare the content of the workbook task with the content of the rest of the lesson), and subjective judgment (to evaluate the usefulness and suitability of tasks). These procedures will produce some hard data and some soft data, but that should be an improvement over the common "flip-through" method of determining the suitability of workbooks. In following the procedures, workbook evaluators may wish to eliminate some of the guidelines and/or create additional guidelines.

If the examination of a set of workbooks by a group of workbook evaluators reveals an unacceptable number of problems and weaknesses in a workbook, then some obvious questions usually come to mind: "Should workbooks be improved?" and "Can workbooks be improved?" The answer to the first question must be yes, because workbooks are relied on so heavily in the teaching of reading. The answer to the second question could be a resounding yes if three groups took it upon themselves to pay concerted attention to workbooks: (1) educational researchers who are interested in classroom practice and curriculum design, (2) publishers of basal reading programs, and (3) teachers who use the workbooks associated with basal reading programs. Some suggestions for each group follow.

Educational Researchers

The developers of workbooks do not have a sophisticated body of research from which to draw when they create workbooks. Researchers have done little to study the relationship of the content of workbooks to the content of teachers' guides and student readers. Almost nothing has been written about the instructional design, the wording of instructions, or the sequence and concentration of activities in workbooks. Such information would be invaluable to the developers of workbook tasks. Even more important, however, is that there has been almost no research regarding the relevance of workbook activities to the acquisition of reading skill. Researchers who are interested in the kinds of materials and activities that facilitate reading acquisiton and in the design of reading programs are urged to carry out research that can be applied to the development of workbook tasks.

Publishers of Basal Materials

Many of the workbooks associated with basal readers seem to have been written separately from the rest of the program and after the fact. So that workbooks can be a more useful part of a program, a great deal of planning time at the outset of program development should be devoted to developing plans for integrating the workbook tasks with the rest of the program. Mechanisms should be developed that will permit the people who write workbook tasks to work regularly with other members of the writing team.

Another suggestion is that materials be carefully tested in small-scale, intensive tryouts before they are published. A simple and feasible procedure is to place preliminary versions of workbooks in two to four classrooms. (Obviously, these should be classrooms in which the rest of the program is being tried out.) As the editors or authors observe in the classrooms, they can record what teachers say as they present tasks, observe students as they do the tasks, and listen to the questions the students ask. By analyzing the completed workbook pages and tallying the errors, workbook designers can identify weak tasks (and poor items within tasks) and either eliminate or remedy them. Such procedures would improve workbooks enormously.

Finally, instead of the current, rather superficial integration of the textbooks, the teacher-directed parts of the lessons, and the workbook tasks, a much deeper level of integration of the workbook and the rest of the lesson is suggested. The following are some ideas for facilitating this integration:

1. New vocabulary from the stories being read, and from stories previously read, can be used in a variety of tasks and in a variety of contexts, not only in the tasks that are about the story. Recent research on vocabulary (Beck, Perfetti, & McKeown, 1982) emphasizes that words must be presented many times and in many different contexts for students to acquire new vocabulary. Workbook tasks seem to be an obvious medium for the application of this research.

2. Since students spend a good part of the reading period reading a story or an expository passage in the textbooks, it seems only sensible that the major portion of the workbook tasks should be based on this reading. Questions in workbook tasks that ask about the salient features of stories (plot, settings, characterizations) and about the important information in expository passages seem to be more valuable than questions about short paragraphs that are unrelated to any other reading the students do. The application of comprehension and decoding skills to the main reading done in the lesson would seem to make the teaching (and use) of these skills much more functional and meaningful. Therefore, the recommendation is that essentially all of the workbook tasks should relate to the current lesson,

should review aspects of previous lessons, or should provide for the application of previously learned information and vocabulary in new but related contexts.

Teachers

The advice to teachers is for the most part obvious. Workbook tasks must be evaluated before they are assigned to students. Teachers should operate not from a position of faith in the printed word but rather from a position of skepticism. Some tasks should be abandoned because they are confusing, because they are not important, or because they are nonproductive consumers of time. Tasks that are valuable, however, should be repeated, and particularly effective tasks can be adopted by the teacher to permit the students to practice further examples or instances of what is being taught. Teachers should become aware of which tasks require additional instructions, which pictures require modification, and which tasks most students can do independently. Teachers should also realize how counterproductive it is for students to spend a long time working on tasks on which they make many errors. Worthwhile but difficult tasks should be done when teachers have time to monitor students as they work on the tasks.

In addition, teachers should make their observations about unsatisfactory workbooks and unsatisfactory tasks known to the publishers of their basal series. Publishers will change their materials as the demands of their markets encourage them to change. Information from teachers to publishers can and will affect the quality of workbooks.

Conclusion

All of the hours students spend working and practicing in their workbooks have to be considered a part of reading instruction. Thus, what is provided in those workbooks should be given the serious consideration of researchers, of publishers of the materials used in classrooms, and of the teachers evaluating those materials.

Reference Note

1. Mason, J., & Osborn, J. *When do children begin "reading to learn"? A survey of classroom reading instruction practices in grades two through five* (Tech. Rep. No. 261). Urbana: University of Illinois, Center for the Study of Reading, September 1982.

References

Beck, I.L., Perfetti, C.A., & McKeown, M.G. Effects of long-term vocabulary instruction on lexical access and reading comprehension. *Journal of Educational Psychology*, 1982, *74*, 506–521.

Osborn, J. The purposes, uses, and contents of workbooks and some guidelines for teachers and publishers. In R.C. Anderson, J. Osborn, & R.J. Tierney (Eds.), *Learning to read in American schools: Basal readers and content texts.* Hillsdale, N.J.: Erlbaum, 1984.

3
Stories in Readers and Trade Books

Bertram Bruce

For many people, the phrase "learning to read" conjures up an image of a group of little children sitting in a circle on tiny chairs, taking turns reading aloud from a book of stories. Similarly, the phrase "reading to a child" invokes an image of a child sitting on a bed or a lap and a parent reading a story to the child. Other images we might create about children and reading would likely have a primary feature in common with these first two: the reading of stories.

Even for children, reading is not confined to stories; there are also poems and cereal boxes, street signs and animal books, letters and instructions for games, arithmetic books and words on the TV screen. Stories, however, seem to be central to the way we think about learning to read, and they certainly play a major role in formal reading instruction. If we want to understand reading and learning to read better, it is essential that we think about the part played by stories. We need to know what stories really are, what it takes to understand a story, and what can be done to facilitate story understanding. We also need to see how story reading relates to other kinds of reading.

There are several tacit assumptions about stories: (1) a story is a natural thing to read; (2) it is an easy-to-read recounting of exciting events; (3) story understanding is similar for children and adults and does not need to be (perhaps cannot be) taught; (4) the form, though not the content, of children's stories is similar to that of the stories adults read; and (5) stories are good preparation for other reading.

There is some truth in each of these assumptions, but there are also ways in which each conflicts with research findings. If we are to have the best possible reading programs, we need to understand stories better. This chapter will explore current research on stories, story understanding, and the teaching of story understanding to see the implications for reading programs.

Stories

In a discussion of the treatment of graphic signals in basal reader manuals, Durkin (1981) points out that the stories given to beginning readers require that they understand a set of complex graphic signals, such as quotation marks, at the very beginning of their reading careers. This observation calls into question the common assumption that stories are good for beginners because they are simple and thus easy to read. Suppose, however, that these graphic signals were not an impediment to reading. Would a story then be the simple form that it is often taken to be? Recent research suggests not; rather, understanding an apparently simple children's story can require a sophisticated knowledge of concepts, social life, and literary forms.

Results of national surveys of children's reading and writing skills (NAEP, Note 1, Note 2) show that our schools have not been fully successful in helping children learn either to comprehend or to appreciate the complexities of the literature they are expected to read. An insufficient appreciation of the nature of stories and of the demands of story understanding is likely to be a contributing factor to this problem. A better understanding would certainly help in formulating strategies for teaching reading.

For an overview of research results on stories, one would need to look at research on schemata in reading (Rumelhart, 1980b), metacognition (Brown & Smiley, 1977), inference (Collins, Brown, & Larkin, 1980), hypothesis formation (Bruce & Rubin, Note 3), text comprehension models (Kintsch & van Dijk, 1978), social plans (Newman, 1980), story schemas (Applebee, 1978; Mandler, 1978), affect in stories (Brewer & Lichtenstein, 1981), background knowledge (Adams & Bruce, 1982), rhetorical structures (Booth, 1961; Chatman, 1978), the author-reader relationship (Bruce, 1981), and literary response (Rosenblatt, 1978). A review of these works would be only a sampling of the many volumes written about stories; by means of a simple experiment, however, we can perhaps develop a sense of what has been learned from the research. We will examine several versions of a story. The differences between these versions demonstrate some of the essential story elements. For the experiment to work, you must keep in mind the salient features of each version, and you must be patient; the early versions may seem like word salad.

What is a story, anyway? This question, which might seem rather simple, has generated considerable research interest in the past few years (Black & Wilensky, 1979; Frisch & Perlis, 1981; Mandler & Johnson, 1980; Rumelhart, 1980a), which has led to new theories and empirical work on story intuitions (Brewer & Lichtenstein, 1981). Our concern here is not to attempt to define some minimal criteria for storyhood but rather to understand the ingredients that blend together in a story. We will highlight some of these ingredients by taking apart a simple children's story and looking at it in altered forms that reveal something of its essence.

The first version is based on the premise that a story is about events; that is, it describes changes in a state of affairs. Typically, these events are caused by intentional agents to whom the events are significant; that is, their outcome matters. The following text describes some significant events in the lives of a dog, a cat, and a mouse:

Version 1

The dog woke up just in time to see the cat cross the finish line. He had teased the cat about being so pokey.

"I get where I'm going as surely as YOU do!" said the cat.

The mouse suggested they run a race to settle the argument. The dog lay down by the side of the path to take a short nap.

If this text seems incomprehensible or boring, don't worry; it should be. Even though potentially exciting events are described—a race, an argument, teasing, and so on—there is a marked lack of coherence. It is difficult to track the order in which the events occurred. Studies that have manipulated the order of events in such narratives (Mandler, 1978; Stein & Nezworski, 1978; Thorndyke, 1977; Baker, Note 4) have shown that narratives are generally easier to comprehend and to recall later if the order in which events are described matches their true order in the world created by the narrative. Thus, the problems in version 1 are at least partly attributable to a scrambling of the sentence order.

Reordering the sentences, we get version 2:

Version 2

The dog teased the cat about being so pokey.

"I get where I'm going as surely as YOU do!" said the cat.

The mouse suggested they run a race to settle the argument. The dog lay down by the side of the path to take a short nap. He woke up just in time to see the cat cross the finish line.

Here, events begin to make more sense. We see teasing as part of an argument that leads to a race. Although a readability formula (Bruce, Rubin, & Starr, 1981; Davison & Kantor, 1982) would assign the same rating to versions 1 and 2, most people would feel that version 2 is more readable. It is also easier to remember—and it is beginning to look like a story.

Version 2 still has problems, however. It seems incomplete, and it is not clear why events happened. Version 2 gives us only a glimpse of the characters' underlying plans. Missing events must be inferred, and the reader does not know enough about the characters' beliefs and goals to make the inferences.

Version 3 is more complete (added words are italicized):

Version 3

The dog teased the cat about being so pokey. *But the dog lost this race. "I get where I'm going FASTER," said the dog.*

The mouse suggested they run a race to settle the argument. *"I'll race you and I'll WIN!" the cat said.*

The race had hardly begun before the dog was out of sight. He lay down by the side of the path to take a short nap. *The cat kept plodding slowly along.* The dog woke up just in time to see the cat cross the finish line.

The point of the story now begins to become clear; it shows a real argument and how the race serves to settle it. From a purely cognitive view, version 3 is an improvement, because it is easier to comprehend and remember. Like the two earlier versions, however, version 3 is unsatisfying. Among other things, it fails to generate suspense, surprise, or curiosity. Brewer and Lichtenstein (1982) have shown that the presence of these features is necessary for the intuitive feeling that a narrative is, in fact, a story. Whatever suspense might have been created in version 3 is lost because the second sentence informs us about the final outcome.

Clearly, revision is needed again. With a few small changes, we get a minimal suspense story:

Version 4

The dog teased the cat about being so pokey.
"I get where I'm going as surely as YOU do!" said the cat.
"But I get where I'm going FASTER," said the dog.
The mouse suggested they run a race to settle the argument.
"I'll race you and I'll WIN!" the cat said.
The race had hardly begun before the *speedy* dog was out of sight. He lay down by the side of the path to take a short nap. The cat kept plodding slowly along. The dog woke up just in time to see the cat cross the finish line *and win the race.*

Highlighting the dog's speediness and not revealing the race winner until the end gives an element of surprise to the final outcome. In addition, we can feel at least a little suspense about the argument and the race. For the first time, we have something that might qualify as a story. Version 4 is a weak story, however. Although it qualifies as a story on technical grounds, it is unlikely that many readers would care about the characters or about who wins the race.

One reason for our discomfort with version 4 is that it is difficult to connect it with the knowledge we had before we read it. Comprehension is a creative process in which a reader constructs new meaning out of old (Adams & Bruce, 1982). Texts function as blueprints or, more typically, as artists' sketches that guide, inspire, and constrain the reader's creative process but never determine it. In our sample text, the sketch is too spare; it fails to stimulate the vast reservoir of knowledge that every reader has about animals and races and thus creates a feeling of pointlessness to the enterprise.

Even in texts as empty as this one, however, a reader can sometimes find meaning. Many readers of versions 1 through 4 have no doubt caught the semblance of a familiar story that makes more sense. By changing the dog into a hare, the cat into a tortoise, and the mouse into a fox, we get this version of Aesop's "The Hare and the Tortoise":

Version 5

The *hare* teased the *tortoise* about being so pokey.
"I get where I'm going as surely you YOU do!" said the *tortoise*.

"But I get where I'm going FASTER," said the *hare*.
The *fox* suggested they run a race to settle the argument.
"I'll race you and I'll WIN!" the *tortoise* said.
The race had hardly begun before the speedy *hare* was out of sight. He lay down by the side of the path to take a short nap. The *tortoise* kept walking slowly along. The *hare* woke up just in time to see the *tortoise* cross the finish line and win the race.

More has changed between versions 5 and 4 than just the characters' names. Whereas we had been reading about three familiar but undistinctive animals, we now have characters whose features enhance the construction of meaning.

The simple change of names has linked the previously impotent story into two immensely powerful sources of knowledge—our knowledge of the real world and our knowledge of stories. The first opens up a realm of concepts and relationships among concepts that is far richer than anything we can infer directly from our simple text. Knowing how fast a hare can be and how slow a tortoise is is incomparably more useful for the construction of meaning than any literally conveyed message, such as "the speedy dog." Similarly, the cleverness of foxes makes a fox more believable as the one who would suggest a resolution to an argument. Certainly, one would not expect a mouse to be telling a dog and a cat what to do. When a story works for a reader, it is partly because associations such as these are tapped by the author's choice of words.

The second source of knowledge tapped by the name changes in version 5 is story knowledge. For both versions 4 and 5, the reader has to step outside ordinary reality to make sense of what is being said—that is, to accept that animals talk as people do. Version 5 invokes story knowledge in a more precise way, however. Hares in stories are often impulsive, bold, and not especially bright (Peter Rabbit, Benjamin Bunny, Bugs Bunny, Huge Harold, the Velveteen Rabbit, the rabbits in the *Watership Down* warrens). Foxes are not only clever but often manipulative as well (the fox in "The Fox and the Rooster"). These concepts and others make the reader's construction of meaning far richer than a simple story would suggest.

Version 5 works better as a story than the previous versions because it describes events in a coherent order, because it describes enough for the reader to fill out the plan schemas, because it is organized to create suspense and surprise, and because it situates the story in a rich environment of real-world and story knowledge. What version 5 lacks is engagement. We do not know what the characters are thinking or feeling, and the text is too short to allow us to infer much about them. We are not engaged with the author, either. There is no ostensible purpose to the text and little sense of style. It is difficult to say what the author feels or wants us to feel about the characters, the race, or the story. Finally, we are not engaged with the story itself. There is little reason to comprehend details or to think about the story's meaning for our lives. An unengaging story such as this may satisfy other goals, but it ultimately fails to do what stories are supposed to do.

Version 6 is the original text (Kent, 1974):

Version 6: "The Hare and the Tortoise"

The hare teased the tortoise about being so pokey.
"I get where I'm going as surely as YOU do!" said the tortoise.
"But I get where I'm going FASTER," said the hare.
The fox suggested they run a race to settle the argument. *The hare laughed so hard at the idea that it made the tortoise angry.*
"I'll race you and I'll WIN!" the tortoise said.
The race had hardly begun before the speedy hare was out of sight. *The hare was so sure of himself* that he lay down by the side of the path to take a short nap. The tortoise kept plodding slowly along. The hare woke up just in time to see the tortoise cross the finish line and win the race.
SLOW AND STEADY WINS THE RACE.

With only a few sentences added to relate the thoughts and feelings of the hare and the tortoise, their actions become more sensible and believable. The inside view afforded by these sentences (Bruce, 1982; Steinberg & Bruce, Note 5) enriches the meaning attached to the more externally observable events. The final sentence is the familiar moral, "Slow and steady wins the race." The author now gives us an inside view of himself. (It seems to be a characteristic of fables to make the narrative portion relatively authorless, so that the reader can focus first on the specific instance and then on its generalization in the moral.) The moral lets us know what the author thinks and what he intends the point of the story to be.

Version 6 is not a perfect story, of course, but it is representative of stories written for beginning readers. It relates goal-directed event sequences in a coherent and relatively complete form. Moreover, it uses a structure that enhances suspense and surprise; it invites the reader to situate the story in a rich environment or real-world and story knowledge; and it makes the characters come alive by allowing insight into their thoughts and feelings. Finally, it becomes what every story must be—a communication, with a purpose, between an author and a reader (Bruce, 1981).

Story Understanding

The various versions of "The Hare and the Tortoise" tell us something about what differentiates a story from other kinds of text. Each improvement in the text points to a skill the reader needs to make sense of any story. Thus, it should be clear that to read and comprehend a story, even one as simple as "The Hare and the Tortoise," the reader needs many sorts of knowledge, including knowledge of events, plans, story structures, real-world creatures, story-world characters, and the rhetorical devices that writers employ, such as inside view and author commentary. This knowledge is in addition to the basic graphemic, lexical, syntactic, and semantic knowledge needed to read a single phrase.

Despite the immense cognitive task implied by the need to have and use diverse sorts of knowledge, however, people do learn to read. For some, reading comes early and seems to progress dramatically, even without formal instruction. For others, learning to read is much more difficult. To make sense of the phenomenon of learning to read, we must examine story understanding more directly.

Prior research on early story understanding has been inconclusive. Some studies (Adams & Bruce, 1982; Mandler, Scribner, Cole, & DeForest, 1980) point to the substantial abilities young children possess for understanding stories. Green and Laff (Note 6), for example, have shown that children as young as 5 years are sensitive to subtle stylistic variations and are able to distinguish, for instance, between the rhymed couplets of Virginia Kahl and those of Dr. Seuss. Brewer and Hay (Note 7) have found that, upon hearing a story, 3-year-olds can make accurate judgments about characteristics of the story's narrator.

Numerous studies, however, have highlighted developmental differences in story comprehension (McConaughy, Fitzhenry-Coor, & Howell, in press; Stein & Glenn, 1979; Sedlak, Note 8). One general finding is that adults seem better at understanding events in psychological rather than purely physical terms. Thus, there is some conflict between one line of research that surprises us with portrayals of the remarkable cognitive capacities of young children and another that continues to elucidate the things these children cannot do.

A parallel conflict can be seen in research on the effect of cultural differences on early story understanding (Brewer, Note 9). Kintsch and Greene (1978) have presented evidence that, for undergraduates in Colorado, native Alaskan narratives were more difficult to summarize or to recall than more culturally familiar stories. Steffensen, Jog-dev, and Anderson (Note 10) have shown a similar effect for descriptions of wedding ceremonies in India and the United States that were read by students in each country. On the other hand, Mandler et al. (1980) found few differences in the patterns of recall when they had Americans and Liberians read Western and Liberian folk tales; they concluded that the structure of folk tales may be a cultural universal.

It is not possible to resolve these conflicts at this time. One reason is that we have only limited models of the process of story understanding (but see Collins, Brown, & Larkin, 1980; Bruce & Rubin, Note 3). Another reason is that our theories of story and discourse are inadequate—although, again, there have been promising attempts to develop these theories further (Brewer & Lichtenstein, 1982; Bruce, 1981; Chatman, 1978). A third reason is that research thus far has generally focused on questions of the form "Can people of group X do Y?" rather than on delineating exactly what a person has done in the act of comprehending. It is this last issue that we will examine here.

Following the pattern of the preceding section, we will carry out another experiment with various texts. There is one important difference between the texts in this section and those in the preceding section, however; these texts are prose renditions of a reader's constructed meaning.

Newman (1980) wanted to be able to describe in detail and thus account for differences among readers in the comprehension of simple stories. He used skits taken from "Sesame Street", all of which featured Bert and Ernie. Using various methods (probe questions, recall, reenactments), Newman uncovered striking differences in children's understandings of the skits. (Full explication of the differences required development of a theory about perspective taking and social interaction that is beyond the scope of this chapter.) We can get some idea of what Newman did by reformulating his formal account as a narrative. We will focus on one of the skits, known as "The Cookie Skit."

In the skit, Bert is about to eat a cookie that he has been saving all day when Ernie appears. Ernie sees the cookie and decides that he wants it. He reaches for it, but Bert pulls away, saying, "Not so fast. This cookie is for me. Um."

Ernie isn't fazed, however. He begins trying to convince Bert to share the cookie. He argues that if he (Ernie) had the cookie, he would share it with Bert.

The ending comes when Ernie has Bert ask him (Ernie) if he would share the cookie with Bert. Ernie responds, "Why yes Bert. I'd be happy to share it with you." Ernie breaks the cookie in half, gives half to Bert, and begins eating the other half as he walks off.

Subject's interpretations of the skit were basically the same up to the ending. Their interpretations of the ending varied, however; they can be described as the con, the trick, or the share interpretation. In the con interpretation, subjects said that Bert was led on by Ernie to believe that Ernie would share a cookie with Bert if Ernie had the cookie. Ernie tried to prevent Bert from being angry, even making him grateful that he, Ernie, gave him half his cookie. In the trick interpretation, the subjects said that Ernie just wanted the cookie and did not care whether Bert was angry. In the share interpretation, Bert was angry only because Ernie took the larger half of the cookie!

Analysis of the three cookie skit interpretations suggests a number of conclusions about story understanding. Even the youngest children's interpretations reflect complex analyses of the events, goals, plans, mutual beliefs, and social interactions portrayed in the skit. The analyses also highlight the crucial role that background information can play in constructing interpretations. Newman's (1980) work shows story understanding as a process that goes far beyond the written text. The cognitive processing of young readers is more elaborate than one might first suppose—and fortunately so, for the stories given to young readers demand more than one might first suppose. Readers form hypotheses to account for what they read on the basis of the text at hand and diverse sources of other information. They integrate this knowledge into structures that have profound effects on their comprehension of or memory for text. These powerful structures are nevertheless fragile, since they are sensitive to the effects of new information. Above all, reading is a cultural process that reflects the cultural beliefs, assumptions, and values of the reader and the author as seen through the text.

Teaching Story Understanding

Research on stories has heightened our awareness of the complexity and variety of stories as a type of text. Research on story understanding has performed a similar service. There can be no simple prescription regarding the teaching of story comprehension or the use of story reading within the larger curriculum. Our understanding of stories has to become part of discussions concerning a wide range of difficult issues: cultural variation among students, text selection, comprehension instruction, and the relation of story reading to other kinds of reading.

Cultural Variation

Many programs within schools focus specifically on the needs of economically disadvantaged children but fail to serve these children adequately. Many of these children inhabit a world with a language, social structure, history, and set of values that are different from those represented by the schools. Intentionally or not, the school system has often turned cultural differences into cultural disadvantages or cultural deficits.

Differences among readers in both their literary and their general cultural experiences may influence what they are able to comprehend in a story (Bartlett, 1932; Bohannan, 1975; Kintsch & Greene, 1978; Steffensen et al., Note 10). These differences may also affect readers' enjoyment of stories, which in turn affects their comprehension (Asher & Markell, 1974; Asher, Note 11; Asher, Hymel, & Wigfield, Note 12). We can respond to cultural differences by making use of stories that are more relevant to particular children and by giving aid to children in bridging the gap from their own experiences to those recounted in stories (Simpkins & Simpkins, 1981).

The task is not an easy one. Not much is known about which characteristics of stories are universal (Asher, 1978; Brewer & Hay, Note 7; Asher, Note 11) or what effects unfamiliar stories have on readers. Recent work on narrative structures in the oral and written traditions of various nonmainstream cultures, such as Athabaskan stories (Scollon & Scollon, 1980), black folk tales and oral narratives (Labov, 1973; Smitherman, 1977), and Hawaiian talk stories (Watson-Gegeo & Boggs, 1977), has shown major differences in style, but these differences are not reflected in children's basal readers (Bruce, 1982).

Teaching about stories raises the cultural difference issue in another way. Recent classroom ethnography studies (for example, Trueba, Guthrie, & Au, 1981) have shown that talking about stories is as much a culturally conditioned activity as reading them is. If actions of a character are not well understood by a particular subculture, for example, then discussion of that character in a culturally unfamiliar way may compound a reader's comprehension difficulties.

There have been attempts to reorganize classrooms to accommodate known cultural differences. Au and Jordan (1981), for example, have reported dramatic results at the Kamehameha Early Education Project (KEEP) in teaching Hawaiian children to read. By devising a classroom participation structure that resembles the Hawaiian talk story, the KEEP program allows children to make use of their prior language and cognitive abilities as they learn to read.

Text Selection

The problem of selecting texts for children is complex. Who, after all, should do the selecting—publishers, reading specialists, teachers, librarians, parents, or the children themselves? Many groups are involved in choosing books; their goals may not always coincide and are sometimes irreconcilable (Bruce, 1982). Different groups have different concerns, including how difficult, interesting, varied, or instructive the books are. Another problem has to do with individual differences. What a story means for one child may not be what it means for another. The difficulty of a story is a function of the reader's interests and prior reading experiences as well as of the text itself (Gilliland, 1972).

It is unlikely that any simple approach to text selection will work. There are research results, however, that provide some guidance. We know, for example, that so-called simplification of a text does not always simplify it (Bruce, Rubin, & Starr, 1981; Davison & Kantor, 1982; Davison, Kantor, Hannah, Hermon, Lutz, & Salzillo, Note 13; Davison, Lutz, & Roalef, Note 14). In particular, rewriting texts to conform to a readability formula often creates more problems than it solves. Using readability formulas as the sole criterion for selecting existing texts is also risky. (Certainly, classification of texts to the first or second decimal place of grade level, such as grade 3.49, is a misguided approach.) There is no substitute for testing a text with the population for which it will be used.

Some recent research provides a picture of the relationship between children's stories in basal readers and trade books and the stories the children are expected to read later in school or later in life. This research cites major differences among reading series, between lower and upper elementary school texts, between basal readers and children's trade books, and between children's trade books and adult books. Various groups of texts were assigned to one of four categories of point of view. A comparison of the differences among categories reveals some interesting overall patterns across types of stories and target grade levels.

The first point of view category is a narratorless story. Narratorless stories are told predominantly in the third person. Apart from the implied author, there is no identifiable narrator. Although the story may follow one character about, it gives at most a minimal glimpse into that character's (or any other character's) thoughts and feelings. The narratorless type of story corresponds roughly to the objective type or the omniscient type with limited inside view in earlier classification schemes (Perrine, 1966). The categories used here are more compatible with recent rhetorical structure research.

The engaged narrator type of story is told in the first person by a character who is engaged in the actions he or she describes. The in-effect narrator type of story falls between the first two types. Although it is told in the third person, much of an in-effect narrator story is seen through the thoughts and feelings of one character. The effect is much like that of an engaged narrator story, even though the narration is technically in the third person.

Many texts cannot be forced into any of these categories and must be placed in the fourth category—other. Also included in the other category are stories with an unengaged narrator—that is, stories told in the first person by a narrator who is not engaged in the action.

Table 3–1 shows that in three best-selling basal reader series, narratorless stories predominate in the early grades; from 83.3 to 96.7 percent of the stories are of this type. As a result, children in these grades read very few stories of the point-of-view types they will encounter later on. As the table shows, the students will experience a general increase in the percentages of engaged narrator, in-effect narrator, and other types of stories as they move to the upper grades, but the differences between the points of view used in basal readers of any grade level and those used in trade books are striking at all grade levels. The differences between basal readers and trade books are probably a result of the efforts of basal series publishers to control vocabulary and reading level and to present stories in a systematic fashion. Table 3–1 shows an unintended consequence of these efforts—the excessive use of one point of view type. Analyses have been made of other aspects of stories, types of conflict, and inside view, and similar conclusions have been drawn. One may debate whether the lack of variety found in basal reader story types is a problem, but it is clear that writing a story to order or altering one will have numerous ramifications on dimensions other than those directly addressed.

Table 3–1
Percentages of Stories Told from Different Points of View

Text Group	N	Narrator-less	Engaged Narrator	In-Effect Narrator	Other
Grades 1–3					
Basal A	30	96.7	3.3	0	0
Basal B	30	93.3	0	0	6.7
Basal C	30	83.3	10.0	6.7	0
Trade	30	63.3	26.7	10.0	0
Grades 4–5					
Basal A	20	75.0	15.0	5.0	5.0
Basal B	20	65.0	15.0	20.0	0
Basal C	20	75.0	15.0	10.0	0
Trade	20	40.0	35.0	20.0	5.0
Adult	50	26.0	28.0	30.0	16.0

Teaching Children How to Read Stories

We have discussed stories with little acknowledgment of the context in which they are read. Even so, we have seen repeatedly how the reading of stories is situated in a framework of the reader's experiences and the social context. Do good readers or older readers understand psychological developments in stories better simply because they have read more stories with high inside view or psychological conflicts, or because they have been taught to think in those terms? Does this understanding develop independently of their reading experiences and formal instruction?

Numerous studies have shown the value of reading stories aloud to children, whether the reader be a parent, a teacher, or a grandparent (Chomsky, 1972; Durkin, 1966). Children who listen to stories learn to think of reading in a positive way, and they learn to value stories. In addition, listening to stories may serve a cognitive function by exposing children to the complexity of author–reader interactions, plot developments, and the story structures they need to understand.

Research on the classroom as a social setting for reading is diverse and extensive. Studies have examined, for example, how schools perform the function of stratifying people for work (Bowles & Gintis, 1976) and how this stratifying function is effected in the classroom, even in a first-grade reading group (McDermott & Aron, 1978).

Instructional practices have been developed to help children learn to read better. Reynolds, Standiford, and Anderson (Note 15) have shown that when relevant questions are inserted in a text, readers are better able to answer those or similar questions after they have read the text. Similarly, Guszak (1972) has found that students can answer best the questions that teachers ask most often. Studies such as these have encouraged other researchers to affect what is comprehended from a story by changing the types of questions that are asked and to get children to ask themselves questions as they read. Hansen (1981) has shown that practice in predicting events in a story and in answering questions requiring inferences improves children's comprehension of stories.

Raphael (1981) developed a method to help children answer questions about what they had read. She taught students how to categorize answers, according to Pearson and Johnson's (1978) taxonomy. (An answer is "right there" in the text; or it requires the reader to "think and search," combining background knowledge with information from various parts of the text; or it has to be answered "on my own," using knowledge not in the text.)

Another approach has involved teaching children how to look for essential features of a narrative. Singer and Donlan (1972) taught children to generate story-specific questions from a general story schema. The general question, "What is the leading character trying to accomplish?" might yield a specific question, such as "Will Charlotte get the role she wants in the school play?" Students who generated their own questions were able to comprehend stories better.

Relation of Story Reading to Other Kinds of Reading

That story reading is not a simple task is a theme of this chapter. There are many kinds of stories and there are many aspects to a story—for example, events, plans, affect-producing structures, cultural contexts, and author–reader relationships. The understanding of these aspects varies and depends on a reader's cultural background, age, and previous reading experiences. Finally, the context in which story reading occurs is as much a part of the process as the story itself. Story reading can be viewed as an activity in which active comprehension skills, including sensitivity to the author's purpose, are developed and made available for other kinds of reading.

Conclusion

This chapter presents an approach to stories and story understanding that facilitates defining the goals of comprehension instruction.

A coherent picture of story reading that shows a transaction involving a reader and a text is beginning to emerge. The transaction is a cultural event—it integrates the cultural background of the reader with that of the author through the characters and their interactions. The transaction is also a product of the reader's active comprehension. Readers gather data, hypothesize, and infer in order to create meaning.

Out of this view of story reading emerge some general guidelines for teaching and research:

1. We need to understand better the effects of cultural diversity, and we need to devise ways of accommodating textual materials and teaching methods to the needs of children from diverse backgrounds.
2. We need to provide meaningful stories for children to read as soon as they are able to read.
3. We need to read to children. Being read to may be as productive for reading comprehension as reading itself.
4. Simplification of stories is not as easy as it seems and is often counterproductive.
5. Children can be taught to predict, to ask questions, and to become more actively involved in their reading.

Reference Notes

1. National Assessment of Educational Progress (NAEP). *Three national assessments of reading: Changes in performance 1970-80* (Report No. 11-R-01). Denver: Education Commission of the States, 1981.

2. National Assessment of Educational Progress (NAEP). *Reading, thinking and writing: Results from the 1979–80 national assessment of reading and literature* (Report No. 11-L-01). Denver Education Commission of the States, 1981.

3. Bruce, B.C., & Rubin, A.D. *Strategies for controlling hypothesis formation in reading* (Reading Education Rep. No. 22). Urbana: University of Illinois, Center for the Study of Reading, June 1981.

4. Baker, L. *Processing temporal relationships in simple stories: Effects of input sequence* (Tech. Rep. No. 84). Urbana: University of Illinois, Center for the Study of Reading, April 1978.

5. Steinberg, C.S., & Bruce, B.C. *Higher level features in children's stories: Rhetorical structure and conflict* (Reading Education Rep. No. 18). Urbana: University of Illinois, Center for the Study of Reading, October 1980. Also in M.L. Kamil & A.J. Moe (Eds.), *National Reading Conference Yearbook*. Clemson, S.C.: National Reading Conference, in press.

6. Green, G.M., & Laff, M.O. *Five-year-olds' recognition of authorship by literary style* (Tech. Rep. No. 181). Urbana: University of Illinois, Center for the Study of Reading, September 1980.

7. Brewer, W.F., & Hay, A. *Children's understanding of the author's point of view in stories.* Paper presented at the meeting of the Society for Research in Child Development, Boston, April 1981.

8. Sedlak, A.J. *An investigation of the development of the child's understanding and evaluation of the actions of others* (NIH Report CBM-TR-28). New Brunswick, N.J.: Rutgers University, Department of Computer Science, May 1974.

9. Brewer, W.F. *The structure of stories in Western culture: Cross-cultural implications.* Paper presented at the Ontario Institute for Studies in Education Conference on the Nature and Consequence of Literacy. Stratford, Ontario, October 2–3, 1981.

10. Steffensen, M.S., Jog-dev, C., & Anderson, R.C. *A cross-cultural perspective on reading comprehension* (Tech. Rep. No. 97). Urbana: University of Illinois, Center for the Study of Reading, July 1978.

11. Asher, S.R. *Influence of topic interest on black children and white children's reading comprehension* (Tech. Rep. No. 99). Urbana: University of Illinois, Center for the Study of Reading, July 1978.

12. Asher, S.R., Hymel, S.C., & Wigfield, A.L. *Children's comprehension of high- and low-interest material and a comparison of two cloze scoring methods* (Tech. Rep. No. 17). Urbana: University of Illinois, Center for the Study of Reading, November 1976.

13. Davison, A., Kantor, R.N., Hannah, J., Hermon, G., Lutz, R., & Salzillo, R. *Limitations of readability formulas in guiding adaptations of texts* (Tech. Rep. No. 162). Urbana: University of Illinois, Center for the Study of Reading, March 1980.

14. Davison, A., Lutz, R., & Roalef, A. *Text readability: Proceedings of the March 1980 Conference* (Tech. Rep. No. 213). Urbana: University of Illinois, Center for the Study of Reading, August 1981.

15. Reynolds, R.E., Standiford, S.N., & Anderson, R.C. *Distribution of reading time when questions are asked about a restricted category of text information* (Tech. Rep. No. 83). Urbana: University of Illinois, Center for the Study of Reading, April 1978.

References

Adams, M.J. & Bruce, B. Background knowledge and reading comprehension. In J. Langer & T. Smith-Burke (Eds.), *Reader meets author/Bridging the gap: A psycholinguistic and sociolinguistic perspective.* Newark, Del.: International Reading Association, 1982.

Applebee, A.N. *The child's concept of story.* Chicago: University of Chicago Press, 1978.

Asher, S.R., & Markell, R.A. Sex differences in comprehension of high- and low-interest material. *Journal of Educational Psychology,* 1974, *66,* 680–687.

Au, K.H., & Jordan, C. Teaching reading to Hawaiian children: Finding a culturally appropriate solution. In H.T. Trueba, G.P. Guthrie, & K.H. Au (Eds.), *Culture and the bilingual classroom: Studies in classroom ethnography.* Rowley, Mass.: Newbury House, 1981.

Bartlett, F.C. *Remembering.* Cambridge: Cambridge University Press, 1932.

Bohannan, L. Shakespeare in the bush. In A. Ternes (Ed.), *Ants, Indians, and little dinosaurs.* New York: Scribner's, 1975.

Black, J.B., & Wilensky, R. An evaluation of story grammars. *Cognitive Science,* 1979, *3,* 213–230.

Booth, W.C. *The rhetoric of fiction.* Chicago: University of Chicago Press, 1961.

Bowles, S., & Gintis, H. *Schooling in capitalist America.* New York: Basic Books, 1976.

Brewer, W.F., & Lichtenstein, E.H. Event schemas, story schemas, and story grammars. In A.D. Baddeley & J.D. Long (Eds.), *Attention and performance IX.* Hillsdale, N.J.: Erlbaum, 1981.

Brewer, W.F., & Lichtenstein, E.H. Stories are to entertain: A structural-affect theory of stories. *Journal of Pragmatics,* 1982, *6,* 473–486.

Brown, A.L., & Smiley, S.S. Rating the importance of structural units of prose passages: A problem of metacognitive development. *Child Development,* 1977, *48,* 1–8.

Bruce, B.C. A social interaction model of reading. *Discourse Processes,* 1981, *4,* 273–311.

Bruce, B.C. A new point of view on children's stories. In R.C. Anderson, J. Osborn, & R. Tierney (Eds.), *Learning to read in American schools.* Hillsdale, N.J.: Erlbaum, 1982.

Bruce, B.C., Rubin, A.D., & Starr, K.S. Why readability formulas fail. *IEEE Transactions on Professional Communication,* 1981, *PC-24,* 50–52.

Chatman, S. *Story and discourse.* Ithaca, N.Y.: Cornell University Press, 1978.

Chomsky, C. Stages in language development and reading exposure. *Harvard Educational Review,* 1972, *42,* 1–33.

Collins, A., Brown, J.S., & Larkin, K.M. Inference in text understanding. In R.J. Spiro, B.C. Bruce, & W.F. Brewer (Eds.), *Theoretical issues in reading comprehension.* Hillsdale, N.J.: Erlbaum, 1980.

Davison, A., & Kantor, R.N. On the failure of readability formulas to define readable texts: A case study from adaptations. *Reading Research Quarterly,* 1982, *17,* 187–209.

Durkin, D. *Children who read early.* New York: Teachers College Press, 1966.

Durkin, D. Reading comprehension instruction in five basal reader series. *Reading Research Quarterly,* 1981, *16,* 515–544.

Frisch, A.M., & Perlis, D. A re-evaluation of story grammars. *Cognitive Science,* 1981, *5,* 79–86.

Gilliland, J. *Readability.* London: University of London Press, 1972.

Guszak, F.J. *Diagnostic reading instruction in the elementary school.* New York: Harper & Row, 1972.

Hansen, J. The effects of inference training and practice on young children's reading comprehension. *Reading Research Quarterly,* 1981, *16,* 391–417.

Kent, J. *More fables of Aesop.* New York: Parents' Magazine Press, 1974.

Kintsch, W., & Greene, E. The role of culture-specific schematic in the comprehension and recall of stories. *Discourse Processes,* 1978, *1,* 1–13.

Kintsch, W., & van Dijk, T.A. Toward a model of text comprehension and production. *Psychological Review,* 1978, *85,* 363–394.

Labov, W. *Language in the inner city.* Philadelphia: University of Pennsylvania Press, 1973.

Mandler, J.M. A code in the node: The use of story schema in retrieval. *Discourse Processes,* 1978, *1,* 14–35.

Mandler, J.M., & Johnson, N.S. On throwing out the baby with the bathwater: A reply to Black and Wilensky's evaluation of story grammars. *Cognitive Science,* 1980, *4,* 305–312.

Mandler, J.M., Scribner, S., Cole, M., & DeForest, M. Cross-cultural invariance in story recall. *Child Development,* 1980, *51,* 19–26.

McConaughy, S., Fitzhenry-Coor, I., & Howell, D.C. Developmental differences in schemata for story comprehension. In K.E. Nelson (Ed.), *Children's language* (Vol. 5). New York: Gardner Press, in press.

McDermott, R.P., & Aron, J. Pirandello in the classroom: On the possibility of equal educational opportunity in American culture. In M.C. Reynolds (Ed.), *Futures of education for exceptional students.* Reston, Va.: Council for Exceptional Children, 1978.

Newman, D. *Children's understanding of strategic interaction.* Unpublished doctoral dissertation, University of California at San Diego, 1980.

Pearson, P.D., & Johnson, D.D. *Teaching reading comprehension.* New York: Holt, Rinehart and Winston, 1978.

Perrine, L. *Story and structure.* New York: Harcourt, Brace and World, 1966.

Raphael, T.E. *The effect of metacognitive awareness training on students' question answering behavior.* Unpublished doctoral dissertation, University of Illinois at Urbana-Champaign, 1981.

Rosenblatt, L.M. *The reader, the text, the poem.* Carbondale: Southern Illinois University Press, 1978.

Rumelhart, D.E. On evaluating story grammars. *Cognitive Science,* 1980, *4,* 313–316. (a)

Rumelhart, D.E. Schemata: The building blocks of cognition. In R.J. Spiro, B.C. Bruce, W.F. Brewer (Eds.), *Theoretical issues in reading comprehension.* Hillsdale, N.J.: Erlbaum, 1980. (b)

Scollon, R., & Scollon, S.B.K. Literacy as focused interaction. *Quarterly Newsletter of the Laboratory of Comparative and Human Cognition,* 1980, *2,* 26–29.

Simpkins, G.A., & Simpkins, C. Cross-cultural approach to curriculum development. In G. Smitherman (Ed.), *Black English and the education of black children and youth.* Detroit: Harlo Press, 1981.

Singer, H., & Donlan, D. Active comprehension: Problem-solving schema with question generation for comprehension of complex short stories. *Reading Research Quarterly,* 1982, *17,* 166–186.

Smitherman, G. *Talkin and Testifyin.* Boston: Houghton Mifflin, 1977.

Stein, N., & Glenn, C.G. An analysis of story comprehension in elementary school children. In R. Freedle (Ed.), *New directions in discourse processing.* Norwood, N.J.: Ablex, 1979.

Stein, N.L., & Nezworski, M.T. The effect of organization and instructional set on story memory. *Discourse Processes,* 1978, *1,* 177–193.

Thorndyke, P.W. Cognitive structures in comprehension and memory of narrative discourse. *Cognitive Psychology,* 1977, *9,* 77–110.

Trueba, H.T., Guthrie, G.P., & Au, K.H. (Eds.), *Culture and the bilingual classroom: Studies in classroom ethnography.* Rowley, Mass.: Newbury House, 1981.

Watson-Gegeo, K.A., & Boggs, S.T. From verbal play to talk story: The role of routines in speech events among Hawaiian children. In S. Ervin-Tripp & C. Mitchell-Kerman (Eds.), *Child discourse.* New York: Academic Press, 1977.

4
Content Area Textbooks: A Research Perspective

Bonnie Armbruster

T he textbook is a cornerstone of American education. During a decade of classroom observations, John Goodlad (1976) discovered: "The textbook predominated throughout as the medium of instruction, except in kindergarten. With each advance in grade level, dependence on the textbook increased" (p. 14). A study in Texas (EPIE, 1974) concluded that students spend 75 percent of their classroom time and 90 percent of their homework time using textbooks and related materials. Given this pervasive influence of textbooks, few people would argue with the following premise: Textbooks should promote understanding and the learning of important information. This chapter presents some research-based guidelines for evaluating how textbooks promote understanding and learning in general and, in particular, encourage the learning of important information. The guidelines are proposed to aid teachers and textbook adoption committees in choosing the best instructional materials.

A Brief Introduction to a Theory of Reading

A little background in reading theory is prerequisite to an understanding of the role of text in learning. A theory of reading of particular interest at the University of Illinois Center for the Study of Reading is schema theory. According to schema theory, a reader's schema, or organized knowledge of the world, provides much of the basis for comprehending, learning, and remembering information in text. Comprehension occurs when the reader activates or constructs a schema that explains events and objects described in a text. As readers first begin to read, they search for a schema to account for the information in the text, and, on the basis of the schema, they construct a partial model of the meaning of the text. The model then provides a framework for continuing the search throughout the text. The model is progressively refined and constrained as the reader gathers more information from the text. Reading comprehension thus involves progressive focusing and refinement of a complete, plausible, and coherent model of the meaning of the text.

Schema theory underscores the importance of the reader's existing knowledge to text comprehension. Indeed, dozens of experiments have verified the role of background knowledge in understanding and recalling information from text. What the reader brings to the text, however, is not the only factor that affects learning from text. Characteristics of the text itself, by influencing the reader's ability to construct a coherent model of the text's meaning, also affect learning outcomes.

Characteristics of the Text That Affect Comprehension and Learning

The most important text characteristic for comprehension and learning is textual coherence. The more coherent the text, the more likely it is that the reader will be able to construct a coherent cognitive model of the information in the text. Texts cohere both globally and locally (Cirilo, 1981; Anderson & Armbruster, 1984). Global coherence is achieved by text characteristics that facilitate the integration of high-level, important ideas across the entire section, chapter, or book. Local coherence is achieved by several kinds of simple links or ties that connect ideas within and between sentences.

Global Coherence

Global coherence is achieved by the overall structure or organization of the text. Generally, *structure* refers to the system of arrangement of ideas in a text and the nature of the relationships connecting the ideas. A few basic text structures, identified by rhetoricians, linguists, and psychologists, appear to capture the fundamental patterns of human thought. The most common structures are as follows:

1. *Simple listing*—a listing of items or ideas in which the order of presentation of the items is not significant;
2. *Comparison/contrast*—a description of similarities and differences between two or more things;
3. *Temporal sequence*—a sequential relationship between ideas or events, considered in terms of the passage of time;
4. *Cause/effect*—an interaction between at least two ideas or events, one considered a cause or reason and the other an effect or result;
5. *Problem/solution*—an interaction similar to the cause/effect pattern in that two factors interact, one citing a problem and the other a solution to that problem.

Another approach to defining text structures has been to identify structures that are somewhat more specialized—that is, appropriate for particular types of of content or text genres (for example, narratives, newspaper articles, or expository text). Story grammars specify the relationship among the story elements (for example, goals, actions, and outcomes) that underlie narratives. Another text structure is used to describe systems. A description of a system (such as the circulatory system of the human body or the exhaust system of an automobile) typically includes information on the function of the system in the larger entity of which it is a part, the components of the system and their individual functions, and the operation of the system. Specialized structures for other kinds of content-area texts are just beginning to be identified (Dansereau, in press; Lunzer, Davies, & Greene, Note 1).

What research evidence is there that structure makes a difference to a reader who must learn from a text? Perhaps the most decisive evidence comes from the research on story grammars. The consistent result of this research is that memory for stories is superior when the content is organized according to a well-known story grammar (Kintsch, Mandel, & Kozminsky, 1977; Mandler, 1978; Mandler & Johnson, 1977; Thorndyke, 1977; Stein, Note 2). When the structure of a story is altered by displacing or deleting story parts, readers not only say that the stories are less understandable but they also do not remember the stories as well (Thorndyke, 1977).

Meyer and Freedle (1984) have shown that changing the structure while leaving the content the same affects memory for text; that is, the same ideas can be remembered better when they are expressed in one type of structure than another. A study by Meyer, Brandt, and Bluth (1980) found that ninth graders who identified the structure of well-organized text and used this structure as the basis of their recall of the content of the text could remember more from a passage than those who did not use the author's structure.

Other research has shown that learning can be affected by how clearly the structure is indicated in the text. Information about structure can be provided in two ways. One way is through signaling information in the text that emphasizes certain ideas in the content or points out aspects of the structure (Meyer, 1979). Types of signaling include (1) explicit statements of the structure or organization; (2) previews or introductory statements, including titles; (3) summary statements; (4) pointer words and phrases, such as "an important point is . . . "; and (5) textual cues, such as underlining, italics, and boldface.

Another means of providing information about structure is through the repeated, consistent use of a particular structure. Readers reading a series of stories, for example, will remember more of the ideas in the later stories if the later stories have the same structure as the earlier stories (Thorndyke, 1977). Presumably, the reader learns the structure in early stories and comes to expect that ideas in later stories will be organized in the same way.

This research indicates that text structure does have an important effect on learning. If readers know to use the author's structure as a tool in building a coherent model of the text, it seems to be true that the better organized the text and the more apparent the structure to the reader, the higher the probability that the reader will learn from reading.

In addition to structure, another important contributor to global coherence is content. (Actually, content and structure are so closely related that content might be considered an aspect of structure, as is the content of a story in a story grammar.) One area of research indicates that learning and memory are improved when people are given information clarifying the significance of facts that might otherwise seem arbitrary (Bransford & Johnson, 1973; Bransford, Stein, Shelton, & Owings, 1980; Dooling & Mullet, 1973). Consider the following simple example from Bransford et al. (1980). College students who read sentences such as "The tall man bought the crackers. The bald man read the newspaper. The old man purchased the paint" tend to perform poorly on such questions as "Which man bought the crackers?" The students rate such sentences as comprehensible, but they have difficulty remembering the sentences, probably because the relationship between each type of man and the action performed by him seems arbitrary. Their recall improves dramatically for sentences such as "The tall man bought the crackers that were on the top shelf. The bald man read the newspaper to look for a hat sale. The funny man bought the ring that squirted water." The elaborations clarify the significance of the relationship between each type of man and the action he performs.

The effect of significance-imparting information also holds for longer text. Drawing once again on the research with story grammars, we know that information about a character's goal and the events that lead up to a goal has a significant effect on comprehension and memory for narratives (Kintsch & van Dijk, 1978; Rumelhart, 1977; Thorndyke, 1977). Presumably, knowledge of the goal and the events leading up to a goal helps readers understand the significance of a character's actions and the consequences of those actions and thus aids the reader's effort to build a coherent model of a text. Bransford (1984) has suggested that the reciprocal relationship between structure and function provides the reader with information establishing the significance of the content.

Evaluating Structure in Textbooks

The proof of the structure is in the reading—and the reading must cover a fairly extensive piece of the text at that. Only by reading an extensive piece of text can an evaluator of a textbook determine whether the ideas hang together in an identifiable, clear, and logical organization.

One way to get a feel for structure, short of reading entire chapters and units, is to examine the author's use of signaling. One kind of signaling device used universally in textbooks is titles and subtitles. A glance at a table of contents or an outline of chapter titles and subtitles can be very revealing. Compare, for example, the following chapter outlines from two American history textbooks. (In this example, and all the following examples, the numbers in brackets refer to the list of excerpt sources that follows the text of this chapter.)

Textbook 1 [1]

What Were the Problems of New Government?
A. The Basic Problem
B. Economic Troubles
   1. An Empty Treasury
   2. Economic Depression
   3. The Money Problem
C. Conflicts Among the States
D. Unfriendly Foreign Countries
E. Calling the Constitutional Convention

Textbook 2 [2]

Growing Cities, Growing Industries
   Early Cities
   More Cities Grow
   Industrial Growth & Immigration
      Americans All
      Labor Unions
      Jane Addams
      Americans Prosper
   Cities Today
   Industrial & Technical Progress
      Progress Through Inventions
      Technology

The chapter outline from textbook 1 suggests a better, clearer structure than the chapter outline from textbook 2. The textbook 1 chapter outline has an overall structure of simple listing; it is easy to predict that each subtopic will probably be cast in a cause/effect or problem/solution structure. It is difficult, however, to determine any logical structure for the topics from textbook 2.

Another signaling device is the introduction to a unit or chapter. Introductions should give the reader a good overview of the content and structure of the ideas to follow. Introductions from three social studies textbooks follow. The first, a good introduction, is from an American history text.

Do you remember that, in Unit 2, we said that part of our nation's heritage was change? A terribly important change began in 1776, with the Declaration of Independence. Before that, the people of America were colonists under the rule of England. But after that, they were citizens of an independent country. This unit will tell you about the causes of the Revolution, the war itself, and the early years of the United States. [3]

The following is the beginning of another good introduction, in which the reader is nicely set up for a compare/contrast structure:

In this chapter, we are going to look at how people in the 13 English colonies lived in the middle of the 1700's. Ways of life differed from colony to colony in 1750. Black slaves in Maryland lived differently from white merchants in Massachusetts. German-speaking farmers in Pennsylvania lived very differently from large land owners living in Virginia.

Yet there were ways many people in the colonies were alike. . . .[4]

Now read the following chapter introduction:

People worked hard to rebuild and unify America after the Civil War. It was time to move ahead. In 1790 the first census (sen's s) of the United States was taken. A census is an official count of people. Every 10 years a census is taken in the United States. In 1790 there were 4 million Americans. Most of them were living in small settlements or on farms. Today the United States has more than 220 million people. Most of these people live and work in or near cities. [5]

This introduction is terribly confusing. The first two sentences lead the reader to believe that the chapter will discuss the post–Civil War years—the reconstruction, perhaps. The third sentence changes the topic and the time frame. The reader is left wondering what the chapter will be about, not to mention what its structure will be.

Another way to evaluate the structure of a text is to look for topic sentences that alert the reader to the organization of upcoming text. The following is a good example of a useful topic sentence as well as the use of markers in the text to reinforce the indicated structure:

There were five main areas of change related to nationalism. Four of these were *domestic* changes. One involved foreign policy.

1. There was a decline in political party struggles. . . .
2. The national government gained more power through legislation. . . .
3. The national government was also strengthened by the decisions of the Supreme Court. . . .
4. The population of the United States began to move west. . . .
5. In foreign policy, the United States began to assert itself as a power in the Western Hemisphere. . . . [6]

Another way to evaluate the global coherence of textbooks is to look at the content itself: Does the author include information that clarifies the significance of facts? The following excerpt on cities of the Middle Atlantic states is an example of text that lacks global coherence because the author has not included information clarifying the significance of the facts:

The capital of Pennsylvania is Harrisburg. A large number of people there work for the government. Many others work in clothing and shoe factories. Steel is also an important industry, as it is in Pittsburgh.

New Jersey's capital is Trenton. It has many factories. Making electrical goods, metal products, machinery, and rubber products are leading industries. Trenton is also a printing and publishing center. About one-third of the people there work for the government.

Newark is New Jersey's largest city. It is the third largest insurance center in the United States and a major banking center. Newark has many factories. The chief industries make electrical equipment, metal products, and processed foods. Newark is a leading New Jersey port and air cargo center.

Wilmington is Delaware's largest city. It is one of our country's largest chemical and petrochemical centers. A petrochemical is made from petroleum or natural gas. Wilmington's factories make automobiles, steel, plastics, dyes, textiles, and rubber and leather products. Dover, the capital of Delaware, is in a rich farming region. Its chief industries are canning, airplane repairing, and rubber products. [7].

This text is really nothing more than a list of facts that could only be learned by rote memorization. Information about the relationships among location, natural resources, and economy would help readers understand the significance of the facts and would thus improve their chances of truly learning something important about cities of the Middle Atlantic states.

We now turn to another aspect of text that influences comprehension and learning—local coherence.

Local Coherence

Local coherence functions like "a linguistic mortar to connect ideas in the text together" (Tierney & Mosenthal, Note 3). Local coherence is achieved by means of several kinds of cohesive ties—the linguistic forms that help carry meaning across phrase, clause, and sentence boundaries. Examples of common cohesive ties are pronoun reference, or the use of a pronoun to refer to a previously mentioned noun ("The doctor will be back shortly. *He's* with a patient now."); substitution, or replacement of a word or words for a previously mentioned noun phrase, verb phrase, or clause ("My pen is out of ink. I need a new *one.*"); and conjunctions or connectives ("I'd give you a hand, *but* I'm busy.").

A rather large body of research has established the importance of cohesive ties in understanding and remembering text. Repeated references that help to carry meaning across sentence boundaries can decrease reading time and increase recall of text as an integrated unit (de Villiers, 1974; Haviland & Clark, 1974; Kintsch, Kozminsky, Streby, McKoon, & Keenan, 1975; Manelis & Yekovich, 1976; Miller & Kintsch, 1980). As an example (Manelis & Yekovich, 1976), people can read faster and remember better sentences such as "Arnold lunged at Norman. Norman called the doctor. The doctor arrived." than sentences such as "Arnold lunged. Norman called. The doctor arrived." Even though the first sentence set is longer, cohesive referential ties render it easier to learn and remember than the second sentence set.

Another area of research has indicated that children prefer to read, are able to read faster, and have better memory for sentences that are connected by explicit conjunctions, particularly causal connectives, than for sentences in which the conjunction is left to be inferred (Katz & Brent, 1968; Marshall & Glock, 1978–79; Pearson, 1974–75). In the study by Pearson, for example, third and fourth graders were asked which of several sentences they would prefer to use in answering a "Why" question. They selected sentences such as "John was lazy. He slept all day." The children also recalled sentences with an explicit conjunction better than sentences in which the connective was left implicit. Thus, sentences with explicit conjunctions produced better comprehension and recall, even though the added conjunction increased the grammatical complexity of the sentence.

The explanation for the consistent finding that more cohesive text is read faster and remembered better goes something like the following. Readers try to find a coherent model or interpretation of the text. When an incohesive text makes this difficult, readers spend extra time and cognitive energy to remediate the incohesiveness. They reread the text to search for the link, or they search through their memories to retrieve the connection, or they make an inference about a possible relationship. With this extra effort, mature readers may be able to form a coherent interpretation of the text. Children, however, have less chance for successfully reading such text. They are less likely to know that rereading text and searching memory are appropriate fix-up strategies (Armbruster, Echols, & Brown, 1982). Children are also less likely than adults to be able to infer connections when coherence breaks down, simply because they have less linguistic and world knowledge to draw upon. Thus, local coherence in the form of strong, explicit cohesive ties is particularly important in textbooks for children.

Evaluating Local Coherence in Textbooks

In seeking coherence, the evaluator should first check to see that relationships among ideas, particularly causal relationships, are stated explicitly in the text. The following paragraph is an excerpt from a sixth-grade textbook. Many of the connectives indicating relationships are missing and left to be inferred.

In the evening, the light fades. Photosynthesis slows down. The amount of carbon dioxide in the air space builds up again. This buildup of carbon dioxide makes the guard cells relax. The openings are closed. [8]

The following paragraph is a more coherent version of the same content; local coherence is improved because the relationships are more explicit.

What happens to these processes in the evening? The fading light of evening causes photosynthesis to slow down. Respiration, however, does not depend on light and thus continues to produce carbon dioxide. The carbon dioxide in the air spaces builds up again, which makes the guard cells relax. The relaxing of the guard cells closes the leaf openings. Consequently, the leaf openings close in the evening as photosynthesis slows down.

In the following pair of examples, the second is more coherent than the first.

Many of the farmers who moved in from New England were independent farmers. Land cost about a dollar an acre. Most men could afford to set up their own farms. Livestock farming was quite common on the frontier. Hogs could be fed in the forests. The cost of raising hogs was low. [9]

Most of the farmers who moved in from New England were independent farmers. Being an independent farmer means that the farmer can afford to own his own farm. Around 1815, most men could afford to own their own farms because land was cheap—it cost only about a dollar an acre. Many of these independent farms were livestock farms. For example, many frontier farmers raised hogs. Hog farming was common because hogs were inexpensive to keep. The cost of raising hogs was low because the farmer did not have to buy special feed for the hogs. The hogs did not need special feed because they could eat plants that grew in the surrounding forests.

The textbook evaluator who is looking for textual coherence should also check for the order of presentation of events. The order of presentation should generally proceed from the first event to the final events, especially in textbooks for younger children. Young readers can become confused if the order of events in the textbook does not match the order of actual occurrence. The temporal sequence may not be so crucial for older readers. For most students, however, it would seem that the text should remain consistent and should not skip around in time. Text that changes the order of events may send the reader on a wild goose chase; the reader may be unwilling to put forth the effort to figure out the temporal or logical order that underlies the order of presentation in the text.

The following paragraph is an example from a textbook that changes the order of events. The sentences are numbered to make the commentary easier to follow.

(1) Adult female alligators make large cone-shaped nests from mud and compost. (2) The female lays from 15 to 100 eggs with leathery shells in the nest and then covers it. (3) The heat from both the sun and the decaying compost keeps the eggs warm. (4) The eggs hatch in about nine weeks. (5) Unlike other reptiles that hatch from eggs, baby alligators make sounds while they are still in the shell. (6) The mother then bites off the nest so the baby alligators can get out. (7) When first hatched, baby alligators are about 15 to 25 cm. long. [10]

Note the many shifts in the temporal sequence. The first four sentences are fine; they present the order of events from earliest to latest. The fifth sentence reverts back to when the baby alligators were still in the shell. The time frame for the sixth sentence is when the baby alligators are sufficiently mature to leave the nest. The final sentence returns to when the baby alligators were first hatched.

Finally, the evaluator should check for clarity of references. The following excerpt illustrates a confusing use of pronoun reference—the pronoun *they*. Does *they* refer to "the people from the North" or "the Bronze Age people"?

The people from the North learned from the Bronze Age people. They were skilled workers and traders. They made fine tools and jewelry from metals. They traded their beautiful cloth and pottery to peoples around the Mediterranean. They kept records of their trade on clay tablets. [11]

The more coherent the text itself, the more coherent the cognitive model of that text the reader is likely to construct. Textual coherence is particularly important for children, who may not have sufficient linguistic experience and background knowledge to infer the content and relationships that are absent in incoherent text.

Characteristics of Text That Affect the Type of Information Learned

One obvious determinant of the type of information that will be learned from text is the type of information included in the text. Although the research evidence on this point is slim, a series of studies by Reder and Anderson (1980) is pertinent. They concluded that helping students focus attention on important points, rather than having them shift attention between main points and details, is an effective way to aid learning. Although the evidence is not conclusive, it suggests that including excessive details in text distracts students from learning important information.

Another determinant of what is learned from text is the type of questions students are asked about the material they are reading. Numerous studies have demonstrated that students tend to study and learn information that they expect to be tested on (see Anderson & Armbruster, 1984). Questions typically appear at the ends of sections or chapters in textbooks, so one line of research examined the effect on learning of questions that are inserted periodically in the text (Reynolds, Standiford, & Anderson, 1979). It was found that such questions have a striking focusing effect on studying behaviors and learning outcomes. Students tend to spend more time studying text relevant to the inserted questions and perform better on posttest items testing the type of information tapped by the inserted questions. The implication of this research is that the questions asked of students should reflect the type of information we want them to study and learn. If we want students to learn important information, we should ask them important questions.

Evaluating Textbooks for Their Role in Imparting
Important Information

The textbook evaluator should compare the relative emphasis given to important and unimportant points, or main ideas and details. To illustrate the variation in emphasis, compare the following excerpts from two fifth-grade textbooks, each about 450 pages long, on the topic "Washington, D.C." In the first textbook, information on Washington, D.C., appears in a section entitled "We have a national government." Here are three paragraphs from this section:

Washington, D.C., is located on the winding Potomac River. At its center is the Capitol Building. Its white dome rises 300 feet (90 m) above the round center of the building. On each side is a large wing. In the right wing an entrance leads to the chamber where the Senate meets. The entrance in the left wing leads to the chamber where the Representatives gather. There are 540 rooms in the Capitol. These rooms include committee rooms, offices, and rooms where visitors can watch Congress at work.

Look at the map of Washington. Notice how the Capitol faces a long mall. This green, park-like mall leads to the tall Washington Monument. It is 555 feet (170 m) high. It is covered with white marble that is 7 inches (18 cm) thick. The inside of the monument is hollow. It has an elevator to carry visitors to the top.

. . . The White House has 132 rooms. Five of these are open to the public. Special dinners and receptions are held in them. The State Dining Room can hold as many as 140 people for dinner. The Blue Room is where the President greets guests. The walls of the Green Room are covered with light green silk. The room is used as a sitting room. So is the Red Room. The largest room in the White House is the East Room. It is 79 feet (24 m) long and 37 feet (11 m) wide. [12]

In this section that purports to be on the vast topic of the national government, more space is devoted to the White House than to the legislative branch of government, and more detail is provided about the Capitol building than about the job of the president.

Contrast the amount of information given in the second textbook:

Washington, D.C., is our nation's capital. The most important business of the city is conducted in the Senate, the House of Representatives, the President's office, and in many other buildings where people work for our government.

Our nation's capital is built on the Potomac River in the District of Columbia. This location was approved by George Washington, and the land was donated to our nation by the state of Maryland. [13]

In evaluating textbooks for their role in imparting important information, the evaluator should also examine the kinds of questions that appear at the ends of chapters and in unit tests. The evaluator should look for a balance between main idea questions about the most important information and questions about facts, details, and supporting information. The danger is that the questions in these textbooks may be teaching students to attend to details at the expense of main ideas.

Conclusion

This chapter has presented evidence that characteristics of text have an important influence on how much and what students will learn from reading a textbook. There is strong evidence that students will understand and learn more from text that is coherent, with a clear overall structure that establishes the significance of the ideas presented and tight ties that bind the ideas together. Students will learn more important information from a textbook that emphasizes main ideas and asks questions about important understandings. One important implication of the work reported here is the need for textbook adoption committees to give serious consideration to factors of coherence and importance when evaluating and selecting textbooks.

Excerpt Sources

[1] Schwartz, S., & O'Connor, J.R. *Exploring our nation's history (Vol. 1): The developing years.* New York: Globe, 1971.

[2] King, A.Y., Dennis, I., & Potter, F. *The United States and the other Americas.* New York: Macmillan, 1982.

[3] Gross, H.H., Follett, D.W., Gabler, R.E., Burton, W.L., & Ahlschwede, B.F. *Exploring our world: The Americas.* Chicago: Follett, 1980, p. 173.

[4] Klein, S. *Our country's history.* New York: Scholastic, 1981, p. 117.

[5] King, A.Y., Dennis, I., & Potter, F. The United States and the other Americas. New York: Macmillan, 1982, p. 126.

[6] Abramowitz, J. *American history* (5th ed.). Chicago: Follett, 1979, p. 231.

[7] King, A.Y., Dennis, I., & Potter, F. *The United States and the other Americas.* New York: Macmillan, 1982, p. 184.

[8] Bendick, J., & Gallant, R. *Elementary science 6.* Lexington, Mass.: Ginn, 1980, p. 71.

[9] Senesh, L. *The American way of life.* Chicago: Science Research Associates, 1973, p. 149.

[10] Berger, C.F., Berkheimer, G.D., Lewis, L.E., Jr., & Neuberger, H.J. *Houghton Mifflin science (6).* Boston: Houghton Mifflin, 1979, p. 55.

[11] Dawson, G.S. *Our world.* Lexington, Mass.: Ginn, 1979, p. 29.

[12] Brown, G.S. *The country.* Lexington, Mass.: Ginn, 1982, pp. 246–248.

[13] Gross, H.H., Follett, P.W., Gabler, R.E., Burton, W.L., & Ahlschwede, B.F. *Exploring our world: The Americas.* Chicago: Follett, 1980, p. 168.

Reference Notes

1.   Lunzer, E., Davies, F., & Greene, T. *Reading for learning in science* (Schools Council Project Report). Nottingham, England: University of Nottingham, School of Education, 1980.

2. Stein, N.L. *The effects of increasing temporal disorganization on children's recall of stories.* Paper presented at the Psychonomic Society Meetings, St. Louis, November 1976.
3. Tierney, R.J., & Mosenthal, J. *Discourse comprehension and production: Analyzing text structure and cohesion* (Tech. Rep. No. 152). Urbana: University of Illinois, Center for the Study of Reading, January 1980.

References

Anderson, T.H., & Armbruster, B.B. Studying. In P.D. Pearson (Ed.), *Handbook of reading research.* New York: Longman, 1984.

Anderson, T.H., & Armbruster, B.B. Content area textbooks. In R.C. Anderson, J. Osborn, & R.J. Tierney (Eds.), *Learning to read in American schools: Basal readers and content texts.* Hillsdale, N.J.: Erlbaum, 1984.

Armbruster, B.B., Echols, C., & Brown, A.L. The role of metacognition in reading to learn: A developmental perspective. *Volta Review,* 1982, *84,* 45–56.

Bransford, J.D. Schema activation and schema acquisition: Comments on Richard C. Anderson's remarks. In R.C. Anderson, J. Osborn, & R.J. Tierney (Eds.), *Learning to read in American schools: Basal readers and content texts.* Hillsdale, N.J. Erlbaum, 1984.

Bransford, J.D., & Johnson, M.K. Considerations of some problems of comprehension. In W. Chase (Ed.), *Visual information processing.* New York: Academic Press, 1973.

Bransford, J.D., Stein, B.S., Shelton, T.S., & Owings, R. Cognition and adaptation: The importance of learning to learn. In J. Harvey (Ed.), *Cognition, social behavior and the environment.* Hillsdale, N.J.: Erlbaum, 1980.

Cirilo, R.K. Referential coherence and text structure in story comprehension. *Journal of Verbal Learning and Verbal Behavior,* 1981, *20,* 358–367.

Dansereau, D.F. Learning strategy research. In J. Segal, S. Chipman, & R. Glaser (Eds.), *Thinking and learning skills: Relating instruction to basic research* (Vol. 1). Hillsdale, N.J.: Erlbaum, in press.

de Villiers, P.A. Imagery and theme in recall of connected discourse. *Journal of Experimental Psychology,* 1974, *103,* 263–268.

Dooling, D.J., & Mullet, R.L. Locus of thematic effects in retention of prose. *Journal of Experimental Psychology,* 1973, *97,* 404–406.

EPIE Institute. *Fits and misfits: What you should know about your child's learning materials.* Columbia, Md.: National Committee for Citizens in Education, 1974.

Goodlad, J.I. *Facing the future: Issues in education and schooling.* New York: McGraw-Hill, 1976.

Haviland, S.E., & Clark, H.H. What's new? Acquiring new information as a process in comprehension. *Journal of Verbal Learning and Verbal Behavior,* 1974, *13,* 512–521.

Katz, E., & Brent, S. Understanding connections. *Journal of Verbal Learning and Verbal Behavior,* 1968, *1,* 501–509.

Kintsch, W., Kozminsky, E., Streby, W.J., McKoon, G., & Keenan, J.M. Comprehension and recall of text as a function of content variables. *Journal of Verbal Learning and Verbal Behavior,* 1975, *14,* 196–214.

Kintsch, W., Mandel, T.S., & Kozminsky, E. Summarizing scrambled stories. *Memory and Cognition,* 1977, *5,* 547–552.

Kintsch, W., & van Dijk, T. Toward a model of text comprehension and production. *Psychological Review,* 1978, *85,* 363–394.

Mandler, J.M. A code in the node: The use of a story schema in retrieval. *Discourse Processes,* 1978, *1,* 14–35.

Mandler, J.M., & Johnson, N.S. Remembrance of things parsed: Story structure and recall. *Cognitive Psychology*, 1977, *9*, 111–151.

Manelis, L., & Yekovich, F.R. Repetitions of propositional arguments in sentences. *Journal of Verbal Learning and Verbal Behavior*, 1976, *15*, 301–312.

Marshall, N., & Glock, M.D. Comprehension of connected discourse: A study into the relationship between the structure of text and information recalled. *Reading Research Quarterly*, 1978–79, *16*, 10–56.

Meyer, B.J. Organizational patterns in prose and their use in reading. In M.L. Kamil & A.J. Moe (Eds.), *Reading research: Studies and applications (National Reading Conference Yearbook)*. Clemson, S.C.: National Reading Conference, 1979.

Meyer, B.J.F., Brandt, D.M., & Bluth, G. Use of top-level structure in text: Key for reading comprehension of ninth grade students. *Reading Research Quarterly*, 1980, *16*, 72–103.

Meyer, B.J.F., & Freedle, R.O. Effects of discourse types on recall. *American Educational Research Journal*, 1984, *21*, 121–143.

Miller, J.R., & Kintsch, W. Readability and recall of short prose passages: A theoretical analysis. *Journal of Experimental Psychology: Human Learning and Memory*, 1980, *6*, 335–354.

Pearson, P.D. The effects of grammatical complexity on children's comprehension, recall, and conception of certain semantic relations. *Reading Research Quarterly*, 1974–75, *10*, 155–192.

Reder, L.M., & Anderson, J.R. A comparison of texts and their summaries: Memorial consequences. *Journal of Verbal Learning and Verbal Behavior*, 1980, *19*, 121–134.

Reynolds, R.E., Standiford, S.N., & Anderson, R.C. Distribution of reading time when questions are asked about a restricted category of text information. *Journal of Educational Psychology*, 1979, *71*, 183–190.

Rumelhart, D.E. Understanding and summarizing brief stories. In D. LaBerge & J. Samuels (Eds.), *Basic processes in reading: Perception and comprehension*. Hillsdale, N.J.: Erlbaum, 1977.

Thorndyke, P.W. Cognitive structures in comprehension and memory of narrative discourse. *Cognitive Psychology*, 1977, *9*, 77–110.

5
How Useful Are Readability Formulas?

Andee Rubin

Consider for a moment the problems of classroom teachers who are trying to choose an appropriate text for their students. The list of relevant questions is long and far-reaching. One set of important questions concerns the students: What are their interests? How motivated are they? What books and stories have they already read? How sophisticated are they as readers? What books have they enjoyed previously? What books have they disliked? Another set of questions involves the text: Is it fiction or nonfiction? Are the characters likable? What is the major subject matter? Is it more likely to appeal to boys or to girls? Does it make extensive use of such literary techniques as flashbacks? How difficult is the vocabulary? In addition, the teacher must try to ensure that every student in the class grows in reading ability (and is able to demonstrate that growth on standardized tests). Answers to these questions must help a teacher choose the right text.

Publishers face even more difficult problems when they are putting together a reading series. They must choose a group of texts that will be appropriate for large numbers of students although they lack precise information about individual students. Furthermore, publishers must be able to defend their choices to the teachers, administrators, and textbook adoption committees who evaluate reading series.

Determining whether a text is appropriate for an individual student, a classroom of students, or a nation of students is clearly a central issue in reading education. That so many of the factors contributing to appropriateness are impossible to quantify makes the task complicated and unwieldy. In studying this problem, educational researchers realized that the difficulty of a text might be more objectively determined than its overall appropriateness. A numerical estimate of the difficulty of a text could be used to predict which children would be able to read it and then to arrange texts in order of difficulty in reading series. During the past several decades, readability formulas have been developed and refined to provide these reflections of text difficulty.

This chapter describes the development of readability formulas, their common applications, the meanings attached to the numbers that result, the limitations of the formulas, and the counterintuitive results that arise when they are used inappropriately. Finally, the chapter returns to the original impetus for the development of readability formulas—determining text appropriateness. The conclusion offered is that readability formulas are based on an image of the reading process that is now being abandoned by researchers; readability formulas are seen as misfits that go against the current direction of reading research.

The History of Readability Formula Development

Over the past 60 years, readability formulas have proliferated, and new versions have been proposed frequently. At least seven formulas are in general use in education (Dale & Chall, 1948; Dolch, 1948; Flesch, 1954; Fry, 1968; Gunning, 1952; Spache, 1978; Sticht, 1972, 1975). The basic assumption underlying all of these formulas is that text difficulty can be computed by calculating a weighted sum of measures of word and sentence difficulty. Most formulas use either word lists or word length as indicators of word difficulty and sentence length as an indicator of sentence difficulty. The resulting number is usually interpreted as a reading grade level, ranging from approximately 1 to 16.

A Sample of Readability Formula Use

The application of the Spache (1978) formula to a sample of primary-grade material is a good illustration of the use of readability formulas. The Spache formula requires choosing three to five 100-word selections from a book, measuring the percentage of uncommon words (based on a 1,040-word list of familiar words) and the average number of words per sentence in the passages, then combining the two numbers according to the following equation:

Reading grade = .082 (% uncommon words) + .121 (average number words per sentence) + .659

Consider, for example, the beginning passage from *Frog and Toad All Year*, a children's book by Arnold Lobel (1976):

Frog knocked at Toad's door. "Toad, wake up," he cried. "Come out and see how wonderful the winter is!" "I will not," said Toad. "I am in my warm bed." "Winter is beautiful," said Frog. "Come out and have fun." "Blah," said Toad. "I do not have any winter clothes." Frog came into the house. "I have brought you some things to wear," he said. Frog pushed a coat down over the top of Toad. Frog pulled snowpants up over the bottom of Toad. He put a hat and scarf on Toad's head. "Help!" cried Toad. "My best friend is trying to kill me!"

In this 104-word passage, there are 16 sentences, for an average sentence length of 6.5. According to the Spache 1,040-word list, there are 4 (3.8%) unfamiliar words; thus, by the Spache formula, we have

$$\text{Reading grade} = .082(3.8) + .121(6.5) + .659 = 1.8$$

The Development of Readability Formulas

Most researchers date the genesis of readability formulas to the publication of Thorndike's (1921) *The Teacher's Word Book*, a listing of 10,000 vocabulary items arranged by frequency in several samples of language data. Not only was this book of practical significance to reading teachers who wanted to introduce words to their students in some justifiable order, but it was also a public introduction of the idea that estimating the difficulty of reading material might be pedagogically useful. In the early days of readability formula research, many factors were considered as possible contributors to difficulty, from the initial letters of words to the proportion of prepositions in the text (Selden, Note 1). In the last several decades, however, attention has focused on word and sentence difficulty. A word is considered difficult either if it is polysyllabic or if it is not on a formula-specific list of familiar words. The difficulty of a sentence is determined by the number of words it contains.

There seem to be two reasons why readability formulas rely only on word and sentence difficulty. First, the formulas produce correlations in the range of .7 to .8 between readability calculated by formula and an independent measure of readability (Dale & Chall, 1948; Fry, 1968; Spache, 1978). Adding additional variables, such as syntactic complexity, does little to increase these figures (predicting between 50 and 65 percent of the variance in readability). A second reason for limiting the variables included in readability formulas has to do with practical considerations. For both teachers and publishers, formulas have had to be easy and convenient to use. Counting syllables and words can be confusing enough, but including counts of syntactic structures, abstract vocabulary, or passive verb forms would make calculating readabilty an impossibly complex task. Since word and sentence difficulty seemed both sufficient and simple, these criteria have endured as the leading variables in readability studies.

In one prominent departure from the common criteria for calculating readability, Flesch (1951, 1954) included a scale of "human interest" along with his "reading ease" scale. The human interest scale was based on the number of personal references and the number of abstract words in the text. This formula never caught on, although its companion reading ease formula is one of the most widely used. Human interest scores are clearly more subjective and more sensitive to the individual reader's characteristics. Since readability formulas are intended to evaluate texts outside of their interactions with readers, Flesch's human interest scale rests on different assumptions than most readability formulas.

Current Uses of Readability Formulas

Over the past several decades, readability formulas have been relied on more and more to judge text difficulty. Readability formulas have their strongest effect on classroom practice through educational publishers, librarians, adoption committees, and text designers. Common standards for the language in basal readers define implicit readability formulas; in addition, most of the series apply explicit formulas—either in writing or in selecting passages. When texts are adapted by publishers for use in educational materials, the adaptation process includes both content editing and readability considerations (Davison & Kantor, 1982). Many writers and editors become so accustomed to the criteria their texts must meet that they produce text with characteristics of the desired readability level without being consciously aware of the process. Designers of reading comprehension tests and other standardized tests use the formulas to ensure that their passages are appropriately normed at the correct grade level. Librarians sometimes attach readability formula estimates to books as an aid to classroom teachers. Although teachers seldom calculate a readability formula estimate on their own, the options from which they choose appropriate texts for their students are narrowly defined by readability formula considerations.

Outside of educational circles, the influence of readability formulas has grown in the past several years. In an effort to make public documents more comprehensible, several states have adopted readability formula criteria for insurance policies and contracts. Both Massachusetts and Minnesota specify criterion scores on the Flesch Reading Ease Scale for insurance policies, and thirty other states have laws or pending bills that define similar standards (Redish, 1979).

The growing use of microcomputers has also increased the possible applications of readability formulas. Instead of counting words and sentences by hand and arriving at the weighted sum by calculator, a microcomputer program can calculate readability estimates on any text that is typed into the machine. Without good reasons to the contrary, readability formula use will probably become even more widespread in the next several years.

Problems with Readability Formulas

There is, however, a long list of "good reasons to the contrary" that forms the basis of an argument against the extensive use of readability formulas. These reasons to the contrary include technical problems with the methods used to calculate and validate readability formulas, inappropriate uses, and cultural and class bias in the formula word lists.

The Omission of Most Crucial Text Variables

Readability formulas obviously take into account only the most limited set of variables in evaluating the comprehensibility of text. A far-from-complete list of the factors they ignore includes degree of discourse cohesion, number and complexity of inferences required, number of items to remember, complexity of the ideas presented, rhetorical structure, dialect, and background knowledge assumed. Many of these determinants of complexity have been combined under the label "conceptual readability." Their influence on comprehensibility in expository text, stories, and other educational materials has been studied by Kantor and Davison (Note 2), Steinberg and Bruce (1980, Note 3), Armbruster and Anderson (Note 4), and Rubin and Gentner (Note 5). Bormuth (1966) argued for the inclusion of new linguistic variables such as word depth (a variable sensitive to the hypothesized complexity of syntactic processing in a sentence) in formulas to increase interformula correlations. In an attempt to incorporate new psycholinguistic research into readability estimates, Kintsch and Vipond (1979) suggested including such variables as the density of propositions and the number of different arguments in a text. They pointed out the centrality to readability of such factors as "the number of long-term memory searches and reinstatements of propositions into short-term memory." To add such complex variables to current readability formulas would surely destroy their practical usefulness, as calculating them would require large amounts of time and, in some cases, specialized linguistic knowledge. Using computers could solve some of these problems, but some of the most sophisticated methods proposed go beyond even current computational potential. Kintsch and Vipond (1979), in fact, offered their highly complex suggestions not as a "perfect formula" but as a "young and blemished model."

The lack of correspondence between factors that affect a text's comprehensibility and those that readability formulas measure has led, predictably, to low correlations between readability formula measures and independently measured comprehension in several experiments. The most often discussed is an experiment performed by Lockman (1957) with 170 naval cadets. He calculated Flesch Reading Ease Scale scores for nine sets of instructions for psychological tests, then had the cadets rate the instructions on "understandability." The correlation between the measurements was relatively high—but in the wrong direction ($-.65$, $p<.05$). In this case, the readability formula seemed to have missed the mark by a wide margin.

More recently, the Army commissioned a study of readability formulas (Kern, Note 6). To the stated question, "How effectively do formulas predict comprehension at targeted reading grade levels?" the study answered with a flat, "Formulas cannot match material to reader." As evidence, Kern synthesized two other military studies (Caylor, Sticht, Fox, & Ford, Note 7; Kincaid, Fishburne, Rogers, & Chissom, Note 8). In both experiments, the authors had developed a readability formula, using military men's performance on a cloze test on passages selected from job and training material, as an independent measure of text difficulty. Kern (Note 6) applied each formula to the passages used in developing the other formula and discovered a large discrepancy in readability estimates. For example, passages with experimental reading grade levels of 11 or 12 that were used in developing Kincaid's formula ended up with formula estimates of 14 to 21 with Caylor's formula.

An example of a text with a low readability formula score that is nonetheless quite difficult to comprehend highlights some of readability formulas' built-in problems. *Yagua Days* by Cruz Martel (1976) is a story about a young boy of Puerto Rican heritage growing up in New York. In the course of the story, the boy travels to Puerto Rico and learns the meaning of the mysterious term "yagua days." (Yaguas, it turns out, are palm fronds; yagua days are rainy days when the grass is slick and children slide down the hills on yaguas.) This book scores 4.8 on the Dale-Chall (1948) readability formula and 5.2 on Gunning's (1952) formula, yet several sixth graders had considerable difficulty understanding it. Steinberg (Note 9) analyzed the book in an attempt to figure out what the true difficulties were. The following is a passage that seemed especially puzzling to some of the students:

> Mailman Jorge sloshed in, slapping water off his hat. He smiled. "Que pasa, Adan? Why the long face?"
> "Rainy days are terrible days."
> "No—they're wonderful days. They're yagua days!"
> "Stop teasing, Jorge. Yesterday you told me the vegetables and fruits in the bodega are grown in panel trucks. What's a yagua day?"
> "Muchacho, this day is a yagua day. And Puerto Rican vegetables and fruits are grown in trucks. Why, I have a truck myself. Every day I water it!"

According to Steinberg, the real problem with this passage does not lie in the words or sentences. The Spanish words are translated in a glossary, and none of her students found them particularly difficult. What complicates this part of the story is the interaction between the characters. Jorge is teasing Adan about vegetables and fruits growing in trucks, *not* about the meaning of "yagua days." Adan ends up believing that neither of Jorge's assertions is true. A child reading the story must understand both what Jorge believes and what Adan believes. Since the reader does not know at this point what yagua days are, he or she must be able later to modify an earlier interpretation of this exchange in light of the new knowledge. In other words, a reader might agree with Adan at this point in the story that Jorge is teasing about yagua days but might realize later that he was not. Readability formulas give us no understanding of this kind of complexity in text.

A readability formula advocate might dismiss such an example of the failure of readability formulas as an isolated case, chosen especially to point out the weakness of the approach. Trying a readability formula on any randomly chosen text is likely to yield similar results, however, since the problem is in the assumptions and methodology of readability formulas—not in the particular text. It is also true, however, that readability formulas seem to be measuring something resembling difficulty in text. The reason they work at all is the following: text that is difficult to understand because it treats complex issues usually contains long sentences and unfamiliar words. Thus, many texts are difficult to understand and contain long sentences and difficult words, but the length of the sentences and the unfamiliarity of the words are not the reasons for the text's difficulty.

For the natural correlation between complex material and long sentences to occur, texts must be written honestly—that is, written naturally. Unfortunately, in many of the cases where readability formulas are used extensively (basal readers, in particular), the texts cannot be considered natural. We have little reason to believe that a readability formula estimate reflects the degree of difficulty a reader would have in understanding these texts.

The Shaky Statistical Bases of Readability Formulas

Despite the shortcomings of readability formulas on theoretical grounds, a strong statistical history could justify their use under some circumstances. Studying the technical development of readability formulas, however, reinforces doubts about their applicability.

Many of the hundreds of formulas in existence were validated only in terms of earlier formulas. The early formulas, in turn, were validated using the McCall-Crabbs (1925) *Standard Test Lessons in Reading.* The McCall-Crabbs lessons, however, were intended only as practice exercises in reading, never as measures of comprehension or text comprehensibility; nor were they intended to be general indicators of reading ability across age, class, or cultural groups. Nevertheless, the most respected formulas have all used the McCall-Crabbs lessons as the criterion of difficulty. The use of these short passages also introduced a bias against including higher-level features from the formulas; the criterion passages were simply too short to exhibit differing global text organizations (Chall, 1955).

Spache (1978) stated the problem succinctly:

> The reading level given by the formula should mean that a child with that level of reading ability could read the book with adequate comprehension and a reasonable number of oral reading errors. *This assumption has seldom if ever been tested in the development of this and other readability formulas.* (p. 199) (Emphasis added)

Although validation studies generally were not performed in the course of developing readability formulas, a fair number were done later. In a comprehensive review of such studies, Klare (1976) noted that only thirty-nine of sixty-five studies demonstrated any positive correlation between readability formula estimates of difficulty and reader performance on independent criteria such as reading speed or comprehension.

In addition, the development of certain readability formulas exhibits an alarming circularity. The Spache (1978), Dolch (1948), and Fry (1968) formulas were validated against publishers' assigned grade levels, which had been assigned either by common sense or by using readability formulas. When publishers used their own judgment, they tended to emphasize precisely those text features that readability formulas measure: sentence length and word familiarity, based on frequency of use in basal reader programs. The danger is that, over time, certain text features become the focus of readability, whether or not they really have any effect on it (Selden, Note 1). Had some early readability formula designer decided, for example, that words containing *y* were particularly difficult, that assumption might now be guiding the writing of basal readers, and Dick and Jane would never have had a sister named Sally.

Inappropriate Use of Readability Formulas

One irony of readability formula use is that the tools dedicated to the identification of appropriate texts are so often used inappropriately. Even readability formula designers have warned against using their products in situations for which they were not intended. The publishers of the *Raygor Readability Estimator* (1979) include the following warning with their product:

> Reader interest level, reader experience, or any other personal or ethnic variables are not measured by this or any other estimators of readability. Readability estimators do not measure style or syntax.
>
> Making materials less difficult by shortening sentences and substituting shorter or more common words for longer and more difficult sentences and words may not, in fact, reduce the difficulty level indicated when the formula is applied to the new material. The new material may appear easier and show a lower grade level with the estimate, but the concept level may still be high. Readability estimates use variables that predict but do not necessarily control the difficulty of the material. Estimates work best on discursive or narrative prose. Applying estimates to poetry, test items, or other types of nonprose material may produce inaccurate results.

Rewriting. Using readability formulas appears at first glance to be an obvious and effective method for simplifying material. A large number of studies have demonstrated, however, that a readability formula–guided approach to adaptation is likely to produce more difficult texts.

One of the most extensive studies of text adaptation from a linguistic point of view was carried out by Davison and Kantor (1982). They compared adapted texts from a supplementary reading series (Parker, 1963) with the originals from which they were derived and identified four major classes of changes: syntactic structure of sentences, content (addition and deletion of information), vocabulary, and style (rhetorical devices). In the following examples that Davison and Kantor examined, readability levels were often lowered by as much as four grades, but not without serious consequences.

One class of changes involved splitting sentences into shorter components (thereby lowering the readability score). This procedure, however, often resulted in a text in which the reader had to infer the correct relation between two clauses rather than having it stated explicitly. Consider, for example, the following text versions:

Original

If given a chance before another fire comes, the tree will heal its own wounds by growing new bark over the burned part.

Adapted

If given a chance before another fire comes, the tree will heal its own wounds. It will grow new bark over the burned part. (p. 192)

In the adapted version, the reader must infer that growing new bark is the means by which trees heal their own wounds. A reader who does not know very much about trees, however, might see healing wounds and growing new bark as separate processes.

Another common adaptation that shortened sentences and deleted difficult words resulted in the deletion of information about the source of information included in the text. Consider, for example, the following pair of sentences:

Original

A railroad freight agent has figured that it would require at least 40 modern flat cars to haul away just the trunk alone. (Emphasis added)

Adapted

And at least forty freight cars would be needed to haul away just its trunk. (p. 203)

Deleting the attribution of this statement to the freight agent effectively lowers the readability score of the passage, but it also gives the student one less opportunity to learn to distinguish between assertions of the writer and opinions attributed to others—an important prerequisite to critical reading.

Other studies have investigated the use of readability formulas for document revision in noneducational settings. In a study conducted by the National Institute of Education, the federal income tax package was simplified by reducing sentence length and word difficulty, thereby lowering readability estimates about four grade levels—from 12 to 8. A reporter got wind of the revision and gave the revised form to an eighth-grade class in San Jose; very few students could fill it out correctly (Selden, Note 1).

A Navy study carried out by Duffy and Kabance (1981) attempted to separate the effects of manipulating word and sentence difficulty in revisions. Using standardized reading assessment passages from the Nelson-Denny (1973) test, they produced three alternative versions by (1) simplifying only vocabulary, (2) simplifying only sentence structure, and (3) simplifying both sentences and vocabulary. The results contradicted almost all the predictions readability formulas would have made: "While simplifying complex sentences produced the greatest improvement in readability score, the vocabulary simplification is what produced the positive though trivial performance effects. Even this effect is lost when the sentences are also simplified" (Duffy & Kabance, 1981, p. 16).

The Document Design Project at Carnegie-Mellon University discovered that the only way to ensure that a given document is comprehensible is to test people's comprehension of the document. In a study designed to test revision strategies on four documents, Swaney, Janik, Bond, and Hayes (1981) found that their expert document designers inadvertently produced a more difficult car insurance policy. A satisfactory version (which was much longer than the original) was achieved only after the revisers listened to subjects "thinking aloud" as they read the policy and answered questions about it.

All of these studies illustrate the same basic point: rewriting text to satisfy readability formula criteria simply does not work. Since readability formula estimates have validity only by virtue of the correlation between conceptual complexity and word/sentence difficulty in honestly written text, tampering with texts effectively destroys that connection.

Producing Educational Materials. Readability formulas play a central role in the preparation of standardized tests, remedial reading texts, and basal readers. Excerpts used for test passages are evaluated according to readability formulas because it is considered crucial to present material at a precise level in order to measure reading achievement accurately. Remedial reading and basal texts are especially vulnerable to readability formulas because, in both cases, a central goal is to produce text that will not overwhelm unsophisticated readers and will guide them to the correct generalizations about symbol–sound correspondences. The results of this approach are sterile, often incomprehensible texts. Sometimes passages are taken out of context with little regard for the effect of excerpting. Basal readers and remedial reading texts are filled with stories whose main claim to coherence is that they use the same vowel in almost every word.

Examples of incoherent basal stories are easy to find. A recent study by Steinberg and Bruce (1980) demonstrates that reliance on readability formulas (and other learning-to-read criteria) results in stories that neglect important story elements, such as the presence and resolution of conflict or access to characters' thoughts and feelings. In a study of 200 stories, they found that about a third of the stories in two of the early basal series (grades 1–3) contained no conflict between characters, whereas all of the trade book stories written for children in the same age group exhibited some conflict. At the fourth- and fifth-grade levels, almost every story in basal readers and trade books contained conflict. Basal stories in the first few grades thus do not prepare children either for trade books or for the stories in their upper elementary readers.

The influence of readability formulas on educational material development leads to a system in which both texts and tests are judged by the same limited criteria. In the crucial early years of learning to read, children are fed a diet of semi-comprehensible texts that lack the qualities that make reading valuable and enjoyable. The tests that evaluate their progress use the same kinds of texts and pose mostly literal comprehension questions. Interpretive, creative reading is discouraged by this system.

Matching Individual Readers and Texts. One of the original motivations for readability formulas was the need to choose texts for individual students; however, this turns out to be an inappropriate use of readability formulas. It is not possible to confidently apply formulas that represent statistically derived averages to individual books and children. Too many factors influence the interaction between a particular child and a particular book to allow us to give much weight to a number derived from mass measures. Because they are measures simply of text, readability formulas cannot reflect any characteristics of readers, such as interests, background knowledge, culture, or motivation. Selden (Note 1) pointedly summarizes the limitations of readability formulas compared with the complex matching task that teachers face. He stresses that experienced teachers' knowledge about their students goes far beyond the students' standardized reading test scores and that their knowledge about reading materials goes beyond what readability formulas tend to measure. He points out that such information is infinitely more useful in matching the book with the child than a technological assessment of the book and the child's reading test score.

Sociological Problems

Thus far, we have considered readability formulas outside the social system within which they were developed and continue to be used. To ignore this context is unrealistic; understanding the interaction between readability formulas and the American school culture is crucial in developing solutions to the problem of choosing texts for students.

Lack of Cultural Considerations. Schools in the United States are strikingly multicultural, especially in urban areas: black, Hispanic, and Asian students often make up the majority of students in city classrooms. Readability formulas, however, make no statements regarding culture. A Hispanic child might have had little trouble with the excerpt from *Yagua Days*; black inner-city children who have never seen a cow might need more help reading stories about farm life than rural children would; and the following excerpt from the *Bridge Series* (Simpkins, Holt, & Simpkins, 1977) might pose problems for white students who are unfamiliar with Black English Vernacular:

> Shine was a stoker on the *Titanic*. The Brother, he shovel coal into the ship furnace to make the engines go. Now dig. Check what went down on the day the *Titanic* sunk. Shine kept on going up to the captain of the ship. He kept on telling the captain that the ship was leaking.
> Shine run on up to the captain and say, "Captain, Captain, I was down in the hole looking for something to eat. And you know what? The water rose above my feet." (pp. 1–4)

Whereas white students often read "Brother" to mean "male sibling," black students found that this passage reflected the language with which they were most familiar. A readability formula would be blind to these differences.

Readability formula designers have recognized the impact changing times and changing culture might have on their formulas. In 1978, Spache developed a revised version of his 1953 formula, stating, "If a readability formula is to continue to reflect accurate estimates of the difficulty of today's books, it, too, must change." Thus, a formula validated with one group of students and one type of text can be considered invalid for the same types of students and texts as conditions change. The effects on validity of the formula for readers who have different cultural backgrounds or dialects must be considerably greater.

Class Bias. Word difficulty in readability formulas is measured either by number of syllables or according to lists of familiar words. The question "To whom are these words familiar?" was asked in a recent study (Bruce, Rubin, Starr, & Liebling, in press). The authors suggest that such lists reflect a white middle-class vocabulary. Comparing the Hall corpus of words spoken by and to children of various racial and socioeconomic backgrounds (Hall, Linn, & Nagy, Note 10) with the Spache (1978) and Dale-Chall (1948) word lists, Bruce et al. (in press) discovered that black and lower-class children's words were underrepresented on the lists. Thus, texts that are judged easy because they contain familiar words may actually be more difficult for black or lower-class children because the words are not familiar to them.

What is the ultimate effect of readability formulas on nonwhite or non-middle-class students? For "poor readers," the formulas will assert that a text is readable, thereby putting the blame on the reader and his or her "vocabulary problem." Standardized tests, which are also constructed according to readability formulas, similarly assert that certain students are failing or are, at least, below grade level. Basal readers are the source for readability formula word lists and the result of applying readability formulas to text; thus, any cultural bias that existed in the original basal readers has been perpetuated through readability formula development.

A New View of the Reading Process

Readability formulas are based on a view of the reading process that is now being rejected by many reading researchers. The most succinct description of this emerging view of reading comes from Rosenblatt (1978): "A text, once it leaves its author's hands, is simply paper and ink until a reader evokes from it a literary work" (p. ix). In a more expanded view, Rosenblatt states:

> The transactional phrasing of the reading process underlines the essential importance of both elements, reader and text, in any reading event. A person becomes a reader by virtue of his activity in relationship to a text, which he organizes as a set of verbal symbols. A physical text, a set of marks on a page, becomes the text of a poem or of a scientific formula by virtue of its relationship with a reader who can thus interpret and reach through it to the world of the work. (pp. 18–19)

Such a view insists that text exists only in its transaction with a person who reads it and constructs meaning from it. Experimental reading research has reinforced the central role of the reader in the reading process. Anderson (Note 11) has emphasized the role of schemata (the individual knowledge structures through which readers view the world) in reading, citing a series of studies demonstrating that features of readers' lives, such as what subject they have chosen as a college major or their cultural background, predictably affect their understanding of ambiguous passages. Other research (Adams & Bruce, 1982; Bruce & Rubin, Note 12; Collins, Brown, & Larkin, Note 13) has described in detail the process by which different readers, relying on their own idiosyncratic fund of knowledge, construct an interpretation of a text. Adams and Bruce (1982) divided this knowledge into three categories: conceptual knowledge, social knowledge, and story knowledge. For each category, they demonstrated how a child's interpretation of a fable might diverge from an adult's interpretation, according to differences in that category of knowledge.

Research on classroom instruction has focused on the role of children's own experiences in reading. As discussed in chapter 21 of this volume, Hansen tested questioning methods that evoke children's relevant background knowledge and demonstrated that these methods increased reading comprehension. Similar studies by Pearson, Hansen, and Gordon (1979) have demonstrated the effectiveness of teaching students to interweave their own knowledge with the information presented in a text.

Related research has emphasized reading as a communicative experience. Bruce (1981) defines a social interaction model that views reading as communication between author and reader, mediated by several levels of implied author, narrator, implied reader, and narratee. Rubin (1980) views reading as a language experience different from but related to engaging in conversations, watching plays, and talking on the telephone. Olson (1977) examines how reading and writing have changed our view of communication by expanding the time and space limitations that previously confined communication to face-to-face settings.

In the midst of this new research, the readability formulas' view of texts as separate from the reading process and analyzable in isolation seems severely out of place. Reliance on readability formulas leads research away from more insightful and complex analyses of the reader–text transaction and exploration of more fruitful methods for producing appropriate texts. Instead of asking, "How difficult is this text?" we should be asking the following questions:

1. What analytic techniques will help us better understand transactions between particular texts and particular readers?
2. How can we help students make the transition from conversation to reading?
3. What classroom activities can improve students' motivation and comprehension?

4. How can we give students enough information so that they can choose their own texts?

Alternative Methods for Choosing Appropriate Texts

Without readability formulas as a screen of objectivity, decisions about text selection will involve opinions and intuition—*educated* opinions and intuitions, of course. Teachers and publishers should understand rhetorical and literary features of text, discover how children make hypotheses about stories, and analyze where children are most likely to misunderstand a text.

The situations that teachers and publishers face are not the same. Teachers have been shown to be relatively good judges of readability. Dale and Chall (1948) report a .9 correlation between teachers' judgments of text difficulty and reading grade levels calculated from a formula (Gilliland, 1972). Teachers have access to many other sources of information to inform their choices. Educational journals and periodicals regularly publish reviews of trade books for children, and basal readers often contain suggested bibliographies of related books. Teachers may also find some of the recent research on children's preferences informative; Zimet and Camp (1974), for example, compared the book choices of first-graders from cities and suburbs.

Publishers, however, must choose texts that are appropriate for children with a wide variety of backgrounds, and they must satisfy the adoption boards and administrators who decide what series will be available to teachers. To do the best job of text selection, publishers must participate in the kind of process teachers experience: watching individuals and groups of children reading and discussing candidate texts. Field testing offers publishers the opportunity to collect aggregate data on students' responses to texts and to interview children of varying cultural backgrounds about their understanding and appreciation of particular texts. Analyzing readers' descriptions of their successes and difficulties, as suggested by Swaney et al. (1981) and Flower and Hayes (in press), can provide the most useful, detailed information to guide text selection and revision. Those who purchase texts—adoption boards, administrators, teachers—must request and support such field testing so that publishers will spend the extra time and money necessary to develop materials that are truly worth reading.

Reference Notes

1. Selden, R. On the validation of the original readability formulas. In A. Davison, R. Lutz, & A. Roalef (Eds.), *Text readability: Proceedings of the March 1980 Conference* (Tech. Rep. No. 213). Urbana: University of Illinois, Center for the Study of Reading, August 1981.

2. Kantor, R., & Davison, A. Categories and strategies of adaptation in children's reading materials. In A. Rubin (Ed.), *Conceptual readability: New ways to look at text* (Reading Education Rep. No. 31). Urbana: University of Illinois, Center for the Study of Reading, September 1981.
3. Steinberg, C.S., & Bruce, B.C. Conflict: An analysis of a higher-level story feature and its application to children's literature. In A. Rubin (Ed.), *Conceptual readability: New ways to look at text* (Reading Education Rep. No. 31). Urbana: University of Illinois, Center for the Study of Reading, September 1981.
4. Armbruster, B., & Anderson, T. Mapping: Representing text structure diagrammatically. In A. Rubin (Ed.), *Conceptual readability: New ways to look at text* (Reading Education Rep. No. 31). Urbana: University of Illinois, Center for the Study of Reading, September 1981.
5. Rubin, A., & Gentner, D. An educational technique to encourage practice with high-level aspects of texts. In A. Rubin (Ed.), *Conceptual readability: New ways to look at text* (Reading Education Rep. No. 31). Urbana: University of Illinois, Center for the Study of Reading, September 1981.
6. Kern, R.P. *Usefulness of readability formulas for achieving Army readability objectives: Research and state of the art applies to the Army's problem* (Tech. Rep. No. 437). Alexandria, Va.: U.S. Army Research Institute for the Behavioral and Social Sciences, January 1980.
7. Caylor, J.S., Sticht, T.G., Fox, L.C., & Ford, J.P. *Methodologies for determining reading requirements of military occupational specialties* (Tech. Rep. No. 73-5). Alexandria, Va.: Human Resources Research Organization, 1973.
8. Kincaid, J.P., Fishburne, R.P., Jr., Rogers, R.L., & Chissom, B.S. *Derivation of new readability formulas for Navy enlisted personnel* (Research Branch Report 8-75). Pensacola, Fla.: U.S. Navy Technical Training Command, February 1975.
9. Steinberg, C.S. *The role of beliefs and character interaction in the analysis and comprehension of children's stories.* Paper presented at the National Council of Teachers of English Annual Conference, Boston, November 1981.
10. Hall, W.S., Linn, R.L., & Nagy, W.E. *Spoken words* (Tech. Rep. No. 177). Urbana: University of Illinois, Center for the Study of Reading, August 1980.
11. Anderson, R.C. *Schema-directed processes in language comprehension* (Tech. Rep. No. 50). Urbana: University of Illinois, Center for the Study of Reading, July 1977.
12. Bruce, B.C., & Rubin, A. Jobs you shouldn't count on readability formulas to do. In A. Davison, R. Lutz, & A. Roaley (Eds.), *Text readability: Proceedings of the March 1980 Conference* (Tech. Rep. No. 213). Urbana: University of Illinois, Center for the Study of Reading, August 1981.
13. Collins, A., Brown, J.S., & Larkin, K.M. *Inference in text understanding* (Tech. Rep. No. 40). Urbana: University of Illinois, Center for the Study of Reading, December 1977. (ERIC Document Reproduction Service No. ED 150 547.)

References

Adams, M.J., & Bruce, B.C. Background knowledge and reading comprehension. In J. Langer & T. Smith Burke (Eds.), *Author meets reader/A psycholinguistic perspective: Bridging the gap from theory to practice.* Newark, Del.: International Reading Association, 1982.

Bormuth, J.R. Readability: A new approach. *Reading Research Quarterly*, 1966, *1*, 79–132.

Bruce, B.C. A social interaction model of reading. *Discourse Processes*, 1981, *4*, 273–311.

Bruce, B.C., Rubin, A., Starr, K.L., & Liebling, C. Vocabulary bias in reading curricula. In W. Hall (Ed.), *Spoken words*. Hillsdale, N.J.: Erlbaum, in press.

Chall, J.S. The measurement of readability. *Education Digest*, 1955, *21*, 44–46.

Dale, E., & Chall, J.S. A formula for predicting readability. *Educational Research Bulletin*, 1948, *27*, 37–54.

Davison, A., & Kantor, R. On the failure of readability formulas to define readable texts: A case study from adaptations. *Reading Research Quarterly*, 1982, *17*, 187–210.

Dolch, E.W. Grading reading difficulty. In E.W. Dolch (Ed.), *Problems in reading*. Champaign, Ill.: Garrard, 1948.

Duffy, T.M., & Kabance, P. *Testing a readable writing approach to text revision*. San Diego: Navy Personnel Research and Development Center, 1981.

Flesch, R. *How to test readability*. New York: Harper, 1951.

Flesch, R. *How to make sense*. New York: Harper, 1954.

Flower, L.S., & Hayes, J.R. Problem solving and the cognitive process of writing. In C.H. Frederiksen, M.F. Whiteman, & J.F. Dominic (Eds.), *Writing: The nature, development and teaching of written communication*. Hillsdale, N.J.: Erlbaum, in press.

Fry, E.B. A readability formula that saves time. *Journal of Reading*, 1968, *11*, 513–516; 575–578.

Gilliland, J. *Readability*. London: University of London Press, 1972.

Gunning, R. *The technique of clear writing*. New York: McGraw-Hill, 1952.

Kintsch, W., & Vipond, D. Reading comprehension and readability in educational practice and psychological theory. In L.G. Nillson (Ed.), *Memory processes*. Hillsdale, N.J.: Erlbaum, 1979.

Klare, G.R. A second look at the validity of readability formulas. *Journal of Reading Behavior*, 1976, *8*, 129–152.

Lobel, A. *Frog and Toad all year*. New York: Harper & Row, 1976.

Lockman, R.F. A note on measuring "understandability." *Journal of Applied Psychology*, 1957, *40*, 195–196.

Martel, C. *Yagua days*. New York: Dial Press, 1976.

McCall, W.A., & Crabbs, L.M. *Standard test lessons in reading* (Books 2, 3, 4, 5). New York: Teachers College Press, 1925.

Nelson, N.J., & Denny, E.C. *Nelson Denny Reading Test*. Boston: Houghton Mifflin, 1973.

Olson, D. From utterance to text: The bias of language in speech and writing. *Harvard Educational Review*, 1977, *47*, 257–281.

Parker, D.A. *SRA reading laboratory* (Secondary Series, 111b). Chicago: Science Research Associates, 1963.

Pearson, P.D, Hansen, J., & Gordon, C. The effect of background knowledge on young children's comprehension of explicit and implicit information. *Journal of Reading Behavior*, 1979, *11*, 201–209.

Raygor, A.L. *Raygor readability estimator*. Rehoboth, Md.: Twin Oaks, 1979.

Redish, J. *Readability*. In D.A. McDonald (Ed.), *Drafting documents in plain language*. New York: Practicing Law Institute, 1979.

Rosenblatt, L.M. *The reader, the text, the poem*. Carbondale: Southern Illinois University Press, 1978.

Rubin, A. A theoretical taxonomy of the differences between oral and written language. In R.J. Spiro, B.C. Bruce, & W.F. Brewer (Eds.), *Theoretical issues in reading comprehension*. Hillsdale, N.J.: Erlbaum, 1980.

Simpkins, G., Holt, G., & Simpkins, C. Shine. In *Bridge series: A crossculture-reaching program* (Booklet 1). Boston: Houghton Mifflin, 1977.

Spache, G.D. *Good reading for poor readers* (Rev. 10th ed.). Champaign, Ill.: Garrard, 1978.

Steinberg, C.S., & Bruce, B.C. Higher level features in children's stories: Rhetorical structure and conflict. In *The National Reading Conference Yearbook*. Clemson, S.C.: National Reading Conference, 1980.

Sticht, T.G. Project realistic: Determination of adult functional literacy skill levels. *Reading Research Quarterly*, 1972, 7, 424–465.

Sticht, T.G. (Ed.). *Reading for working*. Alexandria, Va.: Human Resources Research Organization, 1975.

Swaney, J.H., Janik, C.J., Bond, S.J., & Hayes, J.R. *Editing for comprehension: Improving the process through reading protocols*. Pittsburgh: Document Design Project, June 1981.

Thorndike, E.L. *The teacher's word book*. New York: Teachers College Press, 1921.

Zimet, S.G., & Camp, B.W. A comparison between the content of preferred school library selections made by inner-city and suburban first grade students. *Elementary English*, 1974, *51*, 1004–1006.

6
Materials Do Make a Difference

Walter H. MacGinitie

To teach reading, teachers must use materials. These materials inevitably make a difference, not only in what is taught but also in how it is taught. The preceding chapters help us understand the ways in which present-day materials influence what teachers do and what students learn.

It is useful to recognize how much we are asking of students when they learn to read, for only then can we appreciate how important appropriate materials and effective instruction can be in helping students become competent, comprehending readers. Reading is an enormously complex activity. The chapters by Bertram Bruce and Bonnie Armbruster illustrate this well. Reading involves a very complex set of cognitive and perceptual processes and requires a rich background of experience with written language and with the physical and social world. Through his experiment with "The Hare and the Tortoise," Bruce has illustrated that the reader needs "knowledge of events, plans, story structures, real-world creatures, story-world characters, and the rhetorical devices that writers employ, such as inside view and author commentary . . . in addition to the basic graphemic, lexical, syntactic, and semantic knowledge needed to read a single phrase" (see chapter 3).

It should be emphasized that readers need this knowledge in a form that they can use, whether or not they are aware of using it. That this knowledge is required does not mean that students need a series of exercises dealing with how events are described or how plans contribute to stories. Most students can best learn these things through independent and guided reading, through listening, and through firsthand experience, rather than through academic exercises.

Research on reading comprehension has made clear that reading comprehension, as distinct from listening comprehension, requires competence in dealing with written language registers, styles, and conventions, which differ considerably from those of most forms of oral language (Maria & MacGinitie, 1982). Most of these differences result not from perverse efforts to make written language more complex but simply from the requirements imposed on written language by lack of intonation, gesture, and shared context.

Also, various types of written language require various types of reading competence. I will illustrate this point with two samples of text from the previous chapters. The following is version 6, the final version of "The Hare and the Tortoise" in chapter 3 (from Kent, 1974). Read this story again; then ask yourself how you know the fox had been listening to the conversation before he spoke. The fox must have been listening to know that there was an argument and that a race might settle it. (Warren, Nicholas, and Trabasso, 1979, call such insights slot-filling inferences.)

Version 6: "The Hare and the Tortoise"

The hare teased the tortoise about being so pokey.
"I get where I'm going as surely as YOU do!" said the tortoise.
"But I get where I'm going FASTER," said the hare.
The fox suggested they run a race to settle the argument. The hare laughed so hard at the idea that it made the tortoise angry.
"I'll race you and I'll WIN!" the tortoise said.
The race had hardly begun before the speedy hare was out of sight. The hare was so sure of himself that he lay down by the side of the path to take a short nap. The tortoise kept plodding slowly along. The hare woke up just in time to see the tortoise cross the finish line and win the race.
SLOW AND STEADY WINS THE RACE.

Now ask yourself how you know that the tortoise was initially a bit irritated at being teased, that the hare is a confident braggart, that the hare rapidly outdistanced the tortoise at first, and that the tortoise passed the sleeping hare. These slot-filling inferences—these "facts"—are at the heart of the story, yet the story does not state them. They come from the reader's own knowledge of what the whole situation must be like, given the parts that are described in the story.

What Warren et al. (1979) call text-connecting inferences are also required. Such inferences are what make it possible for you to know that the argument was between the hare and the tortoise, that the argument concerned a question of superior locomotion, that the idea was that they should run a race, and so on. It is characteristic of stories that a very large proportion of what we might consider the story itself is actually created by the reader through the cues given by the author.

Expository writing often puts to the test a different side of reading competence. An example of expository writing from chapter 4 (Armbruster) illustrates this point:

What happens to these processes in the evening? The fading light of evening causes photosynthesis to slow down. Respiration, however, does not depend on light and thus continues to produce carbon dioxide. The carbon dioxide in the air spaces builds up again, which makes the guard cells relax. The relaxing of the guard cells closes the leaf openings. Consequently, the leaf openings close in the evening as photosynthesis slows down.

Inferences are required in this type of story, too, but the characters, their characteristics, and the situations are new to us. Therefore, we must take time to construct images, to remember their strange characteristics, and to modify and interrelate them in the ways new sentences in the text suggest. We do not have ready-made images and expectations for leaf openings and guard cells, as we do for hare and tortoise. We must bring our images and expectations up to date with each new sentence, or we are lost.

When we read the sentence, "The carbon dioxide in the air spaces builds up again, which makes the guard cells relax," we must remind ourselves what air spaces and guard cells are like, where they are found, and what their functions are, so that the new information about them will make sense to us. Carbon dioxide "builds up," we must infer, because it does not get used up in photosynthesis, which has slowed down. Each new sentence in the paragraph requires this review of relations, functions, and images so that they can be verified, modified, and added to.

Being a good reader requires not only a rich knowledge of the world and of written language but an enormous amount of experience in reading itself. Imagine two boys in the fifth grade who are equal in their ability to play basketball. Over the next few years, one of these boys practices every day. He joins the basketball team in junior high and high school and receives good coaching. The other boy plays basketball only during physical education class. Consider the great difference that will exist in the ability of these two boys to play basketball by the time they are seniors in high school. Reading with understanding is certainly no less complex than playing basketball and probably responds no less to good coaching. If you substitute reading for basketball in the preceding vignette, you would expect a similarly large difference in ability to result. Reading comprehension is seldom taught, however, and is practiced much less than we think. We will see how current school materials contribute to this lack of a central experience.

That reading comprehension is seldom taught is supported by the findings that Dolores Durkin has reported in chapter 1. She found that teachers spend a good deal of time giving assignments in workbooks and similar materials and a good deal of time asking the students questions about the stories and other selections they read. Durkin refers to the latter activity as "assessment," assuming, perhaps, that the purpose of the questioning is to find out what students have understood and what they need. This may be a charitable assumption, for it is a rare teacher who uses the students' responses as a basis for instruction.

In following this pattern of recitation without instruction, the teacher is doing just what the instructional materials suggest. As Durkin points out, basal reader manuals contain many, many questions for the teachers to ask the students in guiding discussion of the reading selection—so many that "if teachers used all the questions found in the manuals, they would be questioning their students constantly." She also points out that "no suggestions are made for what to do if students are unable to [answer], nor are teachers ever encouraged to link what is being done with reading." When students cannot answer a question or when they give a wrong answer, the manuals have almost no suggestions for instruction that would help the students.

What does a teacher ordinarily do when a student gives a wrong answer or no answer? My informal observations suggest that what the teacher does depends a good deal on the age of the student and on whether the written material is from a story in the basal reader or from a chapter in a content area textbook. If the question concerns a story in the basal reader, the teacher is most likely to refer the question to another student. If the student's answer reveals a lack of understanding about some material in a content area textbook, however, the teacher will usually restate the content and provide an explanation in his or her own words, without asking the student to refer to the text. Such explaining is particularly characteristic of high school teachers, but it can be seen in elementary schools when teachers adopt a subject matter teaching mode (MacGinitie, 1983). Whether they are reading in a basal reader or in a content area text, students are seldom helped to learn how to use the text to answer the questions they are asked.

The chapters in this section also illustrate how current instructional materials provide much less practice in reading comprehension than one might expect. Durkin's observational study (chapter 1) and Osborn's examination of workbooks (chapter 2) show that large amounts of student time are given over to receiving assignments and doing exercises. Although these exercises contain some reading, they are, for the most part, far from sustained, meaningful reading. Much of the time students spend on workbooks and related exercises is spent writing the letters of right answers, coloring circles, and underlining words; and much of the time teachers spend in "teaching reading" must be spent in checking to see that the right letters have been written and the right circles colored in.

One would suppose that, in subjects such as social studies and science, students would get great amounts of practice reading, but such is often not the case. Students have often learned that many teachers will explain all the material in class and that there is no need to do the reading (MacGinitie, 1983). Students have also learned that exams and recitations will be based not on the reading but only on what is discussed in class.

Somehow, the idea has developed that a good presenter is a good teacher. The good teacher is seen as a good explainer, rather than as someone who is good at helping students become competent learners on their own. The ultimate futility of making children dependent on their teachers seems not to be considered.

Another reason that students have limited experience with reading is that the texts they read are often not matched to their abilities. The range of reading ability in a typical classroom is enormous. The range in difficulty of reading materials in the typical classroom is much smaller. Typically, for both the better readers and the poorer readers, the available materials do not provide good practice in reading. If the materials are appropriate in difficulty for the average reader in a classroom, they are so difficult for the poorer readers that they provide little practice in comprehension. A student cannot practice comprehension with incomprehensible text. Materials that are truly suited for the average student also do little to extend the reading experience of the better readers.

There is much pressure to require that all textbooks be written at grade level. The application of readability formulas, however, does not assure the matching of students and textbooks. Materials that are impossible for poor readers and pedestrian for top readers will not be made more appropriate for them simply by adding a grade level readability index. Furthermore, in chapter 5, Andee Rubin has made abundantly clear how crude readability formulas are and how inappropriate they are for developing or assessing reading materials.

Appropriate reading must be provided for all students. What is appropriate depends, of course, on topic, purpose, student background, the help the student receives, and other factors. When students receive effective help with reading comprehension, the range of materials appropriate for each student increases. Materials that are too difficult for independent practice in comprehension become comprehensible with good comprehension instruction.

The requirement that texts conform to readability formulas has at least two undesirable side effects on the quality of textbook writing. One of these side effects, clearly illustrated by Rubin, is that conformity to vocabulary and sentence-length limits often overrides concern for careful, logical, and communicative writing. The second undesirable side effect is that such writing leads to the emasculation of ideas. Writing to a formula tends to oversimplify ideas. Rubin cites an example of this in which qualifying statements expressing opinion or doubt were omitted.

Curriculum guides typically include a vast array of topics. Many textbooks, trying to cover all these topics while conforming to demands for simple language, become lists of meaningless facts. This page about birds from a fifth-grade science text is a clear example:

Birds. All birds have feathers. No other kind of animal has feathers.

Birds are warm-blooded, too. A bird's body temperature tends to stay the same, even in cold air.

Birds' eggs are hard shelled. They are not like the eggs of snakes, turtles, and lizards, which have soft shells.

In many ways, the wings of birds are like your arms. The long bones in the wings are similar to your arm bones. But birds' bones are hollow. This makes them light.

One of the largest bones in a bird is the breastbone. The large muscles needed for flying are fastened to it.

Birds have no teeth for chewing. Their food is ground up after they swallow it. Besides food, birds swallow small stones. These help to grind up the food. (Rockcastle, Salamon, Schmidt, & McKnight, 1977, p. 50)

As Armbruster has indicated, in chapter 4, a good text will make clear the significance of the information it presents. The foregoing text does not develop any of the topics enough to make them either meaningful or interesting. The result of writing that says too little about too much is that any meaningful content must be provided by the teacher. Thus, the opportunity to learn by reading, and about reading, is reduced, and the students' dependence on the teacher is increased. It would be far better for textbooks to cover fewer topics interestingly and well.

If we want students to become effective readers, we need to know what we would like students to be able to learn by reading and to experience through reading. We must give recognition to the enormous ranges of ability, interests, and backgrounds of students. Students need to experience clear exposition and imaginative, stimulating expression in their texts and other books.

We have learned from the chapters in this section that many materials currently used in classrooms provide too little real instruction in reading comprehension and too little reading practice. Our first task is to decide what we can reasonably expect students to read and to learn from reading. Our next task is to learn how to help students when they have difficulties with what they are reading. When we give significant but reasonable assignments and give help with difficulties, then can we hold students responsible for what they should learn from reading, and they will gain confidence in their ability to accomplish the reading tasks we give them.

References

Kent, J. *More fables of Aesop*. New York: Parents' Magazine Press, 1974.

MacGinitie, W.H. Readability as a solution adds to the problem. In R.C. Anderson, J. Osborn, & R.J. Tierney (Eds.), *Learning to read in American schools*. Hillsdale, N.J.: Erlbaum, 1983.

Maria, K., & MacGinitie, W.H. Reading comprehension disabilities: Knowledge structures and non-accommodating text processing strategies. *Bulletin of the Orton Dyslexia Society*, 1982, *32*, 33–59.

Rockcastle, V.N., Salamon, F.R., Schmidt, V.E., & McKnight, B.J. *Stem science* (Metric ed.). Menlo Park, Calif.: Addison-Wesley, 1977.

Warren, W.H., Nicholas, D.W., & Trabasso, T. Event chains and inferences in understanding narratives. In R.O. Freedle (Ed.), *New directions in discourse processing* (Vol. 2). Hillsdale, N.J.: Erlbaum, 1979.

Part II
The Organization of Classrooms, Schools, and Instruction

7
The Executive Functions of Teaching

David C. Berliner

T he purpose of this chapter is to remind everyone that classrooms are complex and dynamic workplaces that require management by an executive of considerable talent. Teachers are not usually thought of as executives; nevertheless, I believe that a conception of classrooms as workplaces and teachers as executives has merit.

Origins of Interest

During a break while attending a meeting on reading instruction at a prominent hotel, I discovered that a business management seminar was under way in an adjoining room. The seminar leader was saying: "One of the most crucial skills in management is to state your objectives—you have to have clearly stated objectives to know where you are going, to tell if you are on track, and to evaluate your performance and that of others." That sounded very familiar to an educational psychologist. I stayed to listen and spent the day at the business management meeting.

This group of managers spent some time on the topic of management by objectives. The instructors quoted Mager and Popham, names familiar to many people in education. The second topic was the use of time, which was described as the greatest single management problem. The relevance of their concerns to those of educators seemed clear. The third topic was motivation. The managers heard a presentation on the benefits of positive reinforcement, the negative effects of criticism and punishment, the uses of graphing, and the beneficial effects of contracts and the positive effects of high expectations. The last topic of the day was evaluation. The parallels between the topics covered in this training session for business and public executives and some of the knowledge and skills needed to run a classroom seemed obvious.

Can the concepts and principles of management and executive training be useful to teachers? The answer to that question requires a careful examination of the relationship between management practice and education.

Management theory, as developed by March and Simon (1958), has brought us a model of the actions of people in organizations that is very compatible with life in educational organizations. Their assertion is that people make decisions that are "satisfycing"—decisions that suffice but are not necessarily optimal. March and

Simon argue that we are too limited in our information-processing capability to do anything more than to make satisfycing decisions—decisions that are good enough to get on with the job.

A compelling case can be made for conceptualizing classrooms as extremely complex and dynamic environments managed by talented and experienced executives. There is a respectable body of knowledge about what teachers do to make a difference in students' performance. Outcome measures can be created for judging whether, in fact, valued kinds of learning are taking place. Finally, we now have a scientific community in education ready to engage in the painstaking research necessary to study educational practice in order to overcome or confirm the practices of the field.

Current Conceptions of Management and Executive Behavior

As opposed to the fiercely profit-oriented, production model of management that ran through business at an earlier time, some surprising trends have developed in management today.

Jean-Jacques Serven-Schreiber (quoted in Levinson, 1981) has said that "management is, all things considered, the most creative of all arts. It is the art of arts because it is the organizer of talent." That statement is not incompatible with educational values. Expressing a similar belief, Peter Drucker, high priest of the corporate society, says of management, "Your job is not to tell someone what to do, it is to enable him to perform well" (in Tarrant, 1976). That, also, is not in conflict with basic educational values.

The modern manager now combines worries about efficiency with worries about people—their feelings of satisfaction, their growth, their contributions to the organization, and other personal issues that once were more characteristic of human service providers than of business executives.

If we can agree that the values of management are not now inherently inappropriate for education, we can move on and ask what managers do—keeping an eye open for any parallels with the role of the classroom teacher.

Huse (1979), author of a current text on management, defines a manager as one who works to accomplish the goals of an organization and who directly supervises one or more people in a formal organization. Other texts define a manager or an executive as the person who does the planning, organizing, directing or leading, and controlling (Flippo & Munsinger, 1978; Koontz, O'Donnell, & Weihrich, 1980). Drucker (1977) adds another point: "The first criterion in identifying those people within an organization who have management responsibility is not command over people. It is responsibility for contribution" (p. 50). According to all of these definitions, teachers are clearly managers. Even an empirical study of business managers has a familiarity for educators. A study of 160 private-sector managers (Huse, 1979) revealed that they had

. . . little time alone to think. On the average, during the four weeks of the study, the managers were alone only nine (9) times for a half-hour or more without interruptions. True breaks were seldom taken. Coffee was drunk during meetings and lunch time was almost always devoted to formal or informal meetings. (pp. 12–13)

Private-sector managers and teachers also share a similar pathology; both groups show high levels of stress and that most dreaded condition of the 1980s, burnout. Thus, in function, responsibility, similarity in the demands of the job, and even pathology, the tasks of teachers and managers are similar. Teachers manage when, using the available resources, they produce changes in the knowledge, skills, and attitudes of their students in an acceptable way. Good teaching, like good management, is getting more or better work done under existing conditions.

The last decade has seen a great increase in our knowledge of teachers and teaching. More effective and less effective teachers have been studied, as have more effective and less effective schools. Among the scores of variables now thought to distinguish between the effective and the less effective are a dozen or so that are also basic management concerns.

Research on Teaching: The Executive Functions

The sociological tradition in educational scholarship, from Willard Waller (1932) to Robert Dreeben (1968) and Dan Lortie (1975), as well as most of the citizenry, has always clearly recognized that schools are workplaces. When schools do not appear to function as workplaces, they tend to be viewed, at best, as places where learning takes place relatively haphazardly and, at worst, as custodial institutions.

We must always remember, of course, that schools and classrooms are not *just* workplaces—they are many other things as well, serving, in particular, social and socialization functions. We should never be so overwhelmed by these other functions, however, that we forget that school is a place where work is to be done—where teachers are expected to add value to students.

In teaching or business, the person who runs the workplace must perform a number of executive functions, including the following:

1. Planning of work;
2. Communicating goals;
3. Regulating the activities of the workplace;
4. Creating a pleasant environment for work;
5. Educating new members of the workgroup;
6. Articulating the work of the workplace with other units in the system;
7. Supervising and working with other people;
8. Motivating those being supervised; and
9. Evaluating the performance of those being supervised.

In business or in government executive positions, there is a tenth executive function—developing budgets and managing money. Teachers do not often engage in this activity. The other nine functions, however, are performed by teachers and corporate executives alike, though for vastly different rates of pay. I will now comment on these nine executive functions as they pertain to teaching, in light of my experience and much of the current research on teaching.

Executive Function 1: Planning of Work

Teachers, like all executives, engage in planning. Yinger (1977) identified five time frames used by teachers as they engage in planning. First is the long-range yearly plan, wherein the general framework of what will be covered is made explicit; second, and slightly more focused, is the term; third is the month, wherein basic units of instruction are specified and such things as movies and field trips can be arranged; fourth is the weekly plan, a more detailed description of what will occur, including (usually for the first time) the time allocations for activities; and finally, there is the daily plan, with its schedule and its requirements for special materials or human resources. Researchers in this new area of study agree that the plans made by teachers early in the year have a profound effect on teaching and learning over the course of the year. The planning of lessons or activities and interactive decision making among teachers takes place within the framework of yearly plans (Joyce, 1978–79).

Among the many long-term managerial decisions that teachers make, four strike me as extremely important: choosing content, scheduling time, forming groups, and choosing activity structures. These decisions have been shown to affect student behavior, attitude, and achievement. Unfortunately, not every teacher is aware of how powerful these long-term managerial decisions can be in determining what is learned in classrooms.

Choosing Content. Chief state school officers, superintendents of schools, school board members, and principals often believe that they determine what is taught in the classrooms of their state, district, or school. They do not. The real arbiter of what is taught in classrooms is the classroom teacher.

What we have learned from a Michigan State University research team (Schwille, Porter, Belli, Floden, Freeman, Knappen, Kuhs, & Schmidt, Note 1) is that the perceived effort required to teach a subject matter area, the perceived difficulty of the subject matter area for students, and teachers' personal feelings of enjoyment while teaching a subject matter area influence the teachers' choice of content. One striking example in their data illustrates this point: an elementary school teacher who enjoyed teaching science taught twenty-eight times more science than one who said she did not enjoy teaching science.

From the same research team, we have also learned that even if text is slavishly adhered to, and finished completely by all students, the overlap between what is tested on a standardized test and what is taught in the classroom is probably only about 50 percent. Even within this set of constraints designed to dramatically underestimate the value of schools and teachers, we find that many teachers do not slavishly follow the prescribed textbook. Sometimes, teachers introduce very useful or very interesting content in a curriculum area. Sometimes, however, their personal choices are indefensible. In the Beginning Teacher Evaluation Study (Fisher, Filby, Marliave, Cahen, Dishaw, Moore, & Berliner, Note 2), we observed one elementary school teacher for more than 90 days. During that time, she taught nothing about fractions, even though fraction instruction was mandated by the state for instruction at that grade. When the teacher was asked why she did not teach fractions she said, "I don't like fractions!" This very human response illustrates two things: the power that teachers have in deciding the content of the curriculum and the failure of our educational system to provide any useful feedback to teachers about what they do. Teachers regularly act as curriculum content decision makers, but they are rarely informed about their performance in this crucial area.

The empirical data relating content coverage or content emphasis to achievement is clear (Berliner & Rosenshine, 1977). With such clear evidence about the powerful effects of the content variable, it is interesting to note the casualness with which such content decisions often are made. Buchmann and Schmidt (Note 3), of the Institute for Research on Teaching, point out that elementary school teachers can be a law unto themselves and that if their personal feelings about subject matter are not bounded by an impersonal conception of professional duties, their students will suffer the consequences. They conclude that responsibility in decision making about content requires that teachers examine their own conduct and beliefs.

Scheduling Time. Related to the issues involved in content decisions are decisions about time allocations for subject matter areas. The elementary teacher allocates that most precious of resources—time. What is important to consider is the incredible variation in the time allocations that are made by different teachers. While observing fifth-grade teachers (Berliner, 1979), we noticed that one teacher could find only 68 minutes a day for instruction in reading and language arts, while another teacher was able to find 137 minutes a day. In the second grade, one teacher allocated 47 minutes a day for reading and language arts, while another teacher managed to find 118 minutes a day—two and a half times more than the other teacher. In mathematics, the same variability was evident. One second-grade teacher allocated 16 minutes a day to instruction in mathematics, while another teacher, constrained by the same length of the school day, somehow found 51 minutes a day to allocate to mathematics instruction. From such data, it is not difficult to infer why scheduling of time is a management issue of great consequence.

Another issue has to do with the way time within a curriculum area is scheduled. One of our fifth-grade teachers, observed for 87 days, allocated 5,646 minutes to comprehension activities (such as drawing inferences, identifying main ideas, and paraphrasing), while another fifth-grade teacher, observed for 97 days, allocated only 917 minutes to those kinds of comprehension activities. The management decisions of teachers that allocate time to particular content areas are causally related to achievement in those areas. This is as true in music, art, and physical education as it is in science, mathematics, and reading. Teacher decisions involving the powerful variable of time must not be made in a casual manner.

Forming Groups. Like other executives who are responsible for supervising more than just a few people, teachers form work groups and decide on the size and the composition of the groups. Grouping decisions are very important because they affect student achievement and student attitude.

Qualitative research by Rist (1973) has shown that irrelevant criteria can be used as the basis for group assignment and that such assignments can be of long duration. Rist described one teacher who formed three work groups on the eighth day of kindergarten. It appeared that what she used as the basis of assignment were those well-known correlates of academic ability—clothing, cleanliness, and body odor. The assignments made at the beginning of kindergarten to the group expected to be lowest in achievement were, for the most part, still in force three years later, when second-grade groups were observed.

Shavelson and Borko (1979), after reviewing teachers' decision making about grouping in reading, found that once students were grouped, the group became the unit for the planning of instruction, not the student. More important, however, was that the plans teachers made for high and low groups differed. Shavelson (1983) noted that while teacher plans for low groups were carried out inflexibly and emphasized reading aloud and decoding skills, teaching of the high groups was characterized by flexibility in procedures and emphasis on comprehension skills. Furthermore, the pacing during interactive teaching with high groups was fifteen times faster than it was with the low groups.

Grouping is a very rational response to what Dreeben (Note 4) indicated as one of the most salient characteristics of classrooms—their collective nature. The evidence suggests that the assignment of students to work groups is occasionally like a life-long sentence and that it always results in students in different groups learning different things while in school. Calfee and Brown (1979; also see Calfee and Piontkowski, in press), after reviewing the literature on grouping, note that the biggest issue to face in this area is who makes these decisions and on what grounds. They conclude that teachers "deserve the training in techniques for rational analysis of this problem that would provide greater clarity and direction."

Choosing Activity Structures. The building blocks of a curriculum are found in the activity structures. These activity or task structures, such as reading circle, or seatwork, or recitation, have functions and operations (rules or norms) associated with them (Doyle, 1977). The activity structures that are characteristically used by a teacher determine teacher behavior (as well as student behavior) and student attitudes and achievement. Bossert (Note 5), for example, notes:

Teachers who relied on recitation were less able to establish close social ties with their students than were teachers who primarily utilized small group and individualized projects. Recitation places teachers at the center of control. It forces them to rely on equitable, impersonal sanctions (usually short verbal desists) and on the authority of office rather than on more personalized influence mechanisms. By contrast, small group and individualized instruction increases opportunities for teachers to covertly "bend" classroom rules to handle individual problems and facilitates teacher involvement in, rather than simply teacher direction of, the activity. (p. 46)

The difference in rapport between teachers and students is clearly noticeable when recitation classrooms are compared to individualized instruction and small group classrooms. Different activity structures in these classrooms give rise to differences in the behavior and the attitudes of the participants in the activity. As Bossert (Note 5) notes:

It was not that the teachers who used recitation were less concerned or less empathic, but rather that recitation precludes the individualization and involvement allowed by other activities. (pp. 46–47).

In a study of seventy-five classrooms from kindergarten to sixth grade, 1,200 activity structures were coded (Berliner, 1983). We were trying to learn the normal operating characteristics of about a dozen activity structures, such as reading circle, silent reading, seatwork, and lecture.

We tried to determine how long each activity structure lasted, the number of students in the activity, whether or not there was an opportunity for teachers to evaluate students, and whether such evaluations were public or private. What was most intriguing about this project was that we discovered that teachers, who make choices about activity structures every day, had almost no ability to describe the different activity structures they used. Furthermore, they were unable to compare the relative costs and benefits of one form of instruction over another, either for different pedagogical purposes or for different kinds of students. We concluded that many teachers might not have the skills necessary to be successful managers in the area of choosing activity structures. This deficit in ability to analyze activities, either in terms of functions and operations or in terms of costs and benefits, probably accounts for why teachers seem to adhere to a few familiar activity structures and do not often change their classroom routines.

The responsibility for making reasonable decisions about instruction does not end at the planning stage. Teachers also must eventually carry out interactive instruction with the students. During interaction instruction, many kinds of decisions are made. The few extant studies of teachers' mental lives during interactive teaching reveals that teachers tend to follow mental scripts or lesson schemata as they maintain the flow of an activity. During lessons, teachers use the students' participation and involvement for self-evaluation of the success of the lesson (Peterson & Clark, 1978). Teachers seem to make conscious decisions to change lesson scripts only when something unusual happens or things go poorly. McKay and Marland (Note 6) estimate that teachers make at least ten nontrivial decisions per hour, and McKay and Marland and Morine and Vallance (Note 7) report that interactive decisions usually involve only two alternatives at a time.

Marland (1977) interpreted his data as showing that teachers' interactive classroom behavior is often guided by five principles. Teachers use the compensation principle to favor shy, quiet, dull, or culturally different students. They follow the principle of strategic leniency, so that they can ignore some of the inappropriate behavior of special children. (This strategy is best described by a teacher cited in Carew and Lightfoot, 1979, p. 119, who said that the best advice she ever got was to "*see* but don't *notice* everything.") Teachers use the principle of power sharing when they selectively reinforce certain students to enlist their aid in sharing responsibility, and the principle of progressive checking when they check the problems and progress of low ability students. Finally, teachers follow the principle of suppressing emotions. Marland's teachers felt that emotion during teaching was inappropriate because it could lead to a higher level of emotionality among students, which creates management problems.

The goal of this discussion of the first executive function—the planning of work—is to make explicit the complexity of the job and the power of the variables under the command of a teacher. Compared to feeding the children, keeping order, correcting papers, or ordering chalk, the planning of work is high-status behavior. That is why it was selected as the first point to make about executive functions in teaching. The other executive functions will not be discussed in as much detail; each of them, however, could be elaborated on and used to illustrate how the job of classroom teachers calls for executive skill.

Executive Function 2: Communicating Goals

Managers in any setting need to communicate their goals to those they supervise. Teachers can fulfill this executive function in two important ways: by structuring and by communicating performance expectations. Empirical research has confirmed that these variables affect achievement.

Structuring Performance Expectations. While analyzing protocols of reading and mathematics lessons during an ethnographic study of more and less effective teachers, conducted as part of the Beginning Teacher Evaluation Study (Tikunoff, Berliner, & Rist, Note 8), we found that we sometimes could not infer the teacher's intent. Sometimes we did not have a clue about why the lesson was occurring, where it fit in the scheme of things, or what students needed to focus on for success. Almost invariably, the teachers we judged to be unclear about communicating their goals and giving directions were less effective in promoting academic achievement. After further data collection (Fisher, Berliner, Filby, Marliave, Cahen, & Dishaw, 1980), we noted that both success rate and attention were improved when teachers spent more time discussing the goals or structures of the lesson and giving directions.

Structuring is especially important in classes where seatwork is used frequently. If children do not have a clear idea of what they are to do, they easily find ways to do nothing. In visits to schools, Jerome Bruner (Note 9) saw that many children were unable to figure out what was expected of them. He believed that some simple attention to this problem would easily improve achievement in classrooms.

Structuring affects attention and success rate. It is sometimes not done at all, sometimes only minimally, and sometimes overdone. A case of too much structuring was reported by Hassenpflug (Note 10). Her field notes documented that reading the directions given for many worksheet assignments in the third grade took longer than the time needed by most of the children to finish the assignment. What is most worth noting is that structuring is the responsibility of those who run the place (whether that place be a classroom or a business) and that structuring affects performance.

Communicating Expectations. A second way in which teachers and other executives fulfill the function of communicating goals is through their communication of expectations to those they supervise. The literature on expectations in education has been reviewed by Brophy and Good (1974) and more recently by Cooper (1979) and by Good (in press). This literature in both industry and education is interpreted consistently: there are effects on performance when supervisors and teachers communicate their goals for performance to those they are supervising. If supervisors or teachers set high but attainable goals for performance, performance usually increases. If supervisors or teachers set low goals for performance, performance usually decreases.

The evidence on the differential treatment accorded to high and low ability students is believed to provide clues to how expectations of performance are communicated. In a summary of the literature in this area, Good (in press) reports that, compared to students for whom teachers hold high expectations, students who are perceived to be low performers are more often seated farther away from the teacher; treated as groups, not individuals; smiled at less; given less eye contact; called on less often to answer questions; and given less time to answer those questions. They also have their answers followed up less frequently, are praised more often for marginal and inadequate answers, are praised less frequently for successful responses, and are interrupted in their work more often. This differential treatment between the students for whom teachers hold high and low expectations appears to influence their performance in predictable ways.

Such expectations are not restricted to classrooms. They can also permeate a school, as indicated in the work of Rutter, Maughan, Mortimore, and Ousten (1979) and others (Brookover & Lezotte, 1977; Edmonds, 1979; Venezky & Winfield, Note 11). Rutter et al. (1979) found that marked differences in the success of secondary school students were attributable to such school-level variables as expectations. Their data revealed: "Children had better academic success in schools . . . where the teachers expressed expectations that a high proportion of the children would do well in national examinations" (p. 188). Furthermore, the beneficial effects of high expectations are felt in areas other than academic achievement; Rutter et al. (1979) also note:

> The findings showed that schools which expected children to care for their own resources had better behavior, better attendance and less delinquency. In a similar way, giving children posts or tasks of responsibility was associated with better pupil behavior. The message of confidence that the pupils can be trusted to act with maturity and responsibility is likely to encourage pupils to fulfill those expectations. (p. 188)

Executive Function 3: Regulating the Activities of the Workplace

The person who runs the workplace—the executive in charge—regulates its activities. What happens in workplaces within organizations is never independent of the other activities of the organization. Similarly, what happens in classrooms is affected by and affects what happens within schools, districts, and states (Barr & Dreeben, in press). It is also true, however, that schools and classes appear to be only "loosely coupled systems" (Weick, 1976) in which the teacher is subject to the bare minimum of organizational control from the superintendent or principal. The control of many factors known to affect student acheivement and student attitude in the classroom resides with the teacher. At least six of these factors are worth noting.

Pacing. The evidence for the power of the pacing variable keeps mounting. The more a teacher covers, the more students seem to learn. The variability across classes is notable: One teacher covers half the text in a semester, while another finishes it all. One teacher covers twenty practice problems in a lesson, while another manages to cover only ten. One teacher's students develop a sight vocabulary of 100 words before Christmas, while another teacher's students learn only 50 words. Barr (Note 12) has completed several studies of pacing and has found that 80 percent of the variance in measures of basal reading achievement could be accounted for by the pace of instruction. It is possible that teachers often mismanage the pace at which instruction takes place.

Sequencing Events. Some sequences of events and some standard routines seem to be more conducive to learning than others. We have learned that the sequencing of positive and negative examples in concept teaching has an effect on learning and that a sequence such as rule-example-rule may have value when principles are to be learned. Beck and McCaslin (1978) have shown how the sequence by which one learns to read letters can influence other learning. Good and Grouws (1979) have shown the positive effects of a sequence in mathematics instruction that starts, daily, with review and then moves on to development of new material. This stage is followed by prompted practice, then seatwork, then a homework assignment. Special reviews are recommended weekly and again monthly.

The nature of sequences for conducting efficient junior high school lessons are discussed by Emmer, Evertson, Clements, Sanford, and Worsham (1981). They discuss in detail each element of the opening stage, the stage of checking or recitation, the stage of content development, the seatwork stage, and the closing of the lesson.

Sequencing of activities is a way in which executives and teachers control activities in the workplace. Sequencing appears to affect achievement and can probably be done in more sensible ways than it is now being done.

Monitoring Success Rate. The Beginning Teacher Evaluation Study provided more evidence about the relationship between high success rates and achievement. For younger students and for the academically least able, almost errorless performance during learning tasks results in higher test performance and greater student satisfaction (Marliave & Filby, in press). After reviewing the data from a number of studies, Rosenshine (1983) has concluded that during the initial phases of learning, success rate in reading should be at about the 70 to 80 percent level, but that when students are reviewing or practicing, their responses should be rapid, smooth, and almost always correct. Brophy's (1983) recent comments on this issue are relevant:

> Bear in mind that we are talking about independent seatwork and homework assignments that students must be able to progress through on their own. These assignments demand application of hierarchically organized knowledge and skills that must be not merely learned but mastered to the point of overlearning if they are going to be retained and applied to still more complex material. Confusion about what to do or lack of even a single important concept or skill will frustrate students' progress, and lead to both management and instructional problems for teachers. Yet this happens frequently. Observational studies suggest that, to the extent that students are given inappropriate tasks, the tasks are much more likely to be too difficult than too easy. (p. 268)

From some of the classes in the Beginning Teacher Evaluation Study, we have data to support Brophy's assertion. Students were coded in some classes as making almost 100 percent errors in their workbooks or during their group work, as much as 14 percent of the time we observed them; that is, students in some classes were observed to experience total failure in their learning activities for many consecutive minutes of the school day. As might be expected, the percentage of time the students spent in activities in which they had high error rates was negatively correlated with achievement.

In summary, we find that success rate appears to be another powerful variable with known effects on achievement. Skillful management is necessary to monitor and evaluate the success (or error) rate of students—both when they are working with the teacher and when they are working independently.

Controlling Time. The management of classroom time has been affected by law and governmental regulations. The shift to federally funded "pull-out" programs has required time management capabilities that would tax any manager of any workplace. In such programs, students enter and leave classes at odd times on an odd schedule to work with reading specialists, speech pathologists, school psychologists, and band directors. Recent changes in the law have also resulted in a return of many children with special needs into regular classrooms, creating enormous time management problems.

Time must be controlled after it is allocated or it will be lost. There are many ways to lose time in classrooms. For example, transition times, the time between activities, can mount up rapidly and can cause large losses of the time allocated for a subject. In the school day of about 300 minutes in a class we studied, we coded 76 minutes of transition time. The teacher had established a listening center, a math facts table, a career education table, a silent reading table, a science center, a cooking station, and more. Students moved in and out of these stations throughout the day according to a complex schedule. This teacher actually was losing one-fourth of the school day to commuting!

The lack of advanced preparation of materials by teachers is another common cause of time loss. A lack of coordination between the teachers and the school administration, such that the school office makes announcements or schedules special events during time the teacher has allocated to subject matter teaching, can add up to a serious time loss.

Simple management suggestions have often been found to make a big difference in controlling time. We suggested that a teacher write the language arts assignments on the board at the start of recess, so that the first student into the classroom after recess could start to work and the teacher did not have to wait until the last student came in to give oral instructions. That simple suggestion resulted in savings of 6 minutes a day in this class. Six minutes a day provides a half-hour more instructional time per week.

Controlling time is considered one of the major management problems in business and in education. Fortunately, techniques for managing time effectively are becoming available in education. The manuals for elementary teachers prepared by Evertson, Emmer, Clements, Sanford, Worsham, and Williams (1981) provide dozens of helpful hints on management. Stallings (1980) has provided guides for the management of time at the high school level. Field trials show remarkably improved efficiency in classes in which teachers used these procedures and do not show any apparent negative effect on students' attitudes toward school.

Running an Orderly and Academically Focused Workplace. The value of order and focus in classrooms and schools is made evident by studies of effective schools. With amazing congruence, these studies indicate higher achievement in classes or schools that have an orderly, safe environment and a businesslike manner among the teachers, as well as a schoolwide system that reflects thoughtfulness in promulgating academic programs. Such schools focus on student achievement, hold students accountable for their achievement, and reward achievement. Where such evidence of order and focus is missing, achievement is lower. Purkey and Smith (1983), after reviewing the literature on effective schools, comment as follows:

> The seriousness and purpose with which the school approaches its task is communicated by the order and discipline it maintains . . . evidence exists indicating that clear, reasonable rules not only can reduce behavior problems that interfere with learning but also can promote feelings of pride and responsibility in the school community. (p. 445)

The findings on order and academic focus, however, constitute a real and present threat to schools and to individuals. These findings can lead to overcontrol and to such a strict academic focus that the arts are denied. There is also a danger that debilitating levels of anxiety may be produced among some students. A lack of order and academic focus, however, have been empirically determined to lead to low levels of achievement and may therefore constitute an equally serious threat to the nation.

The power of the order and academic focus variables is clear. The ability to balance forces (to know, for example, that playfulness and order are not incompatible and that individual and societal needs must both be kept in perspective) requires considerable executive-level skill from teachers.

Preventing or Controlling Behavior Problems. We should note, first, that there really are few classes that are totally out of control, even though the media would sometimes have us believe otherwise. There are many classes, however, in which behavior problems occur frequently enough to cause teacher stress, a loss of significant amounts of time, and a break in the orderliness and flow of life in the classroom.

Jacob Kounin (1970), in an enormously influential work, has given us a set of concepts to help us understand the process of maintaining a workplace in which students attend to their assignments. Kounin's concepts are "withitness," describing how effective managers nip behavioral problems in the bud; "overlappingness," describing how effective classroom managers handle more than one thing at a time; the need for "signals" for academic work; the effects of "momentum" and "smoothness" in lessons on student behavior; and the positive effects on attention of "group alerting," "accountability," and "variety" in teaching. These variables, for the most part, have been verified or appropriately qualified in the work of Brophy and Evertson (1976) and Anderson, Evertson, and Brophy (1979), among others. Borg and Ascione (1982) have modified and developed these concepts into teacher training materials, and their work provides clear evidence of changed teacher and student behavior as a function of this kind of training.

Executive Function 4: Creating a Pleasant Environment for Work

A function of executives is to create a convivial atmosphere for work. In teaching, as in business, this means a workplace characterized by politeness, cooperation, mutual respect, shared responsibility, humor, and a number of other dimensions that we value in human social life. In several classroom studies, researchers have characterized the most effective classrooms as convivial places (Fisher et al., Note 2). In the last few years, researchers have developed the technology to help teachers enhance the interpersonal relationships between members of different social classes, races, sexes, or ability groups. Slavin's (1980) "Teams—Games—Tournaments," Cohen's classroom tasks to enhance the status of individuals (Cohen & Roper, 1972), and Aronson's techniques (Aronson, Blancy, Sikes, Stephens, & Snapp, 1978) all provide some evidence of success in creating more cooperation and interdependency among the students in a class.

Executive Function 5: Education of New Members of the Workgroup

The fifth managerial function—educating new workgroup members—takes place systematically in some business settings but is virtually ignored in education. New students in a classroom enter a new culture and need to be socialized to that culture. Three managerial tasks stand out in this function. The first task is assessment of the students' entering ability. The second task is assessment of the students' metacognitive functioning; that is, do they know how to think about what they are doing in school tasks? Metacognitive awareness is a high-level cognitive skill that is needed for efficient learning; without such awareness, real learning may not occur.

The third managerial task involves the teaching of rules. Most rule setting takes place during the first few days of the school year (Tikunoff & Ward, Note 13). Who is responsible, however, for communicating the rules to the new members of the class? Some rules may be communicated in subtle ways. Green and Smith (1983), reviewing the sociolinguistic studies of classrooms, note that the rules for speaking in class are both explicit and tacit and that the tacit dimension of the rule structures may require considerable time to learn. Morine-Dershimer and Tenenberg (Note 14) found the same to be true about the rules for classroom questions. They reported that students have to watch other students to learn how to play the questioning game—a sophisticated game with rules that shift as contexts change.

Executive Function 6: Articulating the Work of the
Workplace with Other Units in the System

All workplaces within organizations fit with other units of the system. Workplaces affect and are affected by what happens elsewhere. In education, the articulation function takes on meaning in two ways. First, teachers must find ways to have classroom processes match the priorities of the school and district. Second, teachers must articulate the present curriculum of the students with previous and subsequent curricula. When teachers have little knowledge of what is taught in the grades below and above them, curricular areas may be repeated or completely missed. Such problems occur when the management of the workplace is done autonomously, without articulation with the rest of the school system.

Executive Function 7: Supervising and
Working with Other People

The common executive function of working with others, which is stressed heavily in schools of management, is not very well addressed in teacher-preparation programs. Without formal training, teachers must learn ways either to govern or to share responsibility with such diverse visitors to the classroom as parent volunteers, paraprofessionals, tutors, school psychologists, itinerant music and art teachers, speech pathologists, school nurses, probation officers, and many others. Because teachers are the executives charged with the responsibility to run the workplace, those teachers who have mastered the problems that accompany the supervision of others find life a good deal easier than those who have not.

Executive Function 8: Motivating;
Executive Function 9: Evaluating

Motivation and evaluation are both topics of importance in education as well as in management, and a rich literature is associated with them. Because of their familiarity, these functions will not be discussed further in this chapter.

Implications and Conclusions

This chapter has provided a description of how a teacher functions as an executive. Mastery of the requisite subject matter areas, together with the managerial skill to meet the demands of complex and dynamic classroom environments, may constitute both the necessary and sufficient conditions for effective teaching.

Although they are almost interchangeable, the term *executive* is preferred to the term *manager*. In education, *management* often refers to classroom control and the techniques for control of deviancy, whereas *executive* is compatible with views of how expert problem solvers in various fields go about their work. The business community takes the notion of executive skill very seriously and honors and pays well for outstanding executive skill. The business community has worked hard at building training programs to equip its personnel with executive skills.

Appropriately modified, such training could be an important part of teacher-education programs. Teachers need to learn how to make decisions in dynamic environments, develop long-range and short-term plans, keep records, supervise others, manipulate bureaucracies, survive in organizational settings, evaluate performance, manage by objectives, and manage time. Teachers might also profit from learning Japanese management styles, currently described as Theory Z (Ouchi, 1981). Schools in the United States have some of the same characteristics as the Japanese corporations described by Theory Z. Teachers, like Japanese workers, have tenure; principals and superintendents, like Japanese managers, usually come from within—from the classroom or the shop; and, as in Japanese corporations, principals and teachers often use the metaphor of a family to describe their schools. Furthermore, certain elements of Theory Z, such as quality circles, shared decision making, and shared responsibility by staff may improve the teaching profession by increasing job satisfaction.

Although classrooms are not the same kinds of workplaces that one finds in business and industry, Drucker (1979) suggests an ideology of modern management that is very compatible with some cherished values in education:

> It may be argued that every occupation—the doctor, the lawyer, the grocer—requires integrity. But there is a difference. The manager lives with the people he or she manages, the manager decides what their work is to be; the manager directs their work, trains them for it, appraises it and, often, decides their future. The relationship of merchant and customer, professional and client, requires honorable dealings. Being a manager, though, is more like being a parent, or a teacher. And in these relationships honorable dealings are not enough; personal integrity is of the essence.
>
> We can now answer the question: Does it require genius, or at least a special talent, to be a manager? Is being a manager an art or an intuition? The answer is: "No." What a manager does can be analyzed systematically. What a manager has to be able to do can be learned (though perhaps not always taught). Yet there is one quality that cannot be learned, one qualification that the manager cannot acquire but must bring with him. It is not genius: it is character. (pp. 58–59)

The apparently useful technology of management, coupled with an ideology of management that is compatible with certain educational values, suggests that the correspondence between management and teaching are worth pursuing, especially from the viewpoint of the teacher as executive.

Root metaphors are powerful forces in shaping human perception. They tend to dominate the way we think about a particular set of operations, skills, or functions. What is now being advocated is a root metaphor that is considerate of the management roles that teachers play. There are several metaphors at the root of people's perceptions of what teaching actually is. Philip Jackson (1968), in his provocative *Life in Classrooms*, clearly recognized the complexity and dynamic qualities of classrooms, but he chose a set of inconsiderate, somewhat authoritarian metaphors to describe his teachers: "supply sergeants," "time keepers," and "traffic cops." Teachers have often been characterized, however, as Mother (or Father) Earth or as information givers. Each label channels our perceptions of what teachers do in some very limiting ways. The metaphor of teacher as Mother (or Father) Earth, for example, connotes behavior that is nurturing and loving. Unfortunately, the metaphor also carries the notion of custodial care, and custodians of children in our society are not accorded either high status or great remuneration. The Mother Earth metaphor may be particularly pernicious for another reason: it may influence the thinking of the predominantly male managers in education (the principals and superintendents), thus preventing elementary classroom teachers (who are predominantly female) from thinking of themselves as members of a managerial class.

Teachers are information givers. Unfortunately, there are negative connotations associated with the division of the people in classrooms into two groups—those who possess knowledge and those who do not. Implied by this metaphor is the limiting notion that *only teachers* teach. With this metaphor, teaching becomes not the managing of information but the providing of it.

From the teaching and managerial functions that have been described in this chapter emerges a much more encompassing metaphor of the teacher—that of executive. The metaphor of the teacher as executive presents a more considerate view of the teacher than the one that is prevalent among the general public or within the teacher education community. This metaphor implies a person who thinks and whose behavior is guided by a set of flexible operating principles. This metaphor suggests a person who manages information and who can reasonably, if not optimally, allocate such scarce resources as time and nurturing behavior. We should begin to train teachers to think of themselves as executives—the first step toward rooting a new metaphor for teaching. Perhaps then teachers can attain the prestige and pay accorded other skilled executives in our society.

Reference Notes

1. Schwille, J., Porter, A., Belli, A., Floden, R., Freeman, D., Knappen, L., Kuhs, T., & Schmidt, W.H. *Teachers as policy brokers in the content of elementary school mathematics* (National Institute of Education Contract No. P-80-0127). East Lansing: Michigan State University, Institute for Research on Teaching, 1981.
2. Fisher, C.W., Filby, N.N., Marliave, R.S., Cahen, L.S., Dishaw, M.M., Moore, J.E., & Berliner, D.C. *Teaching behaviors, academic learning time and student achievement: Final report of Phase III-B, Beginning Teacher Evaluation Study* (Tech. Rep. V-1). San Francisco: Far West Laboratory for Educational Research and Development, 1978.

3. Buchmann, M., & Schmidt, W.H. *The school day and teachers' content commitments* (IRT Research Series #83). East Lansing: Michigan State University, Institute for Research on Teaching, 1981.
4. Dreeben, R. *The collective character of instruction.* Paper presented at the annual meeting of the American Educational Research Association, Toronto, March 1978.
5. Bossert, S.T. *Activity structures and student outcomes.* Paper presented at the National Institute of Education's Conference on School Organization and Effects, San Diego, January 1978.
6. McKay, D.A., & Marland, P.W. *Thought processes of teachers.* Paper presented at the annual meeting of the American Educational Research Association, Toronto, March 1978.
7. Morine, G., & Vallance, E. *A study of teacher and pupil perspectives of classroom interaction* (Tech. Rep. 75-11-6, Beginning Teacher Evaluation Study). San Francisco: Far West Laboratory for Educational Research and Development, 1975.
8. Tikunoff, W.J., Berliner, D.C, & Rist, R.C. *An ethnographic study of the forty classrooms of the Beginning Teacher Evaluation Study known sample* (Tech. Rep. No. 75-10-5). San Francisco: Far West Laboratory for Educational Research and Development, 1975.
9. Bruner, J. *On instructability.* Paper presented at the annual meeting of the American Psychological Association, Los Angeles, August 1981.
10. Hassenpflug, A.M. *The use and understanding of school time by third graders: An ethnographic case study* (Tech. Rep. No. 574). Madison: Wisconsin Research and Development Center for Individualized Schooling, May 1981.
11. Venezky, R.L., & Winfield, L.F. *Schools that succeed beyond expectations in teaching reading* (Final report, National Institute of Education, Grant No. NIE-G-78-0027). Newark: University of Delaware, College of Education, 1979.
12. Barr, R.C. *School, class, group, and pace effects on learning.* Paper presented at the meeting of the American Educational Research Association, Boston, April 1980.
13. Tikunoff, W.J., & Ward, B.A. *A naturalistic study of the initiation of students into three classroom social systems* (Report A78-11). San Francisco: Far West Laboratory for Educational Research and Development, 1978.
14. Morine-Dershimer, G., & Tenenberg, M. *Participant perspectives of classroom discourse* (Executive summary of final report, Contract No. NIE-G-78-0160). Syracuse: Syracuse University, Division for Study of Teaching, 1981.

References

Anderson, L.M., Evertson, C.M., & Brophy, J.E. An experimental study of effective teaching in first grade reading groups. *Elementary School Journal,* 1979, *79,* 193–223.

Aronson, E., Blancy, N., Sikes, J., Stephen, C., & Snapp, M. *The jigsaw classroom.* Beverly Hills, Calif.: Sage, 1978.

Barr, R., & Dreeben, R. A sociological perspective on school time. In C.W. Fisher & D.C. Berliner (Eds.), *Perspectives on instructional time.* New York: Longmans, in press.

Beck, I.L., & McCaslin, E.S. *An analysis of dimensions that effect the development of codebreaking ability in eight beginning reading programs.* Pittsburgh: University of Pittsburgh, Learning Research and Development Center, 1978.

Berliner, D.C. Tempus educare. In P.L. Peterson & H.J. Walberg (Eds.), *Research in teaching*. Berkeley: McCutchan, 1979.

Berliner, D.C. Developing conceptions of classroom environments: Some light on the T in classroom studies of ATI. *Educational Psychologist*, 1983, *18*, 1–13.

Berliner, D.C., & Rosenshine, B. The acquisition of knowledge in the classroom. In R.C. Anderson, R.J. Spiro, & W.E. Montague (Eds.), *Schooling and the acquisition of knowledge*. Hillsdale, N.J.: Erlbaum, 1977.

Borg, W.R., & Ascione, F.R. Classroom management in elementary mainstreaming classrooms. *Journal of Educational Psychology*, 1982, *74*, 85–95.

Brookover, W.B., & Lezotte, L. *Changes in school characteristics coincident with changes in student achievement*. East Lansing: Michigan State University, College of Urban Development, 1977.

Brophy, J.E. Classroom organization and management. *Elementary School Journal*, 1983, *83*, 265–285.

Brophy, J.E., & Evertson, C.M. *Learning from teaching: A developmental perspective*. Boston: Allyn and Bacon, 1976.

Brophy, J.E., & Good, T.L. *Teacher-student relationships: Causes and consequences*. New York: Holt, Rinehart and Winston, 1974.

Calfee, R., & Brown, R. Grouping students. In D.L. Duke (Ed.), *Classroom management* (Seventy-eighth Yearbook of the National Society for the Study of Education). Chicago: National Society for the Study of Education, 1979.

Calfee, R.C., & Piontkowski, D.C. Grouping for instruction. In T. Husen & T.N. Postlethwaite (Eds.), *International encyclopedia of education*. Oxford, England: Pergamon Press in press.

Carew, J., & Lightfoot, S.L. *Beyond bias*. Cambridge, Mass.: Harvard University Press, 1979.

Cohen, E.G., & Roper, S.S. Modification of interracial interaction disability: An application of status characteristic theory. *American Sociological Review*, 1972, *37*, 643–657.

Cooper, H. Pygmalion grows up: A model for teacher expectation communication and performance influence. *Review of Educational Research*, 1979, *49*, 389–410.

Doyle, W. Paradigms for research on teacher effectiveness. In L.S. Shulman (Ed.), *Review of research in education* (Vol. 5). Itaska, Ill.: Peacock, 1977.

Dreeben, R. *On what is learned in schools*. Reading, Mass.: Addison-Wesley, 1968.

Drucker, P.F. *People and performance: The best of Peter Drucker on Management*. New York: Harper & Row, 1977.

Drucker, P.F. Comment. In M. Zimmet & R.G. Greenwood (Eds.), *The evolving science of management*. New York: Amacom, 1979.

Edmonds, R. Some schools work and more can. *Social Policy*, March/April 1979, *26*, 1–5.

Emmer, E.T., Evertson, C.M., Clements, B.S., Sanford, J.P., & Worsham, M.E. *Organizing and managing the junior high school classroom*. Austin: University of Texas, Research and Development Center for Teacher Education, July 1981.

Evertson, C.M., Emmer, E.T., Clements, B.S., Sanford, J.P., Worsham, M. E., & Williams, E.L. *Organizing and managing the elementary school classroom*. Austin: University of Texas, Research and Development Center for Teacher Education, 1981.

Fisher, C.W., Berliner, D.C., Filby, N.N., Marliave, R.S., Cahen, L.S., & Dishaw, M.M. Teaching behaviors, academic learning time and student achievement: An overview. In C. Denham & A. Lieberman (Eds.), *Time to learn*. Washington, D.C.: U.S. Department of Education, National Institute of Education, 1980.

Flippo, E.B., & Munsinger, G.M. *Management* (4th ed.). Boston: Allyn and Bacon, 1978.

Good, T.L. Classroom research: Past and future. In L.S. Shulman & G. Sykes (Eds.), *Handbook of teaching and policy*. New York: Longmans, in press.

Good, T.L., & Grouws, D. The Missouri Mathematics Effectiveness Project: An experimental study in fourth-grade classrooms. *Journal of Educational Psychology*, 1979, *71*, 355–362.

Green, J.L., & Smith, D. Teaching and learning: A linguistic perspective. *Elementary School Journal*, 1983, *83*, 353–391.

Huse, E.F. *The modern manager*. St. Paul: West, 1979.

Jackson, P.W. *Life in classrooms*. New York: Holt, Rinehart and Winston, 1968.

Joyce, B.R. Toward a theory of information processing in teaching. *Educational Research Quarterly*, 1978–79, *3*, 66–67.

Koontz, M., O'Donnell, C., & Weihrich, H. *Management* (7th ed.). New York: McGraw-Hill, 1980.

Kounin, J. *Discipline and group management in classrooms*. New York: Holt, Rinehart and Winston, 1970.

Levinson, H. *Executive*. Cambridge, Mass.: Harvard University Press, 1981.

Lortie, D.C. *School teacher: A sociological study*. Chicago: University of Chicago Press, 1975.

March, J.G., & Simon, H.S. *Organizations*. New York: Wiley, 1958.

Marland, P.W. *A study of teachers' interactive thoughts*. Unpublished doctoral dissertation, University of Alberta, 1977.

Marliave, R., & Filby, N.N. Success rate: A measure of task appropriateness. In C.W. Fisher & D.C. Berliner (Eds.), *Perspectives on instructional time*. New York: Longmans, in press.

Ouchi, W. *Theory Z: How American business can meet the Japanese challenge*. Reading, Mass.: Addison-Wesley, 1981.

Peterson, P.L., & Clark, C.M. Teachers' reporters of their cognitive processes during teaching. *American Educational Research Journal*, 1978, *15*, 555–565.

Purkey, S.C., & Smith, M.C. Effective schools: A review. *Elementary School Journal*, 1983, *83*, 427–452.

Rist, R.C. *The urban school: A factory for failure*. Cambridge, Mass.: MIT Press, 1973.

Rosenshine, B. Teaching functions in instructional programs. *Elementary School Journal*, 1983, *83*, 335–351.

Rutter, M., Maughan, B., Mortimore, P., & Ousten, J. *Fifteen thousand hours*. Cambridge, Mass.: Harvard University Press, 1979.

Shavelson, R.J. Review of research on teachers' pedagogical judgments, plans, and decisions. *Elementary School Journal*, 1983, *83*, 392–413.

Shavelson, R.J., & Borko, H. Research on teachers' decisions in planning instruction. *Educational Horizons*, 1979, *57*, 183–189.

Slavin, R. Cooperative learning. *Review of Educational Research*, 1980, *50*, 315–342.

Stallings, J. Allocated academic learning time revisited, or beyond time on task. *Educational Researcher*, 1980, *9*(11), 11–16.

Tarrant, J.J. *Drucker: The man who invented the corporate society*. Boston: Cahners, 1976.

Waller, W. *The sociology of teaching*. New York: Russell and Russell, 1932.

Weick, K. Educational organizations as loosely-coupled systems. *Administrative Science Quarterly*, 1976, *21*(1), 1–19.

Yinger, R.J. *A study of teacher planning: Description and theory development using ethnographic and information processing methods.* Unpublished doctoral dissertation, Michigan State University, 1977.

8

Ability Grouping and Differences in Reading Instruction

Courtney Cazden

Before children sit down with a teacher to get help in learning to read, they have been classified many times. All children receive assignments to a school, a grade, and a homeroom, then to a reading level, and then usually to a reading group. In addition, some children are further classified to receive additional reading-related services.

Surveys reported by Austin and Morrison (1963) and Wilson and Schmits (1978) agree that children are tracked in ability groups for reading instruction in about four-fifths of elementary classrooms. How is instruction differentiated between high-group and lower-group children? What are the likely outcomes of such differentiation? What causes such differentiation, and where are the best hopes for change? In this chapter, these questions will be addressed in turn, but only the first can be answered fully.

How Is Instruction Differentiated?

Before turning to the results of recent observational research on differential instruction in reading groups, it is important to state what does *not* happen. There is no consistent evidence that teachers favor high group children in amount of instructional time or in more advantageous time during the school day; there is also no consistent evidence that teachers praise one group more than another. The differences that do turn up in all systematic observations of instruction are both more subtle and more closely related to qualitative aspects of reading itself.

Differential instruction occurs not only in reading, as evidenced, for example, in Michaels's (1981) study of sharing time in an ethnically mixed California first grade. Frequently, in sharing time, the teacher tries, through comments and questions, to help children clarify and expand their narrative accounts. Michaels points out that when the child's narrative style matches the teacher's style and expectations, this sharing collaboration promotes the development of a literate discourse style. For such a child, sharing time can become a kind of oral preparation for literacy. In contrast, when a child's narrative style differs from the teacher's, sharing is often unsuccesful and may, over time, have an adverse affect on school performance. Michaels concludes:

> Sharing time, then, can either provide or deny access to key literacy-related experiences, depending, ironically, on the degree to which teacher and child start out "sharing" a set of discourse conventions and interpretive strategies. (pp. 423–424)

Recent observational studies include both survey research (in which teacher and student behaviors are coded and counted in a number of classrooms) and more detailed qualitative case study analyses of instruction (from audiotape or videotape recordings in one or just a few classrooms). Ideally, information of both kinds is available in a single study (Light & Pillemer, 1982), but where that has not happened, findings from separate studies can be integrated.

Consider Allington's (1980) survey of teachers' responses to children's oral reading errors in twenty primary classrooms in three school districts in New York. Table 8–1 summarizes his findings.

Table 8–1
Group Differences in Twenty Primary Classrooms

	Lowest Reading Group	Highest Reading Group
Percentage of teacher interruption of all student errors		
Immediately, at error	66	22
Later	8	9
Total	74	31
Percentage of teacher interruption of semantically appropriate errors	55	11
Percentage of teacher interruption of semantically inappropriate errors	79	48
Percentage of various types of cues supplied by teacher (totaling 100% within each group):		
Graphic/phonic	28	18
Semantic/syntactic	8	32
Teacher pronounce	50	38
Other	14	12

Note: From Allington (1980, tables 2–4; and personal communication, 1982), with group norms translated into percentages. Copyright © 1980 by the American Psychological Association. Adapted by permission of the publisher and author.

Note, first, that there is a difference in the overall rate of teacher correction of the errors: more than two-thirds of the poor readers' errors were corrected, whereas less than one-third of the good readers' errors were corrected. Second, there were differences in the timing of the interruptions: teachers were more likely to interrupt poor readers immediately at the point of error, rather than waiting for the next phrase or clause boundary. Third, this difference in the timing of corrections applies to the categories of both semantically appropriate and semantically inappropriate errors. Although more of the inappropriate errors are corrected in both groups (79 percent versus 55 percent and 48 percent versus 11 percent), the percentages are higher for both categories for the poor readers. The difference is especially notable for the category of semantically appropriate errors: whereas only one-tenth of such errors made by the good readers are corrected, more than half of such errors made by the poor readers are corrected.

Because low reading groups are apt to have a disproportionate number of ethnic minority children, the influence of dialect differences and non-English accents on teacher behaviors should be considered. Cunningham (1976–77) investigated whether teachers' attitudes toward children's semantically appropriate errors differed for dialect-related errors (for example, reading "Here go a table" for "Here is a table") and nondialect errors (for example, reading "I will be home at 5:00" for "I shall be home at 5:00"). In response to a questionnaire, 214 students in university graduate reading courses in four regions of the United States indicated that they would correct 78 percent of the dialect errors but only 27 percent of the nondialect errors. Because the students could not recognize the dialect errors as such, Cunningham infers that the students acted out of ignorance—for example, not understanding that "Here go . . ." really does mean "Here is . . ." to many black children. Moll, Estrada, Diaz, and Lopes (1980) observed the reading instruction of second- and third-grade bilingual children in a California district bordering Mexico who were taught in Spanish by one teacher and in English by another. In general, the children were in the same relative groups in the two situations, but "the overriding concern of the lessons in English is decoding, pronunciation, and other forms related to the sounds of the second language" (p. 57). Moll et al. believe that the English reading teacher mistook nonnative pronunciation for erroneous decoding and so subverted the children's progress in reading for the sake of another lesson in English as a second language.

A fourth difference shown in the Allington (1980) study is in the kinds of clues teachers provide to help the children read the right word: for the poor readers, the clues are more likely to be graphemic/phonemic (that is, related to the spelling or sounds of the letters in a word), whereas, for the good readers, the cues are more likely to be semantic or syntactic (related to the meaning of words or sentences).

Collins (1980) found similar differentiation between good and poor readers in how time was spent during first-grade reading lessons (see table 8–2). Whereas the good readers spent half their time on passage reading, the poor readers spent only one-third of their time on passage reading and another third on sound/word identification.

Table 8-2
Group Differences in Time on Task in One First-Grade Class, in Minutes and in Percentage of Total Time

	Low Group	*High Group*
Dictation/Penmanship	24.5 (16%)	0
Sound/word identification	48.5 (31%)	10.5 (17%)
Sentence completion	24.5 (16%)	8.0 (13%)
Passage reading	49.0 (31%)	29.5 (49%)
Comprehension/Questions	9.0 (6%)	13.5 (21%)

Reprinted with permission from James Collins, *Differential Treatment in Reading Instruction* (Berkeley, Calif.: Language Behavior Research Laboratory, 1980).

Some narrative descriptions from two first-grade case studies will provide a more qualitative picture of children's experiences in these contrasting low and high group reading lessons. The first is from McDermott (1978):

> [In the top group] occasionally, the children create problems by word calling instead of reading for meaning, and the teacher's main pedagogical task is to convince the children that there is living language. . . . Thus, one child reads, "But Ricky said his mother . . ." in a dull monotone, and the teacher corrects her. "Let's read it this way, 'But Ricky, said his mother'."
>
> With the bottom group, the teacher has rather different problems. . . . The children in the bottom group do not read as well as the children in the top group, and the teacher attends less to the language on the book's pages and more to the phonics skills needed to interpret any given word in the text. Thus, there are many more stopping places in the children's reading, and the story line which is to hold the lesson together is seldom alluded to and never developed.

The second description is from Gumperz (1970):

> We observed a reading session with a slow group of three children, and seven fast readers. . . . With the slow readers she [the teacher] concentrated on the alphabet, on the spelling of individual words. . . . She addressed the children in what white listeners would identify as pedagogical style. Her enunciation was deliberate and slow. Each word was clearly articulated with even stress and pitch. . . . Pronunciation errors were corrected whenever they occurred, even if the reading task had to be interrupted. The children seemed distracted and inattentive. . . .
>
> With the advanced group, on the other hand, reading became much more of a group activity and the atmosphere was more relaxed. Words were treated in context, as part of a story. . . . There was no correction of pronunciation, although some deviant forms were also heard. The children actually enjoyed competing with each other in reading and the teacher responded by dropping her pedagogical monotone in favor of more animated natural speech. (p. 140)

It might be argued, as Alpert (1975) does in her study of reading instruction in fifteen second grades, that such differences in instruction between low and high reading groups constitute pedagogically appropriate differentiation and that low group children will receive the high group kind of help at some later time. To confirm or disconfirm this possibility, we would need longitudinal studies following both the instruction and the progress of low group children. Only one such study is available, and that is confined to observations within a single school year. Collins (1980) analyzed segments of lessons in which low group children were reading stories comparable in difficulty to those the high group children had read earlier in the year. In one of his comparisons, the two groups were taped while reading different parts of the very same story. A child in the high group read the following:

"John, I have your boat," said Liza.
"And I have a fly for your frog, too."
"But you can't have your boat or the fly if I can't come in!"
John looked at his frog, and he looked at Liza.
Then he said, "Come in, Liza. Come in."

Later in the year, a child in the low group read a passage from the same story:

He ran out of the house with his things.
And then he threw his boat into the garbage can.
Liza was there. And she saw what John did.

The Collins (1980) transcription of the tapings (with intonation marks deleted) is as follows (C = child, T = *teacher):*

High Group

1	C	John I have your boat/said Liza and
2	T	and
3	C	And I have a fly for your frog too / /
4	T	What's she mean by that
5	C	For the frog to eat / /
6	T	Okay / /
7	L	but . . . I . . . but
8	T	wait a minute till she gets through/ /
9	L	but but
10	T	watch your books watch your books
11	C	But you can't . . . have your boat/or the fly/if I can't come in/ /
12		John looked at his frog/ and he looked at Liza/ . . .
13		Then he said come in Liza
14	T	What did he say/ /
15	C	Come in
16	T	How'd he say it / /
17	C	Come in Li-
18	T	Did he say come in Liza come in/ / Or did he say . . .
19	C	Come in Liza/ come in/ /
20	T	Come in/ Liza

Low Group

```
 1   M   Here    he/ . . . ran/ . . . out/ . . . of/ . . .
 2   T        he
 3   M   the house . . . wuh-    with his things/ /
 4   T                    with
 5   M   And then . . . he . . .                    threw his
 6   T                         sound it out/ thr:ew
 7   M   bu- (boat) boat/ . . . into the . . .    gahbag can/ /
 8                                          guh-
 9   T   gar:bage/ / Say garbage/ /
10   M   gahbage
11   T   Don't say gahbage/ look at me/ /Say ga:r:bage/gar:/ Say it/ /
12       Everybody say it/ /
13   CC  gar: bage
14   T   Celena/say it/ /
15   Ce  gar:bage
16   T                  Right/ /Marlon/ Liza
17   M   Liza . . .                    was . . .          there and she was
18   T            where are we Sherrie        there
19   T   What
20   M        she was          saw what . . .
21   T                  no/ /sss . . .              how does -j- sound/ /
22   M   juh/ /
23   T        What's the boys' name / / . . . John
24   M   John . . . said
25   T                    did/ / She saw what John did/ / Marlon/ what did he
         do/ /
26   T   She saw what he did/ /Now what did he do/ /
27   M   He threw his things in the gahbage
28   T                              gar:bag/ / Right/ / Go on/ /
```

As Collins points out, the teacher helped the two readers in very different ways. With the high group child, she interpolated one comprehension question (line 4), and she corrected the intonation necessary for indicating a clause boundary (line 2) and for separating a spoken message from addressee (lines 14, 16, 18). By contrast, with the low group child, she gave not only more help but qualitatively different kinds of help: directions to use phonic cues (lines 6, 21) and a protracted attempt to correct the reader's pronunciation of one word (lines 9–15, 28), after which even the teacher lost her place.

Because of the consistency of the findings of these studies that otherwise vary by researcher, methodology, and location, the classrooms studied presumably can be considered representative of any larger sample that might be observed.

What Are the Likely Outcomes of this Differentiation?

Existing research suggests two ways in which the kinds of differentiation of instruction just described can restrict the progress of the low group children. First, there is the effect of the more immediate timing of corrections. McNaughton and

Glynn (1981a) conducted an experimental study of the effect of the timing of teacher correction—immediate (before the next word) or delayed (for 5–10 seconds)—on children's self-correction behavior and reading accuracy scores. Immediate correction depressed both children's self-correction and their accuracy scores, even on a second passage when no experimental correction occurred. McNaughton and Glynn (1981b) suggest that teacher correction may interfere with children's progress by maintaining their "instructional dependence."

Second, there is the effect on low group readers of decreased attention to text meaning. The currently dominant model of the reading process contends that reading is neither just a "bottom-up" process, driven by a reader's perceptions of letter, nor just a "top-down" process, driven by the reader's hypotheses about what the text may contain. Rather, the contention is that processing of different levels of text structure proceeds simultaneously and interactively. I believe that most beginning readers do need to have their attention focused, temporarily but explicitly, on syllables and letters, as Resnick (1979) argues. I also believe, however, that even temporary focus must be balanced by a complimentary focus on the higher levels of text essential for meaning.

An important definition of the much used word *context* is the mental context—a context in the mind—provided by the reader's understanding of a larger unit of text than is being read at any one moment. Because of differences in preschool literacy experiences, children arrive at school with that context in the mind developed to a greater or a lesser degree. All children in a literate society have experience with what has come to be called environmental print (labels, signs, and so forth), but that experience is not sufficient for building the context in the mind that is essential for reading larger units of connected text in books. It seems tragic that attention to understanding larger meaningful units of text is most neglected during instruction for the very children who may need it the most.

There may be individual stylistic differences in how children approach the task of learning to read. Bussis, Chittenden, Amareli, and Klausner (in press) found such differences in an 18-month longitudinal study of forty children (two-thirds black, one-third white) in first and second grades in New York City and Philadelphia. About half of the children showed a clear stylistic preference in their initial approach to reading:

> [Some children] tended to put their primary energies to the task of upholding momentum, . . . [and] freely offered substitutions based on memory of the story line, picture clues, partial word analysis (analysis of letter-sound correspondences or of overall spelling configuration), grammatical knowledge, awareness of rhythmic structures, or some combination of these resources. Each one of these tactics enabled a child to say something when faced with uncertainty and thus to keep the reading performance moving.

> [Other children] presented a striking contrast in their early reading behavior to the strategy just described. Initially, at least, these children attended to every word in a text and seemed determined to get each one correctly. They rarely

showed signs of reading ahead or of attending to spans of print larger than a word. If they didn't know a word, they tended to wait for help, to remain silent while they tried to figure it out for themselves, or to engage in a head-on struggle of phonic analysis.

As the children progressed, these differences diminished, and there was never any relationship between these styles and race, sex, teacher, or reading achievement at the end of the 18-month period. Because the Bussis et al. study focused on children's learning, it provides little information on how teachers in these relatively open classrooms accommodated—if at all—to these stylistic differences in their students (just as in most research on teaching, there is little information on how children learn). The authors recommend that teachers provide children with knowledge about information encoded in writing but not "try to change or otherwise predetermine how children organize information and orchestrate knowledge" for themselves. Such differential responsiveness to individuals is not the same as differential instruction to homogeneous ability groups.

Possible Causes of Differentiated Instruction

If we assume that most teachers are dedicated to helping all children learn, how does the seemingly pervasive phenomenon of neglected comprehension in instruction for low group children come about? Before speculating on possible sources, a recent conceptualization of the problem may be helpful. Ann and Harold Berlak's (1981) *Dilemmas of Schooling* describes teachers' resolutions of particular tensions and contradictions, or dilemmas, inherent in all teaching. Although any teaching act can be seen as a simultaneous resolution of multiple dilemmas, each dilemma is a separate lens for examining the teaching process. Three of the Berlaks' dilemmas are especially relevant to differential instruction.

The first teaching dilemma is whether to respond to the ways in which children are alike or the ways in which they differ from one another. Differentiation of instruction by reading groups seems to indicate that teachers consider level of reading ability within a classroom as an indication of categorical differences in the ways children learn to read.

The second dilemma expresses the tension between conflicting theories about how people learn: by holistic practice or by attention to molecular parts. From the accumulated evidence, teachers seem to resolve this dilemma differently for different groups of children—believing that learning must be more molecular for those who have achieved less and can be more holistic for those who have achieved more.

The third dilemma involves how teacher and students should share responsibility for setting standards, monitoring progress, and correcting errors. If we assume that the goal of education is, in Marie Clay's (1979) felicitous words, to help students become "self-improving systems," teachers seem to believe that different groups of children need different kinds of help toward that end. The errors of children in high reading groups are more likely to pass uncorrected. The errors of children in low reading groups, by contrast, are corrected more consistently and more immediately, as if the teachers were acting out of fear that the errors of these children (like the children themselves) might get out of control.

At first, this use of dilemma language as a conceptualization of differentiated instruction may seem like the older "teacher expectations" literature phrased in other terms. Whereas teacher expectations differ in amount—a teacher expects more of some children, less of others—the dilemma language helps us see how the realizations of those expectations in actual teaching behaviors differ in complex, qualitative ways.

Influences on teaching can be categorized as preactive and interactive, to use Jackson's (1968) terms, depending on their temporal relationship to the teaching act. Preactive influences are the dilemma resolutions, scripts, and pedagogical theories that teachers bring to the moment of teaching. They are conscious ideas, accessible in an interview and often detectable in a teacher's written plans. Interactive influences, in contrast, are generated in the "in-flight" interactions with students. They are less conscious and may not result from decisions in the usual reflective sense. (See Shavelson & Stern, 1981, for a general research review.)

Preactive Influences

If teachers do have differential theories of instruction, based on perceived needs of students, where do such theories come from? Are they explicitly taught in pre-service or in-service teacher education? Are teachers told that low achieving children are more likely to develop bad habits and that, therefore, their errors should be corrected more frequently and more promptly? With respect to reading, are they told that low achieving children need more attention to decoding skills and less to comprehension?

Whatever the answers to these questions, messages about how to plan instruction for different groups of children can also be transmitted more implicitly—for example, through the design of materials. In her comparison of two beginning reading programs, Distar (used more frequently in poor and minority communities) and Open Court, Bartlett (1979) speculates about the possible effects of features of these programs on teachers' conceptions of literacy. First, does the altered alphabet and simplified orthography used in Distar 1 convey the impression to teachers that the children in Distar groups cannot cope with "the real thing"? Second, does the more limited set of Distar comprehension tasks—locating and remembering specific information in the immediately preceding text—depress teacher's expectations about the kinds of questions the children are capable of answering?

Interactive Influences

Whether or not teachers' conscious pedagogical plans are influenced explicitly or implicitly toward a differentiation of instruction, that differentiation can be maintained, even generated in the first place, in moment-to-moment "in-flight" interactions in the classroom. The best-laid plans may go awry because no lesson is under the teacher's unilateral control. Teacher behavior and student behavior reciprocally influence each other in complex ways.

The clearest analyses of reading groups from this perspective examine how teachers allocate turns to read and generally try to keep the attention of the reading group members focused on the reading task. One of the striking contrasts McDermott (1978) found in his contrastive study of high and low reading groups in a first-grade classroom was in the turn-taking procedure: in the high group, children read in turn around the group, and no time was lost "off-task" between readers; in the low group, children bid for a turn, and considerable time was lost after each child had finished. Shulman (Note 1) has reviewed turn-taking research and argues against the century-old pedagogical lore that "pupils should be called upon promiscuously, and not in rotation" (Stoddard, 1860). Shulman's arguments are based on exactly what McDermott found: promiscuous assignment means unequal opportunities and substantial time spent attending to the turn-taking process rather than reading.

Research can help us understand not only which teacher behaviors are best according to some criterion, but also why other behaviors continue to exist. McDermott (1978) assumes that the bidding process exists because it is functional for the teacher with the low group in that it helps her avoid calling on children in the group who basically cannot read. Then, because of the time off-task between readers while turns are negotiated, the low group is more interruptable and is actually interrupted more frequently than the higher group by other children who approach the teacher for help.

In a related first-grade study, Eder (1981) also focuses on joint teacher-student production of attentiveness. In the first grade Eder observed, children were assigned to reading groups by the teacher after a conference with the kindergarten teachers, who discussed maturity (attention span and listening skills) as well as reading readiness. Thus, Eder notes, "lower reading groups are likely to have more inattentive behavior due in part to the fact that students who are perceived to be immature and inattentive are often assigned to lower groups" (p. 154). Then the problem escalates: inattentive behavior generates further inattentiveness. When the teacher shifts her attention from the reading lesson to the inattentive children, the lesson loses coherence and interest.

Teachers, like their students, are subject to the effects of reinforcement. McNaughton and Glynn (1980) suggest, for example, that hearing children read the right word correctly following immediate correction is a powerful reinforcer for such correcting behavior, especially with children who are making slow progress, even though there may be unfortunate longer-term effects on the children's progress.

Teachers may also be affected by children's text-reading style. Collins (Note 2) reports a linguistic analysis of differences in the ways children use intonation to signal units of information while reading aloud. He notes:

As low-ranked students read with a prosodic style which made it difficult for larger units to be discerned, the teacher responded with a pedagogical strategy which focused on small text units and seemed to compound any tendency to fragmented text-processing on the part of students. (p. 52)

Where Are the Best Hopes for Change?

The message to be gained from observational research is simply that it will take special efforts to counteract widespread and powerful patterns if we are to make sure that good teaching gets to the children who need it most. Where, then, are the best hopes for change?

Confronting teachers with the observational research, in the hope that self-awareness will be enough, is a first step. None of the research on differential instruction has included discussions with teachers, followed by some kind of monitoring of their deliberate attempts to change their behavior, and such an effort is certainly worth trying. The Kamehameha Early Education Program (KEEP) has developed one such monitoring system, designed to ensure that teachers focus all children's attention on comprehension (see chapter 20). Such a monitoring system may be especially helpful if it is perceived by teachers not as an imposed policing by some evaluator, but as an observation examination done by one teacher for another.

If the present patterns are functional for teachers in important ways in their present context, then change may be difficult to achieve, and even more difficult to sustain, unless the context itself is changed. A change from the traditional round-robin oral reading to silent reading to find answers to questions, for example, as KEEP has done, should significantly decrease the excessive correction of errors with low group children. As Allington (in press) points out, silent reading is judged by the adequacy of the reader's comprehension, whereas oral reading is more open to evaluation on the accuracy of the oral reproduction of the text.

Reference Notes

1. Shulman, L.S. *Educational psychology returns to school*. Invited address to the meeting of the American Psychological Association, Los Angeles, August 1981.
2. Collins, J. *Linguistic perspectives on minority education* (Tech. Rep. No. 275). Urbana: University of Illinois, Center for the Study of Reading, May 1983.

References

Allington, R.L. Teacher interruption behaviors during primary grade oral reading. *Journal of Educational Psychology*, 1980, 72, 371–377.

Allington, R.L. The reading instruction provided readers of differing reading abilities. *Elementary School Journal*, in press.

Alpert, J.L. Do teachers adapt methods and material to ability groups in reading? *California Journal of Educational Research*, 1975, *26*, 120–123.

Austin, M.D., & Morrison, C. *The first R: The Harvard report on reading in the elementary school*. New York: Macmillan, 1963.

Bartlett, E.J. Curriculum, concepts of literacy, and social class. In L.B. Resnick & P.A. Weaver (Eds.), *Theory and practice of early reading* (Vol. 1). Hillsdale, N.J.: Erlbaum, 1979.

Berlak, A., & Berlak, H. *Dilemmas of schooling: Teaching and social change*. London: Methuen, 1981.

Bussis, A.M., Chittenden, E.A., Amarel, M., & Klausner, E. *Inquiry into meaning: An investigation of learning to read*. Hillsdale, N.J.: Erlbaum, in press.

Clay, M.M. Theoretical research and instructional change: A case study. In L.B. Resnick & P.A. Weaver (Eds.), *Theory and practice of early reading* (Vol. 1). Hillsdale, N.J.: Erlbaum, 1979.

Collins, J. *Differential treatment in reading instruction*. Berkeley, Calif.: Language Behavior Research Laboratory, 1980.

Cunningham, P.M. Teachers' correction responses to black-dialect miscues which are non-meaning-changing. *Reading Research Quarterly*, 1976–1977, *12*, 637–653.

Eder, D. Ability grouping as a self-fulfilling prophecy: A micro-analysis of teacher-student interaction. *Sociology of Education*, 1981, *54*, 151–162.

Gumperz, J.J. Verbal strategies in multilingual communication. In J.E. Alatis (Ed.), *Georgetown University Round Table on Languages and Linguistics 1970*. Washington, D.C.: Georgetown University Press, 1970.

Jackson, P.W. *Life in classrooms*. New York: Holt, Rinehart and Winston, 1968.

Light, R.L., & Pillemer, D.B. Numbers and narrative: Combining their strengths in research reviews. *Harvard Educational Review*, 1982, *52*, 1–26.

McDermott, R.P. Pirandello in the classroom: On the possibility of equal educational opportunity in American culture. In M.C. Reynolds (Ed.), *Futures of exceptional children: Emerging structures*. Reston, Va.: Council for Exceptional Children, 1978.

McNaughton, S., & Glynn, T. Behavior analysis of educational settings: Current research trends in New Zealand (*Delta Research Monograph* No. 3) Wellington: New Zealand Association for Research in Education, 1980.

McNaughton, S., & Glynn, T. Delayed versus immediate attention to oral reading errors: Effects on accuracy and self-correction. *Educational Psychology*, 1981, *1*(1), 57–65. (a)

McNaughton, S., & Glynn, T. Low progress readers and teacher instructional behavior during oral reading: The risk of maintaining instructional dependence. *Exceptional Child*, 1981, *28*(3), 167–176. (b)

Michaels, S. "Sharing time": Children's narrative styles and differential access to literacy. *Language in Society*, 1981, *10*, 423–442.

Moll, L.C., Estrada, E., Diaz, E., & Lopes, L.M. The organization of bilingual lessons: Implications for schooling. *Quarterly Newsletter of the Laboratory of Comparative Human Cognition*, 1980, *2*, 53–58.

Resnick, L.B. Theories and prescriptions for early reading instruction. In L.B. Resnick & P.A. Weaver (Eds.), *Theory and practice of early reading* (Vol. 2). Hillsdale, N.J.: Erlbaum, 1979.

Shavelson, R.J., & Stern, P. Research on teachers' pedagogical thoughts, judgments, decisions, and behavior. *Review of Educational Research*, 1981, *51*, 455–498.

Stoddard, J.F. *Stoddard's American intellectual arithmetic.* New York: Sheldon, 1860.

Wilson, B., & Schmits, D. What's new in ability grouping? *Phi Delta Kappan,* 1978, *59,* 535–536.

9
Characteristics of Effective Schools: Research and Implementation

Ronald Edmonds

Review of the Research

A number of studies are most explicit in identifying and advocating particular school characteristics. Weber (1971) was an early contributor to the literature on the school determinants of achievement with his study of four instructionally effective inner-city schools. Weber intended his study as an alternative to Coleman, Campbell, Hobson, McPartland, Mood, Weinfeld, and York (1966), Jensen (1969), and other researchers who had satisfied themselves that low achievement by poor children derived principally from inherent disabilities that were characteristic of the poor. Weber focused on four characteristics of successful schools: (1) "strong leadership," exemplified by a principal who is instrumental in setting the tone of the school, helping to make decisions on instructional strategies, and organizing and distributing the schools' resources; (2) "high expectations" for all students (Weber is careful to point out that high expectations are not sufficient for school success but that they are certainly necessary); (3) an orderly, relatively quiet, and pleasant atmosphere; and (4) a strong emphasis on students' acquisition of reading skills, with careful and frequent evaluation of pupil progress.

In 1974, the New York State Office of Education Performance Review published a study that confirmed some of Weber's major findings. Two New York City public schools were studied, both of which were serving a predominantly poor pupil population. One of the schools was high-achieving and the other low-achieving. An attempt was made to identify the differences that seemed most accountable for the achievement variation between the two schools. The following findings were reported:

1. The differences in student performance in the two schools seemed to be attributable to factors under the school's control.
2. Administrative behavior, policies, and practices in the schools appeared to have a significant impact on school effectiveness.
3. The more effective school was led by an administrative team that provided a good balance between management and instructional skills.

4. The administrative team in the more effective school had developed a plan for dealing with reading and had implemented the plan throughout the school.
5. Many professional personnel in the less effective school attributed children's reading problems to nonschool factors and were pessimistic about the school's ability to have an impact; whereas, in the more effective school, teachers were less skeptical about their ability to have an effect on children.

These findings reinforce the relevance of leadership, expectations, and atmosphere as essential institutional elements affecting pupil performance.

In a more rigorous and sophisticated version of the Weber and New York studies, Madden, Lawson, and Sweet (Note 1) studied twenty-one pairs of California elementary schools that were matched on the basis of pupil characteristics and differed only in pupil performance ratings according to standardized achievement measures. When compared to the low-achieving schools, the high-achieving schools displayed greater principal support, greater teacher effort, a more orderly and task-oriented classroom atmosphere, more time spent on such subjects as social studies, noninstructional use of teacher aides, greater access to materials, highly limited faculty influence on overall instructional strategy, more support services from district administration, and greater job satisfaction among teachers.

In 1977, Brookover and Lezotte published their study, *Changes in School Characteristics Coincident with Changes in Student Achievement*. This work's inquiries and analyses reinforce certain of the Weber (1971) and New York (1974) findings. The Michigan Department of Education's (1976) *Cost Effectiveness Study* and the Brookover and Lezotte (1977) study both focused on educational variables that are liable to school control and important to the quality of pupil performance. In response to these studies, the Michigan Department of Education asked Brookover to study a set of Michigan schools that were characterized by consistent pupil performance improvement or decline. The Brookover (1979) study is broader in scope than these earlier studies and explicitly intended to profit from the methodological and analytical lessons learned.

Since the early 1970s, the Michigan Department of Education has annually tested all Michigan pupils in public schools in grades four and seven. The tests used are criterion-referenced standardized measures of pupil performance in basic school skills. The data from these tests were used by the Michigan Department of Education to identify elementary schools characterized by consistent pupil performance improvement or decline. Brookover and Lezotte (1977) chose eight schools to be studied (six improving, two declining). The schools were visited by trained interviewers who conducted interviews and administered questionnaires to many of the school personnel to identify which differences between the improving and declining schools seemed most important to pupil performance.

The results of this study indicate that the staffs of improving schools accept and emphasize the importance of basic reading and mathematics objectives and believe that all of their students can master the basic objectives. These staffs hold high levels of expectations with regard to the educational accomplishments of their students and are much more likely to assume responsibility for teaching basic skills. With the greater emphasis on reading and math objectives in these schools, the staffs devote much more time to achieving these objectives. They evidence a greater degree of acceptance of the concept of accountability and are further along in the development of an accountability model. The principal is more likely to be an instructional leader and more of a disciplinarian and, perhaps most important, assumes responsibility for evaluation of the achievement of basic objectives.

It is interesting that these researchers found teachers in the improving schools to be less satisfied with their jobs than the staffs in the declining schools. The higher levels of reported staff satisfaction and morale in the declining schools seem to reflect a pattern of complacency and satisfaction with the current levels of educational attainment, whereas the staffs of improving schools appear more likely to experience some tension and dissatisfaction with existing conditions.

The Edmonds and Frederiksen (1978) study focused on city schools that are instructionally effective. The thesis was that all children are eminently educable and that school factors are crucial in determining the quality of the education provided. The project began by asking the following question: "Are there schools that are instructionally effective for poor children?" In September of 1974, Lezotte, Edmonds, and Ratner described their analysis of pupil performance in the twenty elementary schools that make up Detroit's Model Cities neighborhood. All of the schools are located in inner-city Detroit and serve a predominantly poor and minority pupil population. An effective school among the twenty was defined as being at or above the city average grade equivalent in math and reading. An ineffective school was defined as below the city average. Eight of the twenty schools were judged effective in teaching math, nine were judged effective in teaching reading, and five were judged effective in teaching both math and reading.

We turned next to the problem of establishing the relationship between pupil family background and increasing effectiveness. Two schools among the twenty were matched on the basis of eleven social indicators. In one, pupils averaged nearly four months above the city average in reading and math; in the other, pupils averaged nearly three months below the city reading average and one and a half months below the city math average.

The similarity in the characteristics of the pupil populations in these two schools permitted us to infer the importance of school behavior in making pupil performance independent of family background. The overriding point here is that, in and of itself, pupil family background neither causes nor precludes elementary school instructional effectiveness.

The second phase of the project (Frederiksen, 1975) was a reanalysis of 1966 Equal Educational Opportunity Survey (EEOS) data. We retained our interest in identifying instructionally effective schools for students from poor families, but we also wanted to study the effects of schools on children from different social backgrounds. Such an inquiry would permit an evaluation of school contributions to educational outcomes that would be independent of our ability to match schools on the basis of the socioeconomic characteristics of the pupils.

We identified fifty-five effective schools, which varied widely in racial composition, per pupil expenditure, and other presumed determinants of school quality. Our summary definition of school effectiveness required that each school eliminate the relationship between successful performance and family background. The Search for Effective Schools Project (Edmonds, 1983) completed its analysis of social class, family background, and pupil performance for all Lansing, Michigan, pupils in grades three through seven. Five Lansing schools were identified in which achievement seems relatively independent of pupil social class. We used both normative and criterion data to identify schools in which nearly all pupils are achieving beyond minimum objectives, including especially children of low social class from families living at the poverty level.

The major finding was that the effective schools share a climate in which it is incumbent upon all personnel to be instructionally effective for all pupils. This is not a very profound insight, but it does define the proper lines of future research inquiry; for example, what is the origin of that climate of instructional responsibility? If the climate dissipates, what causes it to do so? If the climate remains, what keeps it functioning? Our tentative observations are as follows: Some schools are instructionally effective for poor children because they have a tyrannical principal who compels the teachers to bring all children to a minimum level of mastery of basic skills. Some schools are effective because they have a self-generating corps of dedicated teachers who are committed to being effective for all the children they teach. Some schools are effective because they have a highly politicized parent–teacher organization that holds the schools to close instructional account. We found no single explanation of school effectiveness for the poor or for any other social class. Fortunately, children know how to learn in more ways than we know how to teach, thus permitting schools to use great latitude in instructional strategy. We also know, however, how to teach in ways that can keep some children from learning almost anything. One of the cardinal characteristics of effective schools is that they are as anxious to avoid strategies that do not work as they are committed to implementing strategies that do work.

The most tangible and indispensable characteristics of instructionally effective schools for poor children are the following: (1) strong administrative leadership, without which the disparate elements of good schooling can be neither brought together nor kept together; (2) a climate of expectation, in which no children are permitted to fall below minimum levels of achievement; (3) an orderly atmosphere—not overly rigid, quiet without being oppressive, and generally conducive to the instructional business at hand (effective schools make it clear that pupil acquisition of the basic school skills takes precedence over all other school activities); and (4) a means by which pupil progress is monitored frequently. Thus, the principal and the teachers remain constantly aware of pupil progress in relationship to instructional objectives.

Programs for School Improvement

The research described in the preceding section underlies the basic reforms I suggested for the policies and programs of the New York City public schools. If the research has taught us anything so far, it has taught us that, although Coleman et al. (1966) are correct in the assertion that pupil performance is highly correlated with family background, they are profoundly incorrect in the conclusion that family background is the cause of pupil performance. The research I describe reveals that school response to family background determines pupil performance. The New York City school system now presumes that all children are educable and that the educability of children derives far more from the nature of the school to which they are sent than from the nature of the family from which they come.

The School Improvement Project being implemented in a cross section of New York City schools is a program of intervention based on these premises.

The School Improvement Project brought together a group of men and women known as school liaisons who were assigned to schools that volunteered to participate in the project. After evaluating a school's relative strengths and weaknesses, the school liaison people conferred with the administrative and instructional personnel of that school and then, in close collaboration with representatives of the school staff, prepared a needs assessment document. This document specified the relative strength and weakness of the instructional leadership, the instructional emphasis, the climate of the building, as well as the other characteristics found in successful schools. The document then became the guide for making decisions about the kinds of technical assistance needed to turn the school into a successful school. For example, because one of our firm conclusions is that the principal of a school has to be the person to whom instructional personnel look for instructional leadership, we offer technical assistance to principals. We have found that principals in successful schools systematically observe in classrooms and systematically respond to the observations. If the principal in a project school rarely observes in classrooms, we would assign an experienced person to work with that principal to teach him or her how to be a sophisticated and consistent evaluator of teacher performance in the classroom. If the needs assessment indicated that the teachers were insecure about the use of achievement data, we would assign a measurement expert to the school to conduct seminars on reading assessment data and evaluating achievement outcomes, or we would assign a curriculum person, trained in how to use achievement data as a basis for program design, to help teachers reformulate the school reading program.

The School Improvement Project's process of intervention does not alter per pupil expenditure, does not add in any permanent way to the resources with which the school works, does not reduce class size, and does not add to the repertoire of services that the school has to offer. The project's goal is to help school people make better use of the resources that are already there.

In New York, one of my most difficult assignments was to design a promotion program for children who, according to objective data, do not demonstrate mastery of a sufficient minimum of school skills. The promotion program that was installed requires that the central administration of the New York schools administer a citywide test in reading, writing, and math to fourth- and seventh-grade children. The program specifies that no child is to move to the next grade unless and until he or she can demonstrate sufficient mastery of the bodies of knowledge and sets of skills that are prerequisite for predictable success in that grade. Lest critics claim that there is no justification for nonpromotion if all that can be offered children is a repeat of what they just did, the promotion program also requires that children who are not promoted participate in a program designed to correct their academic difficulties.

Reading and mathematics achievement scores have risen dramatically in New York City in the last four years. Aggregate pupil performance is now above national norms, as measured by the California Achievement Test. Disaggregation of school data shows that although the gain has been citywide, it has been greatest in districts that have the largest proportions of low income children. There also have been dramatic improvements in the individual schools participating in the School Improvement Project.

Programs of school improvement have taken place in several other cities. Milwaukee, Wisconsin was the first school district to launch a formal project of school improvement based on the findings of the Search for Effective Schools Project. In 1978, the Milwaukee school system began a program of instructional improvement in twenty Milwaukee elementary schools designated by the superintendent as ineffective. Whereas the School Improvement Project schools in New York City relied on volunteers, the RISE schools in Milwaukee did not. There are other differences in the two projects but one striking similarity: the gains in achievement in the Milwaukee schools have been as dramatic as those in the New York schools.

Other school improvement projects are getting under way in other parts of the United States. In St. Louis, the Danforth Foundation has been working with St. Louis schools to implement a program of school improvement in four inner-city elementary schools. The St. Louis design is heavily focused on staff development and on an elaborate process for broad consultation and shared decision making.

The New Jersey Education Association School Effectiveness Training Program, under the auspices of the teachers' union, is available on teacher demand and uses staff development as the major instrument of intervention. The state offers small grants to local districts to encourage projects of school improvement. State education department personnel are available to local school district personnel to teach the techniques of assessing the five characteristics of successful schools.

These projects will have an impact not only on students, teachers, and schools but also on our knowledge of how school districts can use research findings as the basis for local programs of school improvement.

Summary Observations

One of the most straightforward and widely disseminated outcomes of the Search for Effective Schools Project is its description of the five factors that characterize instructionally effective schools: leadership, climate, expectations, instructional emphasis, and assessment.

Although we can be reasonably confident that the five characteristics are correlates of school effectiveness, we do not know whether they are *causes* of school effectiveness. The outcome of the school improvement projects in New York and Milwaukee are sufficient to demonstrate the efficacy of a school intervention strategy based on correlates. What is now needed is research that seeks to integrate school effects, teacher effects, and organizational development.

Two bodies of knowledge offer immediate opportunities for strengthening strategies of school intervention. The discipline of organizational development adds sophisticated process to the substance of the five factors, and the information that has derived from certain studies of teacher effects also has immediate applicability to the design of programs of school improvement.

Finally, the activities reported in this chapter are of little importance unless educational decision makers express an interest in using what we have learned about the characteristics of effective schools. After all, one of the characteristics of effective schools is that the principals and teachers care about the quality of teaching and learning for all of their students. Unfortunately, we know far more about the desirability of such caring than about the means by which it can be brought about.

Reference Note

1. Madden, J.V., Lawson, D.R., & Sweet, D. *School effectiveness study: State of California*. Paper presented at the annual meeting of the American Educational Research Association, San Francisco, 1976.

References

Brookover, W. *School Social Systems and Student Achievement*. South Hadley, Mass.: Bergin and Garvey, 1979.

Brookover, W.B., & Lezotte, L.W. *Changes in school characteristics coincident with changes in student achievement*. East Lansing: Michigan State University, Institute for Research on Teaching, 1977.

Coleman, J.S., Campbell, E.Q., Hobson, C.J., McPartland, J., Mood, A.M., Weinfeld, F.D., & York, R.L. *Equality of educational opportunity*. Washington, D.C.: U.S. Office of Education, National Center for Educational Statistics, 1966.

Edmonds, R. *Final report on the research project: Search for effective schools*. East Lansing: Michigan State University, 1983.

Edmonds, R.R., & Frederiksen, J.R. *Search for effective schools: The identification and analysis of city schools that are instructionally effective for poor children.* Cambridge, Mass.: Harvard University, Center for Urban Studies, 1978.

Frederiksen, J. *School effectiveness and equality of eductional opportunity.* Cambridge, Mass.: Harvard University, Center for Urban Studies, 1975.

Jensen, A. How much can we boost IQ and scholastic achievement? *Harvard Educational Review,* 1969, *39* (1), 1–123.

Lezotte, L., Edmonds, R., & Ratner, G. *Remedy for school failure to equitably deliver basic school skills.* Cambridge, Mass.: Harvard University, Center for Urban Studies, 1974.

Michigan Department of Education. *Cost Effectiveness Study.* Lansing: Michigan Department of Education, 1976.

State of New York, Office of Education Performance Review. *School factors influencing reading achievement: A case study of two inner city schools.* Albany: New York Office of Education Performance Review, March 1974.

Weber, G. *Inner-city children can be taught to read: Four successful schools.* Washington, D.C.: Council for Basic Education, 1971.

10

The Logistics of Educational Change

Douglas Carnine and
Russell Gersten

Many theories have been offered to explain why children from impoverished backgrounds have difficulty in learning to read, and many methods have been tried to improve reading performance. One method that has a reasonable amount of empirical support is a mode of teaching that has been labeled *direct instruction*. Rosenshine (1976) introduced the term into the mainstream of educational research. His synthesis of many classroom observation studies concluded that students consistently demonstrate higher reading achievement scores when their teachers do the following:

1. Devote adequate time to active instruction in reading, including a good deal of small group instruction.
2. Break complex skills and concepts into small, easy-to-understand steps and systematically teach in a step-by-step fashion.
3. Ensure that *all* students operate at a high success rate.
4. Provide immediate, useful feedback to students about the accuracy of their work.
5. Conduct much of the instruction in small groups to allow for frequent student–teacher interactions.

More evidence of the suitability of direct instruction procedures has emerged from a host of classroom research studies (Anderson, Evertson, & Brophy, 1979; Cooley & Leinhardt, 1980; Fisher, Berliner, Filby, Marliave, Cahen, & Dishaw, 1980; Leinhardt, Zigmond, & Cooley, 1981; Stallings, 1980). Despite the quantity of this research and the consistency of its findings, the description of direct instruction that has emerged from the research is probably too vague to be of immediate use to those who are interested in school improvement. Administrators and teachers who want to improve the effectiveness of their school organization and their classroom procedures are likely to need step-by-step guidance on what to do and clear feedback about how they are doing. Without such information, their efforts are likely to be less than successful.

Knowledge about effective educational practice is of limited interest if it cannot be disseminated in schools and classrooms. Reading educators must face two sets of challenges: they must design effective instructional systems for the teaching of reading, and they must develop a delivery system that will get the instructional system to teachers and students. There is a pressing need to tie together the fragments of these less well researched areas and to begin taking a rigorous, comprehensive look at the research issues that emerge from the implementation of reading programs in actual classroom settings.

The remainder of this chapter describes a comprehensive, yet manageable, instructional system. The system evolved out of the 14-year school improvement effort conducted by the University of Oregon Direct Instruction Follow Through Project.

The Direct Instruction Follow Through Model

The suggestions that the best way to demonstrate understanding of an educational or social problem is to intervene and solve it is exemplified in the Follow Through Program, which was initiated in 1967 by the U.S. Office of Education. Innovative educational models were to be set up in a variety of communities, in classrooms of low income kindergarten, first-, second-, and third-grade students. The educational models represented a full spectrum of the early childhood education programs that had been developed in the United States, mostly in university settings. Among the programs selected were a language experience model, a Piagetian model, a bilingual model, a behavior modification model, and the direct instruction model. At the time of its inception, Follow Through was the largest educational field experiment ever undertaken by the U.S. Office of Education (or, to our knowledge, by any other educational agency or institution).

The primary objective of the Direct Instruction Model was to close the gap in academic achievement between educationally at-risk students and their middle-class peers. The model was implemented in twenty communities, ranging from inner-city areas in New York City and East St. Louis, Illinois, to Indian reservations in North Carolina and South Dakota, to rural communities in Arkansas, Texas, and South Carolina.

The National Evaluation

For the national evaluation, a sample of Follow Through children were tested upon entry to the program on the Wide Range Achievement Test, or WRAT (Jastak & Jastak, 1965). In addition, demographic information (sex, family income, mother's education, ethnicity, home language) was collected. In each school district implementing a Follow Through (FT) model, a non–Follow Through (NFT) comparison group was identified. Two cohorts of children were included—those who began Follow Through in 1970 and those who began in 1971.

Major analyses were performed on end-of-third-grade reading scores on the Metropolitan Achievement Test (MAT). (Statistically adjusted comparisons, which have generated extensive debate—see House, Glass, McLean, and Walker, 1978—are not presented here.) Figure 10–1 presents median third-grade total reading scores for students in the full 4-year Follow Through program (kindergarten through third grade) for each of the major sponsors. The performance of the direct instruction students is within ten percentile points of the national average and is closer to the national norms than that of students taught on the other models. These effects are corroborated by more intricate statistical analysis (Carnine & Gersten, Note 1; Stebbins, St. Pierre, Proper, Anderson, & Cerva, 1977).

These results have been maintained—and in some cases enhanced—since the national evaluation. Table 10–1 presents mean third-grade achievement scores in total reading for all direct instruction urban sites with a full 4-year program. Note

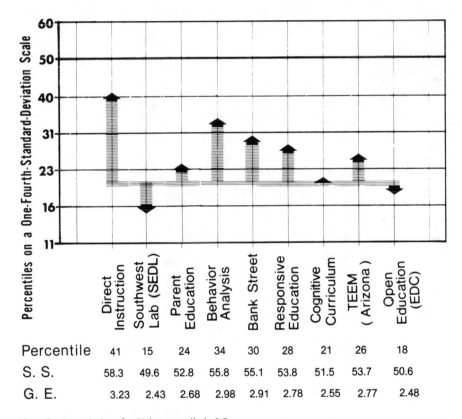

	Direct Instruction	Southwest Lab (SEDL)	Parent Education	Behavior Analysis	Bank Street	Responsive Education	Cognitive Curriculum	TEEM (Arizona)	Open Education (EDC)
Percentile	41	15	24	34	30	28	21	26	18
S. S.	58.3	49.6	52.8	55.8	55.1	53.8	51.5	53.7	50.6
G. E.	3.23	2.43	2.68	2.98	2.91	2.78	2.55	2.77	2.48

Note: Grade equivalent for 50th percentile is 3.5

Source: Reprinted with permission of Wesley C. Becker, Note 12.

Figure 10–1. Median Third-Grade MAT Total Reading Scores

Table 10-1
Stability of Effects: Percentile Equivalents for End-of-Third-Grade Total Reading Scores for Urban Black 4-Year Direct Instruction Follow Through Projects

	Cohort Percentile								
Site	*II* (1973)	*III* (1974)	*IV* (1975)	*V* (1976)	*VI* (1977)	*VII* (1978)	*VIII* (1979)	*IX* (1980)	*X* (1981)
E. St. Louis, Ill.	—	42	35	41	36	—	54[a]	55[a]	66
Flint, Mich.	34	35	40	40	34	46	53	52	42[c]
New York, N.Y.	36	52	42	46	40	33[b]	36[b]	46[b]	47
Washington, D.C.	34	30	40	34	30	44[c]	44[c]	—	—

Note: Mean standard score was converted to percentile. The mean score for non–Follow Through low-income students in large Northeast cities corresponds to the twenty-eighth percentile on the M.A.T. The M.A.T. (1970 elementary) was given at all sites for cohorts III to VI (1974 to 1977). In the 1978–1980 period, a variety of standardized tests were administered, depending on local policy. The Anchor Tables and some of our own research established the comparability (within two to three percentile points).

[a]CAT
[b]SAT
[c]CTBS
[d]SRA

that in some of the sites, average performance of students is actually above grade level; all are consistently within sixteen percentile points of the national norm and are significantly above expected performance of low-income urban students (twenty-third to thirty-first percentile).

In summarizing the results of their evaluation of Follow Through, Stebbins et al. (1977) concluded:

> The Direct Instruction Model is specific in stating that children participating in the Follow Through program are expected to, on the average, perform at the same level as their middle-class peers by the end of third grade. (pp. A-168–A-169)

A Closer Look at Classroom Processes

To understand more fully the observable differences between the Follow Through models and the effects of these differences on student outcomes, Stallings (1975) designed a study that looked intensively at classroom processes in a subsample of the Follow Through sites. She developed a classroom observation system that was sensitive to key variables of each of seven Follow Through models. Table 10–2 presents the segment of her research that is most relevant to the analysis of variables contributing to effective reading instruction. The models are rank-ordered in terms of percentage of observed academic engaged time in reading for the third grade. The amounts of academic engaged time for the Direct Instruction and Be-

Table 10–2
Stallings' Classroom Observations of Follow Through Sponsors

Model	Percentage of Engaged Time in Reading[a]	WRAT Mean Pretest (Fall 1971)	End-of-Third Grade MAT Total Reading Raw Score		Unadjusted Percentile	Relative Difference in Adjusted Percentile Points[b]
			Mean	Standard Deviation		
Behavior analysis (Kansas)	59	35.16	42.21	9.99	34	− 2
Direct instruction (Oregon)	58	33.50	46.63	11.70	41	+ 7
Language experience (Arizona)	42	28.20	32.95	2.05	22	− 4
Responsive (Far West)	41	40.78	47.20	8.40	42	− 2
Psychodynamic (Bank Street)	38	32.42	35.34	11.44	24	− 10
Open classroom (EDC)	37	26.38	32.09	10.12	20	− 5

Source: From Stallings (1975, p. 81). Note that the high scope model is omitted, since there were no third-grade data.
[a]From Rosenshine (Note 2) and Stallings and Kaskowitz (1974, pp. R–3, R–4).
[b]Adjusted for WRAT pretest.

havior Analysis models are virtually identical (59 and 58 percent) and substantially higher than the amounts for the other four sponsors. There is a difference of nine adjusted percentile points on the Metropolitan Achievement Test favoring the direct instruction students, however (corresponding to one-fourth standard deviation). These data at least suggest the importance of variables other than amounts of engaged time. One of the main differences between the Direct Instruction and Behavior Analysis models was the curriculum used to teach reading. The Behavior Analysis Model trained teachers in the principles of behavior modification but used traditional, commercially available reading series. Direct instruction teachers used some behavior modification techniques but also utilized a specially developed curriculum that was constructed to teach reading and language.

Summary of the Follow Through Findings

Stallings's (1975) findings suggest that improvements in reading achievement require more than increased academic engaged time and that curriculum plays a vital role. Although identifying the precise set of variables that account for the Follow Through results is probably not possible, a program in which low-income students are scoring within nine percentile points of the national median demonstrates what can be done in schools. Achievement scores are not the only indication of the students' success, however; the Direct Instruction Follow Through students also scored higher on affective measures (Singer & Balow, 1981) and were perceived by their parents as doing better academically (Haney, 1977).

These improvements in reading achievement did not come easily. The Direct Instruction Model required major organizational changes in each school—in the nature of the curriculum, in how that curriculum was taught, and in the quality and quantity of feedback that teachers gave students and that supervisors gave teachers. Schools that adopted the model changed their inservice training and supervisory procedures. Perhaps most important an elevated level of effort was required of and given by teachers and students. In addition to organizational changes, conceptual changes occurred: teachers began to change how they thought about children and about learning (Gersten, Carnine, Zoref, & Cronin, Note 3).

The Design of Curriculum

The key principle in the design of direct instruction curriculum is deceptively simple: for all students to learn, both the curricular materials and the teacher presentation of these materials must be clear and unambiguous. Lessons must be designed so that the concepts the teachers expect the students to learn can be clearly communicated—that is, so that the students will learn what the teacher assumes they are learning.

Until recently, most of the teacher effectiveness literature avoided one of the most crucial issues in teaching—the analysis of curriculum. Numerous studies indicate that the contents of commercial basal reading programs account for most of the reading instruction in most elementary school classrooms (Durkin, 1981; Mason, Note 4; Osborn, Note 5). Our strong suspicion is that the shortcomings of most major basal reading programs have contributed to the high incidence of reading failure among low-income students.

In the last few years, an increasing number of researchers have turned their attention to examinations of widely used basal reading texts and workbooks (Beck, 1981; Durkin, 1981; Osborn, Note 5). Perhaps the major issue raised by these researchers is the lack of clarity in basal reading programs. Durkin (1981) claims that the suggestions made for teaching various skills are unclear and are reflected in such vague phrases as "help the children understand that," "guide the children in seeing that," "explain why," and "point out how." In Durkin's view, the teachers' guides to the major basal programs "offer precise help when it is least needed; they are obscure or silent when specific help is likely to be required" (p. 63).

Beck (1981) has noted that basal series often assume too much background knowledge on the student's part. Consider, for example, a fifth-grade story about the antebellum South. Comprehension of the story would be likely to suffer unless students have an appropriate background in which to fit such concepts as Quakerism, underground railroad, free states, overseer, trader, bloodhounds, runaway, patrol, and hammocks.

Another topic investigated by reading researchers is the quality and quantity of practice, review, and application exercises in basal reading materials. For most children (and for most adults), learning something new requires practice. Most basal reading programs lack systematic attention to practice, review, and application. Durkin (1981) observes that suggestions for review in the basal programs tend to be nonspecific and that the frequency and spacing of review is often unrelated to either the importance or the difficulty of the material. She questions, for example, whether it is sensible to offer information about ellipses (three dots) as early as grade 1 (as did two series), or as early as grade 2 (as did two others), and then restate that information on twenty-four subsequent occasions?

Englemann and Steeley (Note 6) analyzed some basal programs and found that some important topics and skills in reading comprehension were slighted. In one program, for example, the important skill of identifying the main idea in a paragraph is introduced once and then reviewed an average of once in every sixty-two lessons. Engelmann and Steeley found the prescribed instruction to be inept, and the set of examples presented to teach the concept of main idea supported an average of four possible interpretations. The most common misrule a student could learn from the examples presented in the text was that "the main idea is the first sentence in the paragraph."

To discount the inadequacies of basal reading programs as minor problems that can be easily compensated for by teachers is to ignore classroom realities. Several classroom observation studies have documented that teachers follow the general lesson plans in the teachers' manuals (Mason, Note 4; Osborn, Note 5). Englemann and Steeley's (Note 6) observations reveal that when teachers do attempt to compensate for programs' ambiguities or shortcomings, they often do not present any clearer communication of the concepts than is found in the teacher's guides they are using.

Components of the Direct Instruction Model

Curriculum Design. What differentiates the Direct Instruction Model from most other educational models is that learning is assumed to be the product of the specific instructional communications presented to the student. The direct instruction curriculum goes well beyond simplistic notions of task analysis and the mechanistic teaching of a hierarchy of skills. The emphasis is not on descriptions of characteristics and the developmental stages of the learner. Rather, the model is based on a rigorous analysis of exactly how curricular materials and lessons should be constructed and particularly on the factors of clarity and practice.

Clarity of Instructional Communications. Direct Instruction curriculum designers observe several principles to ensure clarity. A first principle is that nothing is assumed about students' prior knowledge; for example, in reading programs, there must be provision for the systematic teaching of necessary vocabulary and background information. Much of the current research in reading comprehension reveals that comprehension involves a constant interplay between the learner's current repertoire of strategies and skills, the learner's background knowledge, and the demand characteristics of the text. It does not take a great leap of the imagination to conclude that young readers will become confused and frustrated when a large number of inappropriate assumptions about background knowledge are combined with a vague or ambiguous presentation of important concepts.

The principle that most clearly differentiates direct instruction from other instructional approaches is that during the initial stages of instruction, every step of every skill, rule, or problem-solving sequence is taught explicitly. Explicit, step-by-step strategies have been developed to teach students to draw inferences from scientific material, to analyze character motives in fictional passages, and to analyze legal arguments (Carnine & Gersten, Note 1). When each step in a complex comprehension process is made explicit, teachers can determine the step in the process during which a student's performance breaks down and can help the student with that step. Corrective feedback becomes much more efficient and effective (Gersten, Carnine, & Williams, 1982).

Because many students have difficulty in applying skills they have just learned to new situations, instruction does not end with explicit teaching. Teachers still must remain available to provide corrective feedback if errors are made. As soon as a student masters a routine, teacher guidance is gradually faded to facilitate independent functioning and transfer of the skill.

Several research studies support the application of this teaching process to a variety of skills: simplifying complex syntactic structures (Kameenui, Carnine, & Maggs, 1980), studying expository prose (Adams, Carnine, & Gersten, 1982), and analyzing faulty arguments (Patching, Kameenui, Carnine, Gersten, & Colvin, 1983). Extensions of this methodology to other areas of reading comprehension are discussed by Jenkins and Pany (1981), Jenkins and Heliotis (1981), and Pearson (Note 7).

Teaching Procedures

Carefully designed curricula *can* influence how well students will learn to read. Programs are taught by teachers, and the way teachers use any program influences its effectiveness. In an intensive study of implementation of direct instruction programs in seven inner-city schools (Gersten et al., Note 3), the correlation between assessed level of classroom implementation and mean gains in reading on the Comprehensive Test of Basic Skills was .80 in kindergarten and .63 in first grade. Implementation was assessed with both direct observation and rating forms filled out by supervisors. All twenty-five teachers in the sample used the same reading program for 30 to 40 minutes per day. The extreme variability in the success rate of the students seemed to result largely from variability in the quality and quantity of teacher–student interactions.

The teaching procedures that influence teacher–student interactions include (1) motivating students to respond, (2) presenting tasks at a rate that will assure high levels of correct responses, and (3) diagnosing and correcting errors. Effective teachers can transform student errors into constructive learning experiences, for example, by analyzing student mistakes and determining which rules, skills, or processes the students are not mastering. This approach contrasts with a correction commonly used in classrooms, which is simply to tell students the correct answer. Such a procedure is often inadequate, especially when students have made an error in applying knowledge they have been taught. A more constructive correction involves prompting the student to apply previously taught knowledge, reminding him or her of previously taught rules and strategies, and helping the student apply these strategies to the problem at hand.

Some of the naturalistic research on correction of student errors by Good and Beckerman (1978), Brophy and Evertson (1976), Fisher et al. (1980), and Stallings (1975) helps highlight the importance of offering students consistent, immediate, and strategic feedback. Open-ended questions (such as "Try another way") usually do not help students and can have just the opposite effect (Fisher et al., 1980). Staying with a problem child for too long and attempting to cajole him or her into answering by offering emotional support can actually impede the student's learning

(Stallings, 1975). Gersten et al. (1982) demonstrated that when teachers do not respond to students who make errors, or merely give the right answers, reading acquisition is not as rapid as when teachers offer clear feedback about the adequacy of student responses, remind them of critical steps or strategies when correcting responses, and, when necessary, model (or prompt) and then test the critical steps (see also Carnine, Note 8).

Although the research on correction is in its infancy, the small amount of data we have confirms our experience: when corrections are based on the analysis of the task and the relationship of that task to what the learner knows, these corrections can be an integral part of the practice, review, and application process—and a part of a constructive learning experience.

The difficulty that teachers have in learning how to correct student mistakes is reflected in the relatively long time teachers and paraprofessionals take to learn to react consistently to student errors. The acquisition patterns for several direct instruction teaching procedures are presented in figure 10-2. Note that relatively simple teaching skills, such as format accuracy (the precise teaching of lessons) and use of signals (procedures used to prompt student responses), tend to be mastered by most teachers and aides within a few months. Other teaching skills, such as the use of correction procedures and the maintenance of high levels of student accuracy during group lessons, took a year (or longer) for the majority of teachers to master. If the teachers in the study—most of whom were experienced classroom teachers but new to direct instruction—had not been given intensive classroom supervision, the acquisition of these skills might have taken longer.

As important as the way in which teachers use time is the amount of time they make available for reading instruction. By making more time available for small- and large-group academic instruction (and by more actively engaging the students), teachers contribute to students' reading achievement (see Fisher et al., 1980; Leinhardt et al., 1981; Stallings, 1980). Numerous studies have shown that the more minutes per day students spend actively engaged in reading instruction, the better their reading performance, and that time spent in transitional activities, announcements, and unrelated supplemental activities, games, class trips, and so forth, is negatively correlated with learning (Baker, Herman, & Yeh, 1981).

In the direct instruction classrooms, supervisors work with teachers during the first week of school to set up schedules that allow ample time for reading. During the year, the supervisors see that the schedules are adhered to and also help teachers maximize reading engaged time and minimize time wasted in transitions and waiting.

Schoolwide Implementation

Many of the findings about the use of time and about teaching techniques come from studies that compared good and poor teachers. Although variability in teaching performance is interesting to researchers, it is often harmful to students; un-

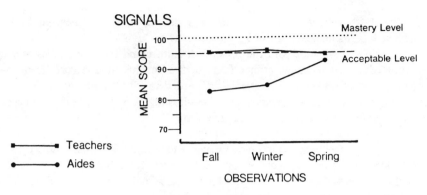

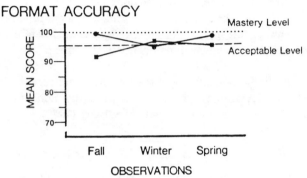

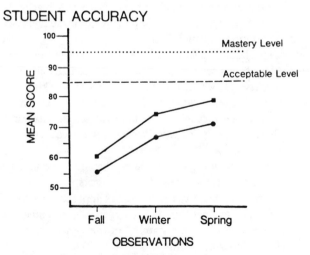

Figure 10–2. Acquisition Patterns for Direct Instruction Teaching Procedures

fortunately, a valiant effort by a second-grade teacher can be negated by the lackluster performance of a third-grade teacher.

A critical review of both the research literature and the case studies of successful educational change efforts leads to the conclusion that core changes—changes that affect the entire school—are needed to ensure that students achieve their capabilities each and every year. The following elements appear to be necessary for an effective schoolwide change effort:

1. Consistent feedback and technical assistance to teachers (Berman & McLaughlin, 1975; Gersten et al., Note 3; Joyce & Showers, Note 9).
2. Incentives and emotional support for teachers from peer groups and administrators (Peterson, 1980; Bredo, Note 10).
3. A system for continual monitoring of student progress (Fullan, 1980) and the use of this information to improve the quality of classroom instruction.
4. High expectations for students' achievement.

It is interesting that some of these elements are very similar to the characteristics of the successful urban schools observed by Edmonds (1979) and Brookover, Beady, Flood, Schweitzer, and Wisenbaker (1979).

Consistent Feedback and Technical Assistance to Teachers

As the Direct Instruction Model has evolved, a shift has occurred in the nature of its teacher training program. In the earlier years, teacher training consisted of out-of-class demonstrations and role playing combined with discussions of philosophy and exhortations on such issues as maintaining high expectations for all students and maximizing engaged academic time. As the years passed, most of the supervisors found that what worked best with students also worked best with teachers; thus, supervisors learned to train teachers by working with them in classrooms—sometimes modeling how to teach a group, other times giving direct feedback about teacher performance. The following guidelines summarize what supervisors have found to be useful when working with teachers:

1. Help teachers organize time so that they spend a good proportion of their school time teaching academic subjects.
2. Use training materials that are at an appropriate difficulty level for each teacher and that systematically break large tasks into small components.
3. Conduct much of the training in the classroom to allow for frequent supervisor-teacher interactions.
4. Provide immediate feedback to teachers about the effectiveness of their teaching, and include specific suggestions for improvement.

An effective supervisor can identify problems, decide which problems are most important, determine remedies, and then describe and demonstrate the remedies.

Monitoring Student Progress

Student progress is measured in two ways—the amount of learning and the quality of learning. The amount of learning can be defined as the content covered; the quality of learning is the level of mastery of the content covered in the weeks of instruction that precede testing.

In each direct instruction classroom, a report on content covered is filled out every 2 weeks. This report shows which lesson each group is working on, the number of lessons gained during the 2-week period, and the number of lessons gained from the start of the school year. Figure 10–3 is an example of such a report. In the figure, we see that group 1 is making good progress. Group 4, however, is only on lesson 40 on the seventieth day of school. This group might complete only ninety lessons by the end of the year. Whether this is acceptable performance will depend on a more careful analysis of how well the students are being taught and an assessment of their level of mastery. This kind of assessment is discussed next.

From the start, the goal of the criterion-referenced testing movement has been to develop test procedures that are directly tied to the goals of instruction. Test performance can then be used for evaluation of instruction as well as for remediation of problems. In the direct instruction program, instructionally referenced tests evaluate the process of instruction throughout the program, not just at the end of the year; results of the tests suggest corrective action when and where it is needed. The tests also use items that have been covered or implied by the program content. Figure 10–4 presents an example of an instructionally referenced, continuous progress test used with third graders and advanced second graders. The skills that are assessed in this section of the test are logical analysis (item 1), memory of important factual information from stories read (items 4 and 7), vocabulary (item 2), applications of concepts taught (item 5), and inference questions (items 3 and 6).

Teacher Thomas   Grade K   School Marshall

Date Dec. 10   Day in School 70

			Reading		
Group	Level	SDIP	LDIP	2-week Gain	Year Gain
1	1	10	90	12	80
2	1	0	70	10	70
3	1	0	60	9	60
4	1	0	40	5	40

Note: L = program level; SDIP = starting day in program; LDIP = lesson day in program.

Figure 10–3. Sample Biweekly Report of Lessons Taught

1. Here's the rule for this game: Every glass has a ball inside it. Circle each object that you *know* has a ball inside it.

2. What tool do we use to measure temperature? (Circle the answer.)

        yardstick   degree   thermometer   odometer

3. What are some of the things that cavemen did *not* have? (Underline the answers.)

        streets   trees   cars   rocks

4. What was Henry Ford's idea for manufacturing cars? (circle the answer.)

    To finish making one car before starting to make another car

    To make parts that would fit any other car he built.

    To make cars that cost a lot of money.

5. Look at the list below. Put an X in front of every object made by people.

    _____ grass
    _____ television
    _____ shoe
    _____ elephant

6. a. Does a molecule of water look the same as a molecule of steam?

   b. Does a molecule of water look the same as a molecule of rubber?

7. What did the enemy army build to help them get inside Troy?

Figure 10–4. Example of an Intructionally Referenced Test (Third-Grade Reading)

Tests of this sort allow for a precise diagnosis of what has been taught and specification of a group's deficiencies. The scores of individual students are reported on a group summary form (see figure 10–5). When it is noted that several students missed items 3, 5, and 6, remediation directions have the teacher reteach these tasks in the program. After a few days of remedial instruction, the students are retested. The continuous progress test scores also alert teachers and supervisors to individual students who are in trouble.

Circle one:

Reading I, II, III
Arithmetic I, II, III
Language I, II, III

Test Section	8
Lesson Number	82
Group	II
Teacher	Voltaire
Date	12/7/80

| | Items | | | | | | | | | | |
Names	1	2	3	4	5	6	7	8	9	10	Percentage Passed
1. Seymour	+	+	−	+	+	+	+				86
2. Lou	+	+	+	+	−	−	+				72
3. Renata	+	+	−	+	+	−	+				72
4. Yolanda	+	+	+	+	−	+	+				86
5. Xavier	+	+	−	−	−	−	+				43
6. Fred	+	−	−	+	+	−	−				43
7.											
8.											
9.											
10.											
Percentage passed	100	84	33	84	50	33	84				

Figure 10–5. Sample Group Summary Form for Instructionally Referenced Test

Reports of content covered and level-of-mastery tests allow supervisors to form hypotheses about which students need remediation and which skills should be retaught to a group as well as about whether individual students should be placed in a slower-paced or a more-advanced group. The supervisors can also form hypotheses about teacher performance. If all students in a group are scoring 100 percent on all the tests, for example, a supervisor might have the teacher go on a skipping schedule so that the students can progress more rapidly through the program. If test scores are low for most students, the supervisor might have the teacher reteach some of the lessons or work on some teaching techniques. In any case, the hypotheses developed while reviewing test results and reports of content covered are verified by direct observation of teachers and students in their classrooms.

Teacher Expectations and Attitudes

Although we agree with the research that maintains that high expectations for all students is a key component of an effective schoolwide reading program, we found that expectations alone are unlikely to improve reading scores reliably. Our experience is that when teachers see high-risk children reading better than the teachers believed possible, their expectations rise. Modeling of effective teaching and management techniques by a supervisor appears to be a realistic way of increasing teacher expectations.

In a description of the evolution of teachers' attitudes toward the Direct Instruction Model during the course of an implementation mandated by court order, Cronin (1980) reported that most of the teachers initially disliked several features of the model. At the beginning of the school year, they disliked using instructional "scripts." They also disliked having virtually no say concerning either the choice of curriculum or how they were to present the curriculum to their students. Many of the teachers reported that they were embarrassed and felt uncomfortable about being observed by supervisors on a weekly basis and being given specific assignments for improvement. After six months, however, the teachers reported that their students were reading at a level they had thought unimaginable for inner-city minority students; the teachers' attitudes toward the direct instruction procedures changed dramatically. To many, the supervision was seen as the most positive aspect of the model. Lortie (1975), Guskey (1982), and Berman and McLaughlin (Note 11) also have reported studies on the relationship between student success and teachers' professional satisfaction.

Conclusion

In our view, one immediate need in education is a relatively objective system for improving instruction. The combination of a detailed procedure for helping teachers in classrooms with a system for monitoring student performance appears to be an effective way to solve the problems of improving reading instruction and raising teacher expectations of students.

A larger problem is getting educators to make changes. It can be difficult for staff members in schools to make the painful admission that things are not as they should be and that teachers and administrators have not been properly prepared to work with children who are having trouble learning to read. Addressing the problem also involves doing some painstaking evaluations of curricular programs. Schoolwide changes imply a great deal of grueling but ultimately satisfying work. Our experience has been that such work is facilitated by providing teachers with materials that emphasize clear instructional communication and by having supervisors who take an active and effective role in the classrooms.

Reference Notes

1. Carnine, D., & Gersten, R. *Direct instruction analysis of reading.* Unpublished manuscript, University of Oregon, 1983.

2. Rosenshine, B. *Direct instruction for skill mastery.* Paper presented at the Learning Research and Development Center, University of Pittsburgh, 1980.

3. Gersten, R., Carnine, D., Zoref, L., & Cronin, D. *Multi-faceted study of implementation of educational change effort in inner city schools.* Paper presented at the annual meeting of the American Educational Research Association, Montreal, April 1983.

4. Mason, J. *Acquisition of knowledge about reading: The preschool period* (Tech. Rep. No. 267). Urbana: University of Illinois, Center for the Study of Reading, December 1982.

5. Osborn, J. *The purposes, uses and contents of workbooks and some guidelines for publishers* (Reading Education Rep. No. 27). Urbana: University of Illinois, Center for the Study of Reading, 1981.

6. Engelmann, S., & Steeley, D. *Implementation of basal reading in grades 4-6.* Unpublished manuscript, Engelmann-Becker Corporation, Eugene, Oregon, 1980.

7. Pearson, P.D. *A context for instructional research on reading comprehension* (Tech. Rep. No. 230). Urbana: University of Illinois, Center for the Study of Reading, 1982.

8. Carnine, D.W. *Barriers to increasing student achievement: What they are, where they come from, and some thoughts on how they can be overcome.* Unpublished manuscript, University of Oregon, 1981.

9. Joyce, B.R., & Showers, B. *Teacher training research: Working hypotheses for program design and directions for further study.* Paper presented at the annual meeting of the American Educational Research Association, Los Angeles, April 1981.

10. Bredo, A.E. *Principal-teacher influence relations in elementary schools.* Paper presented at the annual meeting of the American Educational Research Association, New York, April 1977.

11. Berman, P.M., & McLaughlin, M.W. *Federal programs supporting educational change: Factors affecting implementation and continuation* (R-1589/7-HEW). Santa Monica, Calif.: Rand Corporation, 1978.

12. Becker, W.C. & Engelmann, S. *Analysis of achievement data of University of Oregon Direct Instruction Follow Through,* Technical Report 76-1. Eugene, Oregon, 1976.

References

Adams, A., Carnine, D., & Gersten, R. Instructional strategies for studying content area texts in the intermediate grades. *Reading Research Quarterly,* 1982, *18,* 27–55.

Anderson, L.M., Evertson, C.M., & Brophy, J.E. An experimental study of effective teaching in first grade reading groups. *Elementary School Journal,* 1979, *79,* 193–223.

Baker, E.L., Herman, J.H., & Yeh, J.P. Fun and games: Their contribution to basic skills instruction in elementary schools. *American Educational Research Journal,* 1981, *18,* 83–92.

Beck, I.L. Developing comprehension: The impact of the directed reading lesson. In R. Anderson, J. Osborn, & R. Tierney (Eds.), *Learning to read in American schools: Basal readers and content texts.* Urbana: University of Illinois, Center for the Study of Reading, 1981.

Berman, P., & McLaughlin, M.W. *Federal programs supporting educational change—Vol. IV: The findings in review.* Santa Monica, Calif.: Rand Corporation, 1975.

Brookover, W.B., Beady, C.H., Flood, P.K., Schweitzer, J., & Wisenbaker, J. *School social systems and student achievement: Schools can make a difference.* East Lansing: Michigan State University, College of Urban Development, 1979.

Brophy, J.E., & Evertson, C.M. *Learning from teaching: A developmental perspective.* Boston: Allyn and Bacon, 1976.

Cooley, W.W., & Leinhardt, G. The instructional dimensions study. *Education Evaluation and Policy Analysis,* 1980, *2,* 7–25.

Cronin, D.P. *Implementation study, year 2: Instructional staff interviews.* Los Altos, Calif.: John Emrick and Associates, 1980.

Durkin, D. Do basal reader manuals provide for reading comprehension instruction? In R. Anderson, J. Osborn, & R. Tierney (Eds.), *Learning to read in American schools: Basal readers and content texts.* Urbana: University of Illinois, Center for the Study of Reading, 1981.

Edmonds, R. Effective schools for the urban poor. *Educational Leadership,* 1979, *37,* 15–24.

Fisher, C.W., Berliner, D.C., Filby, N.N., Marliave, R., Cahen, L.S., & Dishaw, M.M. Teaching behaviors, academic learning time and student achievement: An overview. In C. Denham & A. Lieberman (Eds.), *Time to learn.* Washington, D.C.: U.S. Office of Education, National Institute of Education, 1980.

Fullan, M. Research on the implementation of educational change. In R. Corwin (Ed.), *Research on organizational issues in education.* Greenwich, Conn.: JAI Press, 1980.

Gersten, R., Carnine, D., & Williams, P. Measuring implementation of a structured educational model in an urban setting: An observational approach. *Educational Evaluation and Policy Analysis,* 1982, *4*(1), 67–79.

Good, T.L., & Beckerman, T.M. Time on task: A naturalistic study in sixth grade classrooms. *Elementary School Journal,* 1978, *78,* 193–201.

Guskey, T.R. The effects of change in instructional effectiveness on the relationship of teacher expectations and student achievement. *Journal of Educational Research,* 1982, *6,* 345–349.

Haney, W. *A technical history of the national Follow Through evaluation.* Cambridge, Mass.: Huron Institute, August 1977.

House, E.R., Glass, G.V. McLean, L.D., & Walker, D.F. No simple answer: Critique of the "Follow Through" evaluation. *Harvard Educational Review,* 1978, *28,* 128–160.

Jastak, J.F., & Jastak, S.R. *The wide range achievement test.* Wilmington: Guidance Associates of Delaware, 1965.

Jenkins, J.R., & Heliotis, J.G. Reading comprehension instruction: Findings from behavioral and cognitive psychology. *Topics in Language Disorders,* 1981, *1,* 25–41.

Jenkins, J.R., & Pany, D. Research on teaching reading comprehension: Instructional variables. In J. Guthrie (Ed.), *Reading comprehension and education.* Newark, Del.: International Reading Association, 1981.

Kameenui, E., Carnine, D.W., & Maggs, A. Instructional procedures for teaching reversible passive voice and clause construction to three mildly handicapped children. *Exceptional Child,* 1980, *27*(1), 29–40.

Leinhardt, G., Zigmond, N., & Cooley, W.W. Reading instruction and its effects. *American Educational Research Journal,* 1981, *18,* 343–361.

Lortie, D.C. *Schoolteacher.* Chicago: University of Chicago Press, 1975.

Patching, W., Kameenui, E., Carnine, D., Gersten, R., & Colvin, G. Direct instruction in critical reading. *Reading Research Quarterly,* 1983, *18*(4), 406–418.

Peterson, S.M. *Implementation study, year 2: Results from administration of pre-stages of concern questionnaire.* Los Altos, Calif.: John Emrick and Associates, 1980.

Rosenshine, B. Classroom instruction. In N.L. Gage (Ed.), *Psychology of teaching: The 77th Yearbook of the National Society for the Study of Education.* Chicago: National Society for the Study of Education, 1976.

Singer, H., & Balow, I. Overcoming educational disadvantagedness. In J.T. Guthrie (Ed.), *Comprehension and teaching: Research reviews.* Newark, Del.: International Reading Association, 1981.

Stallings, J. Implementation and child effects of teaching practices in Follow Through classrooms. *Monographs of the Society for Research in Child Development,* 1975, *40* (7-8, Serial No. 163).

Stallings, J.A. Allocated academic learning time revisited, or beyond time on task. *Education Research,* 1980, *9,* 11–16.

Stallings, J.A., & Kaskowitz, D. *Follow Through classroom observation evaluation, 1972–73.* Menlo Park, Calif.: Stanford Research Institute, 1974.

Stebbins, L.B., St. Pierre, R.G., Proper, E.C., Anderson, R.B., & Cerva, T.R. *Education as experimentation: A planned variation model, Vol. IV. An evaluation of Follow Through.* Cambridge, Mass.: Abt Associates, 1977.

11

Can Minimum Competency Tests Have a Positive Impact on Education?

Roger Farr

The minimum competency movement has grown out of concern that all citizens be educated sufficiently for playing a successful role in society. Concern for education has been fired by more than a complex about our relatively youthful experience as a nation. We have a much more idealistic commitment to educating our citizens and making them literate than most nations. In much of the world, education is a privilege—not a right.

Since the time of Thomas Jefferson, who saw education as a means of equalizing opportunity and maintaining democracy, educating all citizens has been viewed as a societal obligation in the United States. We have developed one of the few comprehensive public educational systems in the world. That development has never been inexpensive, and, consequently, Americans have always been concerned about their investment in education.

The return on the investment has been substantial: there are now data to indicate that, beyond the physically and mentally incapacitated, fewer than 1 percent of Americans are illiterate (Cook, 1977; Fisher, 1978). The ongoing research of the National Assessment of Educational Progress (NAEP) (Brown, 1981) shows encouraging gains in reading by 9-year-olds between 1971 and 1980—particularly by black students. Other related indicators are also impressive:

1. In a 40-year span (1941–1981), our college population increased 733 percent, while our total population increased 72 percent ("How U.S. Has Changed," 1981).
2. Between 1950 and 1980, the average grade level completed by a U.S. citizen rose from 9.8 to 12.5 (*The American High School*, 1980).
3. Between 1976 and 1980, the percentage of U.S. children in school rose from 89 to 96.8 (*The American High School*, 1980).
4. Between 1962 and 1979, the percentage of U.S. students completing high school rose from 64.2 to 74.3 (*The American High School*, 1980).

The forces now having an impact on the schools are without historical precedent. In fact, the problems school organizations confront and the manner in which the organizations are governed has led to a "new sociology" of education. This new sociology has raised questions about a number of issues, including how policy choices are made, how goals and objectives are formulated, how courses of action are implemented, how resources are allocated, how organizational structures are established, who controls the decision-making process, and, finally, how evaluation procedures (such as minimum competency testing) are articulated, executed, and utilized.

In response to forces seeking accountability, many states have enacted legislation calling for some sort of minimum competency testing programs. The concept is not new. Jaeger (1982) cites precedents in Boston and New York more than 100 years ago. By 1978, the number of states with such legislation had jumped to thirty-five or more, depending on the survey used as a source. Eighteen states use the tests to determine eligibility for high school graduation (McCarthy, Note 1). In other states, minimum competency test scores determine whether children are promoted from grade to grade.

Even as the number of states with minimum competency legislation was increasing, some state legislators had begun showing signs of disenchantment (Clague, 1979), and educators at all levels were questioning the movement. Various other groups—some representing minorities—and individuals were challenging minimum competency testing programs in the courts (Neill, 1979). While the debate and controversy over the effectiveness of these programs rages in professional journals, as well as in the public media, the general public consensus seems to be that the testing programs are a good idea because they establish at least some form of accountability.

Test Score Declines

A related influence on minimum competency programs is the general belief that the schools are disgorging millions of illiterate young people each year and that these young people possess high school diplomas that are worthless pieces of paper. More importantly, the public seems to believe that students are being deprived of an education sufficient to permit them to function successfully in the job market and in the general society.

This broad public belief is strongly reinforced by a number of popular writers who have been overwhelmingly negative about the accomplishments of the schools. Armbruster (1977) wrote that, although the United States spent more on education than on defense in 1976, "the more the parents have spent on schools, the less their children have learned" (p. 55). Marvin Stone (1981) also sounds a note of gloom, predicting that the increasing proportion of illiterates in the U.S. population "could bring about a cleavage in society that carries with it the seeds of great tragedy" (p. 76). During the past fifteen years, these sentiments have been fed by reports of declining test scores. A close look at those declines as indicators reveals the following, however:

1. As far as basic literacy is concerned, the test performance of our nation's children is not declining but is improving—as it has continually throughout the history of our country (Farr & Fay, 1982).
2. The real concern about declining ability among our youth should be focused on levels of comprehension that far exceed anything that could be called basic or minimal (Farr & Olshavsky, 1980).
3. Our valid concern for developing readers who are better reasoners and thinkers needs to be tempered by a full understanding of factors that considerably qualify the score declines; for example, the American determination to make higher education more accessible has led to more students taking college entrance exams.

By the 1960s, data produced by tests were held in such high regard that the public tended to look on tests as absolute evaluations rather than as the limited indicators they are. The public ignored other encouraging indicators, however, such as the schooling levels completed, the number of children staying in school, and the fact that book publishing, lending, and reading had mushroomed during the years of the score declines (Cole & Gold, 1979). In addition, encouraging data about basic literacy were ignored as we correlated our concern for basic literacy to data produced on tests measuring relatively high levels of reading comprehension.

Thus, the critics have been saying that scores produced by such tests as the Scholastic Aptitude Test (SAT) announce our schools' failure to teach basic or minimum literacy; and we have hurriedly established accountability programs to attempt to ensure that such literacy is developed. Our rush to do this endorses our mistaken faith in tests as a complete evaluation technique, and it may also relate to our tendency to covet European educational systems. In many countries, national qualifying exams traditionally have selected those whose tested intelligence and aptitude qualify them for higher levels of education; this selection process begins in the primary grades. We have once again confused our Jeffersonian goal with elitist systems and lumped functional literacy with higher levels of comprehension.

Some Unanswered Questions

Are the score declines on the tests that measure the highest and most sophisticated types of comprehension a valid rationale for the minimum competency movement? Can such tests help produce Americans who are more critical, careful readers— readers who can identify and respond to nuance, mood, and tone and who can spot a strong or weak argument when they read? There are many similar questions that ought to be answered if the minimum competency movement is to have any positive impact on education in this country. The most important of these questions include the following:

1. Is it necessary to test millions of children who are observed daily in the classroom to identify those very few who cannot read well?
2. How are the minimum levels of tests determined? How closely do they match the curricula? Is the minimum competency movement changing curricula in any significant way? If so, is designing curricula to conform to the tests what we really want or ought to be doing?
3. Can minimum competency tests actually evaluate the reading act, which theorists are just now beginning to define convincingly (Johnston, Note 2)?
4. Other than determining which children will repeat instruction (that is, will fail the test), can minimum competency testing produce information that teachers can apply to specific instruction? Can such tests yield other than gross distinctions? Are minimum competency data used often as diagnostic guides? Do teachers find the data useful?
5. How autocratic are the data being produced by minimum competency testing in educational decision making? Are these data a contributing indication in a broader evaluation program that incorporates assessment of teacher judgment and other tests? What impact, if any, has the minimum competency movement had on other kinds of educational evaluation?

Where Are We Headed?

We cannot be sure where the movement is going next. The minimum competency movement might gain more strength as federal support of education decreases and each state seeks more educational accountability. As the federal influence diminishes, however, the states might feel more relaxed about the evaluation regulations that grew, in part, from the federal education legislation of the 1960s and 1970s.

There are important reasons that the topic of minimum competency testing should be of prime concern to us. At present, minimum competency testing is legislated in a majority of states, and such legislation may ensure the retention of such programs for years to come. Educators must try to influence developments so that minimum competency programs accomplish worthwhile ends for education. In discussing the future of minimum competency testing, Clague, (1979) said: "Minimum competency testing is not a dead horse, but it may become, during the course of its grooming, a horse of a different and more healthy color" (p. 509).

Current minimum competency programs may leave a great deal to be desired. It would be foolish and inaccurate, however, to suggest that those who have promoted their development have had as their goal the destruction of public education or the reestablishment of an elitist school system of the type that offended

Thomas Jefferson. The reality of the situation requires that we accept the competency movement as a sincere effort to improve education and to provide a yardstick that will enable the general public to understand the accomplishments of the schools. To accomplish these ends, educators must look more carefully at some of the issues of the minimum competency movement.

Minimum Competency Testing Should Be One Instructional Tool in Complete Assessment

The two most general uses of minimum competency testing are for promotion denial and for remedial assignment (Jaeger, 1982). The charge that both of these uses are misuses is valid if the tests are used as the sole determiner of whether a student fails or is to be given special instruction. Whether these tests can do more—that is, whether they can diagnose reading weaknesses and strengths and inform instruction—is contingent on test construction, on the state of the art of reading research and theory, and on the state of the art in responding to that theory and research (Farr & Tone, 1982; Johnston, Note 2).

Minimum Competency Testing Should Be an Instructional Aid—Not a Punishment

Common sense should tell us that it is illogical to ignore all the information available from educating a child for 12 years and rely on an hour or two of assessment. That is exactly what is done by a program in which a single test determines whether or not a student will be graduated from high school.

If educational decisions are made on the basis of a test, we turn our backs on teacher expertise as though it were far less trustworthy than a test designed by individuals who have never met the student and are unlikely to have visited—let alone lived in—the particular environment in which the child will have to succeed.

Teacher observation allows evaluative judgment that is highly sensitive to a wide range of abilities that no battery of tests—and certainly no single test—can cover. Teacher observation ought to be able to report on the application of any competencies measured by a test in thousands of instances—not on just a very limited set of items. In the case of reading, observation is the only method of determining how a student actually uses what is read and comprehended.

The public needs to be educated regarding both the limitations of testing and the value of evaluation that incorporates relevant information of all types. This educational process should involve a systematized evaluation program that can be fully described, explained, and rationalized—one in which specific procedures depict the exact point at which test data are produced and incorporated in decision making that affects the individual student. When teacher judgments and a test score are not in agreement (which will be about 15 to 30 percent of the time, according to studies), the procedure can require that teachers examine and delineate the reasons for the discrepancy.

In such an analysis, minimum competency testing could lead to either reaffirmation of instructional priorities or recommendations that they change. In this way, even a test that is highly insensitive to the specifics of a student's performance (as many minimum competency tests are) could direct teachers to use other, more specifically focused formal tests and informal assessment techniques, including observation, to identify instruction that the test can only indicate might be needed.

Since minimum competency tests seem to have as their goal the identification of the poorest readers, it seems a waste of student and teacher time, as well as money, to administer such tests to all students. Classroom observations, and the results of studies, indicate that teachers or other school staff can quickly and easily identify the poorest readers in a classroom or in a school. More important, teachers can provide specific information about the materials that students can be expected to read. It should be possible for teachers to identify large numbers of students who do not need to take a test. The implementation of this recommendation could save many dollars and much time in minimum competency programs now in existence.

Using minimum competency testing as one, but not the only, indicator in a diagnostic evaluation program requires that the test be given in time for remediation to take place. This means testing while instruction is in process—not at the end of the semester or the year. It means pinpointing specific competencies to reinstruct, not forcing a child to repeat a whole semester's or year's unit, which surely includes material he or she has already mastered. It means not using minimum competency programs as punishment.

As an instrument of denial, the minimum competency test is a form of threatened punishment that intimidates the student to study harder. If the rash of criticism of our schools is valid, the use of minimum competency testing to deny success to a student is clearly an attempt to blame—not help—the victim, as many critics of such programs have noted.

Jaeger (1982) discusses how the movement could shift the burden from the child to the schools:

> The mere existence of competency testing programs might satisfy the public desire for educational accountability—at least for a time. And, since failing a competency test is most often treated as a student's problem, and not the school's problem, teachers are further relieved of responsibility. It is not surprising that teachers might welcome a lowering, or at least a redirection of the heat. (pp. 238, 239)

Minimum Competency Testing Is Inadequate as the Sole Determiner for Remedial Instruction

The use of minimum competency testing to determine remedial assignments is equally subject to concern. Responsible schools use whole batteries of tests to make such determinations. School psychometricians are aware that test results are but one piece of information to use in evaluating students. To assume that the results of a competency test can stand alone to direct remedial assignment is naive if not ludicrous.

Another Limitation in Using Minimimum Competency Tests

There is another point that stresses the folly of using a single test as the sole basis for an educational decision. The absolute criterion scores produced by minimum competency tests promote their most serious misuse. A single standard for all pupils does not make educational sense and flies in the face of all we have learned about child development. The setting of criterion levels is arbitrary, since we have no clear notion of what it means to be minimally competent as a reader in a diverse society.

In his recent book, *The Mismeasure of Man*, Stephen Gould (1981) debunks much of the so-called scientific effort to measure human intelligence. Gould does not call for the banning of IQ tests; he sees them as tools that may help us understand human behavior. Neither should reading tests be banned, but we do need to see them for what they are—additions to the ongoing evaluation techniques of teachers. A position taken by the International Reading Association regarding the use of minimum competency tests is a reasoned and useful guide for the use of such tests (IRA Board, 1981):

> No single measure or method of assessment of minimum competencies should ever be the sole criteria for graduation or promotion of a student. Multiple indices assessed through a variety of means, including teacher observation, student work samples, past academic performance, and student self-reports, should be employed to assess competence.

> Furthermore, every effort should be made through every possible means to remediate weaknesses diagnosed through tests. Retention in grade or non-promotion of a student should be considered as only one alternative means of remediation and one that should be considered only when all other available methods have failed.

How One State Has Built Its Accountability Program

In Indiana, the statewide accountability program is the Comprehensive Assessment and Program Planning System (CAPPS). This program is significant because it stands in stark contrast to testing-only programs. The CAPPS program is a broad and encompassing approach to assist local school corporations in planning and evaluating their own educational programs.

The CAPPS program is an attempt to ensure that each school district reviews its present educational programs; utilizes school personnel at all levels (as well as representatives from the community) to set goals and objectives; engages in in-depth needs assessment and pupil diagnosis; selects instructional strategies that include teaching/learning activities, educational materials, and teacher in-service; and reports on these activities to the state and to the local community on a regular basis. All school corporations do not set the same goals or use the same instructional strategies, but each school corporation must demonstrate how it is holding itself accountable to students, parents, and the citizenry.

The CAPPS program accommodates a variety of assessment tools within and across local educational settings. It allows for flexibility in the interpretation of instructional methods and the selection of materials. In essence, the rationale behind the CAPPS program promulgates the belief that local school corporations can best deliver educational services to their individual constituencies if they develop a framework for identifying and evaluating local priorities.

The challenge to Indiana educators to convince the public that they have an exemplary accountability system is partially solved by the system's involvement of public representatives at the local level. This involvement reminds the public that the responsibility for promoting a literate citizenry belongs to the public at large. Accountability must include a study of the effort that society is making to provide adequate educational programs.

Minimal Assessment Tests That Profess to Assess Reading Should Attempt to Report on the Reading Process

Regardless of how effective other evaluation techniques in an accountability program are, the minimum competency test should attempt to be the most valid assessment of reading that we are capable of developing. The continuing quest for a definition of functional literacy that will determine minimal levels for survival in society is a misguided effort. We have ample evidence that the relationship between a specific level or type of literacy and life success is not great (Eckland, 1980). Conversely, failure on a minimum competency test does not necessarily imply that a student lacks the skills to survive or function.

How minimal should a minimum competency measure of reading be? The minimum competency movement has sometimes been associated with the most reactionary elements of the "back-to-basics" crusades. If such a measure is limited to decoding skills that never rise to the meaning of text, how can it indicate in any way whether the student who takes it is going to be able to understand actual tasks? As Jaeger (1982) puts it:

> It is widely accepted by curriculum theorists, if not by constructors of minimum competency tests, that a curriculum consisting solely of language mechanics . . . cannot produce functionally literate high school graduates, for the term itself suggests the ability to succeed with the language demands of the adult world.

Furthermore, to focus on the most minimal reading comprehension skills may be so inefficient as to be detrimental to the improvement of education. Amarel

(1980) suggests that students' inability to master language mechanics is not the cause of functional illiteracy; rather, their problem is their inability to comprehend—to recover and reconstruct meaning that is embedded in text. She also suggests that if teachers are limited by accountability to teaching mainly the mechanics, they cannot teach students to comprehend.

The minimum competency tests that have been developed thus far focus on minimal literal comprehension and word recognition skills—precisely those aspects of reading instruction for which we have observed continuous improvement. Indeed, those aspects of reading are the skills being assessed on minimum competency tests. This suggests that if we focus the skill requirements low enough on such measures, we can guarantee student success and assure that the testing program is nothing but a political exercise and a waste of time.

The problem with this emphasis is that it detracts from the very area of reading instruction that the national tests have identified as a problem—reading comprehension and particularly the higher reading/thinking abilities. In fact, as Amarel (1980) suggests, the emphasis in the lower grades on the teaching of word recognition skills and the neglect of the teaching of reading comprehension may explain the declines that are suggested by the reading comprehension scores at the upper grade levels. Research by Durkin (1978–79) clearly demonstrates that the teaching of reading comprehension is currently being neglected.

This discussion leads to an all-important consideration of the potential impact of the minimum competency phenomenon on the curricula of our schools. When students fail the tests, the school is eventually affected by that failure as teachers reorganize their instruction to correspond with what is on the test to guarantee future student success.

One might say that that is exactly what we want to happen, but is it? Can such a test even begin to measure all we want to teach? Conceivably, teachers could accept the test as the sole measure of their accountability—especially if that is the way the public sees it. Then the limitations of what the test can and does measure would become the curriculum itself. We can expect a startling decline in SAT scores if that were to happen!

Meanwhile, there is no question that the existence of a set of minimal reading skills on a mandated state test could become the driving force behind the curriculum. Instructional programs could be developed to help students score better on the tests. So long as a skill is tested, there will exist a rationale for drilling on that skill—whether or not the skill helps a student become a better reader. The school may then continue to neglect the teaching of reading comprehension to develop critical readers and thinkers.

The ultimate consequence for the reading curriculum, when mere drill of basic reading skills becomes the major focus, would be that teachers would no longer be able to deal with ideas in reading or to develop critical readers. Surely, students would become convinced that reading is a tedious and useless activity.

What we are learning from the emerging psychological model of reading indicates that reading is much more than isolated basic skills. Once we determine what processes make up the reading act and how they interact, we have much work to do to develop tests that measure the processes in ways that will provide teachers with instructional information (Farr & Tone, 1982; Johnston, Note 2). It bears repeating that no matter how good the tests become, we must understand—and help the public understand—that tests can never be the final word in a responsible educational evaluation program.

Reference Notes

1. McCarthy, M.M. *Report on research to the H.L. Smith conference on research in education.* Bloomington: Indiana University, School of Education, 1982.
2. Johnston, P. *Implications of basic research for the assessment of reading comprehension* (Tech. Rep. No. 206). Urbana: University of Illinois, Center for the Study of Reading, 1981.

References

Amarel, M. Comments on H. Brundy's "Impact of minimum competency testing on curriculum." In R.M. Jaeger & C.K. Tittle (Eds.), *Minimum competency achievement testing: Motives, models, measures, and consequences.* Berkeley, Calif.: McCutchan, 1980.

The American High School: A Statistical Overview. Washington, D.C.: National Center for Education Statistics, 1980.

Armbruster, F.E. What's wrong with our schools? *Sunday Herald-Times* (Syndicated column). Bloomington/Bedford, Ind., September 18, 1977, 49, 55.

Brown, R. *Literacy in America: A synopsis of national assessment findings.* Denver: National Assessment of Educational Progress, 1981.

Cole, J.Y., & Gold, C.S. *Reading in America 1978.* Washington, D.C.: Library of Congress, 1979.

Clague, M.W. Competency testing and potential constitutional challenges of "Everystudent." *Catholic University of America Law Review,* Summer 1979, *28*(3), 469–509.

Cook, W.D. *Adult literacy education in the United States.* Newark, Del.: International Reading Association, 1977.

Durkin, D. What classroom observations reveal about reading comprehension instruction. *Reading Research Quarterly,* 1978–79, *14*(4), 481–533.

Eckland, B.K. Sociodemographic implications of minimum competency testing. In R.M. Jaeger & C.K. Tittle (Eds.), *Minimum competency achievement testing: Motives, models, measures, and consequences.* Berkeley, Calif.: McCutchan, 1980.

Farr, R., & Fay, L. Reading trend data in the United States: A mandate for caveats and caution. In G.R. Austin & H. Garber (Eds.), *The rise and fall of national test scores.* New York: Academic Press, 1982.

Farr, R., & Olshavsky, J.E. Is minimum competency testing the appropriate solution to the SAT decline? *Phi Delta Kappan,* April 1980, *61*(8), 528–529.

Farr, R., & Tone, B. *Text analysis and validated modeling of the reading process (1973–1981): Implications for reading assessment.* Washington, D.C.: National Institute of Education, 1982.

Fisher, D.L. *Functional literacy and the schools.* Washington, D.C.: U.S. Department of Health, Education and Welfare and National Institute of Education, 1978.

Gould, S.J. *The mismeasure of man.* New York: Norton, 1981.

How U.S. has changed in four decades. *U.S. News & World Report,* December 7, 1981, 52–53.

IRA Board. *Positions statement. Minimum Competency in Reading.* Newark, Del.: International Reading Association, 1981.

Jaeger, R.M. The final hurdle: Minimum competency achievement testing. In G.R. Austin & H. Garber (Eds.), *The rise and fall of national test scores.* New York: Academic Press, 1982.

Neill, S.B. A summary of issues in the minimum competency movement. *Phi Delta Kappan,* February 1979, *60,* 452–453.

Stone, M. Soon, a nation of illiterates? *U.S. News & World Report,* September 7, 1981, p. 76.

12
The Representation of Reading Instruction

Richard Venezky

For more than 150 years, American educators and psychologists have attempted to describe reading instruction. The Reverend Burton (1833) for example, expressed in narrative form the ABC method as he recalled it from his childhood. Horace Mann (1950), writing in 1844, also used narrative form to describe the steps in a reading lesson he had observed the summer before in a Prussian school. Narrative representations such as these continued to be the main vehicle for instructional descriptions until after World War II, when the study of reading instruction began to focus on a wider range of instructional variables than just teacher-directed activities.

Beginning in the early 1960s with the educational technology movement, more systematic and more formal representation schemes were designed (Romiszowski, 1981). Through the work of Gilbert (1961, 1967) in England, Landa (1974) in Russia, and Gagne and his colleagues in the United States (Gagne, 1968; Gagne & Briggs, 1974), a variety of techniques were developed for analyzing and representing instruction. These techniques generally followed a common process model for instructional design. This model, as defined recently by Briggs and Wager (1981), has the following initial steps:

1. State objectives and performance standards.
2. Develop tests for these objectives.
3. Analyze objectives for structure and sequence.
4. Identify students' entry-level abilities.
5. Prepare pretests and remedial instruction.
6. Select media and write prescriptions.
7. Develop first-draft materials.

Initially, the structure of a knowledge or skill domain for step 3 was represented by tree structures (Gibbons, 1971) and related hierarchical displays (Gagne & Briggs, 1974). These are more efficient representations than narratives or tables for complex data sets, yet by themselves they are not totally adequate for representing all phases in the design and implementation of reading instruction.

Consider, as an example, the logical processes involved in planning instruction for decoding skills in a basal reading program. First, a reasonably complete list of decoding skills is developed. Then, the interdependencies among the skills are defined and a subset selected for instruction, based on a variety of criteria and constraints (for example, reading selection vocabulary, time allocated for skill lessons, instructional strategies).

Then, however, based on task analyses for each skill, further decisions need to be made, including definition of prerequisites, lesson steps, and teaching approaches. Finally, review, assessment, and maintenance are planned and the entire sequence is integrated with other skill sequences and mapped onto physical components (pupil book, teacher's guide, supplementary materials, and tests). The types of information that must be represented vary from stage to stage of the planning process. Lists may be adequate for the initial choice of skills to teach, but even tree diagrams are inadequate for clearly delineating interrelationships among skills so that, for example, prerequisites can be easily determined. A different representation scheme is needed for scanning lesson sequences to determine the adequacy of practice and review lessons. The issue here, however, is not simply one of representation of lesson sequences; communication is involved, in that the manner of representation for a curriculum determines how easily teachers, evaluators, and designers can deal with the details of the instructional plan, either for fully adapting it for classroom use or for ensuring its integrity. Romiszowski (1981) remarks: "A visual representation of the structure [of a subject] is an aid both to the analysis of complex subject matter and to the communication of what is worth teaching and learning (to other teachers and also to students)" (p. 133).

How to define and represent a curriculum systematically is the primary goal of the work reported here. In the sections that follow, the motivations for structured or formal descriptions of instruction are defined. A sketch is presented of instructional design and implementation, and a scheme for representing the content of instruction and the anatomy of lessons is proposed and explained. The reader should be aware, however, that what is presented here does not attend to the entire span of instructional representation; rather, it involves the underlying structure of the knowledge base from which instruction is planned and the anatomical features of instructional methodology.

The Need for Instructional Representation

The intent of this chapter is to define a systematic organization and representation for the major steps in planning reading instruction. The scope of this foray into visual communication extends from the listing of instructional goals for a curriculum to the specification of steps within a lesson for accomplishing these goals. Included between these endpoints are all of the topic and skill relationships that are relevant to the curriculum, the definition of instructional methods, and the specification of physical components for conveying a logical structure thus defined. Although the perspective here is that of the curriculum designer, the intent is to evolve a representation scheme that would also serve the needs of someone who might need to analyze and evaluate instruction for educational or legal ends.

The primary motivation for this work is the need to provide a systematic procedure for planning curricula that contain large numbers of skills and topics and then representing these curricula in a manner that makes them accessible for evaluation by a wide range of people. Reading programs typically are planned and written by specialists who contribute selected portions to the whole program. To ensure that everyone's task is properly specified and that all skill introductions, practices, assessments, and reviews are properly placed and correctly written is an enormous task. The task of evaluating a reading program to determine whether it gives adequate coverage to a district's or state's reading objectives is also enormous. At present, the only representations of a program's instructional content are publisher-provided scope and sequence charts. The utility of these charts typically rates somewhere between a stringless bow and a rubber crutch.

A second motivation for this work derives from a recent legal decision involving instruction. A U.S. district court ruled recently that the Florida Department of Education must demonstrate that its schools teach the various skills assessed in the state minimum competency tests (*Debra P.* v. *Turlington*). This case, which centered on the denial of high school diplomas to minority students who failed the tests, has raised an issue that is fundamental to education. In its most unqualified form, this issue is "What is adequate instruction for teaching a specified skill?"

Consider, for example, a ninth-grade English teacher who tells her students at the beginning of each semester that they are responsible for learning, on their own, the meanings of the new vocabulary words they encounter in the text for the course. Assuming that some study methods are suggested and occasional vocabulary tests are given, would such instructional practice qualify as adequate vocabulary instruction in the ninth grade? Would it qualify as such in the sixth grade? Consider a reading program that provides a total of six lessons in grades four through eight in which cause and effect are taught. Assuming that there is excellent instruction in each of these six lessons, plus midyear and end-of-year tests in which cause and effect are assessed, would such a program ensure that most students would be able to recognize cause and effect relationships on a ninth-grade comprehension test?

Educators have developed, mostly by tradition, curricular sequences and time allocations for the teaching of reading skills. If pressed for reasons for these sequences and allocations, however, these educators would probably be no more able to justify them than highway planners could justify driving on the right-hand side of the road. To justify any plan on the grounds that it seems to work is simply to beg the issue; minimum competency testing has arisen because so many students have been failing to learn from current schooling practices. The state of Florida attempted to deny high school diplomas to those who failed to meet minimum standards, but a court has ruled that the state must first show that its schools are meeting minimum instructional standards. This ruling returns us to the questions raised by the two foregoing examples.

To assess instructional adequacy, we must first have clear descriptions of the content, structure, and processes of instruction. These factors do not, by themselves, guarantee answers to the questions raised, but they are essential in any attempt to relate instruction to student outcomes.

Representing a Reading Program

Current design procedures for creating a nationally distributable instructional program generally proceed as follows:

Stage 1: Information is gathered on classroom needs and wants, standardized test objectives, district and state objectives, children's reading interests, and existing program contents. From these sources, possible skills, topics, selections, and instructional approaches are abstracted. Tentative decisions are made on an instructional plan and on program content.

Stage 2: The skills are organized according to topics or strands and then according to their interrelationships. Tentative decisions are made on the physical components of the program (books, chapters, pages), and reading selections are obtained or written and sequenced within books.

Stage 3: The skills are sequenced within books. Skill instruction is planned, and practice, assessment, and review (maintenance) placements are designated.

Stage 4: The lesson structures are designed. Lessons are outlined and written, and art is designed.

Stage 5: The teacher's guide is developed, along with tests, management tools, and supplementary materials.

Stage 6: The various components are evaluated, pilot-tested, revised, and produced.

The representation of information for stage 1 does not pose serious problems. Ordinary lists, outlines, and tables are totally adequate for organizing, analyzing, and communicating at this stage. For stages 2, 3, and 4, however, different schemes are needed. We might assume that a tree diagram would be adequate for organizing skills in stage 2, especially since skills are often designated as hierarchical and trees are convenient devices for representing certain types of hierarchies. Illustrating the assumption that the prerequisites for learning a skill are the skills pointing to it from above, figure 12–1 shows that the idea of a sentence is a prerequisite for learning each of the three sentence types—declarative, interrogative, and imperative—and that knowledge of the sentence types is a prerequisite for learning punctuation. Since, strictly speaking, a tree allows only a single predecessor for each node, relationships in figure 12–1 could not be represented by a tree diagram.

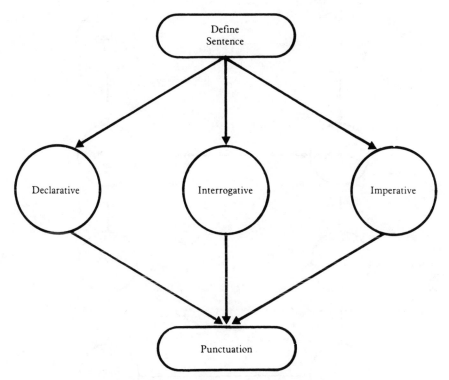

Figure 12-1. A Grammar Sequence

Figure 12-2 also shows where tree diagrams, in the formal sense, are inadequate. A simple sequence of decoding skills is shown on the left side of the figure and a similar sequence of writing skills on the right side. According to the instructional plan represented here, instruction for each letter is to precede introduction of the first decoding pattern involving that letter. The writing strand has both an internal structure, represented as a vertical sequence, and a direct relationship to another strand (decoding) on a one-to-one basis. This pattern also violates the formal definition of a tree.

To overcome the limitations of trees and other strictly hierarchical representation systems, a variety of structures have been borrowed from mathematics and cognitive psychology. Most of these structures have been types of networks or maps, an example of which is shown in figure 12-3. Neil (1970; cited in Romiszowski, 1981) was the first to note the limitations of these newer schemes, particularly their inability to distinguish different types of skill relationships. Neil also expressed a need for construction rules that would encourage "clear visual presentation and organization" of the resulting model.

A formal structure that achieves these goals is a directed graph, which is composed of a finite set of nodes interconnected by arcs. The arcs represent directed

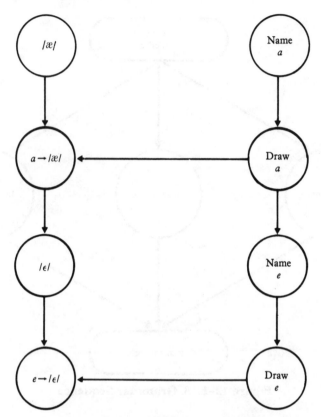

Figure 12-2. A Decoding Sequence

relationships between nodes and may vary according to user definition. Figure 12-4 shows, as an example, a directed graph for a small set of decoding skills. Solid arcs indicate prerequisites that should be taught to all learners, while broken arcs indicate prerequisites that must be taught only to some learners. Through labeled arcs, a rich set of relationships can be portrayed in a relatively uncomplicated manner. Directed graphs are applied in the next section to the representation of information for stage 2, as defined earlier.

Subject and Instructional Networks

The first step in organizing reading skills is to derive one or more subject networks: directed graphs that represent intrinsic skill relationships (skill relationships based on subject matter properties as opposed to instructional decisions). Figure 12-5 shows a subject network for a subset of decoding skills. Depending on its complexity, a subject network might be derived in a general form first, and then one or more nodes would be expanded into more detailed subject networks.

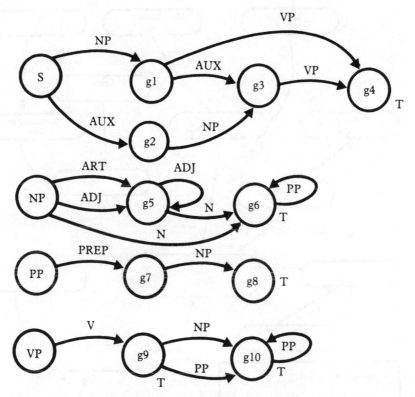

Source: R.F. Simmons, Semantic networks: Their computation and use for understanding English sentences. In R.C. Shank & K.M. Colby (Eds.), *Computer models of thought and language* (San Francisco: Freeman, 1973), p. 83. Reprinted with permission.

Figure 12–3. A Finite State Transition Network for a Simple Grammar

The next step in deriving a formal representation of instruction is to develop an instructional network that defines and links subskills and other prerequisites for each skill identified in the subject network. These subskills represent the instructional steps to be used in teaching each program skill. A skill goal in a study skill subject network might be outlining, for example. In the instructional network, however, outlining might be expanded to the following subskills:

Identifying main topics

Identifying subtopics

Identifying further subtopics

Format mechanics

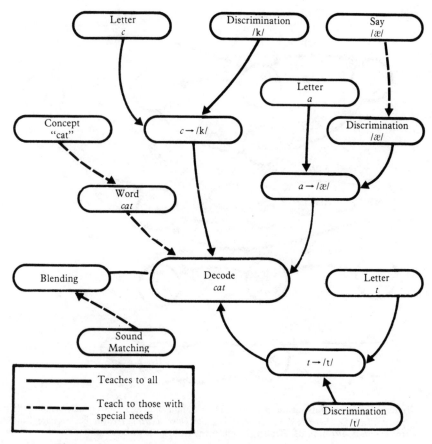

Figure 12–4. A Directed Graph for Decoding *cat*

Furthermore, identifying main topics and identifying subtopics are successor skills to skills associated with finding main ideas and supporting details in a comprehension strand, and format and mechanics is a successor skill to various punctuation and capitalization skills.

What is crucial to an instructional network, and what distinguishes it from a subject network, is the inclusion of instructional decisions. This requires, of course, that a full instructional plan, including treatment of specific topics, be developed along with the subject network.

Typically, the subskills for a reading strand are presented in a scope and sequence chart. Such representation fails, however, to show both logical and instructional relationships among subskills. An example of this is shown in table 12–1, which contains the decoding scope and sequence for *Monroe's New Primer,* first published by Cowperthwait & Co. in 1882.

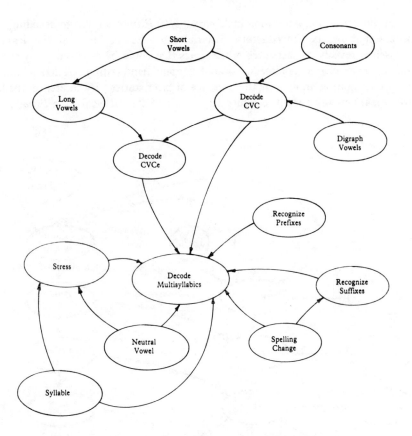

Figure 12-5. Sample Subject Network—Decoding

Table 12-1
Decoding Scope and Sequence for *Monroe's New Primer* (1882)

m	*p*	*q*
n	Short *i*	Two syllables
Short *a*	Short *u*	Silent *e*
Long *i*	Hard *g*	*v*
r	*d*	Long *u* in *you, your*
Long *e* (*e, ee*)	*b*	*zz*
s sharp or hissing	*l, ll*	Long *o* (*o, ow*)
Hard *c*	*k*	*sh*
t	Short *e*	*y* (consonant)
Short *o*	Long *y*	Silent *b*
Sharp *x* (*ks*)	*w*	*th* (vocal)
f	*j*	Long and short *y*
h	Silent *h*	Italian *a*
s flat or buzzing	*ck*	Soft *c*

Although primary attention in *Monroe's New Primer* is given to decoding, an examination of the introductory materials for the teacher and the lessons themselves reveals at least three other topics that could be represented by scope and sequence charts: readiness, vocabulary, and handwriting. (A fourth topic, comprehension, is implied by the presence of brief stories.) By inference, the instructional network shown in figure 12–6 can be constructed for the *Primer.*

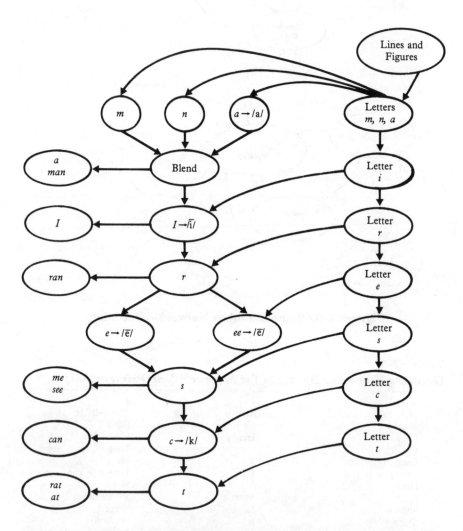

Figure 12–6. Instructional Network for Introductory Skills, *Monroe's New Primer, 1882*

Lesson Sequences

The resulting course that *Monroe's New Primer* represents can be viewed as a mapping from the instructional network onto a linear lesson sequence. The mapping function, however, does not perform a strict one-to-one mapping of subskills onto lessons. Sometimes, several subskills are introduced in a single lesson; occasionally, a review is included; and introductions to single subskills sometimes are mapped onto two or more lessons. Part of the lesson sequence for *Monroe's New Primer* is shown in figure 12–7. Notice, in this program, that letters are introduced as needed, that decoding patterns are applied frequently after they are introduced, and that children are writing full sentences by lesson 3.

Lessons Scores

The final task in deriving a formal representation of instruction is to represent the content of individual lessons. A lesson in this context corresponds to a sequence of events that possess coherence—that is, relate to a common goal or set of goals—and that are not interrupted by sustained, nonrelated events.[1] A 50-minute university lecture usually qualifies as a lesson, as does a 5-minute addition drill in primary school. Two sessions on outlining, separated by instruction in other subjects, comprise two different lessons, however. The representation of lesson events makes up a lesson score. Lesson scores consist of three major types of events: organizational, evaluative, and pedagogical:

> *Organizational events* relate to the bureaucracy of instruction: taking roll, giving information on how final grades will be determined, assigning homework, and so forth.

> *Evaluative events* provide information about the learner. They may be formal or informal tests, recitations, or any other mechanisms that measure properties of the learner.

> *Pedagogical events* are the "everything else" of lessons, the subject-related exchanges between teachers and students that are intended to change the internal state of the learner. Pedagogical events include statements of concepts and principles, explanations of how to work problems, corrective feedback, questions to learners, demonstrations, and much more. Pedagogical events can be either introduction, practice, application, or review.

Instructional activities used to present a subskill for the first time are called introduction. Instructional events coming after an introduction but before mastery are called practice, which is the repetition of a task with or without varying content. Application events are characterized by tasks that require the use of one or more subskills to achieve a higher-level goal, usually in a natural or quasi-natural context.

	1	2	3	4	5	6	7	8	9
Readiness	Lines and Figures	Letters m, n, a	Letter i	Letter r	Letters e, s	Letter c	Letter t	Review	Letters o, x
Decoding		m→/m/ n→/n/ a→/a/	I→/ai/ Practice a→/a/ m→/m/(B) n→/n/(B)	r→/r/ Practice a→/a/ n→/n/ m→/m/	e→/ē/ ee→/ē/ s→/s/ Practice I→/ī/	c→/k/ Practice c→/k/ e→/ē/ ee→/ē/	t→/t/ Practice	Review	o→/o/ x→/ks/
Vocabulary		a man	I, am Practice a, am	ran, an Practice man, a	me see Practice I man	can Practice see me	rat at Practice can	Review	ox
Writing		a man	I am a man.	A man ran.	See me, see me.	Man, see me.	I can see a rat.	Can I see a cat?	An ox can see me.

Note: Unless stated otherwise, lesson events involve introduction and practice.

Figure 12-7. Initial Lesson Sequence for *Monroe's New Primer*

Review involves practice, but it is practice after a subskill is assumed to have been learned. Review might occur just before an assessment or for maintenance at various later points. Review differs from application in that it involves direct, overt attention to a single subskill. Organizational and evaluative events may be instructional; however, their primary goals are not to change the state of the learner but to facilitate the delivery of the pedagogical events selected to do this.[2]

Notice that, even without specifying instruction paradigms for the lessons, a first-pass evaluation of a reading program could be made to see that all subskills are contained in at least one of the instructional events and that the proper orderings are observed—for example, practice before assessment. Many published programs would fail this test for more than a few subskills, especially if the minimum number of practice events for each subskill were set to two or more.[3]

A Reconstructed Reading Lesson from 1882

To demonstrate the representation of lessons through event sequences, a reading lesson has been reconstructed from *Monroe's New Primer* (Monroe, 1882). This lesson would have been taught to first graders early in the sequence of reading lessons and corresponds to lesson 3 in figure 12–7 (featuring the letter-sound correspondence, $I \rightarrow$ /ai/). The lesson is presented first as a script, representing what an observer might have recorded from observation, and then in the form of a lesson score.[4]

Monroe's New Primer Lesson Script

1-2. The teacher asks the students to take out their primers and writes the letters *m, n,* and *a* on the board. She asks if everyone remembers what these are called. She then writes *am, a,* and *man* and asks students to read each word.
3. The teacher engages students in conversation to elicit the pronoun *I.* After this occurs, students are told to open their primers to page 12 and look at the picture. The teacher says the word *I* and the students repeat it several times. The letter *I* is written on the board, and students say /ai/ whenever the teacher points to it. The name of the letter is then introduced and practiced.
4. The words in the lesson are read and the teacher reinforces the correspondences for *I, a, m,* and *n* whenever they occur.
5. Students say *am* slowly, sound by sound, then more quickly. Then they take turns reading *I am a man.*
6. Students copy *I am a man* from their primers. The teacher walks around the room correcting mistakes.
7-8. The teacher concludes the lesson by having the students enunciate *I* carefully several times, then encourages them to listen for *I* in conversations they hear.

The lesson score for this script is shown in figure 12–8.

			Lesson Step					
Event	1	2	3	4	5	6	7	8
Organize	Introductory lesson (page, etc.)							Encourage listening for *I*
Evaluate								
Introduce			*I* → /ai/					
Practice			*I* → /ai/	Reading Words			Pronounce *I*	
Apply					Read Sentence	Write Sentence		
Review		*m, n, a* *am, a,* *man*						

Figure 12–8. Lesson Score for Monroe's New Primer, Lesson 3

Recapitulation

To summarize, a complex knowledge structure or ability is organized for instructional purposes into networks of topics, represented as directed graphs. Within these topic graphs are skills, defined sufficiently in terms of subskills to be realized in instruction. The basic instructional unit is the lesson, which is composed of a linear sequence of instructional events. For management purposes, sequences of lessons are commonly organized into courses.

The topics for a complex subject such as reading are represented in a subject network. When instructional strategies, derived from an instructional theory, are added, a new directed graph, called an instructional network, is obtained. By mapping the instructional network into a linear set of lessons, the lesson sequence is obtained. Finally, the events that comprise any single lesson are represented in a lesson score. The complete representational scheme is shown diagrammatically in figure 12–9.

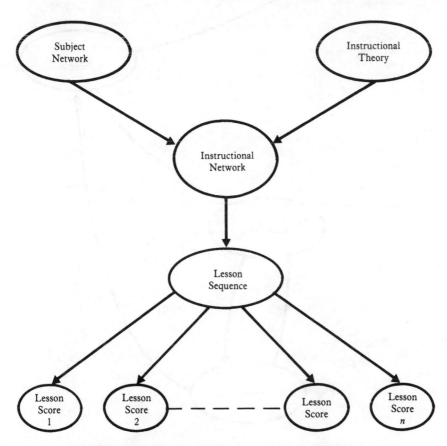

Figure 12-9. Complete Representational Scheme

In an ideal instructional environment, subskills are mapped onto courses that acknowledge considerations of instruction time, learner characteristics, and sub-skill relationships. Thus, for reading, some subskills will be mapped onto courses for grades one through three that deal exclusively with reading. Others will be mapped onto courses for grades four through eight that teach not only reading but also literature and grammar. Others might be mapped onto library lessons or con-tent area lessons.

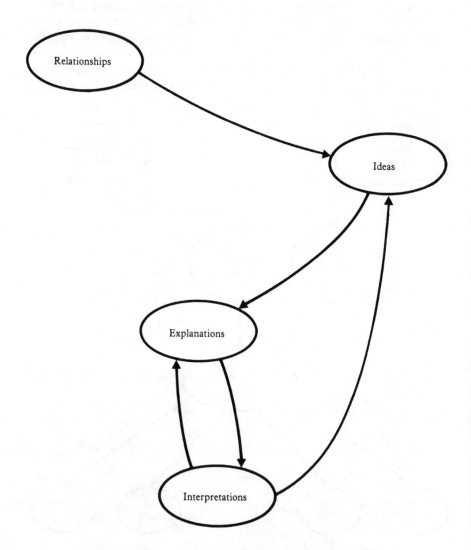

Figure 12-10. Four Strands for Comprehension

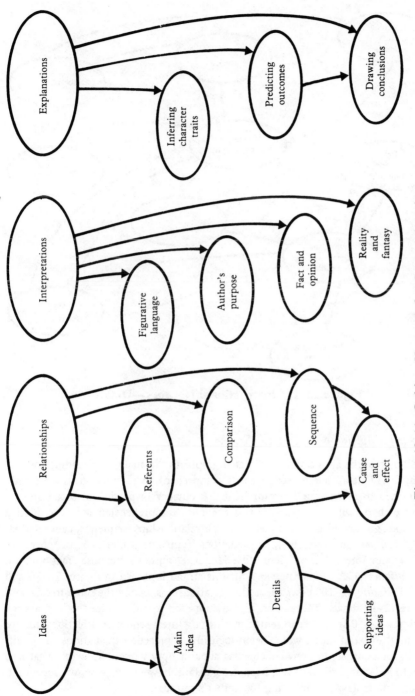

Figure 12-11. Subject Network for Comprehension

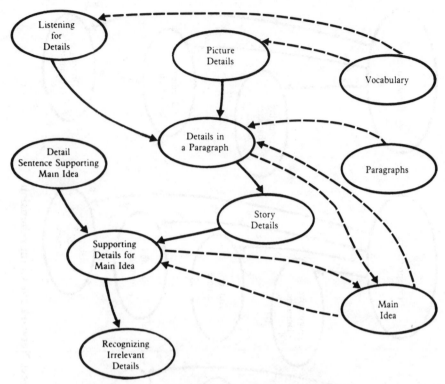

Figure 12-12. Instructional Network—Details

A Sample Application of Directed Graphs

To illustrate the application of directed graphs to the analysis of reading instruction, I will detail a representation of comprehension instruction in a recently published basal reading program (K–8). A cursory inspection of scope and sequence charts will reveal that, in this program, comprehension skills are divided into four groups: ideas (main idea, details), relationships (sequence, cause and effect, comparison, referents), explanations (outcomes, conclusions, character traits), and interpretation (figurative language, author's purpose, fact/opinion, reality/fantasy). A subject network for this strand is shown in figures 12–10 and 12–11. Figure 12–10 shows theoretical relationships among the four strands, and figure 12–11 shows skill relationships within each strand. Notice that the strands in figure 12–10 are not represented in a strictly linear sequence. Relationships are required to build ideas, which seem logically to precede explanations. (It is difficult, for example, to draw conclusions about a story without knowing what it is about.) Relating main ideas and supporting details, however, may require separating reality and fantasy and inferring the author's purpose.

| | \multicolumn{8}{c|}{Lesson} |
	1	2	3	4	5	6	7	8
Introduce	supporting details (paragraph)							
Practice	details	details		find irrelevant details		find irrelevant details		
Apply		science fiction story						
Assess			details				details	details
Review								

Figure 12–13. Partial Lesson Sequence—Ideas (Grade 6)

Similarly, the relationship between such skills as inferring character traits and drawing conclusions, on the one hand, and inferring the author's purpose, on the other, is symmetrical. The first two could be prerequisites for the third, or the reverse.

An expansion of the ideas strand into an instructional network is shown in figure 12-12. Notice that the concept of "details" is introduced through listening and analysis of pictures and that main ideas and details support each other.

The projection of part of this instructional network onto a lesson sequence is shown in figure 12-13. This sequence would normally require about ten instructional days. Lessons divided by a vertical line have two main parts: (1) a reading selection and (2) a sequence of unrelated skill activities. Other lessons involve either a single main skill (for example, a study skill), review, or assessment. When assessment occurs, suggestions are given for reteaching of skills that were not mastered. Notice, first, the patterning of initial instruction—introduction, practice, and assessment. Then observe that the main comprehension skills being taught in this sequence are often neglected in reading selections.[5]

Evaluation

An evaluation of this approach to comprehension instruction would begin with the subject network. The primary focus would be on determining the degree to which the skills portrayed (and their relationships) were consistent with theoretical and empirical investigations and whether or not they represented a complete skill set for the goals of the program. The instructional network, which represents an instructional approach superimposed on the subject matter, would then be evaluated for appropriateness for the intended audience. Finally, the lesson sequence would be evaluated for adequacy, and corresponding lesson scores would be evaluated for coherence. These latter evaluations would require tests for the existence of minimal sets of instructional activities for each skill (for example, introduce, practice, assess, apply) as well as judgments of the effectiveness of the lessons themselves.

The determination of adequate instruction for a test objective would be a function of the frequency and placement of different types of instructional activities. Thus, for complex skills, we would expect to see introductions of each skill at several grade levels, frequent practices, occasional assessment, and application and review. For less complex skills, fewer instructional activities would be expected. Implied here is a relationship between instructional emphasis and learning—namely, that skills that receive frequent attention will be learned better than those that receive less attention. This argument is different from the time-on-task argument in that accumulated lengths of lessons is not the sole evaluative factor. Instead, the actual content of lessons is considered, along with the types of instructional activities involved.

Not included here are suggestions for evaluating the actual implementation of the lesson scores by classroom teachers and the potential effects of these scores on student learning. The procedures proposed could lead to hypotheses about teacher behavior and student learning that could guide analyses of classroom procedures and of student outcomes. The lesson scores, for example, establish a set of expectancies for instructional practice. Evaluation of these scores might lead to such hypotheses as the following:

Lesson x exceeds the average attention span of its intended audience.

Lesson y covers too many different skills and will therefore confuse students performing below grade level.

In lesson 7, insufficient practice is provided for skill b.

Although the representations presented here do not cover actual classroom activites and do not yet suggest how cognitive outcomes of instruction might be predicted, they give an organization to instructional design and evaluation that has been lacking until now, and they help clarify the underlying assumptions of an instructional program.

Notes

1. The types of graphs that are of interest here are antireflexive, antisymmetric, and transitive. Most are also acyclic.

2. This definition is similar to that given by Scheffler (1960), who defines a lesson as "a continuous teaching interval that is not itself part of some other continuous teaching interval" (p. 64). In contrast to these definitions, Herbert (1967) defines a lesson as an instructional relationship between students and a teacher, wherein the teacher controls the essential lesson components (subject matter, media, grouping and location, and so forth). This definition promotes a primary focus on process, whereas the one adopted here is content-oriented.

3. The use of the term *instructional events* here contrasts with the use advanced by Gagne and Briggs (1974), wherein instructional events include such activities as "gaining attention," "presenting the stimulus materials," and "providing feedback." Although the events presented here might be recast in Gagne and Briggs terms, the need would still exist for a level of curriculum planning higher than that of the behavioral events so described. In other words, the approach described here requires attention to the overall pattern of introduction, practice, application, assessment, and review for each skill or topic before decisions are made on such micro-level issues as gaining attention and giving feedback.

4. An introduce, practice, evaluate, and review sequence of events provides an initial basis for automatic generation or evaluation of instruction. We might, for example, define a limited range of paradigms for each of these events in relation to each type of subskill, along with estimates of how many practice events are minimally sufficient for different types of learners. We might also define how often application and review events must occur to prevent

forgetting. Then, either an existing course could be evaluated or a new curriculum could be generated, at least to the level of specifying sequences of subskills and instructional paradigms. Obviously, much more must be specified to make this into a lesson generator.

5. The model lesson given in the introduction to the *Primer* shows a strong Pestalozzi influence. For a prototype of such a lesson, see Horace Mann's *Seventh Annual Report* (Mann, 1950, pp. 86ff.).

References

Briggs, L.J., & Wager, W.W. *Handbook of procedures for the design of instruction* (2nd ed.). Englewood Cliffs, N.J.: Educational Technology Publications, 1981.

Burton, W. *The district school as it was.* Boston: Lee and Shepard, 1833.

Gagne, R.M. *The conditions for learning.* New York: Holt, Rinehart and Winston, 1968.

Gagne, R.M., & Briggs, L. *Principles of instructional design.* New York: Holt, Rinehart and Winston, 1974.

Gibbons, M. *Individualized instruction: A descriptive analysis.* New York: Teachers College Press, 1971.

Gilbert, T.F. Mathetics: The technology of instruction. *Journal of Mathetics,* 1961, 1–2.

Gilbert, T.F. Praxeonomy: A systematic approach to identifying training needs. *Management of Personnel Quarterly,* 1967, *6* (3).

Herbert, J. *A system for analyzing lessons.* New York: Teachers College Press, 1967.

Landa, L.N. *Algorithmization in learning and instruction.* Englewood Cliffs, N.J.: Educational Technology Publications, 1974.

Mann, H. *Seventh annual report, covering the year 1843* (Facsimile ed.) Washington, D.C.: National Education Association, 1950. (First published, 1844.)

Monroe, L.B. (Mrs.). *Monroe's new primer* (Monroe's New Series—First Book). Philadelphia: Cowperthwait, 1882.

Romiszowski, A.J. *Designing instructional systems.* London: Kogan Page, 1981.

Scheffler, I. *The language of education.* Springfield, Ill.: Thomas, 1960.

Simmons, R.F. Semantic networks: Their computation and use for understanding English sentences. In R.C. Shank & K.M. Colby (Eds.), *Computer models of thought and language.* San Francisco: Freeman, 1973.

13
A Conceptual Framework for Reading Instruction

Robert Calfee

P receding chapters in this part have touched on the task of improving the school's capacity to establish and maintain a quality program for instruction in literacy. In this chapter, I want to present a conceptual framework designed to integrate some of these ideas and to serve as a practical tool for aiding practitioners in the task of helping their students become literate.

The Main Themes

In chapter 12, Richard Venezky presents a broad view of the primary elements that must be included in the design of a reading curriculum:

1. A structural representation of the subject matter.
2. An instructional model of the stages of teaching and learning.
3. A network that combines elements of the subject matter structure with the stages of the instructional model to form a series of lessons.

Venezky then proceeds to apply this representational scheme to several instructional situations, using a relatively informal version of graph theory. The examples rapidly become complex; the graphs take on a complicated appearance, largely because the various elements interact with one another.

In Ronald Edmonds's chapter (chapter 9) we have a story of success in schools where failure is predicted. His equation for success is fairly simple:

Leadership + emphasis on reading + frequent assessment + proper atmosphere + high expectations = High levels of student achievement

When this equation works, a result emerges that deserves emphasis: *The local school has within itself the capacity to ensure that it is effective in educating all its students.*

The process of school improvement, as Edmonds describes it, is from external assessment (to revitalize local leadership) to a final stage in which school-based assessment is an ongoing task of teachers as part of their professional responsibilities. Edmonds does not spell out how to accomplish these jobs. He seems to rely considerably on an apprenticeship approach, and he acknowledges substantial variation from one site to another.

In chapter 10, Douglas Carnine and Russell Gersten also report a success story, different on the surface from Edmonds's but with some remarkable similarities. Scattered throughout chapter 10 are the pieces of an equation that strikes me as parallel to Edmonds's—and I trust I am not doing the authors a disservice in my decision about how to assemble the pieces:

Technical assistance and support + school leadership (?) = Emphasis on reading + high academic learning time + appropriate materials + small-group interaction with the teacher + assessment and feedback = Higher levels of student achievement in reading + higher expectations by teachers

Carnine and Gersten differ from Edmonds most noticeably in the matter of who specifies the details of the reading program. For Edmonds, the building of lessons is a task of the local school, and the principal is vital. For Carnine and Gersten, this job is best carried out by a central corps of curriculum designers, whose responsibility is to spell out—in complete detail, step by step, with precise guidelines—everything that the teacher is to do. The goal is to create curriculum materials designed so that students learn exactly the objectives of the program. The major responsibility of local leadership is to ensure that the program is implemented as designed.

In chapter 11, Roger Farr looks at school effectiveness from the output side. His focus is on competency tests, but his comments apply with equal force to the entire range of standardized tests used to measure reading achievement throughout the United States. Farr discusses some successes, notes some problems, and expresses some concerns:

1. Reading scores are improving at the lower levels of primary education, especially for children from impoverished backgrounds.
2. For the last two decades, there has been a continuing decline in performance on tests of higher-level skills, for high school graduates in general and for college-bound students in particular.
3. Testing, including proficiency exams, is here to stay. The public believes that, through such programs, schools may be held to some standard of accountability.
4. There may be too much low-level testing.
5. As tests are increasingly relied on for decisions about individuals and programs, the issue of adequate test validity becomes increasingly important.
6. Given the increasing reliance on tests, the influence of tests on curriculum and instructional practices needs to be monitored vigilantly.

Farr expresses some reservations, which I share (Calfee, Note 1), about current practices in high school competency examinations. Most competency testing programs, though well intentioned, (1) are badly timed (they come too late in the student's school career); (2) are based on scanty and often inadequate information; and (3) lead to no-win decisions that do not help anyone. In my opinion, such programs would do better (1) to focus on student performance at the end of elementary school; (2) to use the full array of information available about student achievement (including test findings but also including data from the instructional program); and (3) to yield decisions about remediation, retention, and program choices.

These recommendations are both educationally defensible and practically workable. Unfortunately, however, it may remain for the courts to decide what schools will actually do.

The Loose Ends

Now I want to pick up a few loose ends. I have selected several I think merit closer examination.

Venezky's description of a lesson is brief and cogent; unfortunately, he does not give us any guidelines for creating a good lesson. His examples are complicated—a feature that is troubling for reasons to be mentioned later. One set of simple guidelines might be taken from his list of instructional elements: introduce, practice, assess, apply, review. (He comments that these elements are the foundation of the Monroe *Primer* lesson that he praises.)

Another comment by Venezky—that an important goal of schooling is to teach independent learning—strikes me as significant and worthy of further thought. What does this statement mean? How might this goal be implemented as part of a literacy program? How can the concept be defined more rigorously than "you know it when you see it," without turning it into behavioral objectives?

No single model explains school effectiveness, according to Edmonds. His basic elements can take many forms, and the underlying process remains unknown. He mentions three potential sources of enlightenment: organizational development research, school effect studies, and teacher effectiveness studies. These three areas presently comprise a collection of bits and pieces, and Edmonds is correct in calling for theory and research that can provide at least a patchwork quilt.

At first glance, everything seems nicely bolted into place in Carnine and Gersten's presentation. Even here though, careful examination reveals a few fluttering threads. Although each individual lesson is thoroughly detailed, the authors note the importance of the demonstrations provided by the training supervisors if teachers are to become successful "orchestrators." Personal observation suggests that teachers do need to see direct instruction in action and that they do ask for explanations—a curious state of affairs, since everything needed is presumably included in the design.

Farr is quite direct in stating his unfinished business—that we have no adequate definition of literacy and that we have serious problems in defining functional literacy. He thinks that intelligent implementation of proficiency testing requires a coherent design for coordinating assessment and instruction, and he worries that educational programs are taking on a Rube Goldberg appearance as one solution is patched onto another.

A common theme running through all these chapters is the call for a coherent conceptual foundation to undergird our thinking about curriculum, instruction, and assessment in reading—the thinking of researchers, teachers, administrators, policymakers, and, perhaps, even students. Note that the issue is not what the *real* structure of reading is. Rather, the question is how we can represent reading and reading instruction simply enough to communicate with one another.

Mental Resources

Step into the shoes of a cognitive psychologist for a moment, and consider the question, "What are the mental resources and powers available to a human being who is trying to comprehend something?" A fable by Herbert Simon (1981) provides an allegorical response to this question:

> We watch an ant make his laborious way across a wind- and wave-molded beach. He moves ahead, angles to the right to ease his climb up a steep dunelet, detours around a pebble, stops for a moment to exchange information with a compatriot. . . .Thus he makes his weaving, halting way back to his home. . . . I sketch the path on a piece of paper . . . a sequence of irregular, angular segments . . . [yet with] an underlying sense of direction, aiming toward a goal. . . . An ant [and likewise a man], viewed as a behaving system, is quite simple. The apparent complexity of his behavior over time is largely the complexity of the environment in which he finds himself. (pp. 63–65)

This fable has several morals. First, the brain is actually quite a simple device in the rudiments of its functioning. It is basically a device that aids in maintaining the balance of the organism; in particular, it examines continuously the relation between present events and previous experiences in order to maintain the balance. (Samuels also notes in chapter 16 the limited ability of the human mind to handle information.)

Second, the human mind, through language, possesses a symbolic capability that allows it to transcend raw experience. We can think about experience, and we can even think about thinking. Here, again, the mind has a limited capacity—a seven-digit telephone number can be remembered easily while it is being dialed, but the task is significantly harder when a three-digit area code is added. The situation is no different when the teacher is asked to think about four basic concepts in reading and then tries to relate these concepts to a scope and sequence chart.

Third, what we remember from experience is an amalgam of the actual experience and our perceptions of it. In varying degrees, human beings try to impose structure on their experiences—an orderly environment is more easily remembered than a random collection of events.

Fourth, thoughts determine actions. We can decide to act by chance ("I'll toss a coin"), by rote automatic response, or by reflective thought; but each of these approaches entails some level of thought. Not even a sleeping person "behaves" without thinking.

These considerations suggest two psychological criteria for any framework proposed to serve as a conception of reading. Because such a conception would be a tool to be used by people (rather than by computers), (1) the conception must consist of a small number of elements, (2) the various parts must be reasonably distinctive, and (3) these parts must be limited by one or more integrative themes.

One key to effective reading instruction is the inculcation in the student's mind of a simple map of the domain of reading. For the school to ensure its success in teaching all students to read, it is important that a common conception be created (the map) to bind together the thoughts and actions of the various participants in the school.

I realize that this proposal runs counter to prevailing views about reading and reading instruction, which generally hold (1) that reading is complex, (2) that each reader (and the teacher) is unique, and (3) that there are many ways to think about reading.

The counterarguments are (1) that everything appears complex until someone finds a simple representation, (2) that uniqueness is easy to find—it is the commonalities that are difficult to appreciate—and (3) that there are only a few ways (perhaps only one) to conceive of reading.

The emphasis on simplicity is of fundamental importance. The choice of how to parse the domain of reading is crucially significant for any coherent conception of reading instruction. We must divide up and analyze, because our minds are unable to deal in a reliable and replicable manner with unanalyzed wholes. We may appreciate and feel deeply about the complexities of reading, but deep feelings are not an adequate basis for problem solving. If there are too many pieces—too many entanglements—we will lose track of where we are going and why.

The Conceptual Framework

Separable Processes

I have suggested (Calfee, 1981) that the task of constructing a workable mental conception of a complex system is something like carving a turkey—it is important to know where the joints are. Figure 13–1 represents a proposal for carving up the area of reading instruction. The first job is to clearly separate the mental domains

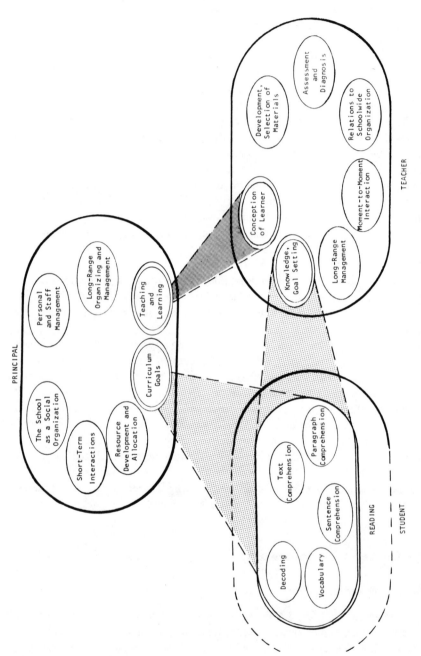

Figure 13-1. The Conceptual Framework of Reading Instruction

of the reader, the teacher, and the principal. Next, each of these domains is divided into a few big chunks (never slice too finely until you have to). The reader's mind, for example, includes five separate domains. Decoding includes knowledge of the principles for expressing spoken language in visual form. Viewed in broad perspective, this domain is not a tangle of inconsistent spelling patterns; rather, it is an incredible tale of how, during the evolution of English, motley languages were melded into an alphabetic writing system that still does a remarkable job of providing cues to the pronunciation, meaning, and origins of each word. Learning phonics is rather dull when it is done by rote from worksheet exercises; by contrast, learning how English is written can evoke the excitement of retracing an important pathway in the development of Western culture.

Vocabularly is a significant part of every reading curriculum. The study of vocabularly seems to move around a great deal, into decoding (the students learning to say the vocabularly words) and into comprehension (studying the words from the reading selection). Most often, vocabulary instruction involves looking up a list of words in the glossary and writing a sentence for each word. Within the separable-process framework proposed here, vocabulary has a clear and distinctive interpretation. It refers to understanding the nature of word meaning. It is useful for students to learn the meanings of individual words, but it is far more important for them to learn that words can be organized into semantic networks and that complex words can be broken down into simple parts. They should learn that the dictionary is a useful tool. When vocabulary instruction becomes a search for ideas, it is an exciting endeavor.

The fundamental task in comprehension is the reconstruction of the structure of a text, whether the text be a sentence, a paragraph, or a passage. In teaching a student the skills of comprehension, the character and clarity of the text matter a great deal; amorphous, incoherent writing is not the best material for training in comprehension. A narrative is dissected very differently from an expository or technical selection. General purpose terms such as *main idea, literal detail, inferences,* and the like, are of little or no value when they are not linked to the structural characteristics of the text. Some types of passages, for example, do not have well-defined main ideas, and it is a mistake to ask students to search for them.

I suggest a concept of the lesson that is quite different from either the variability of the typical basal lesson, as seen by Venezky, or the fixed routine of a direct instruction lesson. The lesson for a particular day focuses on one of the aforementioned domains, and the entire lesson is built around that domain. During the instructional period, the teacher introduces the content of the lesson and then leads the group of students through a problem-solving discussion of the issues, with systematic attention to the need for assessment, practice, application/transfer, review, and reflection.

My colleagues and I are engaged in a school improvement project based on this approach (Calfee, Henry, & Putnam, Note 2), and the results are encouraging. Teachers report that they have a better grasp of the lesson goals, and students are enthusiastic about the small-group discussion format. In some ways, the method resembles Hansen's "think while you read" strategy (see chapter 21) but encompasses the entire lesson. As in the direct instruction model, a key feature in our work has been the development of a consistent and well-articulated design that provides guidelines for the teacher in shaping the discussion and keeping it focused on a single domain (Calfee & Associates, Note 3).

I have emphasized the separability of the mental components in reading because I think it is easier to design and implement a coherent instructional program when the significant building blocks are clearly identified. The accomplished reader joins these building blocks into a dynamic, interactive whole that reflects the demands of the task, the strategy selected for the situation, and the developmental maturity of the reader. Lesgold and Perfetti (1981) describe the contrast as "the structural independence and the functional interdependence of reading skills."

In our analysis of the psychology of reading instruction, we have been examining the mental activities of the student; now we can say a few words about the mind of the teacher. Teaching, like reading, is an "unnatural" act and, as such, has a decomposable structure (see figure 13–1). The task of the teacher is defined to fit sociocultural needs, and training, preparation, and thought are needed to do a competent job. Some ways of laying out the job are more efficient than others. I will illustrate by focusing on the component labeled "moment-to-moment interaction." In handling exchanges with the students, teachers must decide how to deal with questions, feedback, praise, and punishment. They can either respond naturally or they can plan their reactions in a rule-based fashion. Because they are providing models that their students will follow in other social settings, teachers' responses should mirror consistent principles—they should be thoughtful and sufficiently well articulated so that the teachers can explain why they are behaving the way they are.

Figure 13–1 also shows the role of the effective principal. To act as the leader of the school, the principal needs to have a coherent conceptual foundation for integrating the resources, the goals, the opportunities, and the problems of the school. The figure shows the main elements proposed for this conceptual foundation, components that provide the basis for a training program for school administrators.

Shared Conceptions

The concept of reading requires that a set of common themes be shared by the principal and the faculty so that the students can experience a coherent program of instruction. When individual teachers hold different ideas about reading, when these ideas are not clear, when the principal lacks a clear notion of what reading is about, or when everyone relies on the reading materials or the achievement tests to define reading, it is virtually certain that students will be confused.

If the principal and faculty share a common ideology about how students learn and about how to handle individual differences, a foundation exists for the school to become effective for all students. In chapter 8, Courtney Cazden presents evidence that some teachers seem to possess different learning models for students from different socioeconomic backgrounds. To what degree do these conceptions guide the teachers' actions? I also suggest that if the principal has a clear awareness of the rules of procedure for the school, and if this awareness is widely shared by the entire school community, the result is likely to be what Edmonds refers to as a "positive atmosphere."

Wrapping Up

The key to improvement in reading instruction at the local school level, according to conceptual framework sketched here, is to bring our full intellectual powers to bear in making the process of schooling rational. This statement is not intended to dismiss the importance of teaching as an art. Ideas are powerful, and the notion of ideas as tools should permeate the experience of schooling for all participants. The acquisition of literacy should be an exploration of the world of ideas. In this connection, I would press home a point that is not made explicit in the chapters of this book but that they exemplify in one way or another: *The most important outcomes of education—the basic skills—are the ability to think, to solve problems, and to communicate with others in the formal style that has evolved in Western culture.*

Thus, the real value of reading, writing, and arithmetic to success in our culture lies in the tutelage the student receives in thinking. The actual skills are secondary to that more fundamental goal. I believe that Edmonds is correct in stating that the goal of competence in thinking and problem solving is achievable for *all* students. Attainment of that goal is not easy, but it is possible and perhaps essential if we are to survive as a civilization.

At its best, education merges discipline and independence, responsibility and freedom. These qualities are not separate from the various subject matters, including the three R's. Teachers can prepare the basic design for formal thought; they can motivate; and they can ensure practice. Eventually, however, students must be pressed to try their own wings.

The task of school improvement is doable. Even more exciting is the prospect that we are close to a deep understanding of why certain techniques for school change are successful—an understanding that can be shared with teachers and administrators. Edmonds closes with the remark: "Unfortunately, we know far more about the desirability of [the school's] caring [about quality teaching and learning for all students] than about the means by which it can be brought about." The knowledge of that means, however, is within our grasp.

Reference Notes

1. Calfee, R.C. *The case against minimum competency testing.* Presentation at the hearing on minimum competency testing sponsored by National Institute of Education, Washington, D.C., July 1981.
2. Calfee, R.C., Henry, M.K., & Putnam, R.T. *A model for school change: The Graystone Project.* Stanford, Calif.: Stanford University School of Education, 1982.
3. Calfee, R.C., & Associates. *THE BOOK* (A generic manual for reading teachers). Unpublished manuscript, Stanford University, 1981.

References

Calfee, R.C. Cognitive psychology and educational practice. In D.C. Berliner (Ed.), *Review of research in education.* Washington, D.C.: American Educational Research Association, 1981.

Lesgold, A.M., & Perfetti, C.A. *Interactive processes in reading.* Hillsdale, N.J.: Erlbaum, 1981.

Simon, H.A. *The sciences of the artificial* (2nd ed.). Cambridge, Mass.: MIT Press, 1981.

Part III
Foundations for Better Reading Instruction

Part III

14
Building Children's Knowledge of Stories

Dorothy S. Strickland

The Child and the Story

In writing about the role of the story in our lives, Garth Brown (1977) states:

> Story . . . is crucial to . . . our . . . ongoing effort to make sense of the world. We resort to story to make an entity of experience. . . . We . . . often modify experience when creating stories of everyday life, and also, often modify our own internal representations of experience when listening to the stories of others (p. 357).

Story or narrative is the most effective and frequently used form we use to order our world (Hardy, 1968). The use of story is characteristic of adults and children. Children use story in their dramatic play; adults and children use story in the retelling of events and in many other aspects of their communication.

The work of Britton (1970) and Applebee (1978) suggests how a sense of story is developed in children. Britton proposes that we use language in two fundamentally different ways. In the participant role, language is used as a tool for exchanging ideas and information in a relatively objective and sometimes impersonal way; in the spectator role, language is used to create an experience. Applebee (1977) describes the participant role as embracing a spectrum ranging from sports broadcasts and newspaper reports to highly technical and esoteric works.

The spectator role embraces all forms of literary experience, from the stories of childhood to sophisticated adult works. The meaning for each individual is determined by personal interaction with the text. Instead of objective truth, the reader looks for internal consistency and a sense of fitness and proportion. It is through the spectator role that the development of story is thought to take place.

Other researchers studying the development of sense of story in children have noted certain developmental trends. Perhaps the first evidence of the spectator role in children is their use of language to create a special or private world. This use of language is thought to lend itself to the kind of make-believe games and dramatic play that are essential to the acquisition of the specific conventions that constitute a sense of story. As children mature, their oral and written stories increase in length and complexity. The characters, settings, and actions become further removed from the here and now of the immediate environment. Children gradually gain greater control over the events in their stories; they move from writing a loose collection of related events to writing tightly structured narratives that link a set of events to each other and to a common theme (Applebee, 1977).

Other research focuses on the nature and internal structure of stories and the relationship of that nature and structure to comprehension. The work of Mandler and Johnson (1977), Rumelhart (1978), Stein and Glenn (Note 1), and Thorndyke (1977) suggests that stories have an underlying structure that can be described by their narrative parts and interrelationships. Although various researchers label story elements differently, the following elements are generally included:

Setting: an introduction to the main characters, time, and setting.

Beginning: an initiating event that leads the main characters to formulate a major goal.

Goal setting: reactions to the beginning and the formation of the major goal.

Attempt: actions of the characters to achieve the goal.

Outcome: the success or failure of the attempt.

Internal response: subgoals, thoughts, and feelings of characters, leading to actions.

Ending: the long-range consequence of actions and the final responses of story characters.

These elements comprise the parts of a story—theme, plot, and resolution. Listeners and readers use their knowledge of story structure as a framework, or schema, to guide them in anticipating the structure of a story. Knowledge of story structure facilitates comprehension and improves the memory of text (Mandler & Johnson, 1977; Stein, 1979; Whaley, 1981; Anderson, Note 2).

A story schema aids in story comprehension by providing a framework for organizing information, for deciding when a portion of a story is complete or incomplete, and for anticipating what types of information may be forthcoming in the story (Mandler, 1978; Mandler & Johnson, 1977; Stein, 1979; Anderson, Note 2). Story schema may aid memory as well by providing a structure for linking specific events and by helping the individual fill in or infer information that might have been forgotten (Mandler, 1978; Mandler & Johnson, 1977).

Bruce (Note 3) suggests that a reader's prior beliefs and expectations are utilized in well-written stories and that the structure of such stories provides a framework for organizing the reader's prior beliefs. He contends that children who have limited experience with real stories may have difficulty in understanding them.

The work of Mandler and Johnson (1977) further indicates that story schema is used to comprehend and recall stories. Their studies also lend support to the developmental nature of the story schema. Although children at different ages develop similar story schemata, older children have more elaborate and complex concepts of stories.

Whyte (1980) reports that the use of storytelling sessions with young children (aged 4–6) has the potential for increasing the development of certain cognitive functions. Her study of young boys from low-income families in Belfast, Northern Ireland, revealed the children's abilities to extract the central theme of an oral folk-tale, recall other important ideas, and retell the events of the story in logical sequence. The results suggest that 4-year-old children can integrate, transform, and synthesize story information. Experiences with stories can develop these skills and stimulate the development of children's cognitive functions.

The Role of the Story in Reading, Writing, Listening, and Speaking

Stories are the best way to introduce literacy into the lives of children. An understanding of stories and an interest in them is fundamental to the development of reading and writing. Children who are exposed to stories are more likely to want to tell stories, write stories, and read stories written by themselves and others.

The research on early reading is replete with evidence of the importance of literary experiences at the prekindergarten and kindergarten levels. Durkin (1966), Torrey (1969), and Price (1976) examined pupils who learned to read before entering school. They concur that the outstanding characteristic of these children—and also of those who make rapid progress once they begin formal instruction—is that they came from homes where reading books was important and where they had been read to consistently during their preschool years.

Other research involving literature and the language of young children supports the idea that systematic exposure to stories improves children's comprehension of stories and interest in reading and expands their repertoire of language.

Chomsky (1973) found that children who were read to and who read more on their own had a greater knowledge of complex language structures than children who were read to less and who read less.

A knowledge of stories is intrinsically related to literacy. When children read and listen to stories, they make predictions about what they will hear or read. Their knowledge of stories provides a guide or framework for constructing meaning from text. As children become familiar with the language of books, they learn to make predictions based on a variety of patterns in language and events. Reading and writing involve the construction of meaning. When children produce oral or written stories, they are engaged in the process of constructing meaning; their knowledge of stories acts as the framework for that construction.

Stories serve as natural vehicles for language arts instruction, and activities using stories help build children's concept of story and assure that they will be more mature learners for the later activities involving stories. Table 14–1 illustrates the various ways in which stories promote the development of reading, writing, listening, and speaking.

Strategies for Developing Knowledge of Stories

The best way to develop a knowledge of stories in young children is to expose them to stories systematically in a variety of ways. Williamson (1981) reminds us that the concept of a story as the telling of an event or series of events is abstract and difficult:

> To separate "the story" from the specific format and situation in which it is presented can be difficult for a young child. . . . a series of experiences with a single story is valuable for young children, for it enables them to extract what is common to the experiences: the story (p. 26).

The following are some suggestions for bringing young children and stories together.

Reading Aloud

A planned program of reading aloud from a wide variety of picture storybooks is the most effective way to build young children's knowledge of stories. Children should be read to each day. After the reading, the books should be made available for them to browse through. Very often they will want to "read" the story on their own, using the pictures as a guide to the text. Favorite stories should be repeated during the reading aloud period. Children develop the ability to predict the events in stories they know well.

Sufficient time must be allocated for literature activities. When teachers schedule time for the entire group to browse through self-selected books, even very young children can engage in sustained silent reading. Prekindergarten and kindergarten classrooms should have an ample supply of picture storybooks that are made accessible to the children by means of a display that changes periodically.

Textless Books

Picture storybooks without words provide an excellent tool for building an understanding of the structure of stories. Children must understand that there is a story to be inferred from the pictures and that they may not invent an unrelated story. They should be assured that there is no specific text or language, however, and they should feel free to use their own language to tell the story.

The teacher should read the title of the book and discuss the picture on the cover to give the children an idea of what the story is about. Next, the children

Table 14–1
The Role of the Story in an Integrated Language Arts Curriculum

	Reading	Writing	Listening	Speaking
Reading	—	Reading stories gives children models for writing their own compositions. Children may read each other's efforts, group efforts, and the work of professional writers.	Listening to stories strengthens children's story comprehension when reading and their ability to listen for special purposes. Listening for enjoyment promotes further interest in reading books.	Stories give children material and models for their own oral composition: storytelling, dramatic play, creative dramatics.
Writing	The children's written stories provide material for group and independent reading. As children read their own stories, they learn about the relationship between speech and print.	—	Written stories may be shared through reading aloud. Tape-recorded stories may be listened to again and again while the children follow along with the text.	Children may read aloud and discuss their own written stories. Oral response to stories builds the concept of story and story comprehension.
Listening	Listening to stories activates the desire to read and serves as the basis for understanding story structure. Abilities associated with reading comprehension can be fostered through listening comprehension activities.	Listening to stories provides a basis for written story development and the use of expressive language.	—	Listening to stories provides a model for storytelling and a basis for other expressive langue activities. Critical discussion of stories strengthens the ability to integrate and synthesize actions and interactions of characters and events.
Speaking	Children's dictated stories may serve as reading materials. Stories, narrative poems, and refrains read aloud by children may serve as the basis for further silent reading.	Storytelling may serve as material for individual or group books. Stories told from textless books may be written down and read later.	Discussions may be held to make predictions before and during the reading. Oral language activities can strengthen the listening experience and aid comprehension.	—

should tell all they can about each picture. A suggestion such as "Tell what is happening in the picture" helps get the language started. Questions should be used only when absolutely necessary. Such questions as "Where is this happening?" "What do you think they are saying (or thinking)?" and "What are they doing?" help develop a sensitivity to setting, dialogue, and action.

Textless books provide a structure for guiding children through a storytelling experience. The books encourage the use of story language and conventions. Children enjoy telling the same stories again and again.

Creative Dramatics

Stories provide an excellent basis for creative dramatics. Children can pantomime as they hear familiar stories. Folktales, such as *Stone Soup*, contain few descriptive passages and a large amount of action and dialogue. Children will eagerly assume the roles of the three soldiers, tired and hungry, or the villagers, hiding their food from the soldiers.

Dialogue can be added to the pantomime. Cumulative tales, with sequential patterns and repetition, are best. The patterned dialogue in Marjorie Flack's *Ask Mr. Bear*, for example, is easily learned by 4-year-olds, who readily join in as the teacher pauses at appropriate places. Dramatizing stories helps children internalize story patterns and strengthens their understanding and enjoyment of stories.

Conclusion

By making young children aware of literature through the techniques of reading aloud, textless books, and creative dramatics, teachers foster a love of stories and a desire to read. Sharing literature needs no justification beyond the important aesthetic and subjective reasons offered by those who recognize the need for literature in our lives. In this age of accountability, however, it is encouraging to know that the time spent reading aloud to children and engaging them in literature-related activities can support their literacy development.

Reference Notes

1. Stein, N., & Glenn, C. *A developmental study of children's construction of stories.* Paper presented at the Society for Research in Child Develoment Meetings, New Orleans, 1977.
2. Anderson, R.C. *Schema-directed processes in language comprehension* (Tech. Rep. No. 50). Urbana: University of Illinois, Center for the Study of Reading, July 1977.
3. Bruce, B. *What makes a good story.* (Reading Education Rep. No. 5). Urbana: University of Illinois, Center for the Study of Reading, June 1978.

References

Applebee, A.N. A sense of story. *Theory into Practice*, 1977, *16*, 342–347.

Applebee, A.N. *The child's concept of story: Ages two to seventeen*. Chicago: University of Chicago Press, 1978.

Britton, J. *Language and learning*. London: Penguin Press, 1970.

Brown, G. Development of story in children's reading and writing. *Theory into Practice*, 1977, *16*, 357–362.

Chomsky, C. Stages in language development and reading exposure. *Harvard Educational Review*, 1973, *42*, 1–33.

Durkin, D. *Children who read early: Two longitudinal studies*. New York: Teachers College Press, 1966.

Hardy, B. *The appropriate form: An essay on the novel*. London: Athlone Press, 1968.

Mandler, J. A code in the node: The use of a story schema in retrieval. *Discourse Processes*, 1978, *1*, 14–35.

Mandler, J., & Johnson, N. Remembrance of things parsed: Story structure and recall. *Cognitive Psychology*, 1977, *9*, 111–151.

Price, E.H. How thirty-seven gifted children learned to read. *The Reading Teacher*, 1976, *30*, 44–48.

Rumelhart, D.E. Understanding and summarizing brief stories. In D. LaBerge & S.J. Samuels (Eds.), *Basic processing in reading: Perception and comprehension*. Hillsdale, N.J.: Erlbaum, 1978.

Stein, N.L. How children understand stories: A developmental analysis. In L.G. Katz (Ed.), *Current topics in early childhood education* (Vol. 2). Hillsdale, N.J.: Ablex, 1979.

Thorndyke, P. Cognitive structures in comprehension and memory of narrative discourse. *Cognitive Psychology*, 1977, *9*, 97–110.

Torrey, J.W. Learning to read without a teacher. *Elementary English*, 1969, *46*, 550–558.

Whaley, J.F. Readers expectations for story structures. *Reading Research Quarterly*, 1981, *17*, 90–114.

Whyte, J. Stories for young children: An evaluation. *International Journal of Early Childhood*, 1980, *12*, 23–26.

Williamson, P.M. Literature goals and activities for young children. *Young Children*, 1981, *36*, 24–30.

15
The Case for Explicit Decoding Instruction

Joanna P. Williams

This chapter is about learning the reading code, a topic that has been somewhat ignored during the last few years. Research has moved to the area of comprehension. The new refrain is, "We know how to teach decoding; let's learn how to teach comprehension," and this refrain has been translated into funding policy. Most reading researchers are currently deep into studies of inference, story schema, text cohesion, and many other promising areas.

Do we really know how to teach decoding? If so, why are we not doing it consistently and doing it more successfully? What is it about decoding that continues to be so controversial? In truth, I think that the evidence is in and the case is closed. I want to explain why we are where we are today with respect to decoding instruction and what, in my opinion, we should do about it. I will begin with a very brief history, discuss one topic within decoding that is new, review the research evidence, and make some recommendations.

Background and Research

First, let us look at some of the evidence that was used to justify the "whole-word," or "look-say," approach that was in vogue for so many years. Experiments (starting with Cattell, 1886) demonstrated that a familiar word is read as a whole and that a short word, presented tachistoscopically, can be read in as short a period of time as is needed to recognize a single letter. A combination of letters that make a word (such as *cat*) can be read in less time than it takes to identify the same letters in a sequence that does not make a word (such as *tca*). Such evidence, however, did not cause the whole-word method to become so well established. Rather, the causes can be attributed to the influences of Gestalt psychology and a philosophy of education that prevailed during the 1920s and 1930s. Gestalt principles emphasized the importance of a meaningful whole, and a word was considered a meaningful whole. Educational philosophers stressed personal adjustment and the "whole child." These beliefs strongly influenced the vigorous promotion of whole-word or look-say instruction.

By the 1950s, however, there was a great deal of concern about children who were not reading well, and many changes were proposed for reading instruction. In *Why Johnny Can't Read*, Flesch (1955) called for a return to "old-fashioned" phonics instruction. New linguistic methods (Bloomfield, 1942; Fries, 1962) began to make headway. Even though these new methods looked suspiciously like earlier phonics instruction, they were considerably more systematic in presentation. In addition, some novel approaches to instruction were introduced, such as Moore's (1963) talking typewriter and Pitman's (Note 1) initial teaching alphabet. During this period, earlier research findings were reinterpreted. The early tachistoscopic work experiments, for example, had used adult subjects, and it was pointed out that literate adults were different from 5-year-old nonreaders. The perennial question of whether or not we should teach phonics remained central to the discussion. Chall (1967) concluded that early emphasis on decoding leads to higher achievement in word recognition and spelling and is as effective as a whole-word approach in prompting interest and involvement in reading. Chall also concluded that children of low socioeconomic level were especially likely to read better when a code emphasis approach was used to teach them.

Since Chall's book, there has been an enormous amount of research about beginning reading. A large number of instructional programs have been developed, the majority of which at least pay lip service to the idea that decoding is important. Some programs subscribe fully to the point of view that decoding is fundamental.

There are still those (Goodman & Goodman, 1979; Smith, 1975) who believe that instruction in how to break the code should not be emphasized for beginning readers. According to their view, getting meaning from the printed page is the reader's main task. They claim that the skilled reader seems never to use phonic cues but, rather, uses syntactic and semantic cues from the text, context, and general knowledge about the world. This view of reading assumes that the processes that occur in the mature, proficient reader are those that should be taught to the beginning reader. The proponents of this view of reading usually advocate instruction that offers a great deal of language activity, interesting reading material, and an emphasis on comprehension from the very beginning. Such an approach to instruction is, in fact, considerably less structured than that of the traditional look-say basal readers, and it requires a great deal of inductive thinking and discovery on the part of the student.

I believe that there are persuasive arguments against this approach to the teaching of reading. First, the ability to use the graphemic information in a word—the letter-sound correspondences—is valuable in adulthood. Proficient readers do run into new, unfamiliar words every once in a while, and when they do, they benefit from an ability to use phonics cues. The second argument has to do with research. Having rejected the old tachistoscopic studies that justified whole-word learning, we should not fall back into the trap of deciding how to instruct children on the basis of what adults do. Although it is easy to see methodological or logical flaws in outmoded research, it is not so easy, it seems, to see equally blatant problems in new research.

My position in "the great debate" is that decoding instruction is absolutely fundamental. I believe that no matter how complex reading is, word identification must be a fundamental instructional objective at the beginning levels of the teaching of reading. As a child learns to read and becomes more familiar with words, words come to be recognized more rapidly and as whole units. Specific phonics cues may be used less and less as the child becomes proficient at reading. This does not mean, however, that the phonics cues were of no importance in the initial stages of word identification. Phonics cues facilitate the identification of unfamiliar words and have been shown to be of great importance in learning to read (La Berge, 1979; Samuels, Miller, & Eisenberg, 1979).

We have enough data to justify teaching decoding explicitly. Guthrie, Martuza, and Seifert (1979) did a reanalysis of the results of the large-scale comparison of reading methods funded by the U.S. Office of Education in the 1960s, the so-called First-Grade Studies (Bond & Dykstra, 1967). They found that children in linguistics programs or in programs combining phonics and linguistics performed better on the word recognition subtest of the Stanford Achievement Test than children in traditional whole-word basal reading programs. In addition, they found that programs that combined a phonics program with a basal program were superior to the traditional basal approaches. Although they did not find differences among the programs on the paragraph-meaning subtest of the Stanford Achievement Test, the conclusion was that, at least in first grade, an emphasis on decoding seemed beneficial.

In the nationwide Follow Through planned variation experiment, different models for educating disadvantaged children were evaluated. The data analysis by Abt Associates (Stebbins, St. Pierre, Proper, Anderson, & Cerva, 1977) compared three instructional models: basic skills, cognitive-conceptual, and affective-cognitive. On the Metropolitan Achievement Test, the students in basic skills models performed better than the students in the other models. Within the basic skills models, the Direct Instruction Model of the University of Oregon appeared most effective. The superiority of this program was clearest at the first- and second-grade levels and no longer appeared at the fourth-grade level.

The Abt report was controversial. House, Glass, McLean, and Walker (1978) objected strongly to the report's conclusion that there were differences among the instructional models. House et al. emphasized that the effectiveness of every one of the teaching approaches varied widely among school districts. They argued that this was the finding that should serve as a basis for educational policy and that local individuality should be honored.

It is interesting to note that these widely varying conclusions about the Follow Through study deal with two entirely different issues: (1) promoting effective reading instruction and (2) giving local districts the opportunity to make their own decisions. (Each of these issues is of major importance. It is not unusual to find important policy issues in conflict. Such conflict usually leads to some sort of compromise, a solution that is often very disappointing to those who have a heavily vested interest in one or the other of the issues involved.)

Findings from another area of research—classroom management—also suggest that decoding instruction is valuable. Recent work indicates that more time spent in instruction and more direct instruction leads to greater achievement in reading, especially for slow learners (Berliner & Rosenshine, 1977). Resnick (1979) has pointed out that the proponents of a code-emphasis approach also tend to recommend direct instruction. When more instructional time is spent on reading in the classroom, the teacher is likely to be engaged in the direct teaching of decoding.

These research studies can be summarized as follows. Sometimes, decoding-emphasis approaches lead to significantly greater achievement on reading tests. The effects, when they occur, show up only in the early grades and are seen only when word recognition is assessed. The effects are more likely to appear when children of low socioeconomic level are studied. Also, the effects, when they occur, are never very large. The empirical evidence, however, never leans in the other direction; there are no studies in which reading programs that do not emphasize decoding are superior.

To argue against a code approach, it would be necessary to claim (1) that there are positive gains from meaning-emphasis programs, but such gains cannot be assessed; and (2) that these gains are more important than the gains we can measure. In my opinion, such arguments are silly. The evidence (Williams, 1979b) suggests that schools ought to provide children with good decoding programs because such instruction teaches basic decoding skill more effectively. Furthermore, although it has not been demonstrated that decoding instruction helps comprehension, there is no evidence that decoding instruction hurts comprehension.

Designing a Decoding Program

A number of issues must be addressed in designing a decoding program. The first issue has to do with the matter of timing. The real question, as Chall (1967) has said, is not whether to teach phonics but when to start and how much to teach. Chall opted for starting at the very beginning of school. During the past 15 years, there has been a shift toward introducing phonics earlier. Currently, this practice does not seem to prompt much discussion; only the Piagetians and neo-Piagetians caution against introducing training in skill areas too early (Case, 1981).

A major program design question is how explicit the decoding training should be. There is a distinction between analytic and synthetic instructional strategies. Analytic strategies start with a word and break it down into letter-sound correspondences, whereas synthetic strategies start with the individual correspondences and blend them into whole words. Generally, these two strategies also differ in the emphasis that is placed on phonics cues—that is, the degree of reliance the child is supposed to put on graphemic information per se. Although reading the word first and then looking within it analytically does provide an opportunity for the child to discover letter-sound relationships, the discovery method is not always effective. The discovery method is least effective with slower children, since such children are less likely to induce relationships on their own. These are the children for whom explicit, direct instruction is essential. In fact, I would propose that explicit instruction, because it is so efficient and effective, is desirable for all children, not just for slow learners.

Another major design question is how much decoding instruction to offer. Intuition suggests that detailed instruction in all possible correspondences might be overdoing it. Research has shown that even proficient adult readers are ignorant of some of the more complex phonics rules (Venezky, 1974). It appears that after direct instruction on a subset of correspondences of a given type, the average child is able to apply what has been learned to other correspondences. Although one cannot ignore the dictum laid down by Thorndike (1913)—that it is unwise to rely too much on transfer—it would be grossly inefficient to try to provide direct instruction on all correspondences.

Which correspondences should be taught explicitly? Easy-to-master correspondences should be taught first, of course, to make the point that there *are* correspondences and also because an easy-to-difficult training sequence usually turns out to be most effective. The correspondences must be productive, too—that is, enough real words can be made up from them to allow for the development of suitable vocabulary to use in stories and other instructional materials.

When should multiple letter-sound correspondences be introduced? It can be argued that this should be done early, on the grounds that such instruction teaches the child an important general concept—that English orthography is not simple. Instruction on multiple correspondences must provide the child with strategies for dealing with underlying patterns, so that the child is not dependent on a simple left-to-right progression in sounding out words. Slow learners, however, probably should not be faced with complex correspondences too early. We should not assume that general insights about underlying patterns come quickly to all children.

How should multiple letter-sound correspondences be introduced? Presenting two sounds for a single letter simultaneously was found to be better than teaching one correspondence first and then teaching the other (Williams, 1968; Levin & Watson, Note 2). Levin has suggested that instruction that involves simultaneous presentation of multiple correspondences promotes a "set for diversity" and helps children understand how English orthography works. These conclusions were based on laboratory studies, however. Systematic comparisons of methods of teaching multiple correspondences within the context of genuine instructional programs have not been made.

Where should we introduce bound morphemes, such as *-ly* and *-ed*? Since these forms provide fundamental information about the underlying structure of the written language and opportunities to expand vocabulary and natural-sounding language patterns for text, it seems reasonable that this instruction should not be put off too long.

What about exceptions to phonics rules? Venezky (1981) claims that good adult readers do not operate as if they know any rule about "hard *g*," probably because of the large number of simple and familiar words, such as *girl, get,* and *give,* that are exceptions to the patterns. Venezky suggests teaching the hard *g* sound and presenting all soft *g* words as exceptions.

Although there do not appear to be definitive answers to all of these questions, there seems an obvious general conclusion about phonics instruction. The instruction must be systematic, explicit, and sufficient, especially for slow learners. It appears that there are several ways to put together a decoding program and that there may be equally effective alternatives in the design characteristics of a decoding program. The program as a whole must be systematic and explicit and must provide adequate practice, including practice on word identification in natural text.

Segmentation is an aspect of decoding instruction that is of interest to current research. Sometimes children have trouble learning to decode because they are unaware that language is segmented—that is, that sentences are composed of words, that words are made up of syllables, and that syllables are made up of phonemes. Nor do such children realize how segmentation is represented in text. The segmentation of words is represented by the white spaces that separate them, and phonemes are represented by the letters (and letter clusters) in sequence. The ability to isolate phonemes is fundamental to learning to use phonics cues, and it is sometimes difficult for children to learn. This kind of segmentation involves more than simply knowing the language; it requires a kind of awareness of how language is put together. (Much of the credit for pointing out the need for segmentation skills in decoding comes from work by Elkonin, 1963, a Russian psychologist. Isabel Liberman, 1973, also has done extensive work documenting the relationship between performance on auditory segmentation tasks and decoding.)

We designed an instructional program that focuses on auditory segmentation and blending skills (Williams, 1979a; 1980) to teach decoding to learning-disabled children. The program was developed to serve as a supplement to any general classroom reading program. An evaluation of the program was conducted in the New York City public schools. Forty teachers of learning-disabled classes in Manhattan, Brooklyn, and the South Bronx were randomly assigned to a program or a nonprogram condition. Each teacher worked with small groups of children for about seven months. The mean IQ of the children was 82.

We found that the children who had gone through our program performed significantly and substantially better than the control children on unfamiliar (untaught) items as well as on familiar (taught) items. This performance indicated that transfer had occurred and, thus, that the instructional program had succeeded in teaching strategies of decoding. These data show clearly that even very slow learners, if they are given systematic instruction, can generalize and learn at least the rudimentary aspects of decoding.

In such work, it is essential to determine whether or not the children can generalize—that is, demonstrate transfer to content that is not included in the instruction. We focused on whether children are able to use decoding strategies on novel materials. Not all program evaluations can address this question because of the problem in monitoring the instruction to ensure that there is no direct training on the content to be used in assessing transfer. Because of the highly structured nature of our program, it was possible to incorporate such a control in the training.

There have been similar programs incorporating different design characteristics and different instructional techniques—for example, Rosner's (1974) pre-reading program on word analysis and Wallach and Wallach's (1976) program, which uses tutoring in the delivery system. Few large-scale programs focus on auditory segmentation, however, either by identifying it as a prerequisite to decoding or by including instruction in it.

Conclusion

Why does everyone not want explicit decoding instruction? It is surely not because of a lack of empirical evidence, since the evidence for explicit decoding instruction is very strong. However, data do not necessarily determine educational practice. A real-life factor is probably relevant. Decoding instruction is often considered boring, uncreative, and hard work, and successful direct instruction decoding programs often use back-up teachers to share the load. Moreover, unless teachers believe that direct instruction in decoding is important, choices will often be made in favor of a teaching procedure that requires less effort. We know that attitude counts and that, over the years, teachers have been convinced that slow learners can achieve. Schools are seeing the results of that attitude. Would that all teachers could be convinced that direct instruction in decoding would increase the reading achievement of their students, but changes occur slowly. We know that no single educational practice is adopted fully by everyone. Perhaps we should be pleased, not frustrated, about the slow but continuing increase in the acceptance of direct instruction in decoding as a crucial ingredient in beginning reading.

What should researchers do? Instructional programs can and must be based on solid theory and general research findings, but highly detailed and specific research findings ordinarily will not be useful for the development of instruction. Currently, for example, there is a great deal of sophisticated research in word recognition that is valuable for cognitive psychology but is not likely to speak directly to matters of instruction. More to the point for instruction are the actual outcomes of field tryouts of programs. We can improve the decoding programs we have now by further refinement and tryouts, but additional tinkering probably will not make for substantially greater effects on achievement. By the same token,

I would rather see some of the newer work in comprehension translated into program development; such work would lead to enormous and dramatic changes in instruction and, perhaps, to substantial gains in reading achievement.

One big problem remains, however. If we do not continue to beat the drums for good decoding instruction, the gains we have made in this area will not be maintained. The danger is that teachers and publishers might not think it important enough to spend the time, money, and trouble to incorporate good decoding instruction into comprehensive reading programs. We must do whatever we can to encourage them to do so.

Reference Notes

1. Pitman, J. *The future of the teaching of reading.* Paper presented at the Educational Conference of the Educational Records Bureau, New York, October 30–November 1, 1963.
2. Levin, H., & Watson, J. The learning of variable grapheme-to-phoneme correspondence. In *A basic research program on reading* (Final report, Project No. 639). New York: Cornell University and U.S. Office of Education, 1963.

References

Berliner, D.C., & Rosenshine, B. The acquisition of knowledge in the classroom. In R.C. Anderson, R.J. Spiro, & W.E. Montague (Eds.), *Schooling and the acquisition of knowledge.* Hillsdale, N.J.: Erlbaum, 1977.

Bloomfield, L. Linguistics and reading. *Elementary English Review,* 1942, *19,* 125–130.

Bond, G., & Dykstra, R. The cooperative research program in first-grade reading. *Reading Research Quarterly,* 1967, *2,* 5–142.

Case, R. Intellectual development: A systematic reinterpretation. In F.H. Farley & N.J. Gordon (Eds.), *Psychology and education: The state of the union.* Berkeley, Calif.: McCutchan, 1981.

Cattell, J.M. The time it takes to see and name objects. *Mind,* 1886, *11,* 63–65.

Chall, J.S. *Learning to read: The great debate.* New York: McGraw-Hill, 1967.

Elkonin, D.E. The psychology of mastering the elements of reading. In B. Simon & J. Simon (Eds.), *Educational psychology in the USSR.* London: Routledge & Kegan Paul, 1963.

Flesch, R. *Why Johnny can't read and what you can do about it.* New York: Harper, 1955.

Fries, C.C. *Linguistics and reading.* New York: Holt, Rinehart and Winston, 1962.

Goodman, K.S., & Goodman, Y.M. Learning to read is natural. In L.B. Resnick & P.A. Weaver (Eds.), *Theory and practice of beginning reading* (Vol. 1). Hillsdale, N.J.: Erlbaum, 1979.

Guthrie, J.T., Martuza, V., & Seifert, M. Impacts of instructional time in reading. In L.B. Resnick & P.A. Weaver (Eds.), *Theory and practice of early reading* (Vol. 3). Hillsdale, N.J.: Erlbaum, 1979.

House, E.R., Glass, G.V., McLean, L.D., & Walker, D.F. No simple answer: Critique of the Follow Through evaluation. *Harvard Educational Review,* 1978, *48,* 128–160.

LaBerge, D. The perception of units in beginning reading. In L.B. Resnick & P.A. Weaver (Eds.), *Theory and practice of beginning reading* (Vol. 3). Hillsdale, N.J.: Erlbaum, 1979.

Liberman, I.Y. Segmentation of the spoken word and reading acquisition. *Bulletin of the Orton Society,* 1973, *25,* 65–77.

Moore, O.K. Autotelic responsive environments and exceptional children. Hamden, Conn.: Responsive Environments Foundation, 1963.

Resnick, L.B. Theories and prescriptions for early reading instruction. In L.B. Resnick & P.A. Weaver (Eds.), *Theory and practice of early reading* (Vol. 2). Hillsdale, N.J.: Erlbaum, 1979.

Rosner, J. Auditory analysis training with prereaders. *The Reading Teacher,* 1974, *27,* 379–381.

Samuels, S.J., Miller, N., & Eisenberg, P. Practice effects of the unit of word recognition. *Journal of Educational Psychology,* 1979, *71,* 514–520.

Smith, F. *Comprehension and learning.* New York: Holt, Rinehart and Winston, 1975.

Stebbins, L.B., St. Pierre, R.G., Proper, E.C., Anderson, R.B., & Cerva, T.R. *Education as experimentation: A planned variation model. Volume IV-A; an evaluation of Follow Through.* Cambridge, Mass.: Abt Associates, 1977.

Thorndike, E.L. *Educational psychology, Vol. II: The psychology of learning.* New York: Teachers College Press, 1913.

Venezky, R.L. Theoretical and experimental bases for teaching reading. In T.A. Sebeok (Ed.), *Current trends in linguistics* (Vol. 12). The Hague: Mouton, 1974.

Venezky, R.L. *Issues in the design of phonics instruction* (Ginn Occasional Papers, No. 14). Columbus, Ohio: Ginn, 1981.

Wallach, M.A., & Wallach, L. *Teaching all children to read.* Chicago: University of Chicago Press, 1976.

Williams, J.P. Successive vs. concurrent training of multiple grapheme-phoneme correspondences. *Journal of Educational Psychology,* 1968, *59,* 309–314.

Williams, J.P. The ABDs of reading: A program for the learning disabled. In L.B. Resnick & P.A. Weaver (Eds.), *Theory and practice of early reading* (Vol. 3). Hillsdale, N.J.: Erlbaum, 1979. (a)

Williams, J.P. Reading instruction today. *American Psychologist,* 1979, *34,* 917–922. (b)

Williams, J.P. Teaching decoding with an emphasis on phoneme analysis and phoneme blending. *Journal of Educational Psychology,* 1980, *72,* 1–15.

16
Automaticity and Repeated Reading

S. Jay Samuels

Factors That Influence Comprehension

The ability to read with understanding is not only an important skill but also, unfortunately, a complex one. The ability to comprehend written text requires complex cognitive processing strategies, and numerous factors are involved. The factors that influence learning to read and comprehension may be divided into two broad categories: inside-the-head factors and outside-the-head factors. Inside-the-head factors include the reader's background, experience, knowledge, degree of automaticity in decoding, language comprehension skills, motivation, and interest. Outside-the-head factors include the text topic, text format, design and organization, readability of the text, clarity of writing style, and such extraneous factors as constraints placed on the time allowed for reading.

Obviously, inside-the-head and outside-the-head factors may interact to influence comprehension. The degree of match between the text topic and the reader's knowledge about the topic, for example, will have some bearing on the amount comprehended and the ease of comprehension. For a more detailed description of factors that influence reading see Samuels and Eisenberg (1981) and Pearson and Johnson (1978).

Automaticity of Decoding and Comprehension Strategies

Although automaticity is a necessary condition for fluent reading, it is not sufficient in itself. Since comprehension is so complex, other factors, such as background and knowledge of a text topic, will determine, in part, the speed and degree to which the text will be understood.

Usually, when people think of automaticity, they think of it in terms of decoding, but this is too restrictive a use of the term. Besides decoding, other text-processing strategies that are important for reading need to be initiated and run off automatically. Imaging a written description is a technique that can aid comprehension. Some students can image only when they are instructed to do so, but some students image spontaneously and automatically. Another example of a processing strategy is the use of anaphoric terms of reference. Skilled readers who encounter an anaphoric term know that it has a referent and automatically look for the referent either in memory or on the page. Unskilled readers, however, usually have difficulty understanding anaphoric terms (Beck, McKeown, McCaslin, & Burkes, 1979). A final example helps make the point that the concept of automaticity should be extended to include comprehension as well as decoding strategies. Skilled readers know that well-written text has a structure and, without conscious effort, will use the structure to help organize the ideas for later recall. Readers who are unaware of text structure do not seem to show any organization in their recall protocols (Taylor & Samuels, Note 1). These examples of how skilled readers automatically use sophisticated cognitive strategies illustrate that automaticity extends beyond decoding.

What Is Automaticity?

Before attempting to define automaticity, an illustration of automatic behavior might be useful. Some years ago, a friend of mine was studying orthopedic surgery, and as part of his training he practiced tying surgical knots. When he began his knot tying, he had to look at his fingers to guide them, and he was not able to talk or listen to conversation while practicing. During the learning stages, the work was so demanding that any other task that required attention disrupted the primary task. Consequently, he would not permit anything else to interfere. A number of years later, I visited my friend, and although he was now a skilled surgeon, he still practiced the surgical knot tying. During the intervening years, several important changes had taken place, however. He was now able to tie the knots without the need to guide his fingers visually, and he could engage in conversation and even watch television while he tied the knots.

The knot-tying example illustrates several important characteristics of skill development. During the beginning stages, (1) there is a shift from inaccurate to accurate behavior, (2) visual guidance may be required, (3) performance is often slow, (4) large amounts of attention and effort are required, and (5) only one task can be undertaken at a time. During the skilled stages of performance, (1) the task can be performed with accuracy and speed, (2) visual guidance is no longer necessary, (3) there is a dramatic reduction in the amount of attention and effort required to perform the task, and (4) more than one task can be performed at a time.

A definition of automaticity can now be given. *A Dictionary of Reading and Related Terms* (Harris & Hodges, 1981) defines automaticity as "response or behavior without attention or conscious effort." Although this definition captures the essence of what is meant by automaticity, it overstates the case when it states that no attention is necessary. Some small amount of attention may always be required for the execution of even well-learned skills. Another approach to the problem of defining automaticity (LaBerge & Samuels, 1974) is to consider two tasks that could not be performed together at unskilled stages. If both tasks can be performed simultaneously after training, at least one of them is automatic.

Attentional Resources, Decoding, and Comprehension

Dividing Attentional Resources

Decoding and comprehension may be thought of as two separate but interrelated processes. They are separate because decoding is a prerequisite for comprehension, and they are interrelated because comprehension may aid decoding. Figure 16-1 shows a developmental model of beginning and skilled reading. Several assumptions about reading are made in the model:

1. The reading process can be separated into decoding and comprehending.
2. Attention is required in decoding and comprehending.
3. Attention may be used simultaneously for decoding and comprehending, so long as the amount of attention demanded by these processes does not exceed an individual's attention capacity.
4. If the combined attention demands of decoding and comprehending exceed attention capacity, the reader can direct attention alternately to decoding and comprehending.

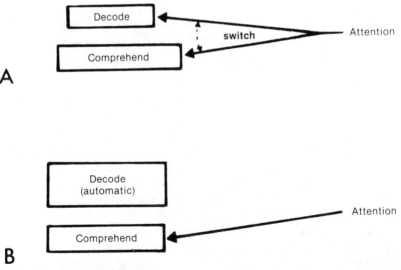

Figure 16-1. A Developmental Model of Reading: (A) Beginning Reading, with Attention Switching between Decoding and Comprehension; (B) Skilled Reading, with Automatic Decoding and Attention on Comprehension

Attention is a hypothetical construct that may be thought of as the energy or effort an individual can exert on such tasks as decoding and comprehending. Each individual possesses an attention capacity that represents the maximum amount of energy or effort that can be called upon in a given unit of time. The stored energy in attention capacity can be allocated in a variety of ways. The energy in attention is like money in the bank: it can be spent in any manner desired, but the amount spent cannot exceed what is in the account.

Decoding and comprehending require a certain amount of attention, depending on such factors as skill of the reader, familiarity with the text topic, and clarity of the text. Skills being learned require large amounts of attention, whereas tasks that have been mastered require considerably less attention. As seen in the beginning stage of decoding (figure 16–1), unskilled readers resort to a strategy of first directing their attention to decoding. When that task is done, they direct their attention to comprehension. By switching attention back and forth between decoding and comprehension, attention capacity is never exceeded, and the job of getting meaning can be accomplished—but at a cost. The cost is that the process is slow and difficult and makes heavy demands on attention and memory systems.

When a reader is fluent, because of the high degree of skill gained through practice, the attention demands required for decoding have decreased significantly. As seen in the skilled stage of figure 16–1, the ability to perform the decoding and comprehension tasks simultaneously and automatically characterizes fluent reading. The student is automatic only for familiar words, however. If unfamiliar words are encountered, significant amounts of attention again may be called upon for decoding them. Thus, it can never be said that readers are fluent with all words; only the words they have encountered many times are decoded automatically.

Stages in Perceptual Learning and Word Recognition

An important aspect of developing decoding skill involves perceptual learning. There are three stages in perceptual learning (see figure 16–2). The first stage involves discovery of those aspects of the features of the stimulus that make it distinctive, distinguishing it from other similar-appearing stimuli. Usually, a stimulus is identified not by a single feature but by a combination of features.

The second stage in perceptual learning is the unitization stage. After the distinctive features are identified, they are joined together with practice to form a unit. There is a certain economy and efficiency to this process of moving from smaller to larger units. Instead of handling the many features in a letter, the reader processes the letter as a single unit. Instead of handling the separate letters in a word, the reader processes the word as a single unit. Gibson and Levin (1975) write: "Economical processing can move in two ways: toward using the smallest distinction in criterion that suffices for a decision, or toward pickup of the largest units that carry structured information" (p. 43). Of course, if there is a need to do so, skilled readers can decompose a unit into its features by focusing their atten-

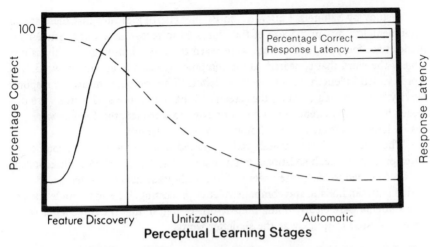

Figure 16-2. Stages in Perceptual Learning, Indicating Changes in Response Accuracy and Speed

tional spotlight on the parts rather than on the whole. In the third and final stage of perceptual learning, stimulus identification is accurate, fast, and automatic.

As seen in figure 16-2, once the student learns the distinctive features of a stimulus, the percentage correct, or accuracy, rises abruptly. Long before the unitization and automaticity stages are complete, the student is at 100 percent accuracy. Unfortunately, many classroom teachers mistakenly believe that learning is completed when the student is near the 100 percent accuracy level. Classroom instructors must remember that the goal is to go beyond accuracy to automaticity and that, to accomplish this, extended practice is required. Just as percentage correct can be used as an indicator of learning, so can speed of response, or response latency. A rule of thumb the classroom teacher can use to determine if the word identification speed is fast enough is that students should be able to identify words as quickly as they can identify their own names.

Unitization in Word Recognition

During the unitization stage, the student tries to use the largest perceptual unit in making a word recognition response. A word may be recognized either through component letter processing or through holistic processing. In component letter processing, the word is recognized by means of its letters, whereas in holistic processing, the word is recognized as a single unit. If a word is recognized through its component letters, short words should be recognized faster than longer words, since each additional letter should add to the time it takes to recognize the word. If words are recognized as a holistic pattern, however, then the time needed to recognize a word should be unrelated to its length, since the word, rather than the individual letters, serves as the unit of processing.

A study by Samuels, LaBerge, and Bremer (1978) indicates that there are developmental trends in the size of the unit used to recognize a word. Students in grades two, four, six, and college were asked to press a button as quickly as possible if the word that appeared on the computer screen was an animal word. The words varied in length from three to six letters. The computer measured response latency between each word on the screen and the button press. If words were processed holistically, latency should be unrelated to word length; if words were processed letter-by-letter, latency should be related to length.

The results with the second graders showed that they were using component letter processing; each additional letter in a word added about 55 milliseconds to the time needed to recognize a word. The fourth-grade data suggested a transition period between holistic and component letter processing. The sixth-grade and college students were clearly doing holistic processing, in that the three-letter words were processed as quickly as the six-letter words.

Studies of the Relationship between
Decoding and Comprehension

Shankweiler and Liberman (1972) found a significant relationship between the ability to read words in isolation and the ability to read words in context: "Our experience suggests that . . . poor reading of text with little comprehension among beginning readers is usually a consequence of reading words poorly (i.e., with many errors and/or a slow rate)." In a study of second graders, McCormick and Samuels (1979) also found significant correlations between accuracy of reading words in isolation and comprehension. Calfee, Venezky, and Chapman (Note 2) report that skill in pronouncing pseudowords was related to other measures of reading skill.

With research results that suggest that accuracy of word recognition is related to comprehension, why are there children who read accurately but with poor comprehension—the children teachers say are "barking at print"? There are two possible explanations: that the decoding is using too much of the attentional resources, or that a student may be as bad at listening comprehension as at reading comprehension. Being able to decode with accuracy will not help much if the problem is not only with decoding but also with comprehension. As discussed earlier, neither decoding accuracy nor automaticity will guarantee good comprehension.

The relationship between the speed of word recognition and comprehension also has been investigated. In the McCormick and Samuels (1979) study, the second graders had to name words presented in isolation, and their speed of recognition was measured. The same words were then put in context, and comprehension scores were obtained. The accuracy of recognition was highly correlated with speed of recognition ($r = -.88$); but, more germane to the topic at hand, the speed at which the words were recognized was significantly related to comprehension ($r = -.55$).

Using a different approach, Perfetti and Hogaboam (1975) studied the relationship between decoding speed and comprehension. A sample of elementary school students was divided into skilled and less skilled readers according to measures of comprehension. Students were shown words in isolation and were asked to identify them as rapidly as possible. These studies indicated consistent differences between the two groups in speed of decoding, with the difference increasing when the words were either low-frequency words or pseudowords.

The findings that accuracy and decoding speed are related to comprehension suggest that one possible way to improve comprehension is to work on the accuracy and speed of word recognition. Several studies have investigated this link between decoding speed and comprehension. In the Dahl and Samuels (1979) study, students in the experimental group were given extended practice in recognizing high-frequency words presented in isolation. The comprehension test contained only a small percentage of the practice words. No significant differences were found between the experimental and control groups in comprehension.

Fleisher, Jenkins, and Pany (1979) trained poor readers in recognizing words in isolation so that the poor readers were as fast at recognizing the words as good readers. The isolated words were then put in context, and both groups read the words in context. Although there was no difference between the two groups in accuracy or speed of recognition, the good readers were superior in comprehension.

Although the Dahl and Samuels (1979) and Fleisher et al. (1979) studies failed to demonstrate that training in rapid decoding can transfer to comprehension, Blanchard's (1980) study demonstrated that such training can have value. In this study, two groups of poor readers were given training in rapid decoding on words in isolation—each group receiving a different list of words. For the transfer comprehension test, the words contained in one of the lists were put into a meaningful text, and both groups had to read the text. Blanchard found that the group that had been given training in rapid decoding on the same words that appeared in the meaningful text had significantly better comprehension than the group that had trained on words that did not appear in the text. This study suggests that automaticity training on words in isolation may have transfer value to comprehension, but only if the words in the practice set appear in a meaningful context.

The finding from the Blanchard study bears a striking similarity to a finding from a study on the unit of word recognition done by Samuels, Miller, and Eisenberg (1979). In this study, skilled readers were asked to recognize common words presented in mirror image. Some of the mirror-image words were presented again and again, and other words were presented only once at the end of training. We were interested in the size of the unit of recognition for the repeated words and for the words seen only once. To understand the importance of this study, recall that the unit of recognition for beginning readers tends to be the letter, whereas the unit of recognition for skilled readers tends to be the entire word. Thus, letter-by-letter processing can signify either that the reader is unskilled or that a skilled reader is processing an unfamiliar word. We found that the unit of recognition became larger with each repeated presentation. If there were broad transfer, one might expect that new words presented only once at the end of training might have units of recognition that were larger than the letter, but this was not the case. The unit for the words seen only once was the single letter, even for the words seen only at the end of the training session. Thus, in this study, as in the Blanchard study, the perceptual training effects were very specific to the words actually used during training.

A major difference in the Fleisher et al. (1979) and Blanchard (1980) studies was that Fleisher et al. used good versus poor readers, whereas Blanchard used two groups of poor readers. Since comprehension is a complex process and decoding is only a part of the process, a plausible hypothesis is that the poor readers in the Fleisher et al. study were deficient in both decoding and comprehension skills. The attempt to solve the decoding problem when there might have been comprehension problems as well could explain why the good readers still surpassed the poor readers. In the Dahl and Samuels (1979) study, the group getting speed training on words in isolation saw only a portion of the words they had trained on in the tests of comprehension. In the Blanchard study, however, the group showing positive transfer to comprehension had all the practiced words in the text used to measure comprehension.

With the experimental evidence before us, we can make some tentative statements about the transfer effects of rapid decoding practice on comprehension. Rapid decoding practice has value, but the development of automatic decoding is but a single factor among the many factors that influence comprehension. Rapid decoding alone cannot ensure skilled reading. Thus, accuracy and speed of decoding are necessary but not sufficient conditions for good comprehension.

Developing Automaticity through Repeated Reading

The claim that "there is nothing new under the sun" is often true. Antecedents to repeated reading occurred in colonial American schools, where reading was taught with short, memorized passages from the Bible and the catechism. These passages were read repeatedly by the students as they learned how to read. The current methods of repeated reading, as developed at the University of Minnesota (Samuels, 1975) and Harvard University (Chomsky, 1978), have some similarities with the procedures used in colonial American schools. The development of repeated reading at Minnesota was an outgrowth of an attempt to apply automaticity theory to reading (LaBerge & Samuels, 1974) whereas the development at Harvard was an outgrowth of Chomsky's attempt to help teachers who were looking for a different way to help poor readers.

The Minnesota studies were guided by several questions:

1. If one takes automaticity theory seriously and wants to help students to become fluent readers, how would one do it?

2. Are there activities and occupations with which the practitioner can develop very complex skills to the level of automaticity?
3. Is there anything different about the training procedures used in the development of complex skills to the automatic level that is different from the methods used to teach reading?

With regard to complex activities in which high levels of automaticity are developed, sports and music come to mind. If the training of athletes and musicians is compared to the teaching of reading, however, an important difference appears. Athletes and musicians practice some small segment of behavior again and again until mastery is reached. In contrast, in the teaching of reading, there is a tendency to introduce new work before mastery of old work has been achieved.

Several other conditions may retard development of automaticity in reading. In some classrooms, follow-up and workbook activities may be unrelated to the teacher-directed portion of the reading lesson. When different parts of the reading lesson introduce different skills, the student may be denied the opportunity to acquire accuracy or automaticity.

A more pernicious problem than the lack of coordination between teacher-directed activities and follow-up and workbook activities arises from the teacher's desire to cover a year's work in a year's time. Sometimes, teachers move students through the reading materials too quickly. With too little time to practice, slow learners may be denied the opportunity to achieve either accuracy or automaticity. With insufficient time to practice, slow learners are denied the opportunity to achieve accurate and automatic decoding. For many students, especially slow learners, each day is another day of failure, rather than an opportunity to master important skills.

Different Ways to Use Repeated Reading

One technique to help beginning readers develop automaticity is repeated reading. The technique consists of having the student reread a short, meaningful passage orally several times until a satisfactory level of speed is reached. With each reading, a record is kept of word recognition errors and speed, and this information is entered on a graph. When the criterion level for speed is reached, the student may then go on to the next passage, and the procedure is repeated.

There are a number of different ways to use repeated reading:

1. In reading with audio support, the student reads a passage silently while listening to a tape-recorded narration over earphones. After a number of re-readings, the audio support is removed, and the student reads the passage without help.
2. The student reads for one minute and counts the number of words read during that time interval. This information is recorded on the student's graph. When the criterion level for speed is reached, the student goes on to the next passage.

3. In peer tutoring, two students of approximately equal ability alternate reading and listening to each other. The student who listens keeps track of the time and, if possible, the word recognition errors. (A better reader can be matched with a poorer reader, and a teacher's aide might keep track of time and errors.)

In one of our studies (Samuels, 1979), mentally retarded students reading at a first-grade level were instructed to choose easy stories that were of interest to them. Then, according to the skill of the student, short selections (50–200 words) were marked off for practice in the books they had selected. The student read the short selection orally to an assistant, who recorded the number of word recognition errors and the reading speed. This information was entered on a graph by the student. Then the student went back to his seat and practiced reading the passage silently until it was his turn to read orally to the assistant again. This alternation of silent and oral reading continued until the speed criterion level was reached. Then the student went on to the next passage.

A graph from one student in this study is shown in figure 16–3. Students in the study were told that they had to reach a speed level of eighty-five words a minute before they could go on to the next passage. Although we wanted them to improve their word recognition accuracy, 100 percent accuracy was not essential. (The reason for placing emphasis on speed rather than on accuracy is that there is a trade-off between accuracy and speed. If the student knows that 100 percent

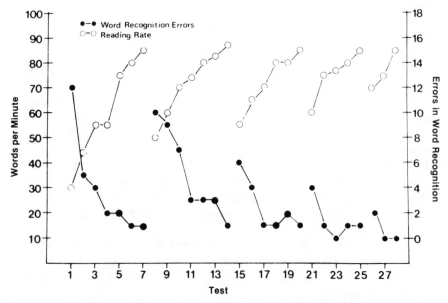

Figure 16–3. Word Recognition Errors and Reading Rate for Five Passages, Using Repeated Reading

accuracy is required in order to advance, he or she will become so fearful of making a mistake that speed will suffer.)

Figure 16-3 shows the progress a student made while reading five selections. Several points worth noting can be seen in this figure. With practice on any of the selections, the word recognition errors decreased and the speed increased. The number of rereadings necessary to reach criterion on speed decreased from seven on the first passage to three on the last one. The initial speed on a new passage increased from thirty words per minute on the first passage to seventy words per minute on the last passage. The number of initial word recognition errors decreased with each new passage. That the initial speed was faster when beginning each new passage suggests that there was a transfer of learning effect.

Several questions have been asked about the method of repeated reading. One question pertains to boredom. Our answer is that, for students who have a history of reading failure, the success they have with this method is exciting. Another question pertains to comprehension. Our answer is that, by rereading a passage several times, the student is helped to understand it. The same practice occurs with college students reading a difficult text: when they do not understand a passage, they reread it. Another question pertains to the need for keeping graphs. Our answer is that repeated reading can be done without graphs (the audio-support method does not use graphs) but that graphs serve a useful purpose by providing the students with feedback about their progress. The final question pertains to the reading skill level for which repeated reading is useful. It appears that this method is useful for beginning readers and for those who may be accurate, but not automatic, at decoding.

Research on Repeated Reading

Dahl and Samuels (1979) did a factorial study that contrasted repeated reading, hypothesis/test training, and recognition of flashed words, along with interaction effects. Results of the tests indicated that training on repeated reading had significant main effects on a cloze test, oral reading speed, and number of word recognition errors, and that there was a significant interaction effect on speed of oral reading for the treatment that combined hypothesis/test and repeated reading.

Herman and Dewitz (Note 3) tested repeated reading over a 5-month period with students at the intermediate grade level. The researchers found that repeated reading was not helpful for the faster readers. For the slower readers, however, the practice significantly improved their reading speed and comprehension.

Carver and Hoffman (1981) used repeated reading with poor readers in high school. They used a computer-based instructional system that used an accuracy criterion rather than a speed criterion. They found that repeated reading was most effective for students who were having trouble with decoding. They state: "Strong support was also found for the notion that the gains resulting from participation in such reading training transfers to new material where the same type of performance is required."

An important theoretical analysis of why repeated reading is an effective tool for developing reading fluency was done by Schreiber (1980). This analysis indicated that repeated reading improves reading by helping students learn how to compensate for the lack of prosodic cues in print (intonation sequences found in speech, such as changes in pitch, stress, and pauses). Schreiber refers to Fries (1963), who writes:

> A large part of learning to read is . . . learning to supply rapidly and automatically the . . . oral signals that are not represented in the graphic signs. It is not simply a matter of speed and fluency. It shows itself in oral reading in what has been called reading with expression. (p. 130)

Measurement and Development of Automaticity

A number of techniques can be used in the classroom to find out if a student is automatic at decoding. The first technique is based on the notion that if a student is automatic at decoding, he or she can decode and comprehend text simultaneously. To use this technique, two passages of the same difficulty level, on topics that are familiar, and of approximately the same length are needed. One passage will be used to test listening comprehension and the other to test reading comprehension. Ideally, there should be matched passages with readability levels starting at grade one and moving upward in difficulty. Then the teacher can select passages at the correct reading level for the student.

The technique involves having the student listen to a passage and then testing the student's comprehension. The student is then instructed to read orally from the second passage, and his or her comprehension of that passage is tested. (Before the student reads, he or she should be told that a comprehension test will be given immediately after reading.) For these test results to be valid, it is essential that the student not be given an opportunity to preview the material.

Since the test provides the teacher with information on listening and reading comprehension, the two modes of information processing can be compared. Also, since the student reads orally, the teacher can record the student's oral reading errors and the extent to which he or she reads with expression. The data from this test of listening and reading comprehension provide the teacher with valuable information. If the student has poor comprehension on the listening test, a general comprehension problem may be indicated. If the listening comprehension level is markedly superior to the reading comprehension level, a decoding problem is present. If, during the oral reading, the student is highly accurate at word recognition but does poorly on the comprehension test, the evidence is that the student is at the accurate level but not the automatic level in decoding.

Another method requires the student to read orally from a passage that is at his or her reading level or somewhat lower. The teacher listens for the amount of

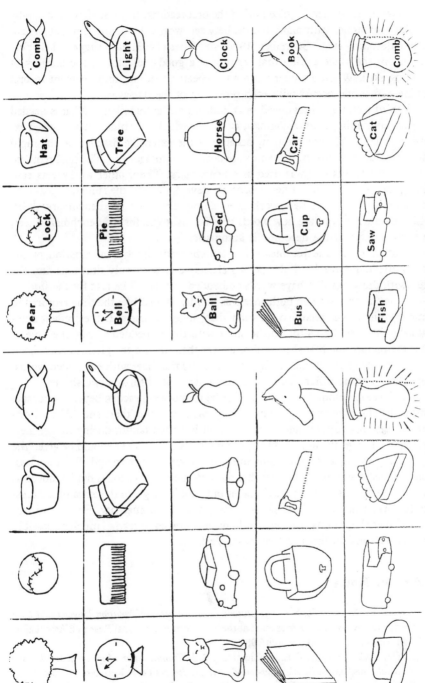

Figure 16-4. A Technique for Measuring Automaticity of Decoding

expression in the student's voice during the oral reading. If the student reads orally in a flat monotone, with many pauses between words, he or she is not at the automatic decoding stage. Schreiber (1980) and Fries (1963) have suggested that expression in the voice during oral reading is a good indicator of the mastery of decoding skill. When a student is doing repeated reading, improvement in oral reading expression occurs with each rereading of the passage.

A third technique uses speed as an indicator of automaticity. What is needed is a page containing a list of common words for which the student has received extensive practice. We assume that, because of the extensive practice on the rapid recognition of these words, the words are decoded automatically. The time required to read these words orally is used as a benchmark. Then, other worksheets containing the same number of new words are developed, and the student's goal is to recognize words on the new worksheets as rapidly as on the benchmark sheet. When the time to read the new words is as fast as it was for the benchmark sheet, we can assume that the decoding is automatic.

Another technique for measuring automaticity involves a variation of the Stroop effect. Figure 16–4 shows two sheets—one with only drawings and the other with drawings that have words embedded in them. The task for the student is to name the drawings on both sheets as rapidly as possible; the time required to name the pictures is recorded for each sheet independently. If the student automatically decodes the words on the sheet with the embedded words, the time to name the pictures on that sheet will be slower than that for the pictures-only sheet. If the student is not automatic with the words on the sheet with embedded words, there should be no difference in picture-naming speed for the two sheets.

To develop automaticity, there must be reinforced practice beyond accuracy. For the developer of curriculum materials, this means that there should be follow-up activities that support and reinforce what has been taught during the teacher-directed portion of the lesson. At regular intervals, the student should be given the opportunity to practice these skills until they have been mastered. For the classroom teacher, the implications are that the slower students should not be moved at too rapid a pace through the basal reader but should be given the extra time necessary for practicing words and skills to the point of automaticity. Finally, all students who are beginning readers should be encouraged to read as much as possible from easy-to-read books. Practice makes perfect.

Reference Notes

1. Taylor, B., & Samuels, S.J. *The utilization of syntactic information by good and poor third grade readers.* Paper presented at the American Educational Research Association Convention, New York, March 1982.
2. Calfee, R.C., Venezky, R.L., & Chapman, R.S. *Pronunciation of synthetic words with predictable and unpredictable letter-sound correspondences* (Tech. Rep. No. 71). Madison: Wisconsin Research and Development Center for Cognitive Learning, 1969.

3. Herman, P.A., & Dewitz, P.A. *The effect of repeated readings on reading rate, word recognition accuracy, syntactic chunking and comprehension.* Unpublished manuscript, University of Toledo, 1982.

References

Beck, I., McKeown, M., McCaslin, E., & Burkes, A. *Instructional dimensions that may affect reading comprehension: Examples from two commercial reading programs.* Pittsburgh: University of Pittsburgh, Learning Research and Development Center, 1979.

Blanchard, J.S. Preliminary investigation of transfer between single-word decoding ability and contextual reading comprehension by poor readers in grade six. *Perceptual and Motor Skills*, 1980, *51*, 1271–1281.

Carver, R., & Hoffman, J. The effect of practice through repeated reading on gain in reading ability using a computer-based instructional system. *Reading Research Quarterly*, 1981, *16*, 374–390.

Chomsky, C. When you still can't read in third grade: After decoding, who? In S.J. Samuels (Ed.), *What research has to say about reading instruction.* Newark, Del.: International Reading Association, 1978.

Dahl, P.R., & Samuels, S.J. An experimental program for teaching high speed word recognition and comprehension skills. In J.E. Button, T.C. Lovitt, & T.D. Rowland (Eds.), *Communications research in learning disabilities and mental retardation.* Baltimore: University Park Press, 1979.

Fleisher, L.S., Jenkins, J.R., & Pany, D. Effects on poor readers' comprehension of training in rapid decoding. *Reading Research Quarterly*, 1979, *15*(1), 30–48.

Fries, C.C. *Linguistics and reading.* New York: Holt, Rinehart & Winston, 1963.

Gibson, E.J., & Levin, H. *The psychology of reading.* Cambridge, Mass.: MIT Press, 1975.

Harris, T.L., & Hodges, R.E. (Eds.). *A dictionary of reading and related terms.* Newark, Del.: International Reading Association, 1981.

LaBerge, D., & Samuels, S.J. Toward a theory of automatic information processing in reading. *Cognitive Psychology*, 1974, *6*, 293–323.

McCormick, C., & Samuels, S.J. Word recognition by second graders: The unit of perception and interrelationships among accuracy, latency, and comprehension. *Journal of Reading Behavior*, 1979, *11*(2), 107–118.

Pearson, P.D., & Johnson, D.D. *Teaching reading comprehension.* New York: Holt, Rinehart & Winston, 1978.

Perfetti, C.A., & Hogaboam, T. The relationship between single word decoding and reading comprehension skill. *Journal of Educational Psychology*, 1975, *67*, 461–469.

Samuels, S.J. The method of repeated readings. *The Reading Teacher*, 1979, *32*, 403–408.

Samuels, S.J., & Eisenberg, P. A framework for understanding the reading process. In F. Pirozolla, & M. Wittrock (Eds.), *Neuropsychological and cognitive processes in reading.* New York: Academic Press, 1981.

Samuels, S.J., LaBerge, D., & Bremer, C. Units of word recognition: Evidence for developmental changes. *Journal of Verbal Learning and Verbal Behavior*, 1978, *17*, 715–720.

Samuels, S.J., Miller, N., & Eisenberg, P. Practice effects on the unit of word recognition. *Journal of Educational Psychology*, 1979, *4*, 514–520.

Schreiber, P.A. On the acquisition of reading fluency. *Journal of Reading Behavior*, 1980, *12*, 177–186.

Shankweiler, D., & Liberman, I.Y. Misreading: A search for causes. In J.F. Kavanaugh & I.G. Mattingly (Eds.), *Language by ear and by eye*. Cambridge, Mass.: MIT Press, 1972.

17

The Problem
of Differential Instruction

Patricia M. Cunningham

Teaching involves more than just managing; it also involves such functions as engaging attention, diagnosing, explaining, questioning, guiding, inspiring, exciting, and caring. These functions must be learned by teachers to make their teaching more effective. These functions are important for teachers because they allow them to engage themselves and their students in teaching and learning.

Imagine that you are a teacher in a multiaged classroom. You have a group of second graders and a group of fourth graders, both reading in the second-grade book, and both groups are appropriately placed. You meet with the second graders and teach a selection from the basal reader. Immediately following that, you meet with the fourth graders and teach the same selection. If someone were observing these lessons, would you appear to be doing things differently with the two groups of students? The research suggests that there would be more differences between the two lessons than similarities. With the fourth graders who read poorly, the major differences would probably be the following:

1. You would be twice as likely to correct oral reading errors.
2. You would be five times more likely to correct semantically appropriate errors (*can't* for *cannot, auto* for *automobile*).
3. You would interrupt immediately to correct an error, rather than waiting until the students finish the phrase or clause.
4. When correcting errors, you would give a graphemic/phonemic cue ("How does that word begin? What sound does the short *a* make?"), rather than the semantic/syntactic cue given your good readers ("Now, how could he sit on a *cheer*? Think about what you're reading!").
5. You would make fewer allusions to the story line that holds the story together.
6. You would spend more time working with isolated words and correcting pronounciations.
7. These students would probably read less than half as many in-context words as the good readers do (Allington, 1983).
8. In-context reading is likely to be done silently (Allington, 1983).

9. The children would probably attend and behave less well.
10. You would be less relaxed than when you are working with the good readers.

The observational data that indicates that the instruction given poor readers is qualitatively different from the instruction given good readers is overwhelming. The issue yet to be resolved is whether the instruction given to poor readers should be different. A related issue is why the instruction is different. Teachers are more alert and anxious and more likely to respond immediately to any errors made by poor readers. These students bring to the reading group a history of failure and a set of adverse behaviors that make the already anxious teacher's job more difficult.

Teachers correct more errors of all kinds when they are working with poor readers because they want the poor readers to be good readers—and good readers do not make many errors. Also, since teachers are looking more closely at the reading behaviors of the poor readers, they are more likely to hear errors that might pass undetected if they were made by good readers. Teachers correct errors with a focus on letters and sounds rather than on meaning because many poor readers do not know their letter-sound relationships very well. Good readers generally do, so a lack of attention to meaning must be the problem of the good readers. Teachers make few allusions to the story line, which would help poor readers gain meaning, because there is limited time and much of it has to be spent in helping them learn words, correcting errors, and trying to keep the students attending and behaving. Poor readers read only half as many in-context words as good readers for the same reason—limited time. Reading by poor readers is done orally rather than silently because they want to read aloud; if you let them read silently, they probably would not read!

What Is Wrong with Correcting All Errors Immediately and with Directing the Reader's Attention to the Letter-Sound Level?

Good readers do not make many errors, but they do make some errors. Have you ever been reading along in a book, newspaper, or magazine, reached a point where the message seemed contradictory, and then glanced back to see that you had read "unnecessary" as "necessary" or "carefree" as "careful"? We have all had the experience of mistaking a word for a similar looking word. Often, these errors are not apparent to us. They become apparent, however, when the sense of what we are reading is violated. When we cannot understand or when what we read in one sentence appears to be contradicted in later sentences, we realize that we have probably made a mistake, and we check and self-correct. This ability to use making sense as a constant self-monitoring device is crucial to successful, fluent reading. Good readers develop this self-monitoring system; poor readers often do not.

Good readers are seldom corrected when they make an error that does not affect meaning. Poor readers are corrected for meaning-changing as well as non-meaning-changing errors. When they make a meaning-changing error, good readers are often allowed to get to the end of the clause or phrase before being stopped. Thus, they often can correct their own error because the words following the error let them know that they have made a mistake and give them a clue about what the word should have been. If you read "I saw" as "I was" but the remainder of the sentence says "the hospital," you will know that you have made a mistake and you will be able to correct it. If I stop you before you can read "*the hospital,*" however, you cannot learn to use making sense to know when to self-correct and you cannot develop an internal monitoring system.

What is Wrong with Devoting Little Attention to the Story Line and Letting Isolated Word Drill Take Up a Larger Percentage of Reading Instructional Time?

Comprehension requires that children relate what they know to what they are reading. Read the following passage (from Tierney & Spiro, 1979) and then close your eyes and summarize what you have read:

Today's Cricket

The batsmen were merciless against the bowlers. The bowlers placed their men in slips and covers. But to no avail. The batsmen hit one four after another along with an occasional six. Not once did a ball look like it would hit their stumps or be caught.

If you are unable to tell what you have read in your own words, you have not comprehended the passage. If you are able to say the words, word identification is not the problem. Rather, the problem is that comprehension requires that we know something about the topic about which we are reading and that we use what we know and try to relate the two. Your problem is not that you do not know how to relate the known to the text but rather that you do not know enough about cricket. If reading instruction focuses too much on words and letters and fails to spend time focusing on what is read and how it relates to what is known, poor readers will get the wrong idea about what reading is and about what you should be trying to do "in your head" as you read. Too much attention to words and letters, which uses up all the time that would be devoted to understanding and thinking in good-reader groups, often results in children thinking that reading is "saying the words right."

What Problems Result If Poor Readers Read Only Half as Much as Good Readers?

For the answer to this question, I refer you to Jay Samuels's chapter (chapter 16). To get good at something, you must practice it a great deal. If poor readers are reading only half as many words during their reading instructional time, it is no surprise that they read at a slow, laborious, halting pace and that they never sound like good readers. Furthermore, most teachers realize that the real amount of in-context reading done by good readers is four or five times greater than that done by poor readers. Good readers, because they are good readers, often choose to read even when they are not in the reading group. Since good readers often finish their seatwork ahead of time, do extra reading during school, often read at home, and have the advantage of having many books available that they are able to read, they obviously read much more than poor readers. It is probable that a student needs more than just a great deal of reading to become a good reader, but it appears clear that, along with instruction, the student must practice regularly if he or she is ever going to get good at it. The observation that poor readers do less than half as much in-context reading as good readers do is probably just the tip of the iceberg.

Why Is It a Problem That Poor Readers Do Most of Their Reading Orally Rather Than Silently?

There are a number of problems with having most reading done orally. Most reading done by children and adults is silent reading. If poor readers are seldom made to read silently, they will probably not learn to do so. The fact that poor readers are reading orally is related to the problems of oral reading errors. A child who is reading silently cannot be stopped for every error, regardless of whether or not the error affects meaning. A child who is reading silently can make an error, read to the end of the phrase or clause, realize that something is wrong, and go back and fix the error. Silent reading is apt to help children develop self-monitoring systems. Oral reading in reading groups is usually done by one child at a time. If seven children read seven pages silently, they have each read seven pages. If they take turns reading the pages orally, they have each read one page. The fact that oral reading is likely to be the mode of instruction in poor-reader groups also suggests that poor readers do not get enough practice reading to become fluent and automatic with word identification.

Should Good Readers and Poor Readers Be Taught Differently?

It seems that there should be some differences in how good readers and poor readers are taught, but that the current differences are the wrong ones. I will recommend some ways in which reading instruction for poor readers should be the same as that for good readers and one way in which it might legitimately need to be different.

Poor Readers, Like Good Readers, Must See Reading as Meaningful and Must Actively Work at Thinking as They Read

Some of the reading instructional time must be devoted to helping children bring what they know to the forefront of their minds. Brainstorming activities such as "What words do you think of when you think of 'skiing'?" and personal experience questions such as "Have you ever been skiing? Do you know anyone who has been skiing? Have you ever seen anyone skiing on the television or in the movies?" will help children call up and share what they know about the topic to be read about.

Children must then have purposes for their reading that help them compare and contrast what they know with what they read. If children have difficulty in formulating purposes, the teacher can let them respond to a forced-choice prereading prediction—for example, "If you think this skiing story takes place in the Swiss Alps, raise one thumb; two thumbs if you think it takes place in the Colorado mountains; thumbs down if you think it takes place somewhere else. Now, read this page and see if you guessed right about the setting."

Most teachers know many ways to help children call up and share what they know and then read actively to see how what they know compares with what is printed on the page. What seems to be needed is not for teachers to learn new strategies, but rather for teachers to realize that poor readers especially need these meaning-focusing activities.

Poor Readers, Like Good Readers, Need a Great Deal of Silent Reading Practice

Some silent reading practice should be in easy materials, and it may take the form of repeated readings. Silent reading practice is crucial to the development of fluency and automaticity in reading and seems to be essential if children are to develop a self-monitoring, making-sense system. In chapter 16, Samuels suggests a number of ways to get children involved in repeated readings. He also suggests that poor readers do as much easy reading as possible.

It is also important that the reading group time be spent as much as possible in silent reading activities. This may be difficult at first, because the children may protest that they want to read aloud. If most of their reading experience has been oral, it is understandable that they will want to do it this way, since reading to them is saying the words aloud. The fact that they want to read orally demonstrates what they think reading is and should make clear to the teacher the need to switch the instructional mode to silent reading for meaning. Accomplishing this with a recalcitrant group of poor readers will require cleverness and persistence on the teacher's part. It is probable that the teacher will have to help children set purposes a page at a time or even, in the face of extreme resistance, a sentence at a time. Directions such as "Read the first sentence and raise your thumb if the day was hot; thumbs down if the day was not hot" (and, in the second sentence, "thumbs up if the boy was happy; thumbs down if not") may be necessary for a short time until the children realize that they can read silently and get information. As quickly as possible, however, the children should move to larger units of text and should help set their own purposes, which will require them to relate self to text.

When Oral Reading Is Conducted as a Whole Class Activity, It Can Be Helpful for the Listeners to Have Their Books Closed

Even assuming that the greater percentage of reading instructional time is spent in silent reading, there is no reason that some time should not be spent in reading orally. Children might first read the story silently for meaning and then choose slips of paper to determine which pages they will "perform and show off" by reading aloud. They should then be given a few minutes to practice their pages. (Notice how repeated readings and automaticity practice sneak in.) As each child reads his or her chosen page the other children and the teacher should have their books closed. The reader should not be interrupted unless the teacher cannot follow what is going on. With this technique, the entire question of which errors to correct is resolved. Errors that do not change meaning ("can't" for "cannot") are never heard, and the reader quickly gets the idea that making sense is the primary purpose of reading. Furthermore, since making sense is the criterion, corrections almost always occur at the clause or phrase boundary, since it generally takes that much additional text to realize that the sense has been violated. Correction would have to be of the semantic/syntactic type ("How could a boy go into a *horse?*") rather than of the graphemic/phonemic type ("Look at the letter. What sound does that make?")

I would make the three preceding recommendations for good readers as well as for poor readers. The final recommendation, however, is solely for poor reader instruction. It allows the first three recommendations to take place.

Add a Second Reading Group Meeting for the Poor Readers

One of the major reasons poor readers do not have as much time focused on meaning is that teachers know that these students need to spend time on word identification skills. One of the major reasons poor readers do not develop fluency and automaticity is that they do not have enough practice. It appears that poor readers need more of everything, but only so much instruction can be squeezed into 25 minutes. Most elementary teachers have some down time late in the day, when work is being finished and the room is being prepared for the next day. Often, the poor readers create problems during this last 30 minutes or so of the day. They do not have work to finish—or will not finish it—and they sometimes interfere with those who do have work to do. Teachers could round up their poor readers for a 15-to-20-minute session each afternoon, focusing on building the word identification skills necessary for the next day's lesson so that all of the next day's time could be devoted to meaning-focused activities. Alternatively, this time could be used for silent reading practice with easy materials. The establishment of a second lesson each day (Allington, 1983) would provide the extra time needed for poor readers to develop both word identification and comprehension abilities.

References

Allington, R.L. The reading instruction provided readers of differing abilities. *Elementary School Journal,* 1983, *83*(5), 548–559.

Tierney, R.J., & Spiro, R.J. Basic postulates about comprehension: Implications for teachers. In J. Harste & R. Carey (Eds.), *New perspectives on comprehension.* Bloomington: Indiana University Language Monographs, 1979.

18

Five Problems with Children's Comprehension in the Primary Grades

Isabel L. Beck

Virtually all people who study reading would agree that reading comprehension is not a simple process. Rather, it is a complex process composed of a number of interacting subprocesses and abilities: decoding accuracy, decoding fluency, vocabulary knowledge, and previous background in the topics in a given text.

To take a deeper look at notions about what it takes to comprehend a piece of text, consider the beginning of a story (Clymer, 1976) from the third-grade reader of a widely used basal program:

The Donkey Egg

The Hodja lived in a small village with his wife, Fatima. They had one little donkey, and how they wished for one more donkey!

The Hodja had a friend, Ali. At times they had quarrels. Then they were not such good friends for a while. One day Ali brought a strange gift to the Hodja. From the folds of his loose coat, he brought it forth. It was large and smooth and round.

He offered the gift to the Hodja and Fatima. "A donkey egg," Ali said. "You must sit on this egg for three weeks."

There is little question that, as a skilled reader, you could recall much of this story and correctly answer questions about it. What needs to be pointed out is that, in comprehending this text, you performed a variety of processes at an unconscious level and applied a good deal of knowledge. In contrast, some third graders are not able to do some of the things you did, and other third graders would have difficulty doing them.

This excerpt is part of an approximately 800-word story that my colleagues and I have worked with in several experiments (Beck, Omanson, & McKeown, 1982). For this story, we have identified more than eighty "difficulty candidates," which fall into two groups: (1) linguistic features in the text and (2) knowledge that must be brought to the text. We have hypothesized that some requisite knowledge is unknown to some third graders and hence negatively affects their processing of the text and their construction of its meaning. Our difficulty candidates are not necessarily instances of low-quality sentences. Rather, they are linguistic and conceptual features of the story that might be difficult for children reading the story.

We have identified three difficulty candidates in the first sentence. First, there are the foreign names, *Hodja* and *Fatima;* although it is probably not important that Hodja and Fatima are pronounced correctly, it is important that they be recognized as names. Even if you had never seen those names before, your experience with foreign names would allow you to tag the words as "names of people," but some children do not have much experience with foreign names. The problem of recognizing the words as names of people may be heightened by our second difficulty candidate, the use of the definite article *the* in *the Hodja.* As an adult reader, you processed *the Hodja* as a title (even if you did not know that *the Hodja* means "the teacher"), so it probably did not disturb you that one character carries a title (the Hodja) and the other a name (Fatima). The third difficulty candidate concerns the separation of the characters. *The Hodja* appears at the beginning of the sentence, and *Fatima* is found at the end of sentence. The separation of the characters perhaps requires reprocessing of the clause; that is, after establishing that *the Hodja* lives in a village, the reader encounters "with his wife, Fatima" and may need to reprocess the sentence to establish that in fact it is *the Hodja* and his wife *Fatima* who live in a village.

We identified two difficulty candidates in the second sentence: "They had one little donkey, and how they wished for one more donkey!" One candidate concerns the motivation for wishing for another donkey. The clause "They had one little donkey" is simply a statement of possession. To relate the possession clause to wishing for another donkey, the reader probably needs to infer from the statement of possession a statement of lack—that is, "They *only* had one little donkey." This inference provides a motivation for wishing. The other difficulty candidate concerns the use of the oral language idiom, *and how.* We suspect that some students have difficulty understanding *and how* because that idiom is unfamiliar in print. Not understanding *and how* may be particularly disrupting to this story, because the expression is used to introduce new information about the wishes of the characters.

Another difficulty candidate occurs in the third sentence: "The Hodja had a friend, Ali." "Ali" is a restrictive clause with an implied verb. The sentence needs to be understood as "The Hodja had a friend *named* (or called) Ali." Because Ali may be unfamiliar as a name, and because there is not a verb to help identify it as a name, we identified this part of the sentence as a difficulty candidate.

What evidence do we have that these difficulty candidates cause problems? The evidence comes from theory, data, children's oral readings, and their recalls. Consider the separation of the characters *the Hodja* and *Fatima* in the first sentence. Much research shows that when two related but noncontiguous concepts need to be integrated to be comprehended, reading time is increased (Carpenter &

Just, 1981; Frederiksen, 1981; Lesgold, Roth, & Curtis, 1979; Perfetti & Roth, 1981). Interruptions can be disruptive to the thread of a text, because the extra time needed to process the connection between concepts takes away from the construction of meaning (Collins & Smith, in press). Indeed, Lesgold and Perfetti (1978) have suggested that in "the non-ideal world of everyday reading, that which takes a long time may not get done."

Do the difficulty candidates prevent children from comprehending effectively? Excerpts from audio tapes of youngsters reading "The Donkey Egg" present evidence that they had problems with certain sentences in the story. Let us look at evidence for difficulty with the foreign names, *Hodja*, *Fatima*, and *Ali*. (It should be noted that the children were given an opportunity to warm up for oral reading. They read the entire text silently, recalled it, and answered thirty-five questions before reading orally.)

Here is how one student, Tamika, read the first sentence. After reading the title, "The Donkey Eggs," she paused, pointed to *Hodja*, and said, "What's this? . . . I forgot this word again." The examiner said, "Hodja." Tamika read "The . . . uh . . . The Hodja lived in a small village with his wife, Fatima. She stopped, pointed to *Fatima* and asked, "What's this word?" The examiner told her, "It's Fatima, you're right."

Although this child pronounced *Fatima* correctly, our conjecture is that the word did not have any specific meaning for her and that she was not able to tag it as a name. She did a kind of double take and then asked about it.

Another child read *Fatima* as *Phantom;* we wonder if this child has knowledge of the word *phantom* and, if so, if he attaches that knowlege to Fatima. Another child's recall suggests that Ali and Fatima have combined into one character she calls *Aliama*. Most of the children were not so overt with their confusions. From the number of pauses and repetitions in their oral reading, however, it is not unreasonable to conclude that some children do mental "huh's" when they get to unfamiliar names.

Tamika's oral reading also provides evidence that she responds to the definite article *the* in *the Hodja*. (When a reader encodes *the*, he or she needs a referent for it. The referent can come from the text or from general knowledge. Since *the Hodja* are the first two words in the text, the referent must come from general knowledge.) Let us consider what Tamika did. First, she asked for a pronunciation of *Hodja*. Then she read "The" (paused and said "uh"), and then she read "The Hodja." It is not unreasonable to suggest that her pause was related to some difficulty connecting *the* with *Hodja*. Had it been *the President*, she probably would not have read "The (uh) The President."

An additional example of oral reading evidence of processing difficulty is related to the sentences, "The Hodja had a friend, Ali. At times they had quarrels." Jamal's reading of this sentence provides strong evidence that he has a problem with the lack of a verb and the unfamiliarity of the name in the first sentence. Jamal read, "The Hodja had a friend (pause) all, all (ignoring the period) at times they . . . " Jamal probably could have handled the sentence, "The Hodja had a friend *called* Ali." Also, he probably would have been able to handle the inferred verb if the sentence were "Tom had a friend, Bob."

The processing requirements for comprehending text are complex, regardless of how obvious and straightforward the text appears to a competent adult reader. The complexity of the comprehension process is magnified for third graders in that few of them have the decoding capabilities of adult readers. Many of the children in our study could be described as accurate but not fluent readers. Even with sentences in which the children pronounced the words correctly and did not get tangled in syntactic structures, they read slowly, haltingly, and nonfluently. While listening to them read, one got a real feeling for how much mental capacity they were using just to get through the words. As Samuels points out in chapter 16 of this volume, the problem is that if a great deal of the children's mental resources are used to get through the words, there might not be sufficient resources left for the children to give comprehension the attention it requires.

Reading comprehension is not a matter of merely extracting meaning from print. Rather, it is an active process in which the reader constructs meaning through a multitude of interactions with a text.

Five Problems in Reading

In an attempt to analyze some problematic interactions, the rest of this chapter is organized around five problems identified from the children's readings and recalls of the Hodja text and their answers to questions about it: word attack, fluency, syntactic structures, word meanings, and background knowledge. In the discussion of the problems, I will relate proposed solutions to what theory and research suggests, and I will then make instructional recommendations for remedies.

Word Attack

Some of the children had obvious word-attack problems; either the examiner had to supply words or the children mispronounced words or sometimes they sounded them out. Teachers often describe such children by saying: "They guess at the pronunciation of words," "They can't remember their sight words," or "They don't know their vowel sounds." In instructional terms, these children have not learned their decoding skills, or they have word attack problems. The children in our study, however, were in the third grade and had had three years of instruction from basal reading programs. Virtually all basal reading programs include instruction in many, if not most, of the English sound–symbol relationships. In the small inner-city school district in which we worked, one-fifth of the 150 third graders who were given a test of decoding, the Wide Range Achievement Test, scored below grade level. To obtain a 3.0 grade-level equivalent score, a child needs to obtain fifty-one points. Twenty-six points are given for writing one's name and finding some letters in the alphabet, and all third graders in the study received those points. Hence, the children needed to read twenty-five words correctly. The child is exited from the test when he or she misses ten consecutive words. To provide a sense of the level of word pronunciation required, the first thirty words on the test are as follows: *cat, see, red, to, big, work, book, eat, was, him, how, then, open, letter, jar, deep, even, spell, awake, block, size, weather, should, lip, finger, tray, felt, stalk, cliff, lame.*

After 22 months of reading instruction, why were thirty students unable to read correctly a list of twenty-five words—all of which are probably in their speaking and listening vocabularies? There are several possible answers to this question: perhaps a child was not ready to learn to read when formal instruction was initiated; perhaps a child encountered stories that were trivial, so that he got turned off to reading; perhaps a child had too much phonics; perhaps a child did not have enough phonics; perhaps a child had the wrong kind of phonics; and so forth.

Depending on their orientation, various reading experts would select different reasons from the foregoing list. From my interpretation of theory, experimental data (Bishop, 1964; Jeffrey & Samuels, 1967), and evaluative research (Guthrie, Samuels, Martuza, Seifert, Tyler, & Edwall, 1976; Stebbins, St. Pierre, Proper, Anderson, & Cerva, 1977), my own analysis of various instructional strategies used to teach decoding (Beck & McCaslin, Note 1), and my clinical experience, I would point to the wrong kind of phonics instruction as the most likely cause of word-attack difficulties. (*Phonics* is here defined as the instructional strategies used to teach sound–symbol relationships and word synthesis.)

The wrong kind of phonics instruction may be characterized as follows:

1. It is too abstract, requiring sophisticated prerequisite abilities; for example, children are expected to extract the /i/ sound by hearing the teacher say, "It is the vowel sound heard in *fish*."
2. It spends time on tasks that do not contribute to reading; for example, children identify pictures of items whose names contain a target phoneme, rather than looking at the phoneme and responding with its sound (Bateman, 1979).
3. It omits components needed for successful decoding; for example, children are not directly taught to blend sounds together.

In contrast, the right kind of phonics instruction contains three elements: (1) direct letter–sound correspondence instruction, which explicitly tells the children what the sound–symbol relationship is; (2) an explicit blending strategy, which teaches children how to synthesize sounds into words; and (3) repeated opportunities to apply learned correspondences and blending to the reading of words in connected text, so that students will learn to read fluently.

Fluency

Most of the children read haltingly, in a monotone, and with many hesitations. Correct but halting reading can be an indication (indeed, I believe it is a good indication) of nonautomated decoding. The word *automatic* is used to describe a skill that can be carried out without overt attention. Automaticity is best understood in the context of the notion that human information-processing capacity is limited; that is, people simply cannot actively attend to too many things at once. The implication for reading is that some of the subprocesses, such as decoding, need to be developed to the point where they are done without direct attention on the part of the reader. If this is not the case, there will not be enough processing capacity for the reader to attend to some of the higher-level processes involved in comprehension (see Samuels, chapter 16 of this volume).

There is empirical evidence that comprehension is weak when texts are read too slowly. Work by LaBerge and Samuels (1974) and Perfetti and Hogaboam (1975) indicates that slow word recognition is related to poor sentence processing and that fast word recognition is correlated with better comprehension. These correlational data have been supplemented by Lesgold and Resnick's (in press) major finding that the causal links between automaticity and comprehension are stronger than those between accuracy and comprehension. These investigators conclude that early weakness in speed seems to be a more serious indicator of later comprehension difficulty than traditional indicators, such as poor achievement test scores. The few intervention studies that have been directed toward the development of decoding automaticity have not yielded completely convincing results, yet the notion that decoding automaticity is needed for efficient reading comprehension is compelling. The theoretical foundation for the notion of automaticity is so well developed that further experiments building on what has been learned can be undertaken with confidence.

Further investigations of decoding automaticity should also provide evidence that direct intervention is helpful (and in some cases required), if automaticity is to develop. The practices that will contribute most effectively to the development of automaticity need to be specified, and practices that work against the development of automaticity should be eliminated. Teachers should stop moving children through reading materials at a constant pace, for example, regardless of the children's ease and fluency in reading. As the selections get harder, the students are confronted with a word pool that is constantly increasing in size and difficulty. There is often little opportunity for rapid word recognition to develop. Children need to have repeated encounters with a set of words. More research could show whether repeated encounters are best accomplished by frequent repetitions of a subset of words that occur in texts written entirely around a limited set of words or by supplemental techniques, such as repeated readings or timed, gamelike activities.

Syntactic Structures

The third reading problem concerns the difficulty many children had with certain syntactic structures. For a long time, there has been a belief that children are linguistically mature by the time they get to school. This belief probably originates from statements by linguists about the extraordinary language accomplishments of very young children (McNeill, 1970; Sloben, 1971). It must be pointed out, however, that although children's accomplishments are extraordinary, they are not complete. Indeed, there is evidence that children's ability to understand syntactic structures continues to increase until at least age 13 (Palermo & Molfese, 1972).

Problems with syntactic structures can arise in two ways. First, children's ability to understand syntactic structures when they are spoken does not guarantee that these same structures will be understood when they are read. This is because print does not have the tone, stress patterns, and other prosodic cues provided by a speaker, nor does print have the support of the real-world context that is present in conversation. Some of the pauses, hesitations, false starts, and rereading heard on our oral reading tapes provide evidence that children use up processing resources to recover the syntactic structure of printed sentences—sentences that would be readily processed as spoken sentences. Second, some syntactic structures are more frequent in speech than in print and are unfamiliar when encountered in print. Such structures may be very treacherous for some young children when they are encountered in print without the cues available in speech.

How should teachers help their students deal with syntactic structures? Teachers can provide direct experience with the structures by reading sentences or passages aloud, with the tone, stress, and pauses that will unravel the meaning of any unfamiliar structures. The children can then imitate the teacher's model by reading the sentences or passages. Next the teacher and children can create new sentences that follow the same structures. Consider the very difficult construction, "From the folds of his loose coat, he brought it forth." After the teacher reads the sentence (perhaps with some theatrical gestures), and the children read what the teacher has modeled, the teacher can then offer sentences more in touch with the child's environment—for example, "From the bottom of his lunch bag, Tom took out a tiny pencil" and then "From the bottom of his lunch bag, Tom brought a tiny pencil forth."

Oral reading is a prevalent part of primary-grade reading instruction, but it is questionable whether the benefits that can be derived from it are always used to advantage. Teachers typically use the oral reading of their children to gather information about word recognition, but they probably do not use oral reading for evaluating and then directly teaching syntactic processing. Children are frequently asked, for example, to read a passage in a way that emphasizes a character's excitement, or sadness, or whatever. In my student-teaching days, the manual I was using frequently suggested that children be told to read with "expression." I followed the suggestion, but the children did not read with expression. I soon realized that the children did not know what *expression* meant and that models of reading with a particular expression (for example, in a way that shows that Henry was frightened or that Louise was happy) were helpful. I also found that children liked to imitate models. Imitation can be playful and fun; it does not have to imply a rigid "read the way I tell you to" approach.

Word Meaning

Many children had difficulty with the meaning of some words. Beginning reading materials include words that are likely to be a part of most young children's speaking and listening vocabularies. This is sensible because, in the course of learning to decode and construct meaning from print, it would be highly inappropriate for children to encounter more than an occasional unknown word. As children progress to the intermediate grades, however, the number and difficulty of words increase. The vocabulary becomes more sophisticated, and word meaning becomes more of a problem.

In the teacher's manuals, words that might cause decoding or meaning difficulties are indicated, and suggestions are made for presenting these words prior to reading. An analysis of the instructional strategies for teaching the meanings of unknown words specified in manuals suggests, however, that these strategies are far from adequate (Beck, McKeown, McCaslin, & Burkes, Note 2). Consider, for example, the strategies provided for teaching some words prior to reading "The Donkey Egg." The teacher is instructed to put a list of potentially troublesome words on the board, including *quarrels, heavens, offered, reply.* Then the teacher reads a sentence—for example, "Arguments are sometimes called _____"—and the children are to choose *quarrels* to fill in the blank. Another sentence is, "If an accident happens, help should be _____" (*offered*). I believe that for children who do not know what *quarrels* or *offered* mean, these fleeting encounters are of very little use. There is little likelihood that the words will be learned, given the lack of power in the context sentences and the single encounter with the words.

The kind of vocabulary control found in the older basal programs is not in evidence in the newer programs. By about the third grade, and certainly by the fourth grade, most of the selections in the newer programs are drawn from independently written materials. Most selections are not created by a publisher for inclusion in a series. Instead, the newer basal readers are virtual anthologies. Authors of the selections are professional writers using the best words available to them to communicate their ideas. They do not draw from an established word pool, nor is the word pool reused from selection to selection. The sophisticated vocabulary found in the selections has both positive and negative potential. The positive is obvious—children can add words to their vocabulary pool. The negative is also obvious—too many unfamiliar words will cause comprehension problems. In addition, the brief encounters with the vocabulary instruction are not likely to increase the vocabulary pool of children with limited vocabularies.

A major finding from my own vocabulary research (Beck, Perfetti, & McKeown, 1982) is that it takes an extended series of fairly intense exposures before one "owns a word"—that is, before a word can be quickly accessed and applied in appropriate contexts. The words that are likely to cause comprehension problems for children in the intermediate grades are not frequently heard in everyday conversation and thus not easily reinforced. Therefore, an effective instructional program must arrange conditions so that words to be learned are reinforced, maintained, and enriched in exciting and playful ways.

In our instructional experiments, fourth-grade children were taught 104 words over a 5-month period. The instruction provided a variety of instances of word concepts and encouraged much discussion of word meanings. The children in our experiment were required to make connections between word meanings, to explore denotations and connotations, to respond to words affectively as well as cognitively, and to elaborate semantic networks. There is evidence that the instructed children were able to apply what they had learned about the instructed words to comprehension tasks. There was also a hint of transfer to other words; that is, the children seemed to learn more untaught words than a comparable control group. This work suggests that reading comprehension may be enhanced by instituting deep and rich vocabulary programs.

The results of our study suggest that it may be better to teach 100 new words well than to present 400 superficially. This brings up a general instructional principle that I think is very important. The schools do fairly well in teaching a little about a lot. Although I do not suggest that this practice be stopped, I do suggest that there also should be times when a lot is taught about a little.

Background Knowledge

Many children did not know what they needed to know to understand the text. In addition, they often did not relate what they clearly knew to what they read.

Recently, there has been a veritable explosion of research about the background knowledge a reader brings to text and its effect on comprehension. The relationship between knowledge and reading comprehension was realized long ago, but the new research has greatly increased our understanding of how background knowledge functions in the reading process. This research has introduced the theoretical notion of schemata—the abstract knowledge structures that provide frameworks for related concepts. A schema brought to bear on a reading task can be thought of as a framework containing slots to be filled by incoming text information. If a reader reads a text about going on vacation, there is likely to be a slot in the vacation schema for packing a suitcase. Statements in the story about folding clothes or carrying bags could then fill the slot and be interpreted as part of packing for a vacation. If a reader did not have a vacation schema with a suitcase-packing slot, the information about clothes and bags in the story might not be so readily understood.

Anderson (Note 3) has distinguished two types of background knowledge problems: one has to do with a reader's lack of specific knowledge; the other has to do with a reader not bringing to bear knowledge that is in his or her repertoire. Various children reading "The Donkey Egg" exhibited one or both of these knowledge problems. Before proceeding to a discussion of some of the apparent sources of knowlege difficulties encountered by the children reading "The Donkey Egg," I will summarize the rest of the story: Ali, the antagonist, has given the Hodja, a gullible character, a pumpkin, and has told him it is a donkey egg that will hatch a donkey if he sits on it. Weeks later, the pumpkin softens and smells, and the Hodja decides he must get rid of it. Still thinking it's a donkey egg, but a rotten one that won't hatch, the Hodja takes it to a hill to dispose of it. It rolls down a hillside, hits a tree, and bursts open, startling a rabbit. As the long-eared rabbit runs off, the Hodja mistakes it for a baby donkey and is horrified over the loss.

Several knowledge domains and specific facts needed for comprehension of this story were either not available or not used by a number of our third-grade children. Some kind of understanding of a practical joke (perhaps of tricks people play on one another) would help children understand the antagonist's plans and goal. Even better would be an understanding that the gullibility of a recipient, combined with fortunate coincidence, can contribute toward the success of a practical joke. The story takes place in old-time Turkey and includes many references to that period; thus, the children would benefit from knowing some Turkish customs or at least from understanding that people living in different cultures and times did some things differently than we do today. Such understanding might reduce potential interference from numerous text references to unfamiliar events, such as the Hodja thanking Ali by kissing his hand and pressing it to his forehead and the marking of time by visits to the public bath house and coffeehouse.

One fact that needs to be understood by readers of the Hodja story is that there is a similarity between rabbit and donkey ears. A very important point in the story is when, because the Hodja mistakes the rabbit for a donkey, he thinks the pumpkin hatched a donkey; yet only six of twenty-four children who read this story got the point. Three children said that the Hodja thought the rabbit had come out of the pumpkin but did not relate that to the Hodja thinking the rabbit was a baby donkey. Two children said that a donkey came out of the pumpkin and was lost to the Hodja. And eleven children simply said that the rabbit came out of the pumpkin.

To discuss why so many children did not construct the appropriate ending to the story, it is important to present the final page of the story (Clymer, 1976):

At the top of the hill he stopped. He put the pumpkin on the ground. To the Hodja, the pumpkin was still a donkey egg. It started rolling down the hillside.
It rolled over rocks and around bushes. It rolled against a tree. It hit a stone and cracked open.

Under that tree a long-eared rabbit was sleeping. When the pumpkin burst open, the rabbit jumped up. He hopped off down the hill and out of sight.

It was a beautiful long-eared rabbit. The Hodja saw him. "Oh," he groaned. "The baby donkey at last! The donkey egg was just ready to hatch. May heaven help us all," he shouted. "Now it has hatched and our baby donkey is lost forever!"

As written, the text is far from explicit. A number of text-connecting inferences and slot-filling inferences must be made if a reader is to comprehend the Hodja's confusion of rabbit ears and donkey ears. To better understand what makes these inferences difficult for children, consider the two youngsters who told us that a baby donkey came out of the pumpkin. Most children probably know that donkeys do not hatch from pumpkins. (In fact, as directed in the teacher's manual, the teacher told these children before they read the story that donkeys do not hatch from pumpkins.) Despite this information, two children either misread the text or ignored the text and told us that a donkey came out of the egg. The question is why this happened.

A reasonable hypothesis is that, in the course of reading, the children had to give direct attention to too many things, and their reading system was overloaded. Let us assume that, in this passage, the two children were expending a great deal of effort on decoding, recovering the syntactic structure of a sentence here or there, attaching meaning to a word here or there, and figuring out some of the references to foreign customs. When these children encountered the sentence in which the Hodja shouted, "Now it has hatched and our baby donkey is lost for-ever!" they processed only a literal interpretation of the sentence. Perhaps they had used up their resources in decoding and determining the literal meaning of the passage and did not have resources left to infer that the last sentence is about what the Hodja thought, not what actually happened. These children did not bring their knowledge that donkeys do not hatch from pumpkins to the text. To do so, they would have had to reject the literal meaning of the sentence, make a text-connecting inference, and bring some knowledge to the text. That is a lot of work after already having done a lot of work.

A number of things could be done to help the children construct the correct ending to the story. First, the text could be more explicit—for example, "From the top of the hill, the Hodja saw the long-eared rabbit and thought it was a baby donkey." During the prereading preparation, the teacher could set up a frame-work to help the children interpret incoming information and discriminate impor-tant from unimportant information. A mistaken identity framework would facilitate construction of an appropriate conclusion to the story. Let us consider mistaken identity as a schema. An important slot in a mistaken identity schema is the similar features of objects whose identity is switched. The information given about the similar features of a rabbit and a donkey is not stated very explicitly in the story. The text simply describes the rabbit as "long-eared." Apparently, this was sufficient for at least four of the six children who constructed the appropriate ending for the story. One would guess that their background knowledge allowed them to relate rabbit ears to donkey ears.

A well-developed mistaken identity schema probably contains a slot that has to do with the proximity of an observer to an object and the amount of time spent observing. If one catches only a glimpse of an object and is at a distance from it, the probability of mistaken identity might increase. There is some weak information in this regard in the story; the Hodja puts the pumpkin down at the top of a hill, it rolls down over rocks and around bushes, then gets to the tree where the rabbit was sleeping. The recalls of two of the children who got the point of the story indicated that they were aware that the Hodja was at a distance from the rabbit and that the rabbit hopped away fast.

A sophisticated mistaken identity schema might also include an understanding of the power of perception over reality—that what one believes can override what is. The text is quite explicit: "To the Hodja, the pumpkin was still a donkey egg." No child's recall indicated that the Hodja's perception was used; however, this does not mean that the children ignored it. If the children had read the last episode with a well-formed mistaken identity schema, some of the text's weak information might have received more attention; or, if the text information had been stronger, a mistaken identity schema might have come into play more easily. For many of the children, the absence of a well-formed schema and strong text information, combined with lower-level processing inefficiency, made for great difficulties in understanding the end of the story.

Texts in which the subject matter is too difficult for many children are easy to spot (for example, a second-grade text about the temperature in the Arctic and the desert, in both Fahrenheit and centigrade; a fourth-grade story that relies on knowledge of the interdependence of animals in nature). The influence of knowledge on reading, however, cannot be limited to having or not having certain knowledge. The examples from "The Donkey Egg" show that even if a child has some story-appropriate knowledge, that knowledge may not be used. Reasons why knowledge is not used include (1) weak reader knowledge, (2) weak textual information, and (3) weak lower-level processes. Reading instruction must strive to prevent all three conditions from occurring simultaneously. What are children learning about reading if they frequently leave their reading lessons without really comprehending the meaning of the story? For such children, reading is probably dull, unrewarding, or frustrating.

Many third graders do not have efficient word-processing skills. Therefore, either the text information in the stories should be explicit and strong or the prereading discussion should activate existing knowledge and provide frameworks for helping readers select important text information. A combination of both approaches would be advantageous. That is not all, however. Assume that the text of "The Donkey Egg" stays the same and that a mistaken identity framework is provided in the prereading discussion. The teacher should also discuss clues that tell how the Hodja concluded that the rabbit was a donkey.

For comprehension instruction to be truly effective, teachers must help students with the specific aspects of reading that are likely to be most difficult. By working through these difficulties with teachers who are able to demonstrate explicitly the steps in the comprehension process, children will begin to learn how to do the thinking themselves.

Conclusion

In this chapter, I have proposed that an interaction of reader and text characteristics may cause a young reader's processing system to become overloaded and that comprehension failure will result. I recommend that primary reading instruction provide practice with lower-level skills for reading fluency, start children thinking in ways that will help them understand what they read, and add to the children's knowledge of the world around them. These seem to be conflicting recommendations; that is, to practice lower-level skills, textual material should be kept conceptually easy and should be about things most children know about. Texts that give children opportunities to think in interesting ways and add to their store of general knowledge are clearly also important. I suggest a two-strand system of reading instruction: (1) a daily reading assignment of an interesting but conceptually easy selection and (2) a regular presentation of conceptually more difficult selections grouped around similar knowledge domains (Beck, 1981). The lower conceptual load of the easy selections would allow children to build reading fluency, and the more difficult selections, with a greater conceptual load, would help build students' knowledge structures. Grouping stories around similar knowledge domains (for example, mistaken identity, nautical life) would help children learn to read more demanding text. Such groupings do not exist in most basal reading programs. Rather, in their attempts to be everything to everyone, publishers have developed series that are a smorgasbord of content. One day children may read a fanciful Turkish tale, the next day a realistic narrative about fishing off the coast of Maine, and the next day a text about the temperature in the Arctic and the desert. Each of the selections requires different background knowledge, but the time to develop this knowledge fully is not available on a daily basis—hence, the strong recommendation for grouping texts around similar domains. There would not be a frequent need, then, to develop new knowledge. Each successive story would reinforce the children's previous knowledge of a topic and then proceed to build on that knowledge base.

Reading instruction in the primary grades has to satisfy many goals: decoding accuracy and fluency, increased word knowledge, experience with various linguistic structures, knowledge of the world, and experience in thinking about texts. Teachers do not always recognize that all these factors influence comprehension; and when there is such recognition, they sometimes attempt to do too much at one time. Unless different lessons and different textual materials are provided by basal series publishers to support different aspects of reading instruction, the instructional and practice time students and teachers invest may not result in the intended skills and abilities.

Reference Notes

1. Beck, I.L., & McCaslin, E.S. *An analysis of dimensions that affect the development of code-breaking ability in eight beginning reading programs* (LRDC Publications 1978/6). Pittsburgh: University of Pittsburgh, Learning Research and Development Center, 1978.
2. Beck, I.L., McKeown, M.G., McCaslin, E.S., & Burkes, A. *Instructional dimensions that may affect reading comprehension: Examples from two commercial reading programs* (LRDC Publications 1979/20). Pittsburgh: University of Pittsburgh, Learning Research and Development Center, 1979.
3. Anderson, R.C. *Schema-directed processes in language comprehension* (Tech. Rep. No. 50). Urbana: University of Illinois, Center for the Study of Reading, July 1977.

References

Bateman, B. Teaching reading to learning disabled children. In L.B. Resnick & P. Weaver (Eds.), *Theory and practice in early reading* (Vol. 1). Hillsdale, N.J.: Erlbaum, 1979.

Beck, I.L. Reading problems and instructional practices. In T.G. Waller & G.E. MacKinnon (Eds.), *Reading research: Advances in theory and practice* (Vol. 2). New York: Academic Press, 1981.

Beck, I.L., Omanson, R.C., & McKeown, M.G. An instructional redesign of reading lessons: Effects on comprehension. *Reading Research Quarterly*, 1982, *17*, 462–481.

Beck, I.L., Perfetti, C.A., & McKeown, M.G. The effects of long-term vocabulary instruction on lexical access and reading comprehension. *Journal of Educational Psychology*, 1982, *74*, 506–521.

Bishop, C.H. Transfer effects of word and letter training in reading. *Journal of Verbal Learning and Verbal Behavior*, 1964, *3*, 215–221.

Carpenter, P.A., & Just, M.A. Cognitive processes in reading: Models based on readers' eye fixations. In A.M. Lesgold & C.A. Perfetti (Eds.), *Interactive processes in reading*. Hillsdale, N.J.: Erlbaum, 1981.

Clymer, T. *Reading 720*. Lexington, MA: Ginn, 1976.

Collins, A., & Smith, E.E. Teaching the process of reading comprehension. In D.K. Detterman & R.J. Sternberg (Eds.), *How and how much can intelligence be increased?* Norwood, N.J.: Ablex, in press.

Frederiksen, J.R. Sources of process interactions in reading. In A.M. Lesgold & C.A. Perfetti (Eds.), *Interactive processes in reading*. Hillsdale, N.J.: Erlbaum, 1981.

Guthrie, J.T., Samuels, S.J., Martuza, V., Seifert, M., Tyler, S.J., & Edwall, G. *A study of the locus and nature of reading problems in the elementary school*. Washington, D.C.: National Institute of Education, 1976.

Jeffrey, W.E., & Samuels, S.J. Effect of method of reading training on initial learning and transfer. *Journal of Verbal Learning and Verbal Behavior*, 1967, *6*, 354–358.

LaBerge, D., & Samuels, S.J. Towards a theory of automatic information processing in reading. *Cognitive Psychology*, 1974, *6*, 293–323.

Lesgold, A.M., & Perfetti, C.A. Interactive processes in reading comprehension. *Discourse Processes*, 1978, *1*, 323–336.

Lesgold, A.M., & Resnick, L.B. How reading difficulties develop: Perspectives from a longitudinal study. In J.P. Das, R. Mulcahy, & A.E. Wall (Eds.), *Theory and research in learning disability*. New York: Plenum Press, in press.

Lesgold, A.M., Roth, S.F., & Curtis, M.E. Foregrounding effects in discourse comprehension. *Journal of Verbal Learning and Verbal Behavior*, 1979, *18*, 291–308.

McNeill, D. The development of language. In P.H. Mussen (Ed.), *Carmichael's manual of child psychology*. New York: Wiley, 1970.

Palermo, D.S., & Molfese, D.L. Language acquisition from age five onward. *Psychological Bulletin*, 1972, *78*, 409–427.

Perfetti, C.A., & Hogaboam, T.W. The relationship between single word decoding and reading comprehension skill. *Journal of Experimental Psychology*, 1975, *67*, 461–469.

Perfetti, C.A., & Roth, S.F. Some of the interactive processes in reading and their role in reading skill. In A.M. Lesgold & C.A. Perfetti (Eds.), *Interactive processes in reading*. Hillsdale, N.J.: Erlbaum, 1981.

Sloben, D.I. *The ontogenesis of grammar: Facts and theories*. New York: Academic Press, 1971.

Stebbins, L.B., St. Pierre, R.G., Proper, E.C., Anderson, R.B., & Cerva, T.R. *Education as evaluation of Follow Through*. Washington, D.C.: U.S. Department of Health, Education and Welfare, 1977.

19

Three Recommendations to Improve Comprehension Teaching

James W. Cunningham

Reading comprehension has been a major concern of educators for the past six decades. Besides building fast and accurate word identification ability, what can teachers do to improve their students' reading comprehension? Research in reading education, teacher effectiveness, and cognitive psychology has provided some answers to this question. Although there is little agreement on the best methods to teach comprehension, some major areas of agreement have emerged from this research. Collectively, this research instructs us that, to help readers comprehend better, teachers should do the following:

1. Have students read easy materials and perform comprehension tasks that can be completed with high success.
2. Teach concepts for topics and words.
3. Use tested interventions to guide students' reading during comprehension lessons.

Easy Material and High Success

Easy Material

Since the 1930s, reading educators have strongly advocated that students be assigned materials that they can read comfortably, regardless of the demands of the curriculum (Betts, 1936, 1941; Whipple, 1939). Betts (1946) recommended that students be taught reading lessons in material that they can read orally without assistance while making no more than five oral reading errors per hundred words. Cooper (1952) found that the easier the assigned reading book was for the children to read orally, the greater their reading gain was for the year. Ekwall (1974, 1976), working in conjunction with a polygraph expert, concluded that third-, fourth-, and fifth-grade students who averaged 7.65 errors per hundred words (not counting pure repetitions as errors) exhibited the same physiological signs as someone who had just been shaken by an automobile accident. Clay (1969) found that beginning readers who made the most progress had a median error rate of 2.7 errors per hundred words read.

Gambrell, Wilson, and Gantt (1981) tested fourth-grade boys of normal intelligence, both good and poor readers, on their ability to read orally from material they had been taught in a reading lesson. The investigator noted the number of unknown words encountered during the oral reading. Not one of the thirty-five good readers ever encountered more than three unknown words per hundred in any of the selections read. Lesgold and Resnick (1981) observed oral reading behavior of a cohort of students as they progressed through first, second, and third grades. The students in the cohort were identified as high-, medium-, or low-ability readers. When reading passages containing sentences closely adapted from the reading materials the children had completed, the high-ability readers averaged between 1.6 and 3.3 errors per hundred words.

High Success

Betts (1946) also recommended that students be taught reading in material that they can read independently and then answer correctly at least 75 percent of the short-answer, closed-book comprehension questions about the material. Betts believed that the teacher's assistance and instruction during the reading lesson should bring the student's comprehension up to 90 percent. Herber (1970) and Graves and Slater (Note 1) state that students need to meet with success in almost all of the school work they do. Jorgenson (1977) and Jorgenson, Klein, and Kumar (1977) found that the easier the material was (relative to their reading ability), the better was the students' classroom behavior.

Teacher-effectiveness researchers have considered student success rate as one variable under the control of the teacher. Powell (1979) has explained that task difficulty is a characteristic not of the curriculum but of the relationship between the task and the individual student's level of skill. If a teacher engaged in direct instruction selects and directs the tasks to be performed (Stevens & Rosenshine, 1981), the teacher has the responsibility to provide students with tasks at a difficulty level that will maximize reading achievement.

Brophy and Evertson (1976) found that there was higher achievement in Title I schools in which students answered questions correctly 80 percent of the time. Gickling and Armstrong (1978) conducted an experiment with first- and second-grade students in which very unsuccessful students were given reading material at various levels of difficulty. The investigators concluded that maximum task completion, task comprehension, and on-task behavior occurred when the student success rate on reading assignments was between 93 and 97 percent. This success rate apparently applied to both oral reading accuracy and silent reading comprehension. The Beginning Teacher Evaluation Study (BTES) documents that, in second- and fifth-grade classrooms, the time students spend on easy instructional tasks in reading is correlated with student reading achievement (Fisher, Filby, Marliave, Cahen, Dishaw, Moore, & Berliner, Note 2). Walberg, Hare, and Pulliam (1981) found that reading task difficulty ratings on the part of elementary students had a statistically significant negative correlation with achievement gains in reading. Stallings (Note 3) reports research findings that senior high school poor readers who spent more time on tasks they could complete correctly also had higher reading achievement. Berliner (1981), discussing the BTES findings, states that the more time students spent on high success tasks, the higher their achievement gains were for the year and the better their retention of learning over the summer. Stevens and Rosenshine (1981) report that the greater the amount of time students spent doing easy work (mean accuracy rate of at least 80 percent accomplished in a short time), the more they gained in achievement; the more time they spent doing hard work, the less they gained in achievement. Gersten, Carnine, and Williams (1982) found that the teachers who were most successful (in terms of the reading gains their students achieved) had students performing tasks with student success rates near 90 percent, while the less successful teachers had students performing tasks with student success rates below 75 percent.

High student success on reading tasks is related not only to student reading achievement but also to student attitudes and motivation. Pupil success rate is related to improved pupil attitudes toward reading in particular and toward school in general (Berliner, 1981; Duffy, 1981; Fisher, Berliner, Filby, Marliave, Cahen, & Dishaw, 1980). Duffy (1981) has succinctly described a relationship between student motivation and success rate:

> Effective teachers apparently motivate by letting pupils know that they are capable of learning, by exuding confidence in their own capacity to provide useful assistance to pupils and by assigning tasks at which pupils can succeed, thereby making the prophecy come true. (p. 124)

This picture of effective teachers using high success rates to develop motivation stands in sharp contrast to the picture of teachers who are unwilling or unable to do so (McDermott & Aron, 1978):

> Not only do the children in the bottom group come to school not knowing how to read, but they have a teacher who expects them to know how to read and who cannot teach them to read while she has 20 other children walking around the room. And it is in this difficult situation that they must overcome the pressure of having the other children taunt them for their performances. Even within the bottom group we hear claims of one child against another. ("Oh, you can't read." "Better than you!") Or we can point to a child in the bottom group who constantly calls for turns to read but, at the same time, appears to arrange her requests in ways that make it difficult for the teacher to call on her. (p. 58)

Students who are consistently given work that is too hard for them will tend to give up on reading and become motivation problems (Brophy, Note 4). In fact, the syndrome of learned helplessness appears to result from having received a steady diet of tasks that cannot be completed successfully, regardless of effort (Thomas, 1979).

Thus, high success rate seems to be related to academic learning time (Berliner, 1981) in two ways. First, it is part of the definition of academic engaged time (Berliner, 1981; Duffy, 1981; Fisher et al., 1980). Second, students are motivated to stay on task longer if the task is easy rather than difficult (Gickling & Armstrong, 1978).

Unlike reading educators and teacher-effectiveness researchers, cognitive psychologists have been more interested in the process of reading and less interested in reading outcomes, such as achievement gains or improved attitudes. Some conclusions can be drawn from cognitive psychology relative to the match between reader ability and text/task difficulty. First, there seems to have been almost universal acceptance of the idea that the more a reader already knows about a given topic or event, the better that reader will comprehend and learn from a text about that topic or event (Anderson, 1977, 1978; Bransford & McCarrell, 1974; Pearson, Hansen, & Gordon, 1979; Rumelhart, 1980; Rumelhart & Ortony, 1977; Stevens, 1980). Moreover, a reader benefits from prior knowledge not only about the content of a text but also about the form in which that content is transmitted (Bartlett, 1978; McDonald, 1978; Meyer, Brandt, & Bluth, 1980; Whaley & Spiegel, Note 5; Bowman & Gambrell, Note 6). If easy materials are those that readers already know much about in both content and form, then we can improve comprehension and learning from text by having students read easy materials.

A great many studies have been completed that compared the comprehension processing of good versus poor readers (Golinkoff, 1975–76; Stanovich, 1980). In these studies, good and poor readers read the same passages. If the poor readers had been reading passages that were relatively as easy for them to read as the passages were for the good readers in the studies, it is certainly possible that the poor readers would have behaved more like good readers (Thompson, 1981). The implication is that if having students read difficult materials causes them to act like poor readers and having them read easy materials causes them to act more like good readers, to get poor readers to act more like good readers, we should have them read easy materials.

Britton and his associates (Britton, Westbrook, & Holdredge, 1978; Britton, Ziegler, & Westbrook, 1980) found that it consistently takes good readers longer to react to distracting clicks when reading easy texts than when reading difficult texts. In combination with theories of automaticity and reading (Perfetti, 1977; Samuels & Eisenberg, 1981), Britton's findings suggest that easy texts engage readers more completely because the readers are not distracted by the processing obstacles presented by difficult texts; that is, while reading easy texts, readers concentrate on meaning, but while reading difficult texts, they concentrate on concentrating. To get students to concentrate on comprehension rather than on comprehending, we should provide readers with easy rather than difficult materials.

Can Materials or Tasks Be Too Easy?

If there is nothing new in a passage for a reader, the reader will almost certainly be bored reading that passage. If a passage is interesting and has something new for a reader, however, it is difficult to see how it can be too easy to read.

Gickling and Armstrong (1978) report that off-task behavior increased for first- and second-grade children when they were given extremely easy tasks. The children's task-completion rate was not lower, however, suggesting that the teachers did not give them enough work to keep them occupied. Other studies have failed to find a ceiling effect on ease of materials (Cooper, 1952; Jorgenson, 1977; Jorgenson et al., 1977).

Reading materials and tasks should be at least somewhat interesting to students and should have something new for the students to learn or experience. A teacher must have enough materials and tasks available to keep students engaged. Beyond that, it is not clear whether materials and tasks can be too easy. In lieu of more research, common sense dictates that students be given the hardest material that is easy for them and the most difficult tasks they can complete with high success.

A Note about Reading Rate and Fluency

Although there has been a long tradition in reading education that developing readers should be instructed with materials in which they can accurately identify most words and comprehend satisfactorily without assistance, there is a more recent belief that learners should also be given materials that they can read fluently and at a satisfactory rate, both orally and silently (Betts, 1946; Durrell, 1956; Gates, 1947). Biemiller (1977–78) has cited data supporting the necessity of attaining an adequate reading speed for successful reading achievement, but reading educators are vague and imprecise on what an adequate speed is. Lesgold and Resnick (1981) found, in their longitudinal study of first-, second-, and third-grade development of a cohort of students, that low-ability readers read familiar passages orally at from thirty to fifty words per minute; medium-ability readers read at from sixty to seventy-five words per minute; and high-ability readers read at from seventy-five to ninety-five words per minute.

Teacher-effectiveness researchers have given some support to the positive relationship between task-completion rate and student achievement, particularly as it relates to content covered (Berliner, 1981; Stevens & Rosenshine, 1981; McDonald & Elias, Note 7).

Research in cognitive psychology that is related to speed and automaticity of word identification (LaBerge & Samuels, 1974; Perfetti, 1977; Perfetti & Hogaboam, 1975; Perfetti & Roth, 1981; Samuels & Eisenberg, 1981) demonstrates that good readers identify words in isolation more quickly than poor readers do.

There is a lack of studies, however, comparing the reading rates of good and poor readers as they read passages that are relatively easy or difficult for them or words in isolation selected from those passages.

Are Teachers Now Having Students Read Easy Materials and Perform High-Success Comprehension Tasks?

Anyone who has spent much time in classrooms will affirm that poor readers are almost always provided with materials from which they read slowly and with a noticeable number of oral reading errors and obviously impaired comprehension. Many teachers in these classrooms seem unwilling or unable to match students with easy materials and high-success comprehension tasks. The literature suggests that this has always been the case (Chall & Feldmann, 1966; Duffy, 1981; Jones, 1948; Kelly, 1967, 1970; Roberts, 1976; Zintz, 1970; Jorgenson & Klein, Note 8).

The tragedy for poor readers, of course, is that they are the victims of a compromise made between their needs and the demands of the curriculum. Although almost all poor readers are assigned materials and tasks that are easier than those received by other students (Arnold & Sherry, 1975), the research cited here indicates that these so-called easy materials and tasks are still too difficult for them. As a result, poor readers suffer the doubly crippling condition of using low-status texts and tasks with which they still cannot succeed.

Concepts for Topics and Words

Reading educators have long held what Anderson and Freebody (1981) have called the instrumentalist position regarding the role of knowledge of word meanings in reading comprehension. Gates (1947) stated the position this way:

> It is necessary to get the meanings of the words, or at least most of them, in a sentence before the sentence as a whole can be understood. (p. 180)

Smith (1963) stated it even more strongly in a paraphrased poem:

> *Words Words Words*
> For want of a word, the phrase is lost.
> For want of the phrase, the sentence is lost.
> For want of the sentence, the paragraph is lost.
> For want of the paragraph, the selection is lost.
> All meaning is lost for want of a word. (p. 278)

This view of meaning vocabulary knowledge as a cause of reading comprehension has received consistent indirect support in the form of factor analyses of reading comprehension tests (Davis, 1944, 1968; Thorndike, 1974), quasi-experimental causal methods (Yap, 1979), and readability research (Klare, 1974–75). A strong relationship between meaning vocabulary and comprehension still obtains, even when intelligence is held constant (Vineyard & Massey, 1957).

Direct support for this view also exists, and it is broadly based. Educators have often found that teaching word meanings improves reading comprehension (Alderman, 1926; Barrett & Graves, 1981; Beck, Perfetti, & McKeown, 1982; Draper & Moeller, 1971; Mickelson, 1973–74). Becker (1977) has argued for the use of a procedure by which words would be selected and taught systematically by direct instruction throughout a student's public school career. Cognitive psychologists (Freebody & Anderson, 1981; Marks, Doctorow, & Wittrock, 1974; Wittrock, Marks, & Doctorow, 1975) have found that replacing content words in a passage with low-frequency synonyms hampers students' comprehension for that passage.

Concept Knowledge

Although reading educators have held that knowledge of word meanings is instrumental to reading comprehension, they also simultaneously have held what Anderson and Freebody (1981) have called the knowledge position:

> Rather than being directly important, possessing a certain word meaning is only a sign that the individual may possess the knowledge needed to understand a text. For instance, the child who knows the word *mast* is likely to have knowledge about sailing. This knowledge enables that child to understand a text that contains sentences which do not even involve the word *mast*, such as, "We jibed suddenly and the boom snapped across the cockpit." (p. 81)

Horn (1937), Smith (1963), and Dechant (1970) are three reading educators who argue the necessity of adequate background knowledge and experience and advocate that teachers take steps to build general background experience for their students. Beck and McKeown (Note 9) and Tierney and Cunningham (in press) have seen the long tradition of building background for the basal reading selection in the teacher's manual lesson plan as direct evidence that reading educators have accepted a causal relationship between background knowledge and comprehension. Correlational research has supported the existence of the relationship, finding that background knowledge is a significant factor in comprehension, regardless of the reading ability or age of the readers (Cantor, 1935; Hilliard & Troxell, 1937; Pearson et al., 1979; Stevens, 1980).

Intervention research by reading educators also supports the existence of a causal relationship between background knowledge and comprehension. McWhorter (1935), cited in Smith (1963), provided enriching experiences to children who were lacking in background information and noted significant improvement in their reading. McDowell (1939), also cited in Smith (1963), improved reading readiness for kindergarten students by providing them with an enriched curriculum. Graves and his associates (Graves & Cooke, 1980; Graves, Cooke, & LaBerge, 1983; Graves & Palmer, 1981) developed previews for short stories that had, as one component, the building of prior knowledge that was important to understanding the selection. These several experiments produced data documenting that reading the previews before reading the stories increased students' learning from stories by a significant and impressive amount. Increased learning from text has been accomplished by teaching relevant background directly (Stevens, 1982) and through analogies (Hayes & Tierney, 1982).

Teacher-effectiveness researchers have not been concerned with the curricular issue of developing background knowledge, either for particular reading passages or for passages in general. It seems safe to say, however, that using direct instruction to build knowledge prerequisite to comprehension would not contradict their findings.

In general, the theory and research of cognitive psychology support the notion that background knowledge affects how much and what information is recalled from reading, as well as readers' perceptions of, for example, an author's background and purposes (Tierney & Cunningham, in press). Ausubel (1963, 1968, 1978), Anderson (1978), Rumelhart and Ortony (1977), Rumelhart (1980), and Spiro (1980) have addressed the role of background knowledge and its relation to text comprehension, particularly as background knowledge applies to the broader issues of processing and recalling information. Schema theorists have concluded from their research that availability of appropriate schemata, access to available schemata, and change or maintenance of appropriate schemata are all necessary for comprehension (Spiro, 1980).

Are the Respective Roles of Vocabulary and Knowledge in Comprehension Too Uncertain and Controversial for Instructional Implications to Be Drawn?

Currently, four positions can be taken regarding the relative and respective roles of vocabulary and knowledge in comprehension. Each of these positions has implications for instruction:

> The instrumentalist position (Anderson & Freebody, 1981), discussed earlier, implies that word meanings should be taught.

> The knowledge position (Anderson & Freebody, 1981), also discussed earlier, implies that background knowledge should be taught.

> The interactive-compensatory position (Stanovich, 1980; Freebody & Anderson, Note 10) states that a knowledge of word meanings can be expected to compensate for a lack of background knowledge and that background knowledge can be expected to compensate for a lack of knowledge of word meanings. This position implies that either word meanings or background knowledge should be taught—whichever is easier to teach.

The interactive-archipelago position states that knowledge of word meanings and background knowledge operate as an archipelago, with the words representing the islands (land above the water surface) and knowledge representing the island chain (land below the water surface). According to this position, words and knowledge function as a unit; knowing a word meaning is knowing the topic as that word relates to it, and vice versa. This position implies that word meanings and background knowledge should be taught at the same time.

Major theoretical distinctions can be made among the four positions; however, if the direct instruction emphasis of much of the teacher-effectiveness research is accepted, something interesting happens when one considers implications of the various positions for instruction in reading. Unless one teaches word meanings and background knowledge at the same time—as a unit—some of the positions are denied. Thus, theory and research support the instructional implications of the interactive-archipelago position. Teaching word meanings and background knowledge at the same time holds the most promise for improving reading comprehension.

Although the simultaneous teaching of background knowledge and knowledge of word meanings is a recommendation with which few reading educators, teacher-effectiveness researchers, or cognitive psychologists are likely to argue, one must not conclude that anything and everything done instructionally will work. Attempts to teach word-meaning skills such as morphemic analysis or use of context or dictionary are probably doomed to failure (Hafner, 1965; Jackson & Dizney, 1963; Otterman, 1955).

There are background knowledge and word-meaning programs that have worked, however, and these are programs in which a topic and the word meanings associated with that topic were taught at the same time (Barrett & Graves, 1981; Beck et al., 1982; Cantor, 1935; Hayes & Tierney, 1982; Lieberman, 1967; McWhorter, 1935; McDowell, 1939; Mickelson, 1973–74; Stevens, 1982). Successful programs have often provided a variety of activities and experiences with the topics and words being learned (Barrett & Graves, 1981; Beck et al., 1982; Draper & Moeller, 1971; Lieberman, 1967) rather than teaching to task in a mastery-learning or trials-to-criterion instructional paradigm (Pany & Jenkins, 1978; Jenkins, Pany, & Schreck, Note 11).

Programs that have worked have generally taught ten or fewer new words per week (Barrett & Graves, 1981; Beck et al., 1982; Lieberman, 1967; Vanderlinde, 1964) and have had a duration of 18 or more weeks (Barrett & Graves, 1981; Beck et al., 1982; Draper & Moeller, 1971; Lieberman, 1967; Vanderlinde, 1964). Less successful programs have generally taught more than ten new words per week and have had a duration of far less than 18 weeks (Pany & Jenkins, 1978; Tuinman & Brady, 1974; Jenkins et al., Note 11).

Tested Intervention

Basal reading series traditionally have employed a directed reading lesson for guiding students' reading (Harris & Sipay, 1980; Beck, McKeown, McCaslin, & Burkes, Note 12). Betts (1946) outlined the steps of a directed reading activity, and many reading education methods textbooks published since that time have presented a version of that general lesson plan (Cunningham, Arthur, & Cunningham, 1977; Dechant, 1982; Dillner & Olson, 1982; Mason, 1981; Wilson & Hall, 1972).

A directed reading activity is most often a set of questions given to students before they read and again after they read. Anderson and Biddle (1975) concluded that before-reading questions facilitate learning for the information sought by the questions and that after-reading questions facilitate learning for all textual information.

Reading educators have proposed alternatives to the wide use of the directed reading activity. Stauffer (1959, 1969) developed the directed reading-thinking activity. Manzo developed the ReQuest procedure (1969, 1970) and the guided reading procedure (1975). These comprehension plans are contrasted by their developers with the directed reading activity. Research has lent some support to the use of the directed reading-thinking activity (Biskin, Hoskisson, & Modlin, 1976; Davidson, 1970; Lovelace & McKnight, 1980; Petre, 1970), the ReQuest procedure (Manzo, 1970), and the guided reading procedure (Bean & Pardi, 1979).

More recently, reading educators have developed and tested other lesson frameworks for guiding students' comprehension during reading lessons. Hansen (1981) compared second-graders' inferential comprehension when they were taught ten basal stories under three conditions: the strategy method, the question method, and the traditional basal method. The strategy method, a directed reading-thinking activity with more teacher direction and a metacognitive component, elicited certain children's experiences and then related them to important ideas from the reading selection. The question method was a directed reading activity wherein all questions asked in the guided reading phase were inferential questions, rather than the standard ratio of five literal to one inferential. When asked inferential questions, students taught by either the strategy method or the question method surpassed students taught by the traditional basal method.

Cunningham, Moore, Cunningham, and Moore (1983) have concluded that all reading comprehension lesson frameworks have at least four steps:

Step 1: Establish purpose(s) for comprehension.

Step 2: Have students read for the established purpose(s).

Step 3: Have students perform some task that directly reflects and measures accomplishment of each established purpose for comprehending.

Step 4: Provide direct feedback about students' comprehension, based on their performance.

Cunningham et al. (1983) have also concluded that many, but not all, comprehension lesson frameworks have an optional readiness step preceding step 1: Cue access to, or develop background knowledge for, information assumed by the text.

How these steps are carried out varies tremendously. In the directed reading-thinking activity (Stauffer, 1969) and the ReQuest procedure (Manzo, 1969), students are led to establish their own purposes, whereas in various other versions of the directed reading activity, students are generally assigned purposes. At present, research findings about the different versions of the four-plus-one-step lesson framework are inconclusive, yet each of these steps is supported by a great deal of tradition and some research.

Reading educators have also used other interventions to guide students' comprehension. Tierney and Cunningham (in press) have classified activities for increasing learning from text or prose into prereading activities, guiding reader-text interactions during reading to learn, and teacher interventions following reading to learn.

A promising prereading activity, discussed earlier, is previewing. Graves and his associates (Graves & Cooke, 1980; Graves et al., 1983; Graves & Palmer, 1981; Hood, 1981; Graves & Slater, Note 1) found that previews consistently increased learning from the stories and also helped students make inferences about the stories.

Another intervention is inducing self-questioning by the readers. Frase and Schwartz (1975) found that high school and college students who produced their own questions for prose recalled the content better than students who just studied the passages. More recent research by André and Anderson (1978–79) and Wong and Jones (Note 13) supports this position.

A third kind of successful teacher intervention is asking students application-type or meaningful learning questions after reading (Anderson & Biddle, 1975; Rickards & Hatcher, 1977–78; Watts & Anderson, 1971).

Teacher-effectiveness research has strongly supported direct instruction (Becker, 1977; Berliner, 1981; Berliner & Rosenshine, 1977; Samuels, 1981; Stevens & Rosenshine, 1981). Direct instruction is characterized by having students work under the direction of a teacher, who selects and directs the student activities. Lessons are structured, and directions are given clearly and frequently to ensure that students understand what they are to do and how they are to do it. Students' attention is monitored by the teacher, and the students are guided and encouraged to stay on task.

Cognitive psychologists have demonstrated and investigated the phenomenon labeled depth of processing (Anderson, 1970; Craik & Lockhart, 1972). They have found that any intervention that induces readers to process textual content more completely and deeply causes them to comprehend and remember that content better (Anderson & Glover, 1981; Burton, Niles, & Wildman, 1981; Kane & Anderson, 1978).

Wittrock and his associates (Doctorow, Wittrock, & Marks, 1978; Linden & Wittrock, 1981; Wittrock, 1981) have investigated the role of attention, particularly selective attention, in reading comprehension. Wittrock (1981) discusses interventions as they relate to attention:

> Different meanings can be constructed from the text by directing the learners to different information in it, and by giving the learners different goals for reading the text. (p. 236)

In her landmark study, Durkin (1978) systematically observed elementary classrooms and found astonishingly little direct comprehension instruction. She learned that "many of the procedures likely to improve comprehension . . . were never seen" (p. 526). Perhaps the teachers she observed were knowledgeable about interventions for guiding comprehension instruction, but their interventions did not show when they were observed.

As a veteran provider of in-service comprehension instruction training, I have yet to find a group of elementary teachers in which many know about the directed reading-thinking activity, the guided reading procedure, or the ReQuest procedure, yet these are only three of a number of tested interventions that are available for teachers to use in guiding students' comprehension during reading lessons. Because research supports the use of these interventions without designating one or another as most effective, the wise teacher would make use of a variety of interventions, keeping in mind student needs and text characteristics as well as instructional goals. Moreover, employing these interventions within the method known as direct instruction can only increase the likelihood that teachers will positively influence readers' comprehension.

Conclusion

This chapter has presented three instructions for teachers who wish to improve the comprehension of their students, especially the poor readers. The instructions imply that teachers should (1) provide students with easy reading materials and comprehension tasks on which they can succeed, (2) teach background knowledge and vocabulary simultaneously, and (3) use tested interventions to guide students' reading. It remains to be seen what improvements in reading comprehension would result from classroom programs that rigorously apply all three instructions, but if this is never done, we will never know.

Reference Notes

1. Graves, M.F., & Slater, W.H. *Some further thoughts on validating teaching procedures to be used by content area teachers.* Unpublished manuscript, University of Minnesota, 1981.

2. Fisher, C.W., Filby, N.N., Marliave, R., Cahen, L.S., Dishaw, M.M., Moore, J.E., & Berliner, D.C. *Teaching behaviors, academic learning time and student achievement* (Final report of phase III-B, Beginning Teacher Evaluation Study, BTES Technical Report Series, Tech. Rep. V-1). San Francisco: Far West Laboratory for Educational Research and Development, 1978.

3. Stallings, J.A. *Teaching basic reading skills in secondary schools*. Paper presented at the meeting of the American Educational Research Association, Toronto, April 1978.

4. Brophy, J. *Recent research in teaching*. Invited address presented at the annual meeting of the Northeastern Educational Research Association, October 1980.

5. Whaley, J.F., & Spiegel, D.L. *Enhancing children's reading comprehension through instruction in narrative structure*. Unpublished manuscript, University of North Carolina, 1982.

6. Bowman, M., & Gambrell, L.B. *The effect of story structure questions upon the reading comprehension of sixth grade students*. Unpublished manuscript, University of Maryland, 1982.

7. McDonald, F.J., & Elias, P. *Beginning Teacher Evaluation Study: Phase II technical summary, final report*. Princeton, N.J.: Educational Testing Service, 1976.

8. Jorgenson, G., & Klein, N. *A comparison of tested reading ability and levels of basal reader used with urban elementary school boys*. Paper presented at the meeting of the American Educational Research Association, Washington, D.C., April 1975.

9. Beck, I.L., & McKeown, M.G. *Trends in instructional research in reading: A retrospective*. Unpublished manuscript, University of Pittsburgh, 1982.

10. Freebody, P., & Anderson, R.C. *Effects of vocabulary difficulty, text cohesion, and schema availability on reading comprehension* (Tech. Rep. No. 225). Urbana: University of Illinois, Center for the Study of Reading, November 1981.

11. Jenkins, J.R., Pany, D., & Schreck, J. *Vocabulary and reading comprehension*. (Tech. Rep. No. 100). Urbana: University of Illinois, Center for the Study of Reading, 1978.

12. Beck, I.L., McKeown, M.G., McCaslin, E.S., & Burkes, A.M. *Instructional dimensions that may affect reading comprehension: Examples from two commercial reading programs* (LRDC Publications 1979/20). Pittsburgh: University of Pittsburgh, Learning Research and Development Center, 1979.

13. Wong, B.Y.L., & Jones, W. *Increasing metacomprehension in learning-disabled and normally-achieving students through self-questioning training*. Unpublished manuscript, 1982.

References

Alderman, G.H. Improving comprehension ability in silent reading. *Journal of Educational Research*, 1926, *13*, 11–21.

Anderson, R.C. Control of student mediating processes during verbal learning and instruction. *Review of Educational Research*, 1970, *40*, 349–369.

Anderson, R.C. The notion of schemata and the educational enterprise: General discussion of the conference. In R.C. Anderson, R.J. Spiro, & W.E. Montague (Eds.), *Schooling and the acquisition of knowledge*. Hillsdale, N.J.: Erlbaum, 1977.

Anderson, R.C. Schema-directed processes in language comprehension. In A.M. Lesgold, J.W. Pellegrino, S.D. Fakkema, & R. Glaser (Eds.), *Cognitive psychology and instruction*. New York: Plenum Press, 1978.

Anderson, R.C., & Biddle, W.B. On asking people questions about what they are reading. In G.H. Bower (Ed.), *The psychology of learning and motivation* (Vol. 9). New York: Academic Press, 1975.

Anderson, R.C., & Freebody, P. Vocabulary knowledge. In J.T. Guthrie (Ed.), *Comprehension and teaching: Research reviews*. Newark, Del.: International Reading Association, 1981.

Anderson, T.N., & Glover, J.A. Active response modes: Comprehension "aids" in need of a theory. *Journal of Reading Behavior*, 1981, *13*, 99-109.

André, M.E.D.A., & Anderson, T.H. The development and evaluation of a self-questioning study technique. *Reading Research Quarterly*, 1978-79, *14*, 605-623.

Arnold, R.D., & Sherry, N. A comparison of the reading levels of disabled readers with assigned textbooks. *Reading Improvement*, 1975, *12*, 207-211.

Ausubel, D.P. *The psychology of meaningful verbal learning*. New York: Grune and Stratton, 1963.

Ausubel, D.P. *Educational psychology: A cognitive view*. New York: Holt, Rinehart and Winston, 1968.

Ausubel, D.P. In defense of advance organizers: A reply to the critics. *Review of Educational Research*, 1978, *48*, 251-257.

Barrett, M.T., & Graves, M.F. A vocabulary program for junior high school remedial readers. *Journal of Reading*, 1981, *25*, 146-150.

Bartlett, B.J. *Top-level structure as an organizational strategy for recall of classroom text*. Unpublished doctoral dissertation, Arizona State University, 1978. (Research report, Prose Learning Series, No. 1, Arizona State University, College of Education, Department of Educational Psychology, December 1978.)

Bean, T.W., & Pardi, R. A field test of a guided reading strategy. *Journal of Reading*, 1979, *23*, 144-147.

Beck, I.L., Perfetti, C.A., & McKeown, M.G. Effects of long-term vocabulary instruction on lexical access and reading comprehension. *Journal of Educational Psychology*, 1982, *74*, 506-521.

Becker, W.C. Teaching reading and language to the disadvantaged—What we have learned from field research. *Harvard Educational Review*, 1977, *47*, 518-543.

Berliner, D.C. Academic learning time and reading achievement. In J.T. Guthrie (Ed.), *Comprehension and teaching: Research reviews*. Newark, Del.: International Reading Association, 1981.

Berliner, D.C., & Rosenshine, B.V. The acquisition of knowledge in the classroom. In R.C. Anderson, R.J. Spiro, & W.E. Montague (Eds.), *Schooling and the acquisition of knowledge*. Hillsdale, N.J.: Erlbaum, 1977.

Betts, E.A. *The prevention and correction of reading difficulties*. Evanston, Ill.: Row, Peterson, 1936.

Betts, E.A. Reading problems at the intermediate grade level. *Elementary School Journal*, 1941, *40*, 737-746.

Betts, E.A. *Foundations of reading instruction*. New York: American Book, 1946.

Biemiller, A. Relationships between oral reading rates for letters, words, and simple text in the development of reading achievement. *Reading Research Quarterly*, 1977-78, *13*, 223-253.

Biskin, D.S., Hoskisson, K., & Modlin, M. Prediction, reflection, and comprehension. *Elementary School Journal*, 1976, *77*, 131-139.

Bransford, J.D., & McCarrell, N.S. A sketch of a cognitive approach to comprehension. In W.B. Weimer & D.S. Palermo (Eds.), *Cognition and the symbolic processes.* Hillsdale, N.J.: Erlbaum, 1974.

Britton, B.K., Westbrook, R.D., & Holdredge, T.S. Reading and cognitive capacity usage: Effects of text difficulty. *Journal of Experimental Psychology: Human Learning and Memory,* 1978, *4,* 582–591.

Britton, B.K., Ziegler, R., & Westbrook, R.D. Use of cognitive capacity in reading easy and difficult text: Two tests for an allocation of attention hypothesis. *Journal of Reading Behavior,* 1980, *12,* 23–30.

Brophy, J., & Evertson, C. *Learning from teaching: A developmental perspective.* Boston: Allyn and Bacon, 1976.

Burton, J.K., Niles, J.A., & Wildman, T.M. Levels of processing effects on the immediate and delayed recall of prose. *Journal of Reading Behavior,* 1981, *13,* 157–164.

Cantor, A. *An historical, philosophical, and scientific study of kindergarten excursions as a basis for social adaptation and reading readiness.* Unpublished master's thesis, University of Cincinnati, 1935.

Chall, J., & Feldmann, S. First grade reading: An analysis of the interactions of professed methods, teacher implementation, and child background. *The Reading Teacher,* 1966, *19,* 569–575.

Clay, M.M. Reading errors and self-correction behavior. *British Journal of Educational Psychology,* 1969, *39,* 47–56.

Cooper, J.L. *The effect of adjustment of basal reading materials on reading achievement.* Unpublished doctoral dissertation, Boston University, 1952.

Craik, F.L.M., & Lockhart, R.S. Levels of processing: A framework for memory research. *Journal of Verbal Learning and Verbal Behavior,* 1972, *11,* 671–684.

Cunningham, P.M., Arthur, S.V., & Cunningham, J.W. *Classroom reading instruction: Alternative approaches.* Lexington, Mass.: D.C. Heath, 1977.

Cunningham, P.M., Moore, S.A., Cunningham, J.W., & Moore, D.W. *Reading in elementary classrooms: Strategies and observations.* New York: Longman, 1983.

Davidson, J.L. The relationship between teachers' questions and pupils' responses during a directed reading activity and a directed reading-thinking activity. (Doctoral dissertation, University of Michigan, 1970). *Dissertation Abstracts International,* 1971, *31,* 6273A–6274A (University Microfilms No. 71-15,124).

Davis, F.B. Fundamental factors of comprehension in reading. *Psychometrika,* 1944, *9,* 185–197.

Davis, F.B. Research in comprehension in reading. *Reading Research Quarterly,* 1968, *3,* 499–545.

Dechant, E.V. *Improving the teaching of reading* (2nd ed.). Englewood Cliffs, N.J.: Prentice-Hall, 1970.

Dechant, E.V. *Improving the teaching of reading* (3rd ed.). Englewood Cliffs, N.J.: Prentice-Hall, 1982.

Dillner, M.H., & Olson, J.P. *Personalizing reading instruction in middle, junior, and senior high schools* (2nd ed.). New York: Macmillan, 1982.

Doctorow, M., Wittrock, M.C., & Marks, C. Generative processes in reading comprehension. *Journal of Educational Psychology,* 1978, *70,* 109–118.

Draper, A.G., & Moeller, G.H. We think with words (therefore, to improve thinking, teach vocabulary). *Phi Delta Kappan,* 1971, *52* 482–484.

Duffy, G.G. Teacher effectiveness research: Implications for the reading profession. In M.L. Kamil (Ed.), *Directions in reading: Research and instruction* (Thirtieth Yearbook of the National Reading Conference). Washington, D.C.: National Reading Conference, 1981.

Durkin, D. *Teaching them to read* (3rd ed.). Boston: Allyn and Bacon, 1978.

Durrell, D.D. *Improving reading instruction.* Yonkers-on-Hudson, N.Y.: World Book, 1956.

Ekwall, E.E. Should repetitions be counted as errors? *The Reading Teacher,* 1974, *27,* 365–367.

Ekwall, E.E. Informal reading inventories: The instructional level. *The Reading Teacher,* 1976, *29,* 662–665.

Fisher, C., Berliner, D., Filby, N., Marliave, R., Cahen, L., & Dishaw, M. Teaching behaviors, academic learning time and student achievement: An overview. In C. Denham & A. Lieberman (Eds.), *Time to learn.* Washington, D.C.: National Institute of Education, 1980.

Frase, L.T., & Schwartz, B.J. Effect of question production and answering on prose recall. *Journal of Educational Psychology,* 1975, *67,* 628–635.

Freebody, P., & Anderson, R.C. *Effects of differing proportions and locations of difficult vocabulary on text comprehension* (Tech. Rep. No. 202). Urbana: University of Illinois, Center for the Study of Reading, May 1981. (ERIC Document Reproduction Service No. ED 201 992)

Gambrell, L.B., Wilson, R.M., & Gantt, W.N. Classroom observations of task-attending behaviors of good and poor readers. *Journal of Educational Research,* 1981, *74,* 400–404.

Gates, A.I. *The improvement of reading* (3rd ed.). New York: Macmillan, 1947.

Gersten, R.M., Carnine, D.W., & Williams, P.B. Measuring implementation of a structured educational model in an urban school district: An observational approach. *Educational Evaluation and Policy Analysis,* 1982, *4,* 67–79.

Gickling, E.E., & Armstrong, D.L. Levels of instructional difficulty as related to on-task behavior, task completion, and comprehension. *Journal of Learning Disabilities,* 1978, *11,* 559–566.

Golinkoff, R.M. A comparison of reading comprehension processes in good and poor comprehenders. *Reading Research Quarterly,* 1975–76, *11,* 623–659.

Graves, M.F., & Cooke, C.L. Effects of previewing difficult short stories for high school students. *Research on Reading in Secondary Schools,* 1980, *6,* 38–54.

Graves, M.F., Cooke, C.L., & LaBerge, M.J. Effects of previewing difficult short stories on low ability junior high school students' comprehension, recall, and attitudes. *Reading Research Quarterly,* 1983, *18,* 262–276.

Graves, M.F., & Palmer, R.J. Validating previewing as a method of improving fifth and sixth grade students' comprehension of short stories. *Michigan Reading Journal,* 1981, *15,* 1–3.

Hafner, L.E. A one-month experiment in teaching context aids in fifth grade. *Journal of Educational Research,* 1965, *58,* 472–474.

Hansen, J. The effects of inference training and practice on young children's reading comprehension. *Reading Research Quarterly,* 1981, *16,* 391–417.

Harris, A.J., & Sipay, E.R. *How to increase reading ability* (7th ed.). New York: Longman, 1980.

Hayes, D.A., & Tierney, R.J. Developing readers' knowledge through analogy. *Reading Research Quarterly,* 1982, *17,* 256–280.

Herber, H.L. *Teaching reading in content areas.* Englewood Cliffs, N.J.: Prentice-Hall, 1970.

Hilliard, G.H., & Troxell, E. Informational background as a factor in reading readiness and progress. *Elementary School Journal,* 1937, *38,* 255.

Hood, M. *The effect of previewing on the recall of high school students.* Unpublished master's thesis, University of Minnesota, 1981.

Horn, E. *Methods of instruction in the social studies.* New York: Scribner's, 1937.

Jackson, J.R., & Dizney, H. Intensive vocabulary training. *Journal of Developmental Reading,* 1963, *6,* 221–229.

Jones, D. An experiment in adaptation to individual differences. *Journal of Educational Psychology,* 1948, *39,* 257–272.

Jorgenson, G.W. Relationship of classroom behavior to the accuracy of the match between material difficulty and student ability. *Journal of Educational Psychology,* 1977, *69,* 24–32.

Jorgenson, G.W., Klein, N., & Kumar, V.K. Achievement and behavior correlates of matched levels of student ability and materials difficulty. *Journal of Educational Research,* 1977, *71,* 100–103.

Kane, J.H., & Anderson, R.C. Depth of processing and interference effects in the learning and remembering of sentences. *Journal of Educational Psychology,* 1978, *70,* 626–635.

Kelly, H. Effects of an in-service education program utilizing simulated classroom procedure on classroom teachers' awareness of pupils' instructional reading levels (Doctoral dissertation, Case Western Reserve University, 1967). *Dissertation Abstracts International,* 1968, *28,* 4026A (University Microfilms No. 68-03315).

Kelly, H. Using an informal reading inventory to place children in instructional materials. In W. Durr (Ed.), *Reading difficulties.* Newark, Del.: International Reading Association, 1970.

Klare, G.R. Assessing readability. *Reading Research Quarterly,* 1974–75, *10,* 62–102.

LaBerge, D., & Samuels, S.J. Toward a theory of automatic information processing in reading. *Cognitive Psychology,* 1974, *6,* 293–323.

Lesgold, A.M., & Resnick, L.B. *How reading difficulties develop: Perspectives from a longitudinal study.* Pittsburgh: University of Pittsburgh, Learning Research and Development Center, 1981.

Lieberman, J.E. *The effect of direct instruction in vocabulary concepts on reading achievement.* Bloomington, Ind.: ERIC Clearinghouse on Reading, 1967. (ERIC Document Reproduction Service No. ED 010 985)

Linden, M., & Wittrock, M.C. The teaching of reading comprehension according to the model of generative learning. *Reading Research Quarterly,* 1981, *17,* 44–57.

Lovelace, T.L., & McKnight, C.K. The effects of reading instruction on calculus students' problem solving. *Journal of Reading,* 1980, *23,* 305–308.

Manzo, A.V. The ReQuest procedure. *Journal of Reading,* 1969, *13,* 123–126.

Manzo, A.V. Reading and questioning: The ReQuest procedure. *Reading Improvement,* 1970, *7,* 80–83.

Manzo, A.V. Guided reading procedure. *Journal of Reading,* 1975, *18,* 287–291.

Marks, C.B., Doctorow, M.J., & Wittrock, M.C. Word frequency and reading comprehension. *Journal of Educational Research,* 1974, *67,* 259–262.

Mason, G.E. *A primer on teaching reading.* Itasca, Ill.: F.E. Peacock, 1981.

McDermott, R.P., & Aron, J. Pirandello in the classroom: On the possibility of equal educational opportunity in American culture. In M.C. Reynolds (Ed.), *Futures of exceptional students: Emerging structures.* Minneapolis: National Support Systems Project, 1978.

McDonald, G.E. *The effects of instruction in the use of an abstract structural schema as an aid to comprehension and recall of written discourse.* Unpublished doctoral dissertation, Virginia Polytechnic Institute and State University, 1978.

McDowell, H.R. *A comparative study of reading readiness.* Unpublished master's thesis, University of Iowa, 1939.

McWhorter, O.A. *Building reading interests and skills by utilizing children's first-hand experiences.* Unpublished master's thesis, Ohio University, 1935.

Meyer, B.J.F., Brandt, D.M., & Bluth, G.J. Use of top-level structure in text: Key for reading comprehension of ninth-grade students. *Reading Research Quarterly,* 1980, *16,* 72–103.

Mickelson, N.I. Associative verbal encoding (a/v/e): A measure of language performance and its relationship to reading achievement. *Reading Research Quarterly,* 1973–74, *9,* 227–231. (Abstract)

Otterman, L.M. The value of teaching prefixes and word-roots. *Journal of Educational Research,* 1955, *48,* 611–616.

Pany, D., & Jenkins, J.R. Learning word meanings: A comparison of instructional procedures and effects on measures of reading comprehension with learning disabled students. *Learning Disability Quarterly,* 1978, *1,* 21–32.

Pearson, P.D., Hansen, J., & Gordon, C. The effect of background knowledge on young children's comprehension of explicit and implicit information. *Journal of Reading Behavior,* 1979, *11,* 201–209.

Perfetti, C.A. Language comprehension and fast decoding: Some psycholinguistic prerequisites for skilled reading comprehension. In J.T. Guthrie (Ed.), *Cognition, curriculum, and comprehension.* Newark, Del.: International Reading Association, 1977.

Perfetti, C.A., & Hogaboam, T. The relationship between single word decoding and reading comprehension skill. *Journal of Educational Psychology,* 1975, *67,* 461–469.

Perfetti, C.A., & Roth, S. Some of the interactive processes in reading and their role in reading skill. In A. Lesgold & C. Perfetti (Eds.), *Interactive processes in reading.* Hillsdale, N.J.: Erlbaum, 1981.

Petre, R.M. Quantity, quality and variety of pupil responses during an open-communication structured group directed reading-thinking activity and a closed-communication structured group directed reading activity (Doctoral dissertation, University of Delaware, 1970). *Dissertation Abstracts International,* 1971, *31,* 4630A-4631A (University Microfilms No. 71-6474).

Powell, M. Difficulty level of student assignments. *Practical Applications of Research,* 1979, *1*(3), 1–2, 6.

Rickards, J.P., & Hatcher, C.W. Interspersed meaningful learning questions as semantic cues for poor comprehenders. *Reading Research Quarterly,* 1977–78, *13,* 538–553.

Roberts, T. "Frustration level" reading in the infant school. *Educational Research,* 1976, *19,* 41–44.

Rumelhart, D.E. Schemata: The building blocks of cognition. In R.J. Spiro, B.C. Bruce, & W.F. Brewer (Eds.), *Theoretical issues in reading comprehension.* Hillsdale, N.J.: Erlbaum, 1980.

Rumelhart, D.E., & Ortony, A. The representation of knowledge in memory. In R.C. Anderson, R.J. Spiro, & W.E. Montague (Eds.), *Schooling and the acquisition of knowledge.* Hillsdale, N.J.: Erlbaum, 1977.

Samuels, S.J. Characteristics of exemplary reading programs. In J.T. Guthrie (Ed.), *Comprehension and teaching: Research reviews*. Newark, Del.: International Reading Association, 1981.

Samuels, S.J., & Eisenberg, P. A framework for understanding the reading process. In F.J. Pirozzolo & M.C. Wittrock (Eds.), *Neuropsychological and cognitive processes in reading*. New York: Academic Press, 1981.

Smith, N.B. *Reading instruction for today's children*. Englewood Cliffs, N.J.: Prentice-Hall, 1963.

Spiro, R.J. Constructive processes in prose comprehension and recall. In R.J. Spiro, B.C. Bruce, & W.F. Brewer (Eds.), *Theoretical issues in reading comprehension*. Hillsdale, N.J.: Erlbaum, 1980.

Stanovich, K.E. Toward an interactive-compensatory model of individual differences in the development of reading fluency. *Reading Research Quarterly*, 1980, *16*, 32–71.

Stauffer, R.G. A directed reading-thinking plan. *Education*, 1959, *79*, 527–532.

Stauffer, R.G. *Directing reading maturity as a cognitive process*. New York: Harper & Row, 1969.

Stevens, K.C. The effect of background knowledge on the reading comprehension of ninth graders. *Journal of Reading Behavior*, 1980, *12*, 151–154.

Stevens, K.C. Can we improve reading by teaching background information? *Journal of Reading*, 1982, *25*, 326–329.

Stevens, R., & Rosenshine, B. Advances in research on teaching. *Exceptional Education Quarterly*, 1981, *2*, 1–9.

Thomas, A. Learned helplessness and expectancy factors: Implications for research in learning disabilities. *Review of Educational Research*, 1979, *49*, 208–221.

Thompson, G.B. Toward a theoretical account of individual differences in the acquisition of reading skill. *Reading Research Quarterly*, 1981, *16*, 596–599.

Thorndike, R.L. Reading as reasoning. *Reading Research Quarterly*, 1974, *9*, 135–147.

Tierney, R.J., & Cunningham, J.W. Research on teaching reading comprehension: An update. In P.D. Pearson (Ed.), *Handbook on research in reading*. New York: Longman, in press.

Tuinman, J.J., & Brady, M.E. How does vocabulary account for variance on reading comprehension tests? A preliminary instructional analysis. In P.L. Nacke (Ed.), *Interaction: Research and practice for college-adult reading* (Twenty-third Yearbook of the National Reading Conference). Clemson, S.C.: National Reading Conference, 1974.

Vanderlinde, L.F. Does the study of quantitative vocabulary improve problem-solving? *Elementary School Journal*, 1964, *65*, 143–152.

Vineyard, E.E., & Massey, H.W. The interrelationship of certain linguistic skills and their relationship with scholastic achievement when intelligence is ruled constant. *Journal of Educational Psychology*, 1957, *48*, 279–286.

Walberg, H.J., Hare, V.C., & Pulliam, C.A. Social-psychological perceptions and reading comprehension. In J.T. Guthrie (Ed.), *Comprehension and teaching: Research reviews*. Newark, Del.: International Reading Association, 1981.

Watts, G.H., & Anderson, R.C. Effects of three types of inserted questions on learning from prose. *Journal of Educational Psychology*, 1971, *62*, 387–394.

Whipple, G. Characteristics of a sound basic reading program. In W.S. Gray (Ed.), *Recent trends in reading* (Proceedings of the Conference on Reading). Chicago: University of Chicago, 1939.

Wilson, R.M., & Hall, M. *Reading and the elementary school child.* New York: Van Nostrand, 1972.

Wittrock, M.C. Reading comprehension. In F.J. Pirozzolo & M.C. Wittrock (Eds.), *Neuropsychological and cognitive processes in reading.* New York: Academic Press, 1981.

Wittrock, M.C., Marks, C., & Doctorow, M. Reading as a generating process. *Journal of Educational Psychology,* 1975, *67,* 484–489.

Yap, K.O. Vocabulary—Building blocks of comprehension? *Journal of Reading Behavior,* 1979, *11,* 49–59.

Zintz, M. *The reading process.* Dubuque: William C. Brown, 1970.

20

The Role of Research in the Development of a Successful Reading Program

Kathryn Hu-Pei Au,
Roland G. Tharp,
Doris C. Crowell,
Cathie Jordan,
Gisela E. Speidel, and
Roderick Calkins

T his chapter discusses the system for reading instruction developed at the Kamehameha Early Education Program (KEEP) in a manner that illustrates the crucial role of research in program development. As we will show, it is difficult, but by no means impossible, to develop and operate a school program based on research findings. Although we emphasize the research conducted at KEEP, the program's development was also shaped by the results of studies reported in other chapters of this volume.

Another purpose of this chapter is to highlight aspects of KEEP's work that have implications for the development of reading programs for disadvantaged minority students. The KEEP reading program was designed specifically to meet the needs of disadvantaged students of Hawaiian ancestry. Although not all of the specific features of the reading program may be appropriate for or readily translatable to other groups of disadvantaged minority children, the process evolved at KEEP—using research to guide program development—is readily generalizable.

Background Information

Hawaiian Students

The term *Hawaiian* refers to descendants of the original Polynesian inhabitants of the Hawaiian Islands, about 17 percent of the population. There are about 30,000 Hawaiians being educated in the public schools. These students, as a group, score dismally on standardized tests of reading achievement. The 1978 administration of the Stanford Achievement Test in the public schools, for example, yielded the following results. In reading, at grade four, 45 percent of Hawaiian students were performing below average, compared to 23 percent nationally; 51 percent were average, compared to 54 percent nationally; and 4 percent were above average, compared to 23 percent nationally. By grade eight, 69 percent of Hawaiian students were performing below average, 31 percent were average, and less than 1 percent had above average scores (Thompson & Hannahs, Note 1). The problems faced by Hawaiians are as serious as those faced by any disadvantaged minority group in the United States.

KEEP and Its Major Lines of Research

The initial focus of KEEP was on developing a reading program that would allow elementary school students to achieve at or near national norms. After about 6 years of work in our laboratory school, a successful prototype reading program was developed. Refining that program and finding ways to disseminate it to public schools has occupied our time for the last 5 years.

The basic research approach can be termed the "least-change" approach (Tharp & Gallimore, 1979), duplicating a public school setting as closely as possible. The laboratory school kept to the same daily and yearly schedule as the public schools. Classrooms were the same size, and the teacher–pupil ratio was the same. There were two major differences, however. First, three-quarters of the students were from families on welfare, a much higher proportion than in any of the local public schools. Second, classrooms were equipped with special facilities for observation and videotaping, so that research could be carried on with minimal disruption of teaching activities. We added classes to the laboratory school until there was one class each in kindergarten through third grade.

For the reading curriculum itself, a middle-of-the-road basal reading program was used first. We implemented it according to the book, even developing criterion-referenced tests for all the objectives in the program. During the early and mid 1970s, our work progressed on two parallel lines. First, we were gaining practical, hands-on experience in teaching reading to Hawaiian children. In this process, we learned what adjustments were needed to help our target students learn to read well. Second, we were conducting formal, focused studies to test a number of hypothetical reasons for the widespread failure of the schools to teach Hawaiian students to read.

At the level of educational policy or administration, the implication of much of KEEP's research is very clear: in designing or implementing programs for disadvantaged, culturally different students, it is extremely important to examine very carefully the assumptions of those programs. What are the supposed reasons for the students' school failure?

Motivation. Perhaps Hawaiian children did not learn to read well because they were not motivated to do so. Perhaps they did not work hard enough at learning to read.

Teachers can be trained to use contingent reinforcement in working with Hawaiian children (Sloat, Tharp, & Gallimore, 1977; Speidel & Tharp, Note 2), so that these children are motivated to read and work hard. In the laboratory school, we achieved rates of time on-task at about 90 percent, some 20 percent higher than in comparison schools (Tharp, Note 3). In a conventional reading program, the children did not learn to read any better than control students, as indicated by scores on standardized tests of reading achievement (Tharp, 1982). Thus, our work indicated that a high level of motivation (or industriousness) might be a necessary but not sufficient condition for learning to read.

Cognitive Skills. Perhaps Hawaiian children did not learn to read well because they lacked certain basic thinking skills necessary for learning to read. An extensive 9-year program of individually administered IQ tests measured specific areas of thinking, memory, and general knowledge. Our students entering kindergarten are not markedly low in any of these areas; by the end of their kindergarten year, they are at average levels on all subtests (Klein, Note 4).

The IQ tests also provide three kinds of summary scores: a verbal score, a performance score, and a total score. Of these three, verbal IQ is generally the most highly related to reading achievement. As with some other populations of disadvantaged minority students, Hawaiian children enter kindergarten with higher performance IQs than verbal IQs. Their total IQ scores are at about 90, approximately 10 points below average. After a year in kindergarten, their total IQ scores rise by about 10 points to the average IQ for nationwide standardization groups. What puzzled us about this finding was that, although IQ tests predict school success, Hawaiian children scored in the bottom third on standardized tests of reading achievement at the end of first grade (Klein, 1981; Tharp, 1982).

Dialect Interference. Perhaps Hawaiian children did not learn to read well because of dialect interference—interference between their nonstandard dialect, Hawaiian Creole English, and the Standard English used by their teachers and in their reading texts.

Parallel work has been carried out by researchers working with disadvantaged black students (Baratz & Shuy, 1969). We conducted a series of studies in this area but found little evidence of dialect interference in reading acquisition. We were able to identify only five pairs of sounds that might be confused by Hawaiian children (Smith, Truby, Tharp, & Gallimore, Note 5). Furthermore, try as we might, we could come up with pitifully few pairs of words incorporating these sounds that might possibly be confused even if used in context. It was hard to see, then, how interference at the phonological level could ever be great enough to account for the children's poor performance in learning to read. In the few instances in which a relationship was found between Hawaiian Creole fluency and reading achievement, the children who performed better on the dialect measure tended to be the better readers. It was clear that bidialectism was not sufficient reason to explain why children were not learning to read.

While discovering what the problem was not, we finally began to get an idea of what it was.

Comprehension. Hawaiian children did not learn to read well because they required a curriculum in which systematic instruction in both comprehension and phonics was provided from the very beginning (Crowell & Au, 1981a).

Reading curricula in basal series generally focus on two major skill areas: phonics (and various other word identification skills) and comprehension. An assumption often made is that most children learn to read best if the focus during their first years in school is on phonics, with relatively less time spent on comprehension. For any group of children, this division is probably artificial and is likely to present a misleading view of the purpose of reading (Crowell, 1982). For Hawaiian children, a focus on comprehension in the early grades is crucial, because they do not see the point of learning letter–sound relationships. They are not accustomed to learning by deduction from rules (Jordan, 1981). Many of them have not been read to, and they do not know that sense can be made of written symbols or that text can yield interesting information (Jordan, 1981). These students need to be involved in the actual act of reading, particularly text comprehension, right from the beginning. Thinking skills emphasized in the reading program seem applicable to listening as well as to reading comprehension (Crowell & Au, 1981a). Thus, before they can read themselves, children are taught to apply these thinking skills to stories read aloud to them. They are then helped to transfer these skills to material they read on their own. We bombard them with questions about the text to teach them that sense can be made of printed stories.

Language Development. Hawaiian children did not learn to read well because of their unfamiliarity with Standard English, not just because they were dialect speakers.

Our initial approach to language research, centering only on dialect interference, was framed too narrowly. We needed to study the children's familiarity with Standard English. In extended oral discourse, the children's comprehension was significantly better when the information was provided in Hawaiian English rather than in Standard English (Speidel, Tharp, & Kobayashi, Note 6). Our students had less knowledge of the rules of Standard English, in morphology and syntax, than children whose primary language code was Standard English. Our students do not acquire Standard English grammar as quickly as average Standard English-speaking children, falling, as a group, one standard deviation below the norm in first grade and three standard deviations below in third grade (Gallimore & Tharp, Note 7; Speidel, Note 8). Familiarity with Standard English is significantly correlated with reading achievement. Knowledge of grammatical rules, at an intuitive level, is an even better predictor of reading achievement than verbal IQ as measured by the Wechsler Intelligence Scale for Children—Version R (WISC-R) (Speidel, Note 8).

The school must accommodate language differences and promote the children's development of competence in Standard English. What teachers should not do is try to teach Standard English rules directly, either through explicit instruction of grammatical rules or through pattern drill (Speidel, in press; Day, Note 9). The teacher's role is to facilitate communication by eliciting speech from the children in the context of a discussion that is meaningful to them and by expanding, refining, and restructuring their speech in a supportive manner. Improving Hawaiian children's general language skills and familiarity with Standard English enables them to progress at the same rate as Standard English-speaking children in mastering features of Standard English grammar (Speidel, Gallimore, Vuyk, & Vogt, Note 10).

Cultural Compatibility. Hawaiian children did not learn to read well because of a serious mismatch between the culture of their homes and communities and that of the school (Gallimore, Boggs, & Jordan, 1974; Jordan, Gallimore, Sloggett, & Kubany, 1968; Jordan & Tharp, 1979).

Sometimes, the world of the child and the world of the school are so different that students consistently encounter serious social and academic difficulties, for reasons that are seldom clear either to them or to their teachers. There seem to be a number of points at which the culture of the school is definitely at odds with the values and standards of behavior of disadvantaged Hawaiian students (Gallimore et al., 1974).

Hawaiian children are often raised in a system of sibling caretaking, whereby older brothers and sisters have a good deal of responsibility for the younger ones. Children learn to orient to other children, and to turn to them rather than to adults, when they are in need of routine help or information. Thus, it is not surprising to find that the students often look to one another for assistance with classroom tasks, rather than approaching the teacher. Teachers sometimes feel that the children are ignoring them and talking to one another too much. The natural impulse is to scold them—a practice that only serves to establish the conflict between the demands of school and home. An important part of our teacher training program helps teachers distinguish when it is appropriate for children to orient to adults and when to children. Teachers are taught to use systematic praise to encourage adult orientation in those contexts where it is necessary (Tharp, Note 3). At other times, we try to build on the children's preference for relating to other children. We encourage teaching and learning interactions among the children around tasks related to learning to read (Jordan, 1981).

From our major lines of research, we learned that it was not very difficult to motivate our students to work hard on tasks related to learning to read. We found that disadvantaged Hawaiian children have the intellectual ability to learn to read, that they apparently do not have any particular cognitive deficit, and that dialect interference is not a major factor in hindering reading development. We also learned that positive outcomes occur with a reading program that stresses comprehension and language development and includes a teacher training program that minimizes cultural conflicts and maximizes learning by building on the children's natural strengths.

Results of Standardized Tests of Reading Achievement

Full reports of standardized test results are presented by Tharp (1982) and Klein (1981; Klein, Troy, Tharp, Gallimore, & Calkins, Note 11). We will attempt here merely to provide illustrative examples of our findings. The test scores of students in our program, as compared to a control group of students of the same background, are shown in figure 20-1 (from Klein et al., Note 11). Although our public school sites serve areas with many Hawaiian families, working with intact classes has meant that we have had the opportunity to teach students of many different ethnic backgrounds. As seen in figure 20-1, students who are not Hawaiian also benefit from our program, although the advantage to them is not so great.

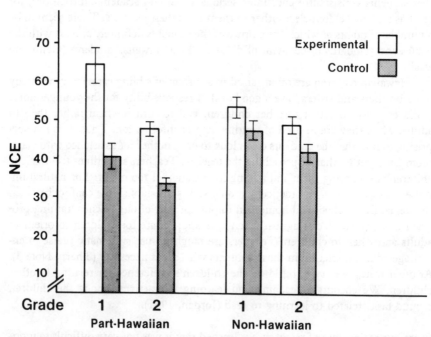

Source: T.W. Klein, M. Troy, R.G. Tharp, R. Gallimore, & R. Calkins, *The role of evaluation in the development and dissemination of the Kamehameha reading system* (Symposium presented at the Evaluation Research Society/Evaluation Network, Austin, October 1–3, 1981).

Figure 20-1. Total Reading Scores on the Metropolitan Achievement Test at All Field Sites, Combined for Spring 1979 and Spring 1980

The overall effects of the KEEP reading program on the performance of our target students in learning to read can be seen in figure 20-2 (from Klein & Troy, Note 12). The scores for control students in vocabulary and comprehension subtests are shown in the top curves. If their scores were as predicted by aptitude tests, they would match the normal curve; but they tend to be grouped to the left, far below the average for students of this age in the general population. In the bottom set of curves, the scores of the target students are almost normally distributed, indicating that they are much closer to achieving at the level expected from their intelligence test scores.

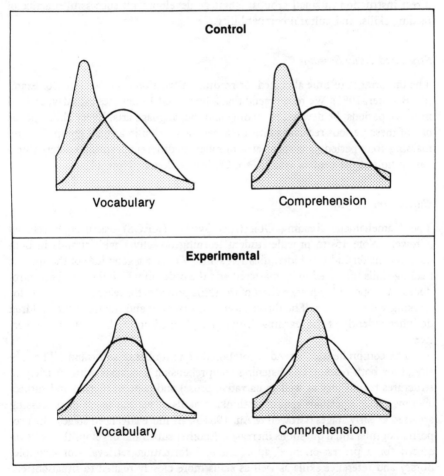

Source: T.W. Klein & M.E. Troy, *Evaluation of the KEEP reading system* (Paper presented at the 60th Annual Meeting of the Western Psychological Association, Honolulu, May 6, 1980).

Figure 20-2. Distributions of Gates-MacGinitie Vocabularly and Comprehension Scores for All Field Sites, Spring 1979.

The KEEP Reading Program

The KEEP reading program is highly structured and is demanding to teach, requiring high levels of teacher preparation time and energy. It has thirty-three specific features (see Appendix 20A, from Au, Note 13). These features are monitored monthly in our classrooms. Relatively few features can be absent if intervention is to be effective. The thirty-three features represent the particular set of conditions that comes closest to ensuring the desired results in student learning.

These thirty-three features are summarized in the following categories: a structured daily schedule; curriculum content; monitoring of student progress; direct instruction in small groups; language development; successful practice of reading skills; and cultural compatibility.

Structured Daily Schedule

The importance of time allocated for reading instruction is known (see, for example, Berliner, 1981). We recommend that 2 hours and 15 minutes each day, divided into five periods, be devoted to reading and the language arts. Every child spends one of these periods receiving direct teacher instruction in a small group. The remaining four periods are spent at a number of different learning centers (for a description of the centers system, see O'Neal & Bogert, Note 14).

Curriculum Content

The Kamehameha Reading Objectives System (KROS) has been developed (Crowell, Note 15) to provide student learning objectives with strands in both comprehension and word identification skills. We have a good idea of the specific reading skills that need to be mastered and the order in which they are best introduced. A scope and sequence chart of the skills provides the teacher a road map for working with students. The direct teacher instruction and the work the children do independently at the learning centers are planned on the basis of these objectives.

The comprehension strand is composed of a number of substrands. The substrand for both reading and listening comprehension uses texts with a variety of structures (expository as well as narrative prose) and content (fiction and subject area material); questions requiring thinking skills at various levels of processing are used at early stages (Crowell & Au, 1981b). At more advanced stages, the proportion of inferential questions increases. Another substrand develops the skills required for a process-oriented approach to information retrieval—for example, library and reference skills as well as skills more closely related to situations encountered in everyday life, such as using a telephone directory. Another substrand centers on vocabulary development and includes knowledge of word meanings, analogies, and the use of context.

Monitoring of Student Progress

Criterion-referenced tests match each of the objectives in our scope and sequence chart. Comprehension testing is done quarterly. Other testing is done at teacher request—optimally, at least once every 2 weeks. We have had enough experience to know whether a class is progressing at the appropriate rate, and we know for each quarter of the school year what the average number of tests passed in different skill areas should be if the class is to score at the fiftieth percentile on a standardized test of reading achievement. Teacher aides carry out the testing program and maintain records of student progress. These records help teachers individualize center assignments. Students are given feedback on their test performance, so that they know when they have passed or failed a test.

Small Group Instruction

A different group of children goes to the teacher for direct instruction during each of the five 20-minute periods. Each of these small reading groups is formed on the basis of the children's performance on the criterion-referenced tests. When observing a teacher during small group instruction, we look over the children's test profiles to see that the teacher is covering the proper skills at the proper level of difficulty. We check to see that the children are attentive nearly 100 percent of the time (and that this attentiveness is of an active sort) and that the teacher is applying specific teaching strategies.

We also check to see how time is distributed across skill areas (Au & Hao, Note 16). During a month, an average of two-thirds of instructional time should be spent on comprehension and the rest on word identification skills.

Language Development

The KEEP reading program increases the children's familiarity with school and textbook language in a number of ways. The children are not given Standard English texts to read during beginning reading instruction. Rather, the teacher engages the children in an activity, such as making peanut butter sandwiches, and encourages them to talk about what is happening. The children dictate a story about this activity to the teacher, who accepts their language patterns, whether in standard or dialect form. This story is used as a text to build reading skills. This language experience procedure (Allen & Halvorsen, 1961) has the advantage of first engaging the children in reading text that is familiar to them in both content and language patterns.

Later, Standard English texts, usually basal reader stories, are introduced. To circumvent potential problems arising from the less familiar language of these texts, teachers may use the experience-text-relationship (ETR) method (Au, 1979). During the experience phase, the teacher has the children discuss background experiences related to the story they will read and introduces unfamiliar words and language patterns from the story. In the text phase, the teacher directs the children's attention to the details of the story with a sequence of questions. Finally, during the relationship phase, the teacher helps the children integrate text information with their background knowledge. Throughout the lesson, the teacher asks questions at several levels of difficulty (Crowell & Au, 1981b) to further encourage the development of text comprehension skills.

The early language experience lessons and the lessons centered on Standard English texts have many of the features of effective language development sessions (Speidel, in press; Speidel & Vuyk, Note 17). The teacher encourages children to put their ideas into words and expands upon and clarifies their utterances. The teacher is constantly modeling different language patterns. The children learn new vocabulary items, concepts, and language patterns from one another. The intent is that the expansion of the children's language skills, particularly their familiarity with Standard English, will be interwoven with reading instruction.

Successful Practice of Reading Skills

While one group of children is with the teacher, the other children work at learning centers. There are ten to twelve centers that provide seating for three or four children each. The centers are numbered, and each is associated with a particular type of activity. The children are not all working on the same assignment at any one center; for example, all the children may be writing answers to questions based on short passages, but some are working with an easy passage and others with a more difficult one. Because the children are mixed heterogeneously, they are able to help one another with assignments. There is usually a great deal of talking going on, most of it about work (Jordan, 1981). Assignments and learning center activities are designed to provide a great deal of successful practice in reading and language arts skills. By the time each center period is over, most children have finished their work and are playing quiet games, chatting with one another, or doing recreational reading or creative writing. At the end of the 20 minutes, the children check their individual schedules to see which center to go to next. In less than a minute, the class has redistributed itself.

The children are able to explain what they have to do to complete their assignment and what skill area they are practicing. Not only does the teacher know where each child stands in learning to read, but the children usually know exactly where they stand and where they are headed.

Cultural Compatibility

Systematic attention has been given to making the program compatible with the culture of Hawaiian children. The KEEP effort was partly generated by intensive and well-documented studies of modern Hawaiian culture, which provided knowledge about the children's home culture (Gallimore et al., 1974; Gallimore & Howard, 1968; Howard, 1974). We wanted to minimize conflicts between the culture of the home and that of the school and to build upon the skills, knowledge, and behaviors that the children acquire in their home culture. We made the fit between school and home culture one of the criteria for selecting classroom practices (Jordan, 1981).

In a KEEP classroom, the children, not the teacher, undertake the fairly complex task of setting out and putting away the material and supplies at each of the learning centers. Although this feature might not, at first, appear to be very important, it builds upon a particular strength in the children's upbringing. From a very young age, many Hawaiian children are taught to assume responsibility for major household chores (Gallimore et al., 1974). Allowing the children to become responsible for similar chores in their classrooms is an extremely effective way to build teacher–student and student–student rapport and also gives students a sense of investment in their classrooms and in their school. We feel that this kind of involvement is a necessary prerequisite to good learning.

The organization of the learning centers allows the children to teach and learn from one another (Jordan, 1981). Centers are a comfortable and productive context for working on school tasks, and peer helping is an effective way of supplementing teacher instruction. In their home culture, the children are accustomed to working in small group settings with indirect adult supervision; they have experience in taking care of younger siblings and learning from older ones. These experiences prepare children to teach and learn from their peers.

A feature of reading instruction is the "talk story" style of interaction in the small reading groups (Au, 1980; Au & Jordan, 1981). "Talk story" in Hawaiian culture is characterized by joint performance, or the cooperative production of responses by two or more speakers (Watson-Gegeo & Boggs, 1977). In reading lessons, the teacher often allows two or more children to cooperate in framing answers to questions. Here, group performance is valued above individual performance.

Researcher-Practitioner Collaboration and the KEEP Reading Program

Detailed discussions of KEEP's educational research and development are available (Tharp, 1981; Tharp & Gallimore, 1979). Here, the importance of the interaction between theoretical and applied levels of research in the development of effective reading programs for disadvantaged minority students will be discussed. Substantial resources are required for the extensive research and development effort of the type conducted by KEEP. School systems working with more limited resources might promote similar kinds of efforts. To encourage such partnerships, we conclude with a discussion of the value of research–practitioner collaboration.

Researchers with both theoretical and applied orientations have contributed many ideas important to the development of the KEEP reading program, and practitioners have worked out specific methods for using these ideas in the classroom. Many ideas, such as the "talk story" style of interaction in reading lessons, came from observations of successful practitioners. Researchers then identified the idea, described it in theoretical terms, and analyzed its inner workings so that methods for teacher training could be developed.

The roles of the researcher at KEEP are to lead and to be led. Researchers doing curriculum studies frequently discuss their ideas with reading consultants and give workshops for teachers. Simultaneously, consultants and teachers identify problems of general concern to researchers.

We had greatly underestimated the difficulty of the job of the classroom teacher in helping disadvantaged Hawaiian children learn to read well. Although many of the ideas underlying the KEEP reading program are very simple, their implementation is complex. Teachers have to plan and prepare five small group lessons per day and plan and prepare for the learning centers. The amount of teacher preparation time required is perhaps our greatest concern. The astonishing thing is that teachers are willing to put in this time once they become convinced that the program will work with their students. At present, there are about forty public school teachers working with the KEEP program at four different schools in largely Hawaiian communities.

The KEEP reading program takes about 2 years for teachers to master; the skills required for successful small group instruction seem most difficult. This period of training is very stressful and includes frequent meetings and visits from a reading consultant. Teaching behavior is coded during small group lessons, and students are tested to see whether they are learning. The teachers must be data oriented, must have high performance expectations, and must be accountable for the performance of the students in their classrooms. As we learn more, we will be able to make our teachers' jobs somewhat easier. By developing more materials in specific skill areas, we will reduce preparation time. Nevertheless, the program will still be demanding and challenging. Teachers must actually engage the children in the process of learning to read; the program relies heavily on their abilities and good judgment.

The KEEP program could not have been developed without extensive research efforts, and we could not operate or improve it without continuing to do research. No matter how capable our practitioners are, they do not have the time (or the data) to sit down and think their way through the many problems. Because the reading consultants and teachers are always seeking new ideas that might help them do their jobs better, researchers sometimes feel that preliminary results of studies are snatched from their desks before the proper stamp of scientific caution has been affixed. Our research at KEEP has not necessarily made the jobs of our practitioners easier, but it has made their success much more likely.

Neither the personal experience and knowledge of the teachers nor the formal contributions of researchers have alone been sufficient to create this program. Only the two together have succeeded. More than anything else, it is this partnership that we recommend to anyone concerned with developing programs for children who are waiting to be taught to read.

Reference Notes

1. Thompson, M., & Hannahs, N. Testimony prepared for the Native Hawaiian Education Act, presented to a joint committee on elementary, secondary, and vocational education and post-secondary education of the U.S. House of Representatives. Honolulu: Kamehameha Schools, November 1979.
2. Speidel, G.E., & Tharp, R.G. *Training teachers in the use of positive feedback* (Tech. Rep. No. 33). Honolulu: Kamehameha Early Education Program, 1975.
3. Tharp, R.G. Peer orientation, industriousness and learning to read: Experience with the Hawaiian child. In D. Jordan, T. Weisner, R.G. Tharp, R. Gallimore, & K. Au, *A multidisciplinary approach to research in education* (Tech. Rep. No. 81). Honolulu: Kamehameha Early Education Program, 1978.
4. Klein, T.W. Personal communication, February 24, 1982.
5. Smith, K.J., Truby, H. Tharp, R.G., & Gallimore, R. *The KEEP phone discrimination test* (Tech. Rep. No. 64). Honolulu: Kamehameha Early Education Program, 1977.
6. Speidel, G.E., Tharp, R.G., & Kobayashi, L. *Is there a comprehension problem for dialect-speaking children? A study with children who speak Hawaiian English*. Manuscript in preparation, 1982.
7. Gallimore, R., & Tharp, R.G. *Studies of Standard English and Hawaiian Islands Creole English: KEEP linguistic research 1971-1976* (Tech. Rep. No. 59). Honolulu: Kamehameha Early Education Program, 1976.
8. Speidel, G.E. *The relationship between psycholinguistic abilities and reading achievement in dialect-speaking children*. Paper presented at the annual meeting of the American Educational Research Association, San Francisco, 1979.
9. Day, R. *The teaching of English to Hawaii creole-speaking children* (Tech. Rep. No. 29). Honolulu: Kamehameha Early Education Program, 1975.
10. Speidel, G.E., Gallimore, R., Vuyk, S., & Vogt, L. *Oral language in a successful reading program for Hawaiian children*. Symposium presented at the Annual Convention for Teachers of English Speakers of Other Languages (TESOL), Honolulu, May 1982.
11. Klein, T.W., Troy, M., Tharp, R.G., Gallimore, R., & Calkins, R. *The role of evaluation in the development and dissemination of the Kamehameha reading system*. Symposium presented at the Evaluation Research Society/Evaluation Network, Austin, October 1-3, 1981.
12. Klein, T.W., & Troy, M.E. *Evaluation of the KEEP reading system*. Paper presented at the 60th Annual Meeting of the Western Psychological Association, Honolulu, May 6, 1980.
13. Au, K.H. *The essential features list of the KEEP reading program* (Language Arts Series No. 3). Honolulu: Kamehameha Early Education Program, 1981.

14. O'Neal, K., & Bogert, K. *Classroom organization for the language arts teacher: A system for meeting learner needs through the use of work areas and small group instruction* (Tech. Rep. No. 78). Honolulu: Kamehameha Early Education Program, 1977.
15. Crowell, D.C. *Kamehameha Reading Objectives System (KROS).* Honolulu: Kamehameha Early Education Program, 1981.
16. Au, K.H., & Hao, R. *A quality control system for reading instruction* (Working paper). Honolulu: Kamehameha Early Education Program, 1978.
17. Speidel, G.E,. & Vuyk, S. *Developing children's discourse skills.* Paper presented to the Hawaii Educational Research Association, Honolulu, 1982.

References

Allen, R., & Halvorsen, G.C. The language experience approach to reading instruction. *Contributions in reading.* Boston: Ginn, 1961.

Au, K.H. Using the experience-text-relationship method with minority children. *Reading Teacher,* 1979, *32,* 677–679.

Au, K.H. Participation structures in a reading lesson with Hawaiian children: Analysis of a culturally appropriate instructional event. *Anthropology and Education Quarterly,* 1980, *11*(2), 91–115.

Au, K.H., & Jordan, C. Teaching reading to Hawaiian children: Finding a culturally appropriate solution. In H.T. Trueba, G.P. Guthrie, & K.H. Au (Eds.), *Culture in the bilingual classroom: Studies in classroom ethnography.* Rowley, Mass.: Newbury House, 1981.

Baratz, C., & Shuy, W. (Eds.). *Teaching black children to read.* Washington, D.C.: Center for Applied Linguistics, 1969.

Berliner, D.C. Academic learning time and reading achievement. In J.T. Guthrie (Ed.), *Comprehension and teaching: Research reviews.* Newark, Del.: International Reading Association, 1981.

Crowell, D.C. Systematic development of thinking skills through a language arts curriculum. In W. Maxwell (Ed.), *Thinking: An interdisciplinary report.* Philadelphia: Franklin Institute Press, 1982.

Crowell, D.C., & Au, K.H. Developing children's comprehension in listening, reading, and television viewing. *Elementary School Journal,* 1981, *82*(2), 51–57. (a)

Crowell, D.C., & Au, K.H. A scale of questions to guide comprehension instruction. *The Reading Teacher,* 1981, *34*(4), 389–393. (b)

Gallimore, R., Boggs, J.W., & Jordan, C. *Culture, behavior and education: A study of Hawaiian-Americans.* Beverly Hills: Sage Publications, 1974.

Gallimore, R., & Howard, A. (Eds.). *Studies in a Hawaiian community: Na makamaka o Nanakuli.* Honolulu: Bernice P. Bishop Museum, 1968.

Howard, A. *Ain't no big thing: Coping strategies in a Hawaii American community.* Honolulu: University of Hawaii Press, 1974.

Jordan, C.E. *Educationally effective ethnology: A study of the contributions of cultural knowledge to effective education for minority children.* Unpublished doctoral dissertation, University of California at Los Angeles, 1981.

Jordan, C., Gallmore, R., Sloggett, B., & Kubany, E. The family and the school. In R. Gallimore & A. Howard (Eds.), *Studies in a Hawaiian community: Na makamaka o Nanakuli.* Honolulu: Bernice P. Bishop Museum, 1968.

Jordan, C., & Tharp, R.G. Culture and education. In A. Marsella, R.G. Tharp, & T. Ciborowski (Eds.), *Perspectives in cross-cultural psychology.* New York: Academic Press, 1979.

Klein, T.W. Results of the reading program. *Educational Perspective,* 1981, *20*(1), 8–9.

Sloat, K.C.M., Tharp, R.G., & Gallimore, R. The incremental effectiveness of classroom-based teacher training techniques. *Behavior Therapy,* 1977, *8,* 810–818.

Speidel, G.E. Creole and Standard English in Hawaii: A comparison of two approaches to language development in Hawaiian Creole-speaking children. In K. Li & J. Lum (Eds.), *Research on Asian and Pacific bilingual education.* Los Angeles: National Dissemination and Assessment Center, in press.

Tharp, R.G. The metamethodology of research and development. *Educational Perspectives,* 1981, *20*(1), 42–48.

Tharp, R.G. The effective instruction of comprehension: Results and description of the Kamehameha Early Education Program. *Reading Research Quarterly,* 1982, *17*(4), 503–527.

Tharp, R.G., & Gallimore, R. The ecology of program research and development: A model of evaluation succession. In L.B. Sechrest (Ed.), *Evaluation studies review annual* (Vol. 4). Beverly Hills: Sage Publications, 1979.

Watson-Gegeo, K.A., & Boggs, S.T. From verbal play to talk story: The role of routines in speech events among Hawaiian children. In S. Ervin-Tripp & C. Mitchell-Kernan (Eds.), *Child discourse.* New York: Academic Press, 1977.

Appendix 20A

Essential Features of the KEEP Reading Program, as of October 1981

1. 2 hours, 15 min. allocated time for reading/language arts.
2. Reading groups meet daily with teacher.
3. Meeting time is 20–25 min. daily.
4. 4 additional center periods of 20–25 minutes.
5. The teacher requests tests at least once every 2 weeks.
6. Over a month's time, at least one test has been requested for every child.
7. Of all the tests requested for all the children in the class, there was an overall pass rate of 70% or better.
8. Feedback is given to students about test results.
9. Children in the class are assigned to homogeneous reading groups on the basis of KROS criterion referenced test results.
10. There are 3 to 7 children in a reading group.
11. The teacher provides instruction at the appropriate level, according to the KROS results.
12. Two-thirds of the time in direct teacher instruction is spent in comprehension, and one-third in word identification skills.
13. Children in the reading group are attentive nearly 100% of the time.
14. The teacher tries to involve *all* children in the group in the discussion.
15. There is a high level of active student participation.
16. The teacher introduces new skills prior to giving centers assignments involving those skills.
17. A variety of appropriate strategies for teaching reading comprehension is being used.
18. The strategies being used are well executed.
19. Instruction in word identification follows the sequence of KROS objectives.
20. Instruction is consistent with the KROS hierarchy of word identification strategies.
21. Phonics is taught by analytic methods.
22. The classroom is organized in learning centers.

From K.H. Au, *The essential features list of the KEEP reading program* (Language Arts Series No. 3). Honolulu: Kamehameha Early Education Program, 1981.

23. There is an introductory period, of teacher directions, for centers work.
24. Three to four children work at centers together.
25. At least half of the work at centers is directly related to the KROS objectives.
26. Centers work is at the children's independent level (i.e., 80% or more of the items in assignments are completed correctly).
27. In general, children are spending 75% or more of the time at centers working on their assignments.
28. One-half of centers time is spent on comprehension activities, with the remaining time divided between word identification skills and other language arts skills.
29. Centers assignments are designed to be consistent with individual children's reading skills, as reflected by KROS criterion referenced test data.
30. Materials and activities in centers are consistent with the stated purpose of the center.
31. Children are responsible for the setting up and cleaning up of learning centers.
32. Teaching/learning interactions occur among children at centers.
33. Talk story-like participation structures are present in small group lessons.

21
Teaching Children to Think as They Read

Jane Hansen

I n September, a first-grade child challenged her teacher: "When you read you don't do *anything*." Readers do think when they read, however. Teachers need to teach thinking processes, and students need to learn these processes; but teachers find it difficult to teach the invisible processes of thinking, and children have trouble learning what they cannot see others do. To teach these processes, teachers need to be aware of their own unconscious processes, and students need to become aware of such processes as they learn to read.

The Reading Process

When readers recall what they read, they recall the meaning of a passage rather than the exact words. Readers construct meaning by combining information found in various parts of a passage, rather than by recalling individual sentences (Bransford, Barclay, & Franks, 1972); they put together a message for the page, rather than taking a message from the page.

Comprehension is not possible if readers cannot interact with a text. Readers may recite the words, but the words in themselves do not necessarily carry meaning. The reading process does not function unless readers can use knowledge outside a text to comprehend a text's meaning.

Bransford and Johnson (1973) gave readers the following passage:

> The procedure is actually quite simple. First you arrange things into different groups. Of course, one pile may be sufficient depending on how much there is to do. If you have to go somewhere else due to lack of facilities that is the next step, otherwise you are pretty well set. It is important not to overdo things. That is, it is better to do too few things at once than too many. In the short run this may not seem important but complications can easily arise. A mistake can be expensive as well. At first the whole procedure will seem complicated. Soon, however, it will become just another facet of life. It is difficult to foresee any end to the necessity for this task in the immediate future, but then one never can tell. After the procedure is completed, one arranges the materials into different groups again. Then

they can be put into their appropriate places. Eventually they will be used once more and the whole cycle will then have to be repeated. However, that is part of life.

Mature readers could not understand this paragraph until the title, "Washing Clothes," permitted them to access previous experience and make the paragraph understandable. This study illustrates two components of reading: readers not only need to have prior knowledge, but they must use that knowledge as they read. Without a title for the passage about washing clothes, readers could not use their knowledge about sorting laundry. Thus, readers use words and other knowledge to put messages together.

Readers create their own meaning for a text when they weave their own knowledge into the passage. In Bartlett's (1932) study, readers from different cultures all read an Eskimo folk tale, but their interpretations differed. Their versions reflected their own culture rather than the Eskimo culture. Similarly, when readers from India and the United States explained a passage about an Indian wedding, the two groups of readers understood the passage differently (Anderson, Reynolds, Schallert, & Goetz, 1977).

The ramifications of such studies are far-reaching. Readers take concepts from the words on a page and use these concepts to construct their own representation of a printed message (Anderson, 1977; Collins, Brown, & Larkin, 1980). Readers actively engage in a process of searching for meaningful, memorable connections between what they see in print and their own prior knowledge. This active nature of the reading process may be the most important aspect of reading that we have confirmed in the last decade (Pearson, 1981).

Thinking While Reading

The connections readers make when they comprehend are frequently called inferences. Because inferences play such a prominent role in an active reading process, teachers should teach children to use inferential thinking skills when they read. Children need to approach printed information with the same spontaneity with which they approach other information in their daily lives. Children crave to understand things that happen around them. They incessantly ask, "Why?" When we explain things to them, we say, "Well, it's sort of like . . ." We connect the unknown to something they know, so that they can understand. Thus, they draw inferences between similar pieces of information.

Young children often do not appear to realize that a text is a source of new information that they could understand if they would make connections between the text and something they already know. (Beck, in chapter 18 of this volume, provides further evidence in support of the notion that children do not spontaneously integrate existing knowledge with text.)

Many researchers hypothesize that comprehension is a deliberate action and that readers need to recognize when to use their various comprehension strategies. Myers and Paris (1978) investigated both primary and upper-elementary students' concepts of what they do as they read. The young children in their study who had comprehension difficulties were unaware of many comprehension strategies. Myers and Paris suggest that beginning readers could profit from instruction about the process of reading.

Educators believe, however, that they should delay the teaching of inferential thinking. Basal readers do not offer nearly as many inferential thinking exercises in their primary-grade programs as they do in their upper-grade programs. School curriculum guides usually do not stress the development of inferential thinking skills in the beginning grades. Although children in the primary grades need to learn how to decode, they also need to learn that reading is a process of creating meaning. If the instructional focus is on decoding and literal comprehension at the expense of a comparable focus on creating meaning, children may not realize the essence of the reading process.

Poor readers receive instruction on decoding and literal comprehension for an even longer period of time than average readers. Gumperz (Note 1) and Allington (1980) found that teachers teach their poor readers differently than they teach their good readers. They teach good readers to consider the overall message of a text, but they teach poor readers to focus on individual words. (This research is reviewed by Cazden in chapter 8 of this volume.)

Canney and Winograd (Note 2) interviewed good and poor readers in grades two, four, six, and eight. In response to the question "What is reading?" the students in grades two and four gave answers focused on decoding. The immediate goal of creating meaning was not uppermost in their minds. By the upper grades, the good students focused more on getting meaning than on decoding, but the poor readers at those levels still did not consider reading a meaning-producing activity. In the second part of their study, Canney and Winograd showed that readers who view reading as a meaning-producing activity comprehend better than other students.

Wixson's (1980) research supports Canney and Winograd. She found that the comprehension of fifth-grade students was inhibited when teachers asked literal questions. In contrast, when the teachers' questions required that the students focus on connections, their comprehension improved.

Currently, when we teach children to read, we ask them to spend a large portion of their time focusing on print rather than on the connections between the print and stored knowledge. It is time to ask the question "What *should* you see when a reading teacher is teaching children to think as they read?" The teacher should help students use the reading strategies of mature readers. A considerable amount of instruction probably should occur before the students read, so that they can use their thinking skills as they read.

Hansen and her colleagues developed a prereading discussion plan modeled on the inferential connections people make between familiar and unfamiliar information (Hansen, 1981a, 1981b; Hansen & Hubbard, in press; Hansen & Pearson, in press). The discussions are based on the idea that children need to actively search, seek, find, and establish connections when they read. Teachers used the plan with average readers in the second grade and poor readers in the fourth grade. The second-grade students answered literal and inferential comprehension questions from ten instructional stories better than students in a control group. The fourth-grade poor readers not only answered inferential questions from the instructional stories better than control students but also answered questions on transfer stories better than the control students.

Within the discussions, students make comparisons between their existing knowledge and the information to be read. They talk about what they have experienced (or learned) and hypothesize how the information they are about to read may be similar to or different from their own stored knowledge. As they share their knowledge, they learn new connections from each other; they now have more possible connections to make when they read. The students also learn that because different people have had different previous experiences, they may draw different conclusions. They learn that different people may interpret a particular piece differently and that various interpretations may be defensible.

These discussions have another crucial element: making connections is not left up to chance. The students talk about inferential comprehension and use the terminology of the process. They talk about the purpose of the connections between the print and their stored knowledge and about how it is easier to understand something when you can find something familiar in it. These students know what they do when they read. They think about calling up their own background knowledge and using it. Poor readers tune in particularly well to these discussions. These students know that they are poor readers, and they are eager to learn about a system that may help them.

A motivational factor emerges from these discussions. Students readily take part, become interested in the stories, and willingly read the stories on their own. One teacher said, "Inference training is an exciting way to introduce a story. The story becomes a new friend that the students have heard about but not met."

Gordon (1980) developed a similar way to teach children to think as they read. Students who use Gordon's "inference awareness" method develop three understandings about inferences: (1) the language necessary to discuss inferences, (2) the purpose of inferences when they read, and (3) the need to draw inferences whenever they read, not just in reading class.

Raphael (Note 3) developed another instructional method in which students learn to make connections. In her lessons, students analyze the process of answering questions. Her system for question answering requires that students decide where the source of an answer is and then decide what the answer is. Students learn three question–answer relationships: (1) text-explicit (when a question is generated from one sentence in a text and the response is in that same sentence); (2) text-implicit (when the response to a question must be created by combining information found in at least two different places in the text); and (3) script-implicit (when the answer to a question can only be found in the reader's script, a script being some knowledge the reader has stored in his or her mind). In Raphael's instructional sequence, teachers gradually lead their upper-elementary students to recognize the three question–answer relationships. After the students articulate the thinking processes involved in answering questions, their abililty to provide correct answers to questions improves.

Palincsar and Brown (chapter 22 of this volume) have extended question-answering skills by adding reciprocal teaching—an explicit method of teaching comprehension in which students stop periodically as they read to interpret and predict. Dialogues with the teacher (or with other students) are an explicit method of comprehension instruction, because the teacher fully informs the students about the nature of the instruction. When the teachers add the dialogues to the question-answering instruction, comprehension on transfer passages improves dramatically.

Each of these procedures for comprehension instruction emphasizes meta-comprehension. The students not only practice a thinking activity, they also learn to use their thinking skills consciously. They learn to use and direct their own thinking processes. Thus, they learn how to learn (Bransford, 1979; Brown, Campione, & Day, 1981). These four procedures demonstrate several ways of teaching thinking. We must teach our students an awareness of various thinking strategies so that they can choose the most effective strategy in a given situation.

Students should spend a large portion of their time thinking when they are in reading class. They need to put together all the pieces of the reading process, because reading is greater than the sum of its parts. We must teach them how to think as they read, because the basic skill of reading is thinking.

Reference Notes

1. Gumperz, J. *Ethnography and controlled experimentation in the study of literacy.* Paper presented at the Reading Comprehension Conference, Center for the Study of Reading, University of Illinois, May 1980.
2. Canney, G., & Winograd, P. *Schemata for reading and reading comprehension performance.* Paper presented at the meeting of the American Educational Research Association, Boston, April 1980.
3. Raphael, T. *Improving question-answering performance through instruction* (Reading Education Rep. No. 32). Urbana: University of Illinois, Center for the Study of Reading, March 1982.

References

Allington, R.L. Poor readers don't get to read much in reading groups. *Language Arts*, 1980, *57*, 872–876.

Anderson, R. The notion of schemata and the educational enterprise. In R. Anderson, J. Spiro, & W.E. Montague (Eds.), *Schooling and the acquisition of knowledge*. Hillsdale, N.J.: Erlbaum, 1977.

Anderson, R.C., Reynolds, R.E., Schallert, D.L., & Goetz, E.T. Framework for comprehending discourse. *American Educational Research Journal*, 1977, *14*, 367–382.

Bartlett, F.C. *Remembering: A study in experimental and social psychology*. London: Cambridge University Press, 1932.

Bransford, J.D. *Human cognition: Learning, understanding, remembering*. Belmont, Calif.: Wadsworth, 1979.

Bransford, J.D., Barclay, J.R., & Franks, J.J. Sentence memory: A constructive versus interpretive approach. *Cognitive Psychology*, 1972, *3*, 193–209.

Bransford, J.D., & Johnson, M.K. Considerations of some problems of comprehension. In W.G. chase (Ed.), *Visual information processing*. New York: Academic Press, 1973.

Brown, A.L., Campione, J.C., & Day, J.D. Learning to learn: On training students to learn from texts. *Educational Researcher*, 1981, *10*, 14–21.

Collins, A., Brown, J.S., & Larkin, K.M. Inference in text understanding. In R.J. Spiro, B.C. Bruce, & W.F. Brewer (Eds.), *Theoretical issues in reading comprehension*. Hillsdale, N.J.: Erlbaum, 1980.

Gordon, C. *The effects of instruction in metacomprehension and inferencing on children's comprehension abilities*. Unpublished doctoral dissertation, University of Minnesota, December 1980.

Hansen, J. The effects of inference training and practice on young children's reading comprehension. *Reading Research Quarterly*, 1981, *16*, 391–417. (a)

Hansen, J. An inferential comprehension strategy. *The Reading Teacher*, 1981, *34*, 665–669. (b)

Hansen, J., & Hubbard, R. Poor readers can draw inferences. *Reading Teacher*, in press.

Hansen, J., & Pearson, P.D. An instructional study: Improving the inferential comprehension of good and poor fourth-grade readers. *Journal of Educational Psychology*, in press.

Myers, M., & Paris, S.G. Children's metacognitive knowledge about reading. *Journal of Educational Psychology*, 1978, *70*, 680–690.

Pearson, P.D. A decade of research in reading comprehension. In V. Froese & S.B. Straw (Eds.), *Research in the language arts: Language and schooling*. Baltimore: University Park Press, 1981.

Wixson, K. *Effects of postreading questions on children's discourse comprehension and knowledge acquisition*. Unpublished doctoral dissertation, State University of New York at Syracuse, 1980.

22
Reciprocal Teaching: A Means to a Meaningful End

Annemarie Palincsar and
Ann Brown

We recently asked a sixth-grade teacher to evaluate a short expository passage. After skimming the passage, the teacher stated emphatically that her students "could read this easily." We then showed her the comprehension questions that accompanied the passage. The teacher said, "You would get the craziest answers to these questions. Sometimes I wonder if we have read the same thing when it comes time for discussion."

This teacher was obviously defining reading in its most narrow sense—as decoding. It is the discrepancy between the ability to decode and the ability to comprehend that is of particular interest to us. This chapter reports on the development and evaluation of a method of comprehension instruction we have been exploring. Our goal has been to teach students four activities designed to foster comprehension and to induce students to monitor their comprehension. These activities include question generating, summarizing, predicting, and clarifying.

Support for the value of question generating while reading has been documented by André and Anderson (1978–79), Frase and Schwartz (1975), Manzo (1969), and Wong and Jones (Note 1). We instruct students to generate, first, questions about main ideas in the text and then questions that would address supporting details.

Although summarization has received less empirical attention (however, see Brown and Day, in press; Day, 1980), this activity provides an excellent opportunity for students to extract and integrate the gist of the material read. Students begin their summaries by stating, "This paragraph was about . . . " They are encouraged to complete their summaries without referring to the text.

Predicting constitutes the third component of this comprehension fostering/monitoring program. Collins and Smith (1982) have advocated that, in addition to making interpretations about what is currently happening in the text (as in summarizing), students should also be taught to make predictions or hypotheses about what will occur in the text. Our students are taught to recognize appropriate opportunities for making such predictions (titles, headings and subheadings, and questions posed in the text). They are also encouraged to make predictions based on the general fund of information that they already possess regarding a topic. As students predict, they establish for themselves a purpose for reading—the confirmation or disproval of their own hypotheses.

Because the failure of poor comprehenders to engage in spontaneous critical evaluation of text has been well documented (Harris, Kruithof, Terwogt, & Visser, 1981; Markman, 1977, 1979), the explicit instruction of clarification is the final activity. Students are first introduced to a variety of reasons why text can be confusing: difficult vocabulary, unclear referents, disorganized text, and unfamiliarity of content. They are then instructed in appropriate fix-up strategies (reread, read on, use context clues, consult a dictionary or a teacher).

The Reciprocal Teaching Procedure

The primary instructional technique employed to teach the four activities is an interactive dialogue in which the teacher explicitly models each of the four activities. The students follow the teacher's model by engaging in the same activities. The teacher prompts and shapes the students' participation by using corrective feedback.

Instruction is preceded by discussion of why we sometimes experience difficulty in understanding what we read. The students are informed that they will learn four activities that will help them keep their attention on what they are reading and also help them ascertain whether they have understood what they have read. The teacher stresses that these activities are to be used not only in reading class but in other academic areas as well—to prepare for tests, complete homework, do book reports, and so forth.

The four activities are then described. Introductory worksheet activities provide sequenced practice with each activity. These worksheets are done on a whole-class basis, and responses are discussed. Following this introduction to the four activities, which takes four class periods, the students and teacher are prepared to begin their dialogue about the text. (It should be noted that the worksheet activities in themselves are not sufficient to promote improved comprehension.)

The teacher first asks the students to predict from the title what content might be included in the text to be read. The students are encouraged to join in freely, speculating from their own backgrounds about what the author might discuss. The teacher notes these predictions and refers to them as the class proceeds through the text. After the group has read the first paragraph silently, the teacher proceeds to model the four activities: first, generating a question or several questions; then, summarizing the text; predicting; and, finally, clarifying anything potentially confusing in the text. The students answer the questions and elaborate on the points the teacher makes. After several paragraphs are completed in this fashion, the teacher assigns a student (preferably a good student) to assume the role of teacher for the next paragraph. The adult teacher prompts as necessary and praises the student teacher's participation. The student teacher assigns the next teacher.

Over time, the adult teacher attempts to turn over more of the instruction to the students but continues to monitor their performance, provide specific feedback, and model for the students when necessary. (For example, "You asked an excellent question about a major point the author is making. Your summary contained more details than are necessary. I would have summarized by saying . . . ").

Several representative transcripts illustrating the reciprocal teaching procedure follow (T = teacher, S = student):

Transcript Illustrating How Sessions Were Begun

T: What is the title of our new passage?
S: The Miracle of Butterflies.
T: Right. What is the miracle of butterflies? Just in your own words, what would you predict this is going to be about?
S: How butterflies fly?
T: So the miracle might be that they fly.
S: How they turn into butterflies?
T: Oh, that's a good prediction!
S: What they do.
S: What season they come out, like summer.
T: O.K. Those are some excellent predictions. Let's begin, and I'll take care of this one.

(All read the first paragraph silently.)

My question is: What have the people of Butterfly City, U.S.A., done to protect the butterflies?
S: They made a law making it illegal.
T: To do what? You are right, Quinton.
S: To kill butterflies.
T: Exactly. Good answer. My summary is that this is about the migration of the monarch butterflies. Do you have anything that should be added to that?

(No answer)

Was there anything unclear in this one?

(No answer)

When it says here, "they call their city Butterfly City," what are they talking about?
S: U.S.A.
T: It's in the U.S.A., but what city is it?
S: California.
T: It's in the state of California.
S: Pacific Grove.
T: There you go! "Their city" refers to Pacific Grove, and apparently thousands of butterflies fly into the city every year. That's interesting, isn't it? All right Marilyn, will you teach us the next one?

Transcript Illustrating How the Teacher Elicits a Comment about an Unclear Meaning

T: Let me ask you something here. Is there an unclear meaning in this paragraph?
S: Yes. Where it says, "Scrawls in wavy light."

T: Now, does the sun ever write a message in the sky?

S: No.

T: No. What is the author doing here?

S: Making up the whole thing in his mind.

T: Alright. Good. It doesn't really happen but the author is using this expression to say that the sun sends us a message and that is that it can be used as an energy source. But certainly you will never look at the sky and see a message written by the sun.

Transcript Illustrating Process of Corrective Feedback

S: Name three different basic methods how salt is produced.

S: Evaporation, mining, evaporation . . . artificial heat evaporation.

S: Correct, very good. My summary on this paragraph is about ways that salt is being produced.

T: Very good. Could you select the next teacher?

(Student selects another student)

S: Name two words that often describe mining salt in the old days.

S: Back to the salt mines?

S: No. Angela?

S: Dangerous and difficult.

S: Correct. This paragraph is all about comparing the old mining of salt and today's mining of salt.

T: Beautiful!

S: I have a prediction to make.

T: Good.

S: I think it might tell when salt was first discovered, well, it might tell what salt is made of and how it's made.

T: O.K. Can we have another teacher?

S: After purification at high temperatures the salt is ready for what?

S: Our tables.

S: That's correct. To summarize—after its purification, the salt is put on our tables.

T: That was a fine job, Ken, and I appreciate all that work, but I think there might be something else to add to our summary. There is more important information that I think we need to include. This paragraph is mostly about what?

S: The third method of artificial evaporation.

S: It mainly tells about pumping water from an underground salt bed that dissolves the salt to make a brine that is brought to the surface.

T: Angela hit it right on the money. This paragraph is mostly about the method of artificial evaporation and then everything else in the paragraph is telling us about that process. O.K. Next teacher.

S: My question is, what are the best people called?

S: The salt of the earth.

S: Why?

S: Because salt and the people have been together so long.

T: Chris, do you have something to add to that? O.K. It really isn't because they have been together so long; it has to do with something else. Brian?

S: (reading) "People and salt have always been together but never has the tie been so complete."

T: Alright, but when we use the expression, "That person is the salt of the earth," we know that means that person is a good person. How do we know that?

S: Because we treasure salt, like gold.

T: Exactly! The whole comparison here is that we treasure people like salt because salt has been treasured like gold. The salt of the earth means that they are very valuable to us. That is the whole punchline of the story ... to understand that while we use salt every day, it is very necessary to our diet and hasn't always been taken for granted.

Evaluating the Reciprocal Teaching Procedure

We have been involved in the evaluation of the reciprocal teaching procedure for several years, in a variety of settings and situations (Brown & Palincsar, 1982; Palincsar, 1982; Palincsar & Brown, Note 2). In this chapter, we will report on its evaluation by four remedial reading teachers who used it to instruct groups ranging from four to seven students.

Students

The four groups participating in this study attended four different rural junior high schools within 20 miles of a middle-sized midwestern city. There were twenty-one students, seven females and fourteen males. Standardized tests administered by each district prior to the initiation of the study (including the SRA (level 2) Diagnostic Reading Test, the Iowa Test of Basic Skills, and the California Achievement Test) indicated that comprehension scores averaged 2 years below grade level and ranged from 0.5 to 5 years below grade level.

In addition to standardized tests, the students were administered an informal screening device to ascertain that they met the criteria established for participating in the study. The criteria focused on identifying a discrepancy between decoding and comprehension skills. The students read a 450-word passage (written at the seventh-grade level) at a rate of at least eighty words per minute correct, with two or fewer error words per minute. These are the rates suggested by Lovitt and Hansen (1976) as predictive of the probable instructional reading level of students. The students answered questions about the passage. A score of 50 percent or less on these questions was regarded as indicative of a comprehension problem. (The mean score on these questions attained by a group of seventh graders identified as good readers was 80.4 percent). The participants in the study averaged 35 percent accuracy on the comprehension questions, a 104 words per minute correct rate, and a 1.5 words per minute error rate.

Material

The passages used for the training sessions were selected from a variety of basal readers frequently used in the schools: *Reading Unlimited*, Scott Foresman (1976); *Keys to Reading*, The Economy Company (1980); *Adventures for Readers*, Harcourt, Brace Jovanovich (1979); *Reading 720*, Ginn and Co. (1976); *Corrective Reading Decoding*, S.R.A. Inc. (1978); and *Serendipity*, Houghton Mifflin (1974).

Design

A multiple baseline design across groups (Hersen & Barlow, 1976) was used to assess the effectiveness of reciprocal teaching. All students experienced baseline, intervention, maintenance, and follow-up phases. The design is presented in figure 22–1.

Experimental Conditions

Baseline. During each day of baseline, the students were given a passage that they were asked to read silently and carefully so that they could answer comprehension questions about the passage. The students were also told to ask for assistance with words they could not read or understand. (There were very few requests for assistance.) After the reading, the passage was collected, and the students were given comprehension questions to answer in writing. A graph indicating the percentage of comprehension questions answered correctly each day was maintained for each student and shared with the students each day of baseline. The total numbers of baseline days ranged from 4 to 10, as illustrated in figure 22–1.

Intervention. During the intervention phase, the reciprocal teaching procedure was introduced and conducted as described in this chapter. After proceeding through the training passage for a period of 25 to 30 minutes, the passages were collected, and the assessment procedure began, as described in the description of baseline. The intervention was scheduled to occur for a maximum of 20 days. Groups 1, 2, and 3 had 20 days of training, while Group 4 had 16 days. During the intervention phase, the students were shown graphs indicating the percentage of comprehension questions answered correctly on a weekly basis.

Maintenance. The maintenance phase began immediately after the last day of intervention. Maintenance occurred for 5 consecutive school days and was conducted in the same manner as baseline.

Follow-up. Eight weeks after the maintenance phase, follow-up probes occurred for 3 consecutive school days and were conducted in a manner identical to that described for baseline. Students were shown their graphs after each of these sessions.

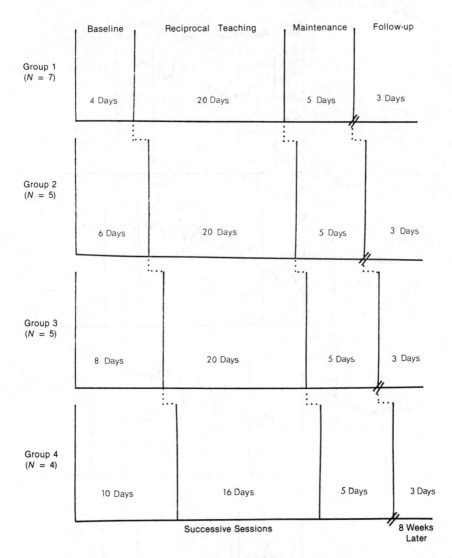

Figure 22-1. Design for Group Reading Study

Results

Of primary interest to us was the students' accuracy in responding to the comprehension questions on the daily assessments. Figure 22-2 depicts the mean performance of each group on these assessments for each day of the study. The data indicate that the students typically were achieving 40 percent accuracy on the comprehension questions during baseline. With the introduction of the reciprocal teaching procedure, their accuracy increased steadily, though gradually, until all

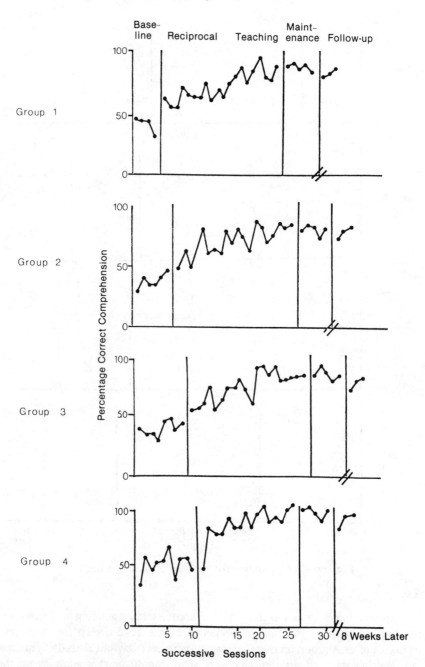

Figure 22–2. Group Mean Percentage Correct on the Daily Assessment Passages

groups were consistently scoring above 70 percent by the fifteenth day of intervention. The students continued to demonstrate gains during maintenance and a slight decrement in performance during follow-up.

These observations were confirmed by the following planned comparisons. Mean accuracy on comprehension questions was significantly greater during intervention than during baseline, $F(1,80) = 482.31, p < .0001$. There was a significant difference between mean performance during the first and second halves of intervention, $F(1,80) = 76.71, p < .0001$. Students continued to gain in accuracy during the second half of intervention. There was also a significant difference between maintenance and the second half of training, $F(1,80) = 5.72, p < .02$. Students' mean performance was better during maintenance than during the second half of the intervention phase. A significant difference was discerned between maintenance and follow-up. Mean performance was higher for those probes that occurred immediately following training than for those that occurred 8 weeks following intervention, $F(1,80) = 7.61, p < .01$. Mean performance during follow-up, however, was significantly greater than mean performance during baseline, $F(1,80) = 534.97, p < .0001$.

We wanted to determine whether the skills acquired during reciprocal teaching transferred to other academic tasks. To ascertain this, the students were asked to complete a variety of tasks prior to beginning the intervention and upon its completion. These tasks included summarizing expository passages, writing sets of questions for expository passages, identifying lines in a story that were incongruous with the title, and rating the idea units of narrative passages for importance. These pretest/posttest measures indicated that, following the intervention, the students experienced greater success in summarizing material, particularly in their ability to recognize main idea information and to extract and invent topic sentences. There were also significant gains in their ability to identify information about which teachers ask questions and to construct clear and complete questions. The students were also significantly more accurate detecting the incongruous lines, suggesting that they were monitoring their comprehension of text more closely. The only task on which the students did not make significant improvement was the rating of idea units in narrative stories. Because this task was the most removed from the skills trained during reciprocal teaching, these results did not altogether surprise us.

Discussion

The results of our investigations suggest that, by using a structured teaching procedure incorporated into a group reading lesson, students' reading behaviors can be modified dramatically. Consistent effects were typically obtained by the twelfth to fifteenth day of training. Furthermore, the students demonstrated improvement on passages independent of the training material. The effects were durable, suggesting that students had assimilated these strategies into their reading routines and continued to use them. Finally, there is evidence that the skills acquired transferred to other important academic tasks.

Other unanticipated benefits have also accrued. During our work with inner-city students and their teachers, the teachers initially expressed concern that the behavior problems presented by their students were likely to interfere with successful implementation of the procedure. This was not the case. In fact, the majority of teachers reported remarkable improvement in general behavior. Students who were formerly failing in paper-and-pencil tasks have responded very well to the opportunity to engage in this structured dialogue. Students particularly enjoy the opportunity to assume the role of teacher, and they report new insights into the difficulties of being a teacher. They mention that it is difficult to ask a question so that everyone understands the information being sought, to teach others the most important information in the paragraph, and to help a student who has missed the point.

We would like to encourage practitioners to include the reciprocal teaching procedure in their repertoires of instructional activities. To facilitate this, we offer several suggestions:

1. To determine that students' reading difficulties are correctly identified as comprehension problems and to ensure that the students are given reading material appropriate to their decoding abilities, the teacher is advised to use the same screening procedure adopted in this investigation. The procedure considers the students' correct and incorrect reading rates and level of comprehension and the readability of the curricular material. For further information regarding this procedure, see Blankenship and Lilly (1981).

2. Engaging in the reciprocal teaching procedure for about 30 minutes per day over 15 to 20 consecutive school days yields very positive results. We found that using well-organized text in the initial sessions facilitated acquisition of the comprehension skills. After the students appear to be comfortable with the procedures, less well organized reading materials were used. To promote transfer to everyday learning activities, we recommend employing the procedure using the basal series or content area texts currently in use in the school.

3. Modeling and corrective feedback are powerful means of teaching and refining comprehension skill. During the initial days of training, the adult teacher should model frequently and should select the more capable students to provide further modeling.

4. Frequent evaluation of progress on comprehension measures is essential to ascertain that the intervention is working successfully. (If the intervention is not effective for particular students, teachers can become more attentive to those students' participation in the training sessions, perhaps assigning them more opportunities to assume the role of teacher.) As important as evaluating the students' progress is sharing that information with the students. This feedback practice

communicates to the students that the activities they are learning pay off, and it maintains student interest in the instructional activity. Students were keenly interested in the graphs we maintained to display their accuracy on the comprehension measures. (Students who were involved in a cross-age tutoring study successfully maintained their own graphs.)

5. Transcripts of the instructional dialogue that were made during the interventions demonstrate that the reciprocal teaching procedure provides an excellent opportunity to identify the obstacles students encounter in their efforts to comprehend text. As the students discuss the content, their difficulties with vocabulary, unclear referents, certain textual constructions, and idiomatic expressions become clear and can be addressed. The teachers indicate that they would continue to record the training sessions and periodically share these recordings with their students to demonstrate progress.

Reference Notes

1. Wong, B., & Jones, W. *Increasing metacomprehension in L. D. normally-achieving students through self-questioning training.* Unpublished manuscript, Simon Fraser University, 1981.
2. Palincsar, A.S., & Brown, A.L. *Instructing reading comprehension monitoring activities through reciprocal teaching.* Unpublished manuscript, University of Illinois, 1982.

References

André, M.D.A., & Anderson, T.H. The development and evaluation of a self-questioning study technique. *Reading Research Quarterly,* 1978–79, *14,* 605–623.

Blankenship, C., & Lilly, M.S. *Mainstreaming students with learning and behavior problems: Techniques for the classroom teacher.* New York: Holt, Rinehart and Winston, 1981.

Brown, A.L., & Day, J.D. Macrorules for summarizing texts: The development of expertise. *Journal of Verbal Learning and Verbal Behavior,* in press.

Brown, A.L., & Palincsar, A.S. Inducing strategic learning from texts by means of informed, self-control training. *Topics in Learning and Learning Disabilities,* 1982, *2*(1), 1–17.

Collins, A., & Smith, E.E. Teaching the process of reading comprehension. In D.K. Detterman & R.J. Sternberg (Eds.), *How and how much can intelligence be increased?* Norwood, N.J.: Ablex, 1982.

Day, J.D. *Training summarization skills: A comparison of teaching methods.* Unpublished doctoral dissertation, University of Illinois, 1980.

Frase, L.T., & Schwartz, B.J. The effect of question production and answering on prose recall. *Journal of Educational Psychology,* 1975, *62,* 628–635.

Harris, P.L., Kruithof, A., Terwogt, M.M., & Visser, T. Children's detection and awareness of textual anomaly. *Journal of Experimental Child Psychology,* 1981, *31,* 212–230.

Hersen, M., & Barlow, D. *Single case experimental designs—Strategies for studying behavior change.* Elmsford, N.Y.: Pergamon Press, 1976.

Lovitt, T.C., & Hansen, C.L. Round one—Placing the child in the right reader. *Journal of Learning Disabilities,* 1976, *6,* 347–353.

Manzo, A.V. *Improving reading comprehension through reciprocal questioning.* Unpublished doctoral dissertation, University of Syracuse, 1969.

Markman, E.M. Realizing that you don't understand: A preliminary investigation. *Child Development,* 1977, *48,* 986–992.

Markman, E.M. Realizing that you don't understand: Elementary school children's awareness of inconsistencies. *Child Development,* 1979, *50*(3), 643–655.

Palincsar, A.S. *Improving the reading comprehension of junior high students through the reciprocal teaching of comprehension monitoring strategies.* Unpublished doctoral dissertation, University of Illinois, 1982.

23
Children Need More Complete Reading Strategies

Carl Bereiter

T here are different degrees of reading comprehension. We may understand the topic of an article but comprehend nothing of what is said about the topic; or we may comprehend a number of details, and even see how they are related to the topic, but fail to comprehend the main argument that these details are meant to support. At a still higher level, we may comprehend an article well enough to answer penetrating questions about its content but not well enough to have thought of such questions ourselves. At this level, we would score well on any normal test of reading comprehension, but we would, in fact, still be lacking something. We would be dependent on someone else—a teacher or questioner—to lead us through the process of interpreting and critically examining what we read.

In many kinds of casual reading, a superficial level of comprehension may suffice. Good readers, however, need to be able to recognize when noteworthy or incongruous information is being presented, and they must then have strategies available for digging out and interpreting the information in a text more completely. It appears that many students lack these higher-powered reading strategies and, therefore, are limited to superficial comprehension. Their cognitive equipment for reading is thus like a tractor that lacks a low gear; it is fine for pulling a drag rake over the surface of a field, but it is no good for deep plowing. The research that I shall summarize briefly in this chapter is concerned with describing a kind of incomplete reading strategy that seems to be common among students in the middle years of school and with considering the rather substantial educational reforms that may be needed to foster more complete reading strategies in these students.

An interesting kind of reading material for investigating comprehension strategies is that which contains incongruous or inconsistent information. One such passage used by Markman (1979)—a passage describing fish and their habitats—contains a sentence stating that there is absolutely no light at the bottom of the ocean. Immediately after this comes a sentence stating that fish living at the bottom of the ocean know their food by its color. Markman found that students as old as 12 tended to overlook such incongruities unless they were specially alerted.

One way to investigate reading comprehension strategies is to have students think aloud as they read such passages (Scardamalia & Bereiter, in press). The thoughts expressed by sophisticated readers indicate that they are doing a great deal of paraphrasing of statements and tying together of ideas encountered in a text. Here, for instance, is how one talented tenth-grader went about reading the aforementioned fish passage. The passage begins with the sentence, "Many different kinds of fish live in the ocean." Three sentences later comes the statement, "Fish live in different parts of the ocean." On reading this, the student remarks, "And [they] couldn't all live in the same part or else there wouldn't be many different kinds of fish in the ocean." The next sentence says, "Some fish live near the surface of the water, but some fish live at the bottom of the ocean," which causes the student to wonder why any fish would live at the surface. The next sentence is the one asserting that there is no light at the bottom of the ocean. The student adds, "which means that these fish that live at the bottom of the ocean live in the dark." This may not be a very profound deduction, but it performs the significant function of tying together the information from two sentences. The student then goes on to infer, "They [the fish] probably can't see much of anything—either that or they have very good vision." When she arrives at the next sentence, which says that fish at the bottom of the ocean know their food by its color, she is in a good position to notice the incongruity and to interpret it in the light of propositions she has already advanced. "And how could they see the color of the food if it's dark," she says, "unless they had really good vision?"

There is nothing remarkable in this student's performance, except in contrast to what we observed in the majority of students. The majority of tenth graders, and virtually all of the younger students we have examined, interpreted each statement as it came along, relating it to the topic (in this case, fish and their habitats) but not to overall arguments or propositions. They would question the plausibility of individual statements (for instance, a statement that some fish have heads that look like alligators), but they would not question one statement in light of another, as is required if one is to notice the incongruity of the statement that fish at the bottom of the ocean know their food by its color.

The following illustration is from a tenth-grade student who seems to be a borderline case. She actively interprets and questions statements, much like the first student, but she does not seem to have any system for putting her interpretations together to achieve a coherent overall understanding of the text. When she reads the statement about no light at the bottom of the sea, she remarks, "So the problem's cold"—a plausible inference, apparently, that fish would suffer from cold in the depths of the sea. On reading the next sentence, about fish knowing their food by its color, she says, "What's color got to do with it? Color—color doesn't mean anything. . . . Color of the food doesn't matter to them. I don't think they can see very good. We did that last year. . . ." Here we see the student struggling to relate the statement to the topic and to what she already knows about fish, but not trying to interpret it in relation to the preceding statement.

This student, we suggest, exhibits an incomplete reading comprehension strategy. The reasoning she performs is as sound as that of the first student, but she applies it within a much more limited framework—a framework that accommodates individual details and general notions of what the text is about but does not accommodate the network of interrelationships that constitute the meaning of the text.

The same incomplete comprehension strategy is revealed when students are given the sentences of a paragraph on separate slips of paper and are asked to arrange them into a good paragraph. Most students in the middle years of school rely exclusively on grouping sentences according to topic and on superficial clues, such as pronouns and connectives (Scardamalia & Bereiter, in press). Among older students, however, we find some who use a very different approach. They work at arranging the sentences so as to produce an overall message that makes sense. The strategy by which they do this involves working at two different levels: at one level, attending to the content of individual sentences; at another level, constructing and revising summary statements of the overall message of the text. This more complete strategy corresponds closely to a well-known psychological model of the comprehension process (Kintsch & van Dijk, 1978). This model involves operating on propositions at different levels—at a detailed level that is concerned with individual text propositions and at a higher level that is concerned with extracting the gist of the text.

Institutional Support for Incomplete Reading Strategies

The investigation of reading strategies referred to in the preceding section is an offshoot of a larger investigation into strategies of written composition (see, for instance, Bereiter & Scardamalia, 1982). In writing, also, we observe an incomplete strategy that appears to be in common use by students. The heart of this strategy consists of turning any writing assignment or question into a topic and then telling what one knows about the topic. Accordingly, we have named it the knowledge-telling strategy (Bereiter & Scardamalia, 1983). The incomplete reading strategy and the incomplete composing strategy appear to share the same limited framework, which confines them to dealing with details as they relate to topics but provides little support for concerns about overall meaning and intent.

Judged on its broad cultural merits, the knowledge-telling strategy is a disaster. It tends to subvert the instructional purposes of essay assignments as well as the most elementary purposes of literary endeavor. It is a strategy well suited to dealing with school demands, however. It is particularly useful for coping with questions one does not fully understand or to which one does not know the answer.

It is not so obvious what survival value an incomplete reading strategy has. If such strategies are as pervasive as we believe, however, they must surely be good for something. Also, it is as true with cognitive strategies as with any other kind of behavior, that if one wishes to change it, one must consider what is supporting it.

The kind of incomplete reading strategy we have been discussing starts to make sense when we consider how it fits in with typical school practices. The prevailing mode of instruction in American schools is question asking (Bellack, Kliebard, Hyman, & Smith, 1966). From the students' standpoint, therefore, the immediate objective of school reading is likely to be to prepare themselves for answering questions that the teacher will ask. Teachers' questions, of course, may cover a wide range, from simple requests for recall to Socratic questions designed to induce critical reflection. Regardless of the level of questioning, however, a topic-plus-detail framework is an economical and effective one for storing text information. Having details filed away under topics is a good organization for simple recall, but it is also a good organization for answering the higher-level questions teachers may ask. Since these higher-level questions are likely to be hard for students to predict, a safe policy is not to interpret information too thoroughly in advance but, rather, to store it in fairly raw form, synthesizing and interpreting it only after one has found out what the question is.

The upshot of such an approach to studying is a strategy that carries comprehension to the point of a logically organized collection of separately understood ideas. Such a form of knowledge, though useful for examinations, has little value in the outside world. The knowledge needs to be further developed into fully formed ideas that are coherently related to other knowledge. That, of course, is the function the teacher tries to perform through questioning and discussion.

Thus, incomplete reading serves the student's purposes in question answering and at the same time serves the teacher's purposes in exerting a guiding influence over the student's knowledge development. With a wise and resourceful teacher, valuable educational growth may occur—but at the risk of making students permanently dependent on someone else to complete the process of transmuting text content into usable knowledge.

Incomplete reading is supported not only by prevailing instructional and testing practices but, seemingly, even by the textbooks students use. Several investigators have noted (see Armbruster, chapter 4 of this volume) that a common structure for textbook paragraphs is a topic sentence that does little more than name a topic, followed by a collection of details related to the topic. Such texts frustrate any attempt to abstract a coherent message and encourage persistence of the topic-plus-detail framework for comprehending expository texts of all kinds.

We should not be hasty, however, in placing blame for the existence of incomplete reading strategies on teachers, on textbooks, or on students. The institution of schooling has evolved over many years, and it is only reasonable to suppose that a mutual adaptation has occurred among the tendencies of all the parties involved. Thus, question asking may have evolved as a teaching practice in response to students' limited comprehension of text material. Textbook structures may have evolved not only in response to what students find easy to understand but also in response to teachers' interest in asking many questions. Whatever the evolutionary history may have been, it is clear that we now have a situation that tends to maintain itself. Textbook structures, teaching practices, and student comprehension strategies reinforce one another, and any effort to change one of these factors is likely to run into trouble from the other two.

Educational Remedies

Simultaneously changing teaching procedures, textbook structures, and student reading strategies may be a very difficult task to manage, but on the basis of present knowledge we can at least formulate a reasonable concept of coordinated change. It would consist of (1) shifting the prevailing teaching practice from emphasis on question answering to emphasis on summarization, (2) producing textbooks that present a coherent argument structure rather than a topically organized collection of details, and (3) teaching students to employ a more complete strategy for constructing meaning from what they read.

Summarization has a great advantage over question answering in that it forces students to do their own abstracting, relating, and discovering of central ideas, rather than being walked through the process under the guidance of teacher questions. Summarizing has unfortunately been associated with regurgitation, and teachers have for many years been led to believe that a higher form of instruction was asking students questions that "make them think." Recent verbal learning research, however, has discovered that summarization is a key to the higher processes of comprehension—formation of a gist or macrostructure—and hence is far more than a simple process of upchucking information (Kintsch & van Dijk, 1978).

There is now substantial basic theory about summarization, and there are some practical approaches to teaching summarization (see Palincsar and Brown, chapter 22 this volume). No one, of course, is recommending summarization as a panacea. It does seem, however, that it offers a desirable alternative to excessive reliance on question asking. The major obstacles to using it as a method of subject matter teaching are the other two factors in our system description—the nature of textbooks and the reading abilities of students.

For students to summarize a text, the text must have a story line or argument that can be abstracted from the supporting details. Such structures are not entirely absent from school texts, but if substantial instructional use were made of summarization, more texts would be needed that have clear propositional structures and that avoid the "basket of facts" approach.

We now turn to the problem of teaching students the reading strategies they would need to go with the summarization of summarizable texts. It is noteworthy that most of the work done on teaching comprehension strategies has dealt with things students do after they read—review, outlining, critical analysis, summarizing, question answering, and the like. The actual reading process is so rapid and automatic that it is difficult for conscious strategies to have an effect on it. Some very promising results have been obtained, however, in recent research by Marlene Bird (1980), who used thinking aloud while reading as a vehicle both for demonstrating reading strategies and for having students practice them.

Bird taught students to summarize complex passages as they read, to backtrack to recover needed information, and to formulate comprehension difficulties as problems and try to solve them. Bird worked with above-average readers in grades seven and eight. During nine class periods of instruction, she demonstrated specific strategies by thinking aloud, had students identify instances of the various strategies, and gave them supervised practice in using the strategies as they thought aloud while reading. The result was that these students showed a significant increase in use of the intended strategies, and they also gained significantly in reading comprehension compared to control groups. Indeed, they were estimated to have gained a 2-year advantage over other groups in reading comprehension scores. Among the groups they surpassed was one group that received intensive question-and-answer practice with questions intended to call upon the same strategies as were taught more directly to the experimental group. Another group that did not fare well received the demonstrations and the thinking-aloud practice but did not get any direct instruction in the strategies. It appears that effective reading comprehension strategies are not readily picked up by osmosis—that is, by mere observation and practice. Direct teaching appears to be needed. Bird's research is valuable in showing a way that direct teaching can be carried out on something so elusive as reading strategies.

Favorable as they are, Bird's results should not be taken to indicate that a sophisticated reading strategy can be taught in nine easy lessons. Some elements of an expert strategy can be taught fairly readily, but others take a long buildup; and it is these more difficult elements that seem to lie closer to the heart of expert competence.

Conclusion

In summary, the research discussed suggests that many students may be developing incomplete reading strategies. This is not merely a phase they go through as students but is, instead, a stable adaptation to the conditions of school instruction, which may leave them permanently limited in their ability to develop knowledge through reading. I have suggested a three-pronged remedial effort, consisting of (1) shifting from question answering to summarization as the primary instructional activity related to learning from texts, (2) shifting to text materials that have clear propositional structures, and (3) direct teaching of more complete reading strategies. Some people might believe that strategy instruction alone should suffice, or that it should be sufficient to alter instructional styles so as to turn more initiative over to students. Some might even argue that just having students do more reading of higher-quality texts would suffice to develop able readers. The problem, as I have tried to suggest, is not that there is anything wrong with these separate approaches. The problem, rather, is that we are dealing with a self-maintaining system involving teachers, texts, and students. To focus efforts on only one part of the system could well mean that any changes produced would eventually be nullified. Recent research, however, offers encouraging prospects for improvement in the overall system within which students acquire the advanced skills of literacy.

References

Bellack, A., Kliebard, H.M., Hyman, R.T., & Smith, F.L., Jr. *The language of the classroom.* New York: Teachers College Press, 1966.

Bereiter, C., & Scardamalia, M. From conversation to composition: The role of instruction in a developmental process. In R. Glaser (Ed.), *Advances in instructional psychology* (Vol. 2). Hillsdale, N.J. : Erlbaum, 1982.

Bereiter, C., & Scardamalia, M. Does learning to write have to be so difficult? In A. Freedman, I. Pringle, & J. Yalden (Eds.), *Learning to write: First language, second language.* London: Longman's 1983.

Bird, M. *Reading comprehension strategies: A direct teaching approach.* Unpublished doctoral dissertation, Ontario Institute for Studies in Education, 1980.

Kintsch, W., & van Dijk, T.A. Toward a model of text comprehension and production. *Psychological Review*, 1978, *85*(5), 363–394.

Markman, E.M. Realizing that you don't understand: Elementary school children's awareness of inconsistencies. *Child Development*, 1979, *50*, 643–655.

Scardamalia, M., & Bereiter, C. Development of strategies in text processing. In H. Mandl, N. Stein, & T. Trabasso (Eds.), *Learning and comprehension of texts.* Hillsdale, N.J.: Erlbaum, in press.

24

Reading Comprehension and School Learning

Paul T. Wilson and
Richard C. Anderson

E ducators today are increasingly concerned with understanding the processes involved in how people read because of the practical consequences
such knowledge can have for classroom instruction. While the debate
continues about how children first learn to read, considerable progress has been
made in understanding the process of reading comprehension. In this chapter, we
will discuss two important facts about comprehension and venture a few suggestions
about how present knowledge should influence instruction in American schools.

A simple model for the school reading situation (adapted from Jenkins, 1979)
would include the reader, the text, the learning activity, and the ultimate required
performance. Each of these components will have an effect on the reader's comprehension. (See Brown, Bransford, Ferrara, and Campione, 1983, for an extensive discussion of these factors. In this chapter, we will confine ourselves to brief comments.)

In chapter 23, Carl Bereiter suggests an interesting relationship between the
learning activity and the required performance. In the all-too-typical learning activity, students attempt to learn topics and lists of details without much understanding. This incomplete learning strategy may leave students equipped to answer
verbatim recall questions in class, but learning topics and details does little to promote constructive, critical thinking. Instead, it leaves students passive and dependent on someone else's ideas about what is important in the material they are studying. Activities described in this volume by Palincsar and Brown, Beck, Au,
Hansen, and James Cunningham would certainly be preferable to this incomplete
strategy if the goal of instruction is to develop students' thinking abilities.

In this volume, both Rubin and Armbruster have discussed problems with the
texts that children are asked to read in school. Armbruster notes in chapter 4 that
paragraphs in many content area textbooks consist of little more than topic
sentences followed by lists of facts. This kind of text organization can only reinforce the incomplete learning strategies Bereiter describes. Particularly insidious,
though, have been the effects of the so-called readability formulas. Their influence
on both the writing and the editing of basal readers and content area textbooks has
been pervasive, and their use has been mandated in the laws for textbook adoption
procedures in many states. The mistaken belief underlying the use of the formulas

is that all we have to do is give students easy materials—short sentences written with short words—and they will learn to read and comprehend better. In chapter 19, James Cunningham concludes from the research evidence that children should be given texts and tasks that they can handle, and there is no doubt that such a view makes sense. There are factors other than readability, however—at least as it is conventionally defined—that have much greater significance in determining the kind of material that children can comprehend. It is these factors that must be addressed much more directly in our educational process.

Our message in this chapter, in fact, is that the reader has been sadly neglected by our present methods of instruction. The tragedy of this is that the reader's interests and prior knowledge have a truly profound impact on how well the reader comprehends what is read and thus on how much he or she will learn.

One way to understand the magnitudes of the effects of interest and prior knowledge is to compare them to the size of other effects that are already known. In a series of studies at the Center for the Study of Reading, measures of how interesting reading materials were accounted for thirty times as much variance in recall as measures of readability and the same amount of variance as an independent measure of verbal ability (Anderson, Mason, & Shirey, in press; Anderson, Shirey, Wilson, & Fielding, in press). In a study by Freebody and Anderson (1983), topic familiarity (that is, prior knowledge) accounted for more than three times as much variance, across several measures of recall, as readability and, again, approximately the same proportion of variance as verbal ability. These are powerful influences, and educators ignore them at their peril.

Interest

Interest can be defined as the capacity of material to evoke an emotional response in children. Anderson, Shirey, Wilson, and Fielding (in press) tested four factors that could contribute to sentence interest. It was expected that children would find materials of interest when they could identify with the main character—a child like them—or when something novel (as opposed to mundane) happened. Life theme and activity level were also expected to influence interest. A life theme was something like a typical experience in the children's lives—such as eating lunch in the school cafeteria. Activity level referred to the intensity of action or feeling in the sentences. Sentences written to ensure independence of the four factors were rated for interest by third-graders. Novelty and life theme accounted for 47 percent and 21 percent of the variance, respectively, in the mean rated interest of the sentences. Contrary to expectations, the children showed a small but significant preference for sentences with adult rather than child characters.

Research by Brewer and Bruce and their respective colleagues is germane because it deals with what makes stories interesting. Brewer and Lichtenstein (1982) have tested a structural affect theory of stories. They claim that stories are a subclass of narratives whose primary purpose is to entertain and, further, that a story is entertaining only if it arouses affect. Their experiments show that people will not call a narrative a story unless it produces an emotional response. Jose and Brewer (in press) evaluated factors that could contribute to the interest of suspense stories. The main factor that made characters interesting was whether they were good or bad, not whether they were adult or male or female. Second graders in particular liked stories with nice characters and happy endings. Sixth graders enjoyed stories in which good characters experienced good outcomes and bad characters got their just deserts. The older children also enjoyed suspense that was due not merely to uncertainty but to uncertainty that had a significant consequence for a character about whom they were concerned. Uncertainty about whether a hiker can get a damp match to light, for instance, will more likely produce suspense for a reader if the hiker is lost in a blizzard.

Bruce (1984) and Steinberg and Bruce (1980) compared stories from basal readers with stories from children's trade books. The basal stories were characterized by low conflict; little inside view of the thoughts, feelings, and plans of the characters; and a detached, impersonal narrator. This was in direct contrast to the features of the trade books, many of which were known to be popular among children because of their appearance on the "Children's Choices" lists published each fall in *The Reading Teacher*. Judged in terms of Brewer's findings, Bruce's observations indicate that the basal reader stories are not very good. Nor do these stories fare very well according to structural criteria for what makes a story, as developed by Rumelhart (1975), Mandler and Johnson (1977), and Stein and Glenn (1979), all of whom have outlined schemata, or models, for the structural organization of stories. Stein and Glenn (1979), for example, argue that stories are structured around the attempts of a character to resolve some kind of conflict or to solve a problem. In chapter 14, Strickland points out the importance of exposing children to good stories from the earliest stages of schooling. Such experiences not only will arouse their interest in stories, they will also help the children learn about the structural and literary characteristics of stories—knowledge that will serve them well as they encounter more difficult stories later in school.

We suggest that children's comprehension and recall of stories will improve if they receive direct instruction about the organization and structure of stories and engage in literary analysis of the stories in their textbooks. In addition, the research findings about interest and suspense must be integrated into the texts that children read in school. Here we wish to implicate not just the writers, editors, and publishers of school materials, but especially the consumers—the administrators, teachers, and adoption committees who make the decisions about how public money is to be spent on textbooks. If the buyers speak with loud, clear voices, the sellers are sure to listen.

The reason that interest is important is that it has a strong effect on learning. Researchers at the Center for the Study of Reading have included interest as a factor in several experiments involving more than 400 third- and fourth-grade students (Anderson, Mason, & Shirey, in press; Anderson, Shirey, Wilson, & Fielding, in press). These studies all used lists of sentences that had been rated for interest by third graders and measured learning of sentence predicates with a cued-recall task shortly after the initial presentation of the sentences. Presentation modes varied, including group and individual listening, silent reading, oral reading with an emphasis on correct decoding, and oral reading with an immediately subsequent prediction task in which the children had to say what would happen next. In all cases, there were strong effects of interest on recall. Boys (who seem to have more problems with reading than girls) were more subject to the influence of interest: their recall was higher for boy-oriented sentences. Girls showed less peaking in their recall of girl-oriented sentences and recalled more of the low-interest material.

Two studies evaluated the possibility that interest effects were due to increased attention to the materials read (Anderson, Shirey, Wilson, & Fielding, in press). Sentences that varied widely in rated interest and measured difficulty were presented, one by one, to individual children seated at a computer terminal. The children's attention was measured by recording their reading time for each sentence and, for some sentences, their response time to a secondary task. These measures may be supposed to reflect duration and intensity of attention (Anderson, 1982). For the secondary task, the children were required to push a button as soon as they heard a beep sound through the headphones they wore while reading. The assumption was that if the children were concentrating on the sentence, it would take longer for them to press the button after hearing the beep.

In both studies, more interesting sentences took longer to read. The response times to the secondary task were also longer for those sentences. These findings may be taken as evidence that the children were paying more attention to the more interesting sentences. Also, the children learned more of the more interesting sentences. There was little or no effect on learning, however, from the extra time spent reading, or from the children's more intense concentration. When the effects of reading time and response time were factored out, there was no change in the effect of interest on learning. Evidently, the interesting sentences that the children learned were not the same ones that they stopped to savor. As Anderson (1982) has expressed it: "The pause to savor an interesting sentence is not the pause that supports the process that gives birth to learning" (p. 301). Interest does not have its effect on learning because of its influence on the duration or intensity of attention. It must be affecting or interacting with different aspects of the comprehension process that remain to be explored.

One possible explanation is that interest effects are due to prior knowledge. Although prior knowledge does not seem to be the main cause of the effect of interest on learning, the picture is not entirely clear. Among the 136 sentences used in the studies just reviewed, a very wide range of topics was covered. One would not expect prior knowledge effects to hold so strongly with many individual sentences as they might have in other studies of the influence of interest on learning from connected text (Asher, 1980; Estes & Vaughan, 1973). Furthermore, all of the interest studies discussed here used a measure of semantic integration as a covariate—that is, an independent rating of the degree of association between the subject noun phrase and the rest of the sentence that may be assumed to capture something of the availability of the information in the sentence. Although semantic integration had a significant relationship to learning, the effect of interest did not diminish at all when semantic integration was factored out, and there was no interaction between interest and semantic integration. Most important, though, as noted earlier, novelty was the main factor in determining the rated interest of the sentences. Where the picture gets a little cloudy is in the finding that life theme also contributed to rated interest, which suggests some influence of familiarity.

Further exploration of possible interactions between novelty and prior knowledge may produce additional educationally relevant findings. It may be that novelty and life theme combine to cause humor, resulting in particularly interesting and memorable sentences, such as "At lunch, the kids slurped up the green slime in the cafeteria" or "The third graders were delighted to have E.T. as their substitute teacher." Another instructional issue to be addressed in the future is how to arouse intellectual interest, as opposed to affective interest, in children. One general conclusion is warranted right now. The effects of interest on learning are pervasive, and children should be provided with the most interesting materials possible if we want to ensure that schools will have a more positive influence on children's intellectual development.

Prior Knowledge

It is common knowledge that, for most children, learning to read is not a natural process. Children need explicit instruction if they are to gain the fluent, accurate command of letter–sound correspondences that is the necessary underpinning for fast, efficient access to word meanings during reading. It would be a grave error, however, to assume that reading instruction should stop at the point where children have mastered letter–sound relations or, indeed, that beginning reading instruction should be directed only toward decoding.

Some children do learn to think on their own when they read, but, as with decoding, thinking while reading does not come naturally for all children, especially for those who are hard to teach. Direct instruction in how to comprehend can help even bright children to be better readers.

Here we will define comprehension as interpreting a message in terms of frameworks—schemata—provided by the knowledge that a reader already has. In other words, what the reader already knows about the topic of a text and the organization and structure of different text genres provides the foundation for what the reader will understand and remember from reading the text. One necessary aspect of comprehension is making inferences—a process for which most present school instruction is inadequate. No text is ever completely explicit. Writing is an act of communication in which the author makes assumptions about what readers already know and anticipates that the readers will supply information that is obvious. Thus, for example, if you read that James Bond rushed to his car and drove to the casino, you do not need to be told that he opened the car door, put the key in the ignition, and so on. You can derive those details effortlessly from your knowledge of cars. In fact, if such details of Bond's starting the car were provided, you would be justified in taking it as a foreshadowing that perhaps there was a bomb in the car.

If readers do not interpret a text in terms of their prior knowledge, they are not playing their role in the act of communication; they are not doing it right. Likewise, authors who make incorrect assumptions about the prior knowledge of their readers are not doing it right either. Textbooks that present information as topics plus lists of facts assume that their readers already possess a considerable amount of relational knowledge about the content, when the purpose of education should be to help the students acquire that knowledge. Many students do not have the appropriate relational knowledge, yet they are given instruction in which the primary thrust is to learn the material as it is in the textbook. For these students, it may be difficult—even impossible—to acquire the relational knowledge that would help further their learning.

When there is a proper match between the author's assumptions and the readers' prior knowledge, readers can make appropriate inferences and elaborations. This is illustrated in a study by Steffensen, Joag-dev, and Anderson (1979) in which American community college students and college students from India read passages about American and Indian weddings. In the passage about the American wedding, the groom turns to the best man, who is about to hand him the ring. Then the passage moves on to other events in the wedding. In recalling the passage, American subjects include the fact that the groom puts the ring on the bride's finger.

In contrast, when there is a mismatch between the author's assumptions and the readers' prior knowledge, the result can often be distortion and incomplete comprehension. In Indian culture, the bride is considered an economic liability to her family. Thus, her family has to give a dowry to the groom's family to persuade them to take over the liability. Strenuous negotiations determine the exact nature and number of the gifts that constitute the dowry. The passage about the Indian wedding describes some of this process and mentions some of the gifts. The American students, though, recalled the gifts being exchanged every which way, as if it were Christmas.

As a result of work by Paris and his associates, it is now known that, even when they possess the requisite prior knowledge, young and less able readers do not spontaneously apply what they know when they read. Paris and Lindauer (1976), for example, gave children such sentences as "The workman dug a hole in the ground." Adults would assume, by default, that the workman had used a shovel, because only an unpredictable method would have to be mentioned. Fifth graders recalled the sentence when they were given the word *shovel* as a cue. First graders and poor readers did not; however, when they were given the learning activity of acting out the sentence, they did recall it when the cue was presented later.

A crucial concept in defining good comprehension is that the reader gets a coherent representation of the information in the text. We can explain what we mean by coherent representation with examples from the Anderson, Mason, and Shirey (in press) study. Third graders were often able to make appropriate predictions about what might happen next when presented with such sentences as "The stupid child ran into the street after the ball." Typically, they might predict that he almost got hit by a car or that his mother got mad at him. These predictions were obviously in keeping with the children's own experiences of similar events. Their performance was different, however, with such sentences as "The tall man picked up the box of crackers." The children might predict that he then put them on the table or that he gave them to his wife. It was the rare child, indeed, who said that the man then set the box on the top shelf. Such a child, though, has a more coherent representation of the information in the sentence. Such a child's prediction uses all the information available and thus produces a superior elaboration of the sentence. If the text says that the man is tall, then the reader has a warrant to infer that the property of height is somehow important; that property, therefore, should be integrated coherently into the mental representation of the information in the sentence. Most young children do not do this with any consistency.

Thinking while reading is not a naturally developing process. Young and less able readers do not spontaneously reason about their reading. They do not actively and constructively apply what they know to connect the information from their reading into a coherent model of what the author is trying to tell them. To help children become better readers, we must start from the earliest stages of instruction to encourage their active, constructive processing of text. This is not as simple as turning on a switch or writing "THINK" on the blackboard. The learning activities described in this volume by Palincsar and Brown, Hansen, and Au are examples of what can be done, and they can be recommended. Others are needed, however. There are many complexities in learning to comprehend well. Young readers must learn to attend to subtle linguistic cues, to discern the limits of the interpretive license that a particular text affords, and to make only those inferences that are truly warranted by a text, not tangential. The child's ability to comprehend must be cultivated over a period of time and requires as its foundation good instruction rooted in directed dialogue with other intelligent people about the meanings of the texts to be studied.

Unfortunately, recent research has shown that there is little effective comprehension instruction in American schools today. There are effective instructional interventions, such as those described in this volume, that embody systematic approaches to teaching and learning. In addition, reading educators such as Betts (1946) and Stauffer (1969) have long recommended a lesson structure that provides not only for comprehension-oriented activities during reading but for pre- and post-reading discussions to integrate children's prior knowledge and to help them evaluate what they have learned. In classrooms, however, such approaches are very seldom seen. As Mason (1983) has put it, "the tail is wagging the dog." Her observations show, as have those of Durkin (1978–79), that most instructional time is actually devoted to evaluation of student learning, rather than to assisting the students with learning. There is little meaningful pre- or post-reading instruction. Durkin's (1978–79) observations demonstrated that out of more than 12,000 minutes of classroom time in reading and social studies, only 45 minutes were spent on comprehension instruction beyond the level of individual words.

In chapter 1 of this volume, Durkin describes her investigation of one cause for the sad state of comprehension instruction. She concludes that the teaching manuals that accompany published materials are very superficial when it comes to providing comprehension instruction. Good suggestions are merely mentioned, often as enrichment after the main part of the lesson has been concluded. The manuals do go into considerable detail on verbatim recall questions, however—the kinds of questions that students can answer by memorizing topics and lists of facts. There is a good reason for this: It is difficult for the writers of teaching manuals to predict what might be said in an intelligent discussion about a text, but it is relatively easy to plan and write questions that ask for verbatim recall. At two conferences conducted by the Center for the Study of Reading, publishers of educational materials have claimed that teachers want manuals that provide the answers as well as the questions. Teachers, say the publishers, do not like to see a note after a question that says, "Responses will vary."

One long-term goal for American education, therefore, is to give teachers the kind of training that will help them be better questioners and better discussion leaders. As teachers acquire these skills, they may well find that it is much more interesting and rewarding to have intelligent discussions with students than it is to have students mechanically parroting topics and lists of facts. In the meantime, we recommend that model lessons such as those developed by Beck and her colleagues be implemented in published school materials and that principals and administrators promote the adoption of more comprehension-oriented activities in the classrooms they supervise.

Conclusion

What we have said about the effects on comprehension of the interests and prior knowledge of the reader has clear implications not only for reading lessons but also for instruction in content area subjects. In concluding, however, we wish to return to the reading instruction that schools provide for young and poor readers. We want to stress that this instruction must be characterized by a proper balance between activities that promote skillful decoding and those that promote skillful comprehension. The tension between these goals continues in American education today. Scholars of reading and reading politicians alike perpetuate what Chall (1967) termed "the great debate." They do so largely in ignorance, we think, of the unhappy influence this tension has on young and poor readers.

It is easy to show that when skilled adult readers are induced to attend to the surface features of language, they exhibit dramatically impaired comprehension of what they have read. Anderson and Hidde (1971) asked two groups of college students to help rate some sentences for use in future experiments. Participants were given 8 seconds to study each sentence. One group was told to rate the pronounceability of each sentence. The other group was told to rate each sentence's capacity to evoke an image. After rating the sentences, subjects were given a cued recall test in which the cue was the subject noun phrase. The pronounceability group had 25 percent recall, whereas the imaging group had 65 percent recall. Typically, however, the instruction given to young and poor readers emphasizes pronouncing and decoding the words—that is, the surface features of the language rather than its meaning. It comes as no surprise, then, that the comprehension skills of these children are poor and that they learn to dislike reading.

In chapter 8, Cazden presents evidence to show that there is actually a different curriculum in school today for those who have been identified as less-able readers. The instruction they receive repeatedly calls their attention to the surface features of the language and ignores the crucial purpose of reading—communication and understanding. Canney and Winograd (Note 1) have found that many less-able readers have no idea that they should be trying to understand the message the author has put in the text; they think they are supposed to be saying the words correctly. We have to wonder about an educational system that not only ignores the interests and prior knowledge of its students but provides them with experiences that have the potential, at least, to discourage if not seriously impair their comprehension abilities. This, surely, is not the foundation for a more literate America—and that is why it must be changed.

Reference Note

1. Canney, G., & Winograd, P. *Schemata for reading and reading comprehension performance* (Tech. Rep. No. 120). Urbana: University of Illinois, Center for the Study of Reading, April 1979.

References

Anderson, R.C. Allocation of attention during reading. In A. Flammer & W. Kintsch (Eds.), *Discourse processing.* Amsterdam: North Holland, 1982.

Anderson, R.C., & Hidde, J.L. Imagery and sentence learning. *Journal of Educational Psychology,* 1971, *62,* 526–530.

Anderson, R.C., Mason, J., & Shirey, L.L. The reading group: An experimental investigation of a labyrinth. *Reading Research Quarterly*, in press.

Anderson, R.C. Shirey, L.L., Wilson, P.T., & Fielding, L.G. Interestingness of children's readng material. In A.E. Snow & M.J. Farr (Eds.), *Aptitude, learning, and instruction: Conative and affective process analyses*. Hillsdale, N.J.: Erlbaum, in press.

Asher, S. Topic interest and children's reading comprehension. In R.J. Spiro, B.C. Bruce, & W.F. Brewer (Eds.), *Theoretical issues in reading comprehension*. Hillsdale, N.J.: Erlbaum, 1980.

Betts, E.A. *Foundations of reading instruction*. New York: American Book, 1946.

Brewer, W.F., & Lichtenstein, E.H. Stories are to entertain: A structural-affect theory of stories. *Journal of Pragmatics*, 1982, *6*, 473–486.

Brown, A.L., Bransford, J.D., Ferrara, R.A., & Campione, J.L. Learning, remembering, and understanding. In J.H. Flavell & E.M. Markman (Eds.), *Handbook of child psychology* (Vol. III). New York: Wiley, 1983.

Bruce, B. A new point of view on children's stories. In R.C. Anderson, J. Osborn, & R.J. Tierney (Eds.), *Learning to read in American schools*. Hillsdale, N.J.: Erlbaum, 1984.

Chall, J.S. *Learning to read: The great debate*. New York: McGraw-Hill, 1967.

Durkin, D. What classroom observations reveal about reading comprehension instruction. *Reading Research Quarterly*, 1978–79, *14*, 481–533.

Estes, T.H., & Vaughn, Jr., J.L. Reading interest and comprehension: Implications. *Reading Teacher*, 1973, *27*, 149–153.

Freebody, P., & Anderson, R.C. Effects of vocabulary difficulty, text cohesion, and schema availability on reading comprehension. *Reading Research Quarterly*, 1983, *18*(3), 277–294.

Jenkins, J.J. Four points to remember: A tetrahedral model and memory experiments. In L.S. Cermak & F.I.M. Craik (Eds.), *Levels of processing in human memory*. Hillsdale, N.J.: Erlbaum, 1979.

Jose, P., & Brewer, W.F. The development of story liking: Character identification, suspense, and outcome resolution. *Developmental Psychology*, in press.

Mandler, J.M., & Johnson, N.S. Remembrance of things parsed: Story structure and recall. *Cognitive Psychology*, 1977, *9*, 111–151.

Mason, J. An examination of reading instruction in third and fourth grades. *Reading Teacher*, 1983, *36*, 906–913.

Paris, S.C., & Lindauer, B.K. The role of inference in children's comprehension and memory. *Cognitive Psychology*, 1976, *8*, 217–227.

Rumelhart, D.E. Notes on a schema for stories. In D.G. Bobrow & A.M. Collins (Eds.), *Representation and understanding: Studies in cognitive science*. New York: Academic Press, 1975.

Stauffer, R.G. *Teaching reading as a thinking process*. New York: Harper & Row, 1969.

Steffensen, M.S., Joag-dev, C., & Anderson, R.C. A cross-cultural perspective on reading comprehension. *Reading Research Quarterly*, 1979, *15*, 10–29.

Stein, N.L., & Glenn, C.G. An analysis of story comprehension in elementary school children. In R.O. Freedle (Ed.), *Advances in discourse processes, Vol. 2: New directions in discourse processing*. Norwood, N.J.: Ablex, 1979.

Steinberg, C., & Bruce, B. Higher-level features in children's stories: Rhetorical structure and conflict. In M.L. Kamil & A.J. Moe (Eds.), *Perspectives on reading research and instruction* (Twenty-ninth Yearbook of the National Reading Conference). Washington, D.C.: National Reading Conference, 1980.

Subject Index

Author Index

About the Contributors

Bonnie Armbruster is assistant professor at the Center for the Study of Reading, University of Illinois. Her areas of specialization are the analysis of content area textbooks, teaching methods, study skills, and instructional development.

Kathryn Hu-Pei Au is a research psychologist and head of the curriculum department at the Kamehameha Early Education Program (KEEP) in Honolulu. She is particularly interested in the reading problems faced by culturally different students, especially in comprehension, and she concentrates on applied research aimed at discovering ways that teachers can work more effectively with these students.

Her coauthors, Roland G. Tharp, Doris C. Crowell, Cathie Jordan, Gisela E. Speidel, and Roderick Calkins, are all members of the multidisciplinary research team at KEEP. Their backgrounds are in educational, clinical, and developmental psychology; anthropology; and psycholinguistics. As a group they have carried out studies of the impact of cultural and language differences on minority children's school achievement, and studies of reading comprehension and writing instruction.

Isabel L. Beck is associate professor of education at the University of Pittsburgh and codirector of the Reading and Comprehension Unit of the Learning Research and Development Center there. In recent years, she has been involved in teacher education, the analysis and evaluation of reading instructional materials, and research on instructional procedures that reflect an understanding of comprehension processes.

Carl Bereiter is professor in the Department of Applied Psychology, Ontario Institute for Studies in Education. His research interests include children's writing and instructional psychology.

David C. Berliner is professor of educational psychology at the University of Arizona. He has written extensively about the findings from and methodology for research on teaching and has studied individual differences in the schools, the problems of teacher evaluation, and the use of time in classes and schools.

Ann Brown is professor in the Departments of Psychology and Educational Psychology and the Center for the Study of Reading, University of Illinois. Her main research interests include memory processes, metacognition, and strategies for understanding discourse.

Bertram Bruce is senior scientist at Bolt, Beranek and Newman, Inc., in Cambridge, Massachusetts, and principal investigator for the BBN contract with the Center for the Study of Reading. His research interests include the study of text and discourse structure, the relationships between oral and written language, and the role that plans and beliefs play in reading comprehension.

Robert Calfee is professor of education and psychology in the School of Education, Stanford University. His main research interests are component skills in reading acquisition, cognitive processes underlying skilled reading, research methods in educational research and evaluation, and determining how teachers think when they teach reading.

Douglas Carnine is associate professor of education at the University of Oregon, where he is also coordinator of the Exceptional Learning Area and director of the Direct Instruction Follow Through Program. His research interests include instructional strategies for the teaching of reading and mathematics and the change processes associated with instructional innovation.

Courtney Cazden is professor of education and chairperson of the Teaching, Curriculum and Learning Environments Program at the Harvard University Graduate School of Education. She is interested in the development of verbal abilities in and out of school and the functions of language in education.

James W. Cunningham is associate professor of education at the University of North Carolina at Chapel Hill. He is currently reviewing reading comprehension instructional research and studying the effects of an original instructional strategy on children's ability to solve word problems.

Patricia M. Cunningham is assistant professor of education at Wake Forest University. Her major research interest focuses on beginning reading instructional alternatives for children who are classified as hard to teach.

Dolores Durkin is professor of elementary and early childhood education at the University of Illinois and senior scientist at the Center for the Study of Reading. Her current work concerns the evaluation of comprehension instruction in classrooms, the content of basal reading programs, and characteristics of minority children who are successful in school.

Ronald Edmonds was professor of education in the Department of Teacher Education, senior researcher at the Institute for Research on Teaching, and professor in the Urban Affairs Programs at Michigan State University. His research interests were desegregation, testing, educational policy, and black history.

Roger Farr is professor of education and associate dean for research and graduate development at Indiana University. His research has concerned reading trends in the United States, the measurement of reading achievement, and the teaching of reading, and he is currently investigating the procedures that states use in adopting basal texts.

Russell Gersten is director of evaluation services for the University of Oregon's Direct Instruction Follow Through Program and adjunct assistant professor of educational psychology. His major interest is in evaluation research, with a particular focus on issues in special and remedial education.

Jane Hansen is assistant professor of education at the University of New Hampshire. Her research has focused on developing ways of improving the inferential comprehension of young children and poor readers.

Walter H. MacGinitie has been professor of education at the University of Victoria. His research has resulted in publications on the structure of language, language development, linguistic and cognitive development in relation to reading, readability, comprehension, and the verbal behavior of deaf children. One of his major research interests has been the measurement of reading achievement.

Andee Rubin is senior scientist at Bolt, Beranek and Newman, Inc., in Cambridge, Massachusetts, and one of the principal researchers on the BBN contract with the Center for the Study of Reading. Her research interests include the relationships among oral and written language experiences, the use of readability formulas, the development of conceptual readability, and the use of microcomputers in teaching reading and writing.

S. Jay Samuels is professor of educational psychology and curriculum and instruction at the University of Minnesota. His research interests include characteristics of outstanding reading programs, the role of automaticity in comprehension, the role of argument repetition in speed of text processing, attentional differences between good and poor readers, and the role of format design in comprehension.

Dorothy S. Strickland is professor of education at Teachers College, Columbia University. Her research interests include reading and language development, reading programs for young black children, and literature for young children.

Annemarie Palincsar is assistant professor in the Department of Counseling, Educational Psychology, and Special Education at Michigan State University. She is particularly interested in instructional strategies to promote listening and reading comprehension and in metacognitive skills of learning-impaired students.

Richard Venezky is Unidel Professor of Educational Studies at the University of Delaware, with a joint appointment in the Department of Computer and Informational Sciences. His current research focuses on the history of reading instruction and its formal representation.

Joanna P. Williams is professor of psychology and education at Teachers College, Columbia University. She has done both applied research and curriculum development in the acquisition of decoding skills and is now interested in children's comprehension of simple expository paragraphs and the design of instructional techniques for teaching main ideas.

About the Editors

Jean Osborn is associate director of the Center for the Study of Reading, University of Illinois, and works in the Follow Through Program as a site consultant to school districts throughout the United States. Her research interests include language teaching, the materials used to teach students to read, and how time is spent in elementary classrooms.

Paul T. Wilson is assistant professor at the Center for the Study of Reading, University of Illinois. His research interests include study skills, the history of instructional methods, the use of pictures in instructional materials, word study techniques, and the role of interest in promoting success in school.

Richard C. Anderson is professor of education and psychology and director of the Center for the Study of Reading, University of Illinois. His major research interests are in instructional and cognitive psychology, particularly learning from text, vocabulary growth, children's interests, and attentional problems.